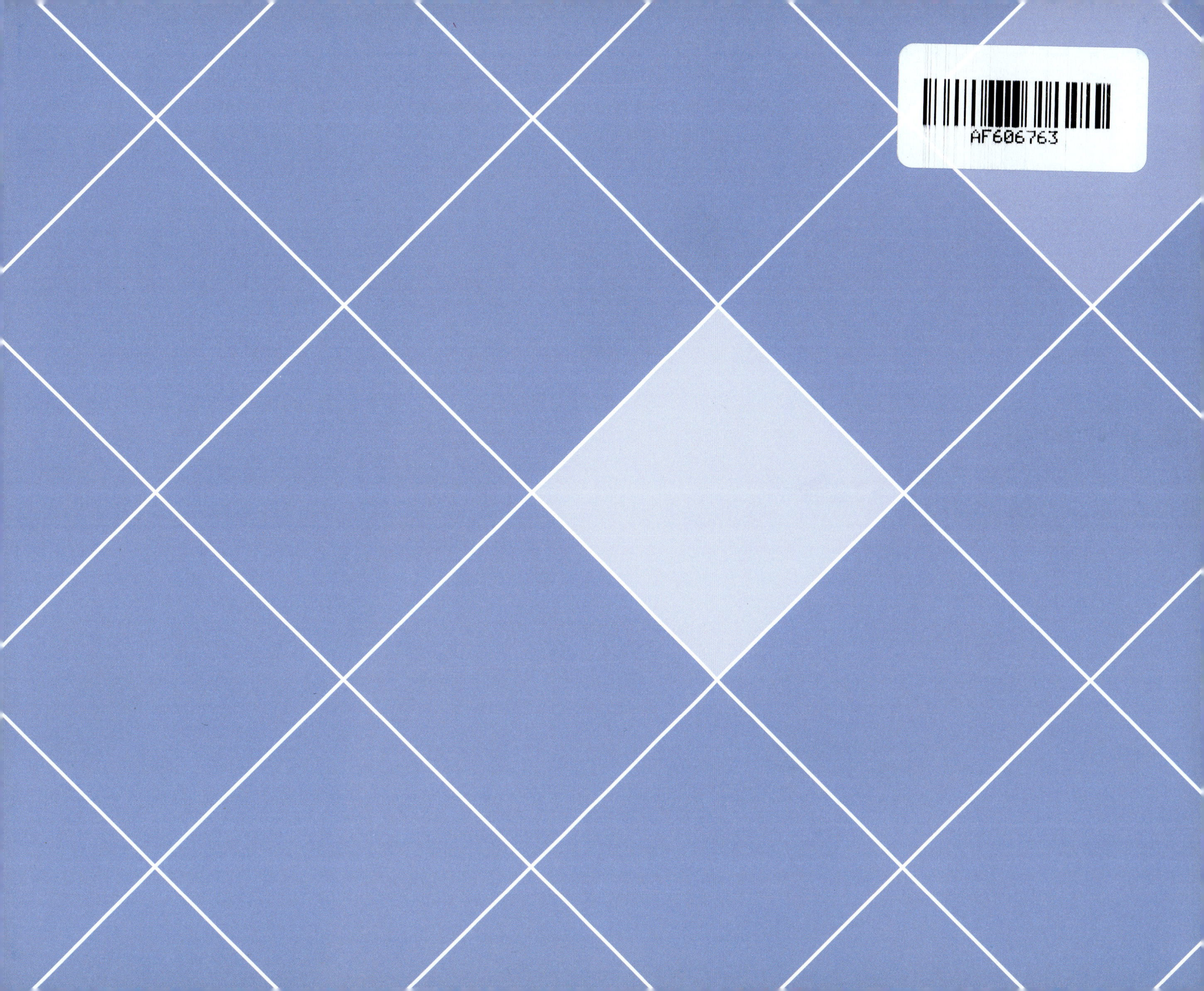

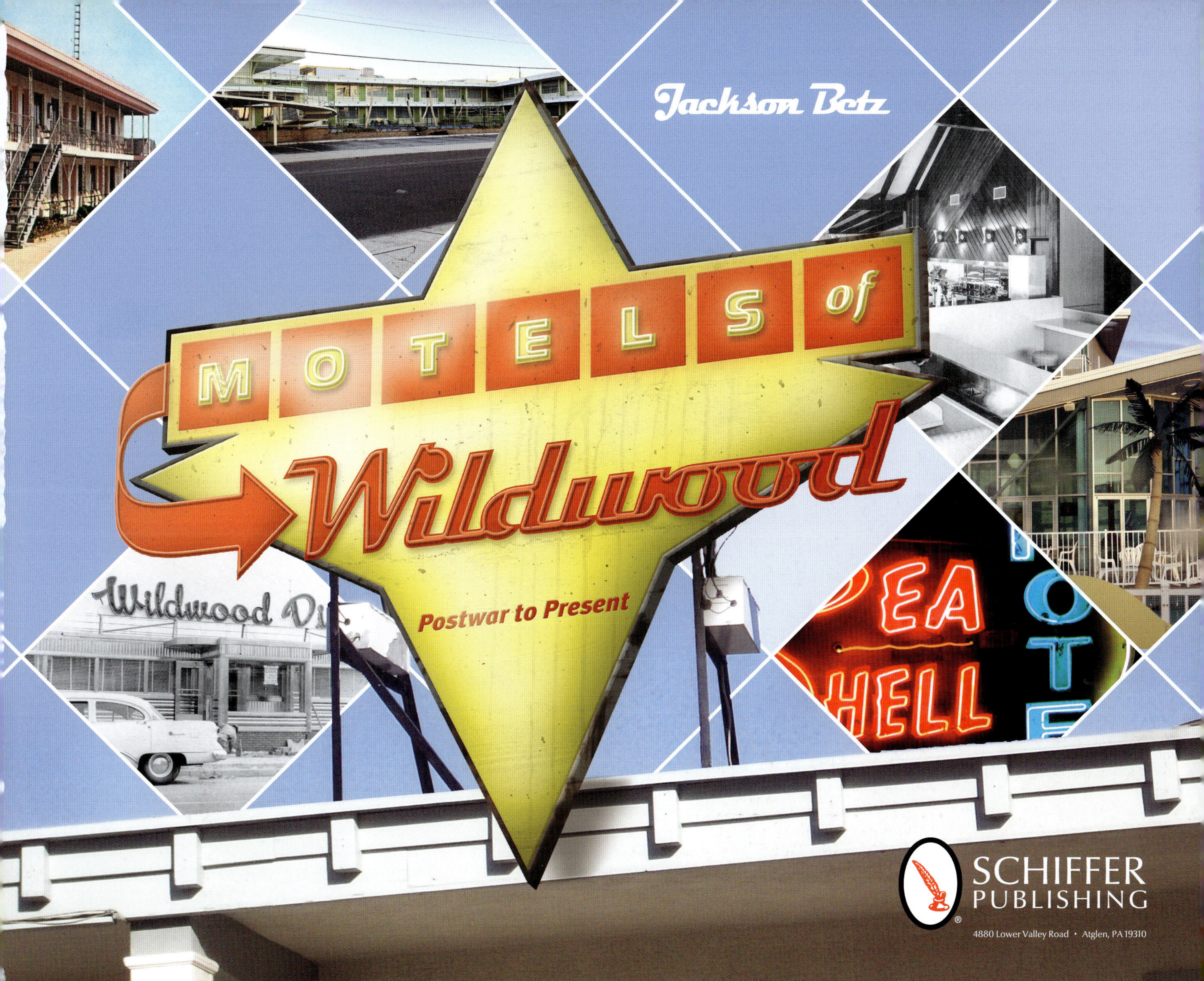
Jackson Betz
MOTELS of
Wildwood
Postwar to Present
SCHIFFER
PUBLISHING
4880 Lower Valley Road • Atglen, PA 19310

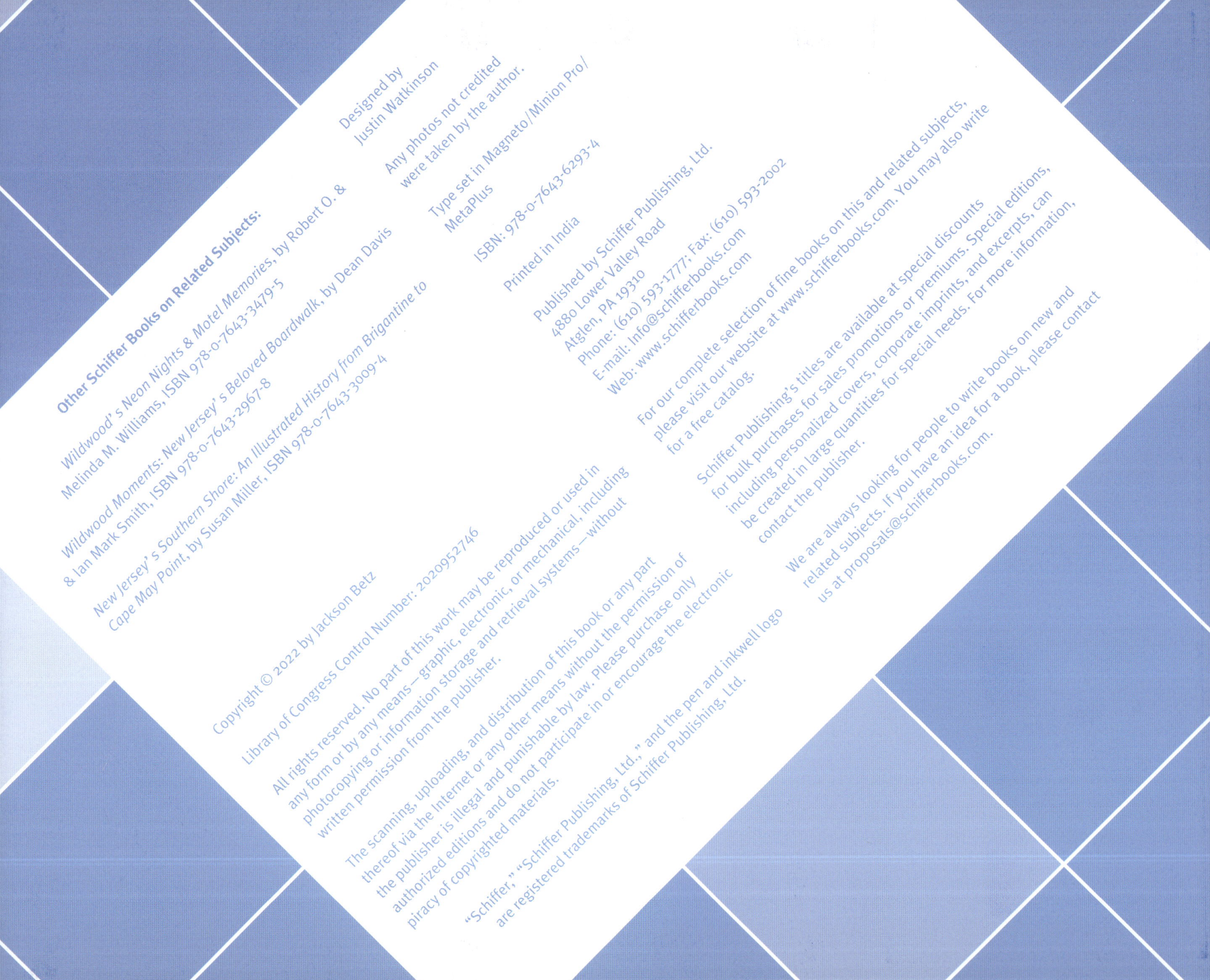

Other Schiffer Books on Related Subjects:

Wildwood's Neon Nights & Motel Memories, by Robert O. & Melinda M. Williams, ISBN 978-0-7643-3479-5

Wildwood Moments: New Jersey's Beloved Boardwalk, by Dean Davis & Ian Mark Smith, ISBN 978-0-7643-2967-8

New Jersey's Southern Shore: An Illustrated History from Brigantine to Cape May Point, by Susan Miller, ISBN 978-0-7643-3009-4

Library of Congress Control Number: 2020952746

Designed by
Justin Watkinson

Any photos not credited
were taken by the author.

Type set in Magneto/Minion Pro/
MetaPlus

ISBN: 978-0-7643-6293-4

Printed in India

Published by Schiffer Publishing, Ltd.
4880 Lower Valley Road
Atglen, PA 19310
Phone: (610) 593-1777; Fax: (610) 593-2002
E-mail: Info@schifferbooks.com
Web: www.schifferbooks.com

For our complete selection of fine books on this and related subjects, please visit our website at www.schifferbooks.com. You may also write for a free catalog.

Schiffer Publishing's titles are available at special discounts for bulk purchases for sales promotions or premiums. Special editions, including personalized covers, corporate imprints, and excerpts, can be created in large quantities for special needs. For more information, contact the publisher.

We are always looking for people to write books on new and related subjects. If you have an idea for a book, please contact us at proposals@schifferbooks.com.

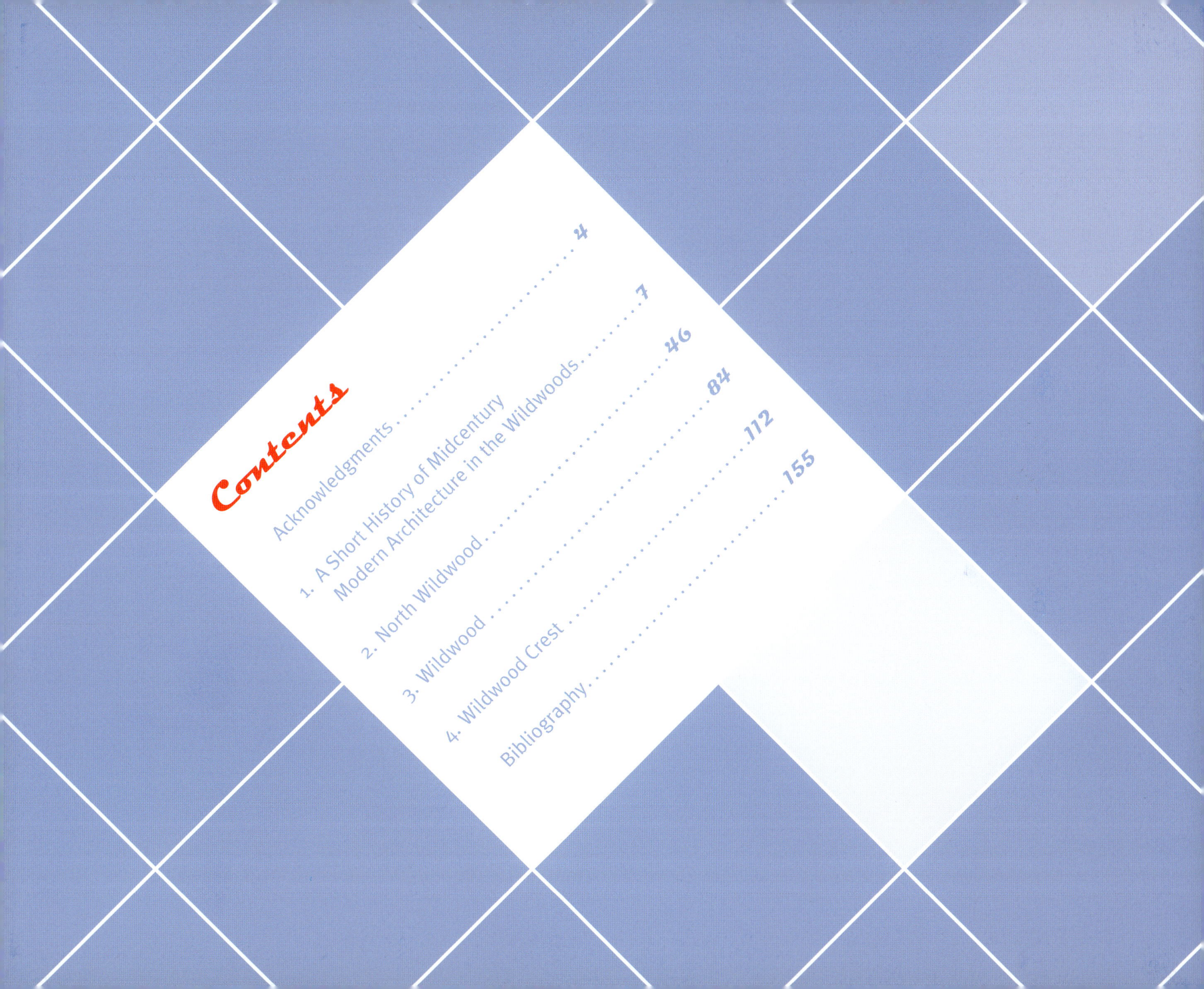

Contents

Acknowledgments

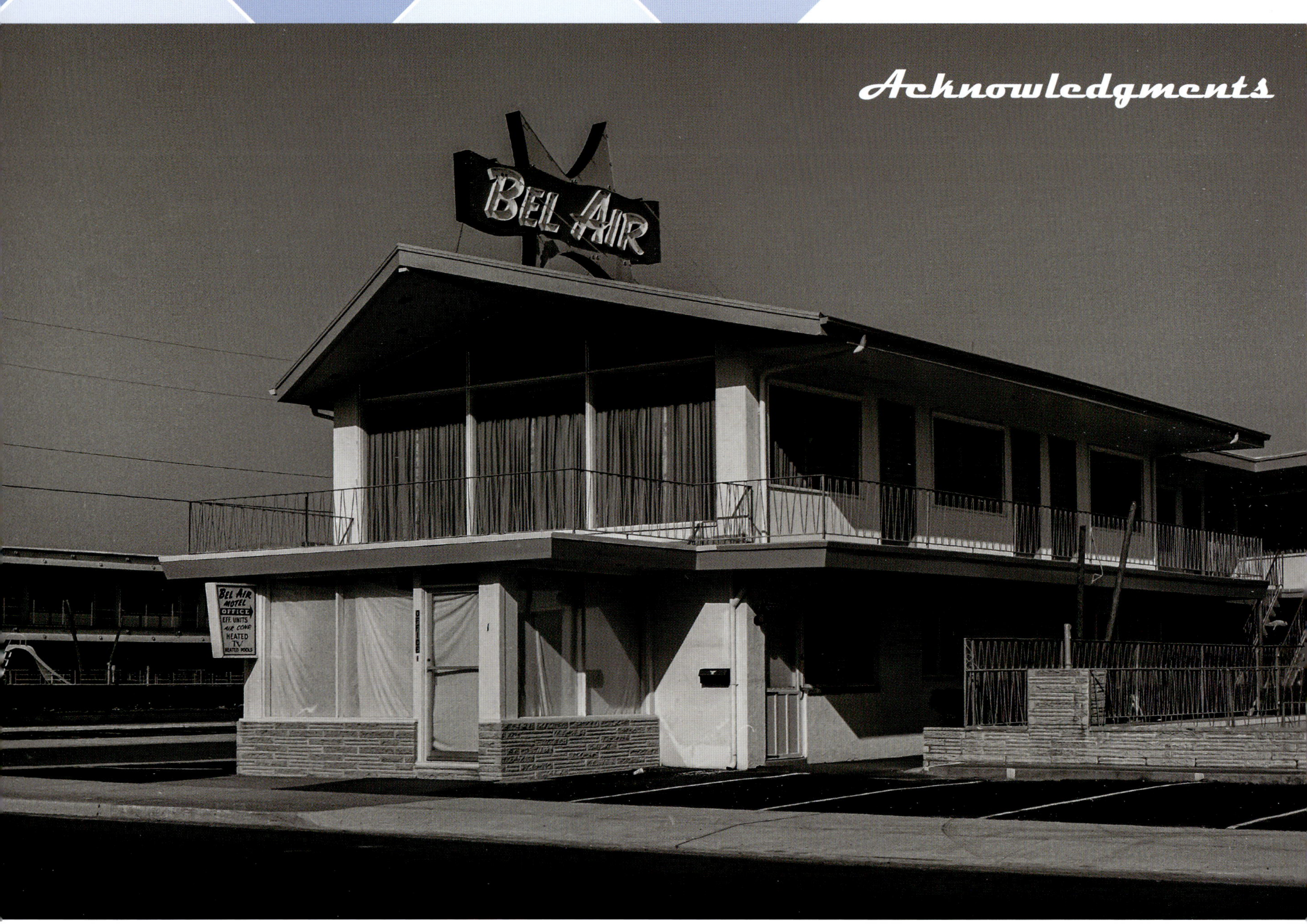

The Bel Air Motel, built in 1956 and expanded eleven years later, combines bright colors and dynamic, asymmetrical architecture in a way that makes it a popular subject for photos, both on- and off-season. *Courtesy of Ed Steinerts*

When I set out to write a history of the classic midcentury architecture of Wildwood, New Jersey, I did not anticipate the number of people who would offer their sincere support and help. My heart is full, and I'd like to acknowledge some people who made this book what it is.

First and foremost, this book would not have happened without the extraordinarily generous funding I received from the University of Pennsylvania's University Scholars Council at the Center for Undergraduate Research and Fellowships (CURF). Thanks to the council and its belief in this project, I spent two summers in the Wildwoods conducting research. Thank you to Harriet Joseph, Nancy Hirschmann, Michael Zuckerman, Amy Hillier, and Emma Hetrick for their help and advice over the years. Also at Penn, a shout-out to Kushol Gupta and Greer Cheeseman for leading the Penn Band, which felt like home during my time there. Thanks also to Marguerite Miller, Alisha George, and Louise Emerick at *Almanac* for giving me the writing and editing experience I needed to pull off a manuscript of this size, and for their support along the way.

In Wildwood, I did research at the Wildwood Historical Society in the George Boyer Museum. There, I dug through binders, boxes, microfilm reels, books, and dusty backrooms in search of pictures, memorabilia, and tidbits of information. Thanks to Jim Adair, Al Brannen, Pam Bross, Kathi Johnson, Dorothy Kulisek, Kathy Skouras, and Anne Vinci for their generosity. Thanks to Al Alven for always being up for a conversation about these dusty old motels and for his help. Thanks also to Chris Tirri for helping with the preservation effort around town and for sharing artifacts he salvaged from demolition sites. I am especially grateful to Taylor Henry, who, when I first knew her, was a volunteer at the historical society but recently became the president (How cool is that?). From looking up facts when I couldn't visit Wildwood to letting me crash on her couch during a couple of intense weekends of fact-finding and photo taking, Taylor has been a staunch advocate for this project. Not only am I grateful to have benefited from her expertise about the Wildwoods and the publishing process, but I am also lucky to call her a friend.

At Schiffer Publishing, thanks to Carey Massimini, Cheryl Weber, Kelly Thomas, and everyone who helped bring this book into focus. In the academic community, I have had the support of several scholars of commercial architecture; these authorities in the field were endlessly supportive and shared many useful photos and nuggets of information. Thanks to Brian Butko, Larry Cultrera, Richard Gutman, Michael Lorin Hirsch, Beth Lennon, and Kyle Weaver. In the Wildwoods: Thanks to Bill DiAntonio for letting me stay at his motel, the Admiral Resort, while I was working on this project (*and* for letting me play the piano in his office, always an enjoyable time). Kieran Linnane, thanks for running Hooked On Books, which kept me supplied with beach reads during the couple of years I spent at the shore. And *major* thanks to Fred Musso. From letting me tag along at job sites to donating many pictures from his collection (several of which appear in these pages) to reading an early draft, Fred has patiently shared his expertise about the Wildwoods' neon signs, and this book is the better for it.

On a personal note, I am lucky to have a fabulous group of friends who have contributed in their special ways to this project, whether asking for updates, just being there, or (in one case) translating Chinese characters on a motel sign! They include Giulia Arostegui, Niyathi Chakrapani,

Walli Chen, Maki Chung, Kyle Ciarrochi, Ash Davis, Richard DiNapoli, Matt Eisenberg, Emily Elenio, Robin Friedman, Alex Harrer, Bradley Herring, Amy Kaiser-Jones, Lisa Kalnik, Reginald Lamaute, Kelly Liu, John McGahay, J. P. McGrath, Morgan McLees, Aaron Mittleman, Juliette Morfin, Andrew Park, Angie Picard, Jenna Pollack, Angela Schmitt, Nicole Tanenbaum, Justin Taylor, Alexis Warner, Galileo West, and Chris Urffer. A few friends deserve special mention for making the writing process fun with funny memes and spot-on music recommendations: Helen Chung, Julie Cohen, Caroline Francois, Caitlin Frazee, Melannie Jay, Shinyoung Hailey Noh, Bernie Wang, Steph Widzowski, and Anyelina Wu. Miles Taylor, it's always an absolute joy sharing music, public transit adventures, and life advice with you; your constant encouragement sustained me through months of writing! (And Taylor Henry, I appreciate you more than words can say, as I mentioned earlier!)

On the home front, thanks to my grandparents for their support over the years. My mom supported this project from its *very* beginnings around 2007, when we would walk around town and take film photos of motels on family vacations. (Whenever my mom found herself in an antique shop over the last few years, she would sift through postcards to find ones from the Wildwoods—several postcards listed as being from my collection in this book are a result of her generosity.) My dad, a professional writer, read a draft of this book, which is the reason there are so few grammatical errors, and my brother has been a constant source of positivity (and in the era before Google Maps, he spotted the Ship Ahoy out the car window when I couldn't for the life of me find the intersection of Baker and Washington Avenues).

A Short History of Midcentury Modern Architecture in the Wildwoods

In 1609, Henry Hudson happened upon the island of Wildwood and dubbed it Half Moon Beach. Yet, it wasn't until 1723 that local plantation owner Aaron Leaming bought a parcel of land and used it to graze cattle. The future Wildwoods remained a sparsely populated, tangled mass of trees and other vegetation until the late 1870s, when growing settlements in neighboring Cape May and Sea Isle City led developers to take a second look at the island.

In 1884, real-estate agent Humphrey Cresse founded a tiny fishing village named Anglesea at the northern end of the island. Two years earlier, developer John Burk had founded the Holly Beach Improvement Company, which developed another village closer to the middle of the island. These early communities contained small, cheaply built beach cottages served by train lines that shuttled vacationers to and from Philadelphia. By 1890, these communities had expanded and spawned two others: Wildwood, near Holly Beach in the center of the island, and Wildwood Crest, the community farthest south. Then, in 1912, Wildwood and Holly Beach merged to become the city of Wildwood, while Wildwood Crest and North Wildwood (formerly Anglesea) achieved borough status in 1905 and 1910, respectively.

Hospitality played an important role in the early development of these resorts. As early as 1885, a small rooming house opened in Anglesea, and in 1890 the Hotel Dayton, a hotel of flagship class, opened in Wildwood. Located at the intersection of Wildwood and Atlantic Avenues, the mock-Tudor Dayton featured an expansive porch that offered its residents prime views of the beach and the ever-growing town. As if to underscore the Dayton's importance to the resort, President Benjamin Harrison attended its dedication ceremony. The Dayton was not the only hotel in the Wildwoods, nor would it remain the most popular or fashionable, but it set the stage for hotels and motels to play a dominant role on the island.

In 1890, an unknown resort entrepreneur hired a construction firm from the neighboring town of Rio Grande to construct a boardwalk along the beach in Wildwood. This temporary boardwalk, which was removed at the end of the summer, proved popular with vacationers, and a boardwalk was laid down every year for the rest of the decade, by turns publicly funded or sponsored by local businesses. In 1899, mayor and prominent developer Latimer Baker proposed a permanent boardwalk, which appeared on the seaward side of Atlantic Avenue the next summer. Proximity to this new boardwalk made several of Wildwood's early hotels more desirable.

Due to a tide condition that, even today, dumps excess sand on Wildwood's beach and chisels away at the beaches of neighboring communities Cape May and Stone Harbor, town leaders decided the boardwalk was too far inland by 1903. Accordingly, the next year the boardwalk was moved east toward the ocean, and businesses and hotels quickly filled the new real estate. This expansion of the island deprived early hotels such as the Dayton of their ocean views, ending the first era of Wildwood lodging and allowing a new generation of hotels to take their place as island landmarks. Entrepreneurs, meanwhile, kicked boardwalk development up a notch.

Copying an idea from Atlantic City, Camden businessmen Charles Reynolds and Herman Buckhorn opened Wildwood's first amusement pier in 1905. Ocean Pier, which put theaters, bowling alleys, a shooting gallery, a carousel, and refreshment stands under a single roof, was designed by prestigious Philadelphia architect Charles A. Brooke. Soon, competing piers such as Casino Pier, Crest Pier, and Blaker Pier opened. As a result, Wildwoods' resort culture shifted to emphasize amusements. This new focus on the commercial would define the island and distinguish it from its more residential neighbors.

By 1910, the town government again moved the boardwalk farther east to follow the shoreline. Its existing piers moved with the boardwalk on pilings, and the rest of the town, including boardwalk shops, underwent a similar upheaval. Undeterred by this modification of the island's map, development continued to thrive. Developer Gil Blaker took advantage of the extra real estate this move generated, building a row of bathhouses and a theater on the boardwalk opposite his Blaker Pavilion. This canny business strategy allowed customers to spend money at a variety of Blaker-owned enterprises. While Blaker's Wildwood empire would not last long, later Wildwood families such as the Hunts and Moreys would make good use of this strategy.

The boardwalk made its last beachward move during the 1920s. Between 1921 and 1928, a new alignment that ran from Cresse Avenue northward to 16th Avenue in North Wildwood was constructed section by section. Once again, most piers and amusements were moved seaward to accommodate the new route.

Another key moment in the resort's evolution happened quietly in 1913, when Camden theater mogul William C. Hunt leased the Blaker Theater. Although this arrangement soon ended in a violent disagreement over rent, Hunt came back to Wildwood with a vengeance, building his own series of movie houses. He bought the Avenue and Comique vaudeville theaters, took over the Blaker (a move he probably relished), and built the Casino, Strand, and Regent Theaters on and near the boardwalk. In 1922, Hunt's Theaters, Inc., was valued at $1 million and encompassed seventeen theaters in Wildwood, Cape May, and Camden. Optimistic, Hunt liquidated his Camden assets to focus on the shore.

Despite his success, Hunt grew restless and in 1925 decided to expand into the amusement industry. He bought a used carousel from the Philadelphia Toboggan Company and installed it on the boardwalk; business was so successful that in 1934, he also bought the aging Ocean Pier. Since the hardships of the Great Depression, this former hub had been floundering. Hunt installed modern rides, added a colorful façade, and transformed the pier into a showplace. Other modern amusement centers such as Marine Pier, between Schellenger and Cedar Avenues, and the Sportland complex, at 24th Avenue, also began taking the place of their outdated counterparts.

Meanwhile, entrepreneurs kept building hotels and apartment buildings on the island. Many were plain, loosely Victorian buildings with clapboard siding, decorative gingerbread, and spacious porches. Names such as Manor, Sheldon, Adelphi-Witte, Fenwick, and Westminster advertised conservative, conventional hotels and rooming houses. Still, business boomed: with the opening of the Wildwood Convention Center in 1927, the town began to host a series of annual and special events that drew large crowds. Festivities such as Wildwood's annual Baby Parade and the 1932 Miss America Parade (a one-off before the event moved to Atlantic City) were so well attended that hotels not only stayed afloat but were also able to expand. During the 1920s and 1930s, hoteliers were among the island's most prosperous merchants.

Architecture Arrives

Amid unexceptional competition on the architectural front, Edward McGarry looked to the future when he opened the Hotel Seville in 1927. While most of the hotel's contemporaries were named after their owners or had names that advertised their beachfront locations (e.g., Ocean Crest), the Seville, located at Ocean and Maple Avenues in a sleepy residential neighborhood, promised an exotic experience. A pink stucco façade exuded a Spanish theme, as did towers capped with tile cupolas, brightly striped window awnings, and a lobby whose entrance allowed patrons to pass through grand arches and classicizing columns. The Seville also departed from the typical Wildwood hotel blueprint by dispensing with the customary porch, substituting a manicured front lawn with the hotel's name spelled out in topiaries. While most hotels of the time advertised relaxation, the Seville took its guests on a journey. This concept would influence later motel builders on the island.

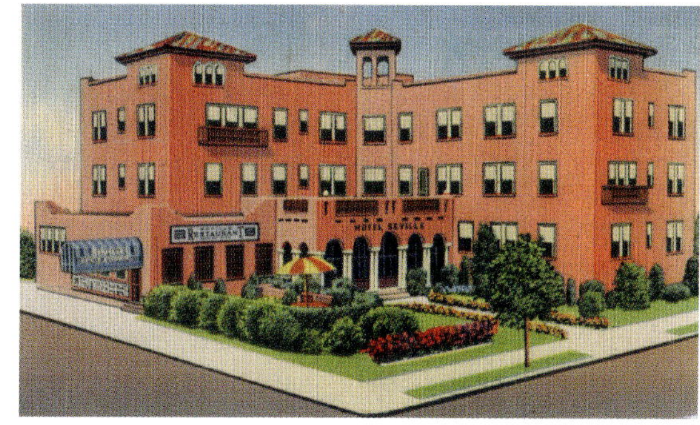

Edward McGarry's Hotel Seville was one of the first hotels on the island to transport its lodgers to an exotic destination. *Courtesy of Vicki Bundschu*

The Seville was a product of a changing architectural culture in the United States. Before the early twentieth century, most architecture had adhered to a Cartesian grid and sober formality. Except for flurries of decoration during the eras of Gothic cathedrals and Victorian gingerbread, architects had seen little reason to deviate from ancient principles of simplicity. By contrast, during the 1920s the art deco movement began to overtake design. It began with Manhattan skyscrapers such as Raymond Hood's American Radiator Building, which opened in 1924, and William van Alen's 1930 Chrysler Building. These buildings featured elaborate, multifaceted façades, blank walls embellished with repetitive patterns, and, in the case of the Chrysler Building, a stunning seven-layered spire. These elements showed designers playing with norms, and a decade later a similar movement began to take place several hundred miles away in Miami.

During the 1930s and early 1940s, Miami architects such as Henry Hohauser and Albert Anis constructed several modest art deco hotel buildings, most four or five stories, in the city's South Beach neighborhood. These buildings borrowed from the extravagant style of urban skyscrapers, but in a simpler way. Streamline moderne, which came to prominence in commercial architecture such as bus stations, movie theaters, and diners, used simple, sleek designs, with porcelain and stainless steel shaped into rounded corners. South Beach architects built dynamic hotels clad in neutral-colored porcelain or white-painted stucco, accented with brightly colored cornices, porthole

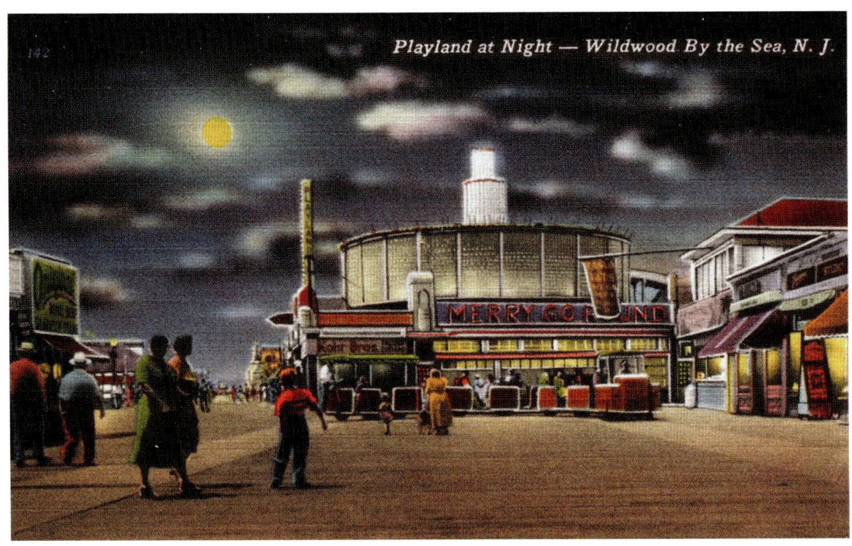

windows, Bauhaus lettering, and other decorative elements (such as the glass-brick lighthouse tower above the corner entrance of the famous Waldorf Towers, topped with a ring of blue neon). These buildings simplified the elite forms of art deco for beach vacationers. By paring down the more outrageous elements of art deco to a pedestrian-friendly scale, these architects also inadvertently influenced the architectural form of the motel, a medium whose peak was still two decades away. The sheer concentration of streamlined hotels on strips such as Beach Drive and Collins Drive created a spectacle. As possibly the world's first hotel district, South Beach set the tone for hotel-filled resorts in decades to come.

While the colorful South Beach hotels captured the public imagination, another neighborhood just 2 miles north influenced architects. Beginning in the late 1940s, Morris Lapidus designed a group of hotels in Miami's Mid-Beach neighborhood (between 23rd and 63rd Streets) that appealed to postwar prosperity and optimism. These hotels, with such exotic names as Eden Roc, Fontainebleau, and Sans Souci, transferred the playful nature

Wildwood's "honky-tonk" boardwalk in the 1940s.
Author's collection

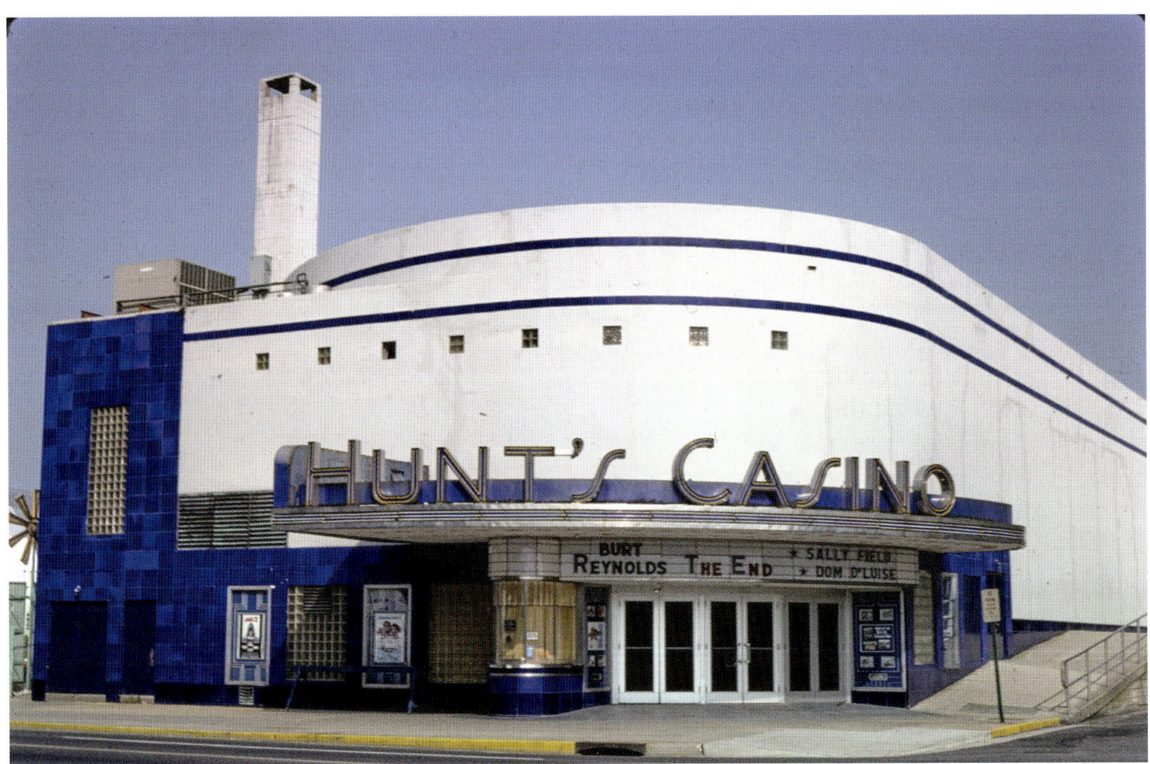

When W. C. Hunt opened the Casino Theater in 1940, he introduced the Wildwoods to streamline moderne.
John Margolies photo

of the smaller South Beach hotels to much-larger buildings. Lapidus designed these hotels not simply to serve as lodging, but also to transport their inhabitants to exotic locales. Lapidus's designs were much more extravagant than the simple and vaguely Spanish decoration at Wildwood's Seville.

Meanwhile, back in Wildwood, William Hunt's Casino Theater burned down in 1939. Rather than admit defeat, Hunt rebuilt, introducing art deco (in the miniature) to the Wildwoods in the process. He also built a new theater called the Shore a block away. Located on Wildwood's well-traveled Atlantic Avenue, the Casino and Shore were pivotal buildings in the resort's history. True to Hunt's instinct, both theaters turned profits and became local landmarks. The Shore and Casino's use of trendy, distinctive, streamlined designs elevated the architecture of one of Wildwood's commercial strips: even though the nearby Dayton, Davis, and Hof-Brau Hotels were instrumental in Wildwood's early development, their aging façades were dreary presences in what was becoming a vibrant and modern resort town.

William Hunt's bad luck was not finished. On Christmas Day 1943, Ocean Pier, which he had painstakingly revitalized nine years earlier, burned down. Then, so did his Strand Theater, perched on the boardwalk at Maple Avenue, in August 1944. Forced by wartime shortages to make choices, Hunt concentrated his first efforts on the Strand. On May 27, 1947, Hunt opened a new Strand Theater on the boardwalk, which, like his earlier theaters on the island, brought art deco to the masses with a chrome roofline, terrazzo flooring, and a shiny neon marquee. Meanwhile, Hunt bided his time and planned a replacement for his Ocean Pier.

Tourist Courts: From Novelty to Mainstay

By the late 1940s, the nature of lodging in the Wildwoods was changing. When veterans returned home from World War II eager to start families (and with disposable income from government GI bills), their opinion of the first generation of Wildwood's hotels was low. Previously cozy rooms now seemed cramped, once-breezy porches now overlooked busy streets, and new safety regulations made Wildwood's hotels' minimal fire precautions seem laughably inadequate. Late 1960s urban renewal would clear the city of many of these out-of-date hotels, but for the time being, changing preferences manifested themselves in new construction.

The first half of the twentieth century had crowded the city of Wildwood with amusements, businesses, apartments, hotels, and houses, but North Wildwood and Wildwood Crest remained relatively sparse. During the forties, landowners and developers began to take advantage of this untapped potential, building a series of tidy one-story bungalows that exemplified the beach culture of the middle of the century. However, in the late 1940s, another form of lodging began to emerge on the island—tourist courts. While the medium had been around for a couple of decades, the earliest courts in the Wildwoods appeared after their peak in the rest of the country. Although past its popular prime, the medium was durable, allowing a family to pull its car up to the front door of a room and circumvent the excesses of hotel life. In the place of hotels' lavish dining rooms and retail space was a grassy courtyard, often supplied with picnic tables. Tourist courts were designed for a new car-oriented culture.

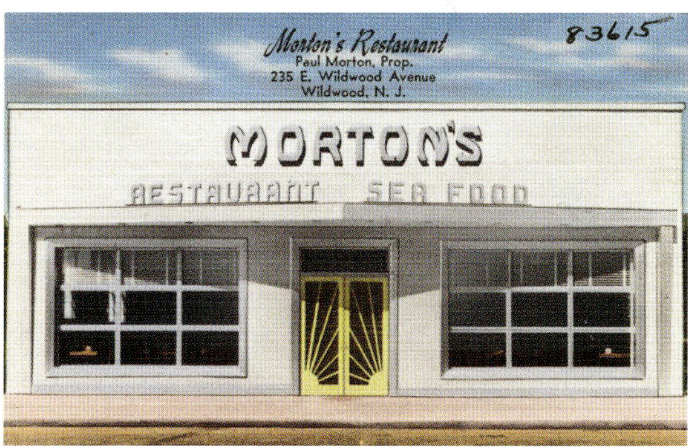

Though it did not become the long-lasting architectural style associated with the island, a few entrepreneurs built art deco businesses in the Wildwoods in the 1940s. *Courtesy of Digital Commonwealth*

The Sea Shell Court, seen in a 1950 postcard, typifies tourist courts of the era. *Author's collection*

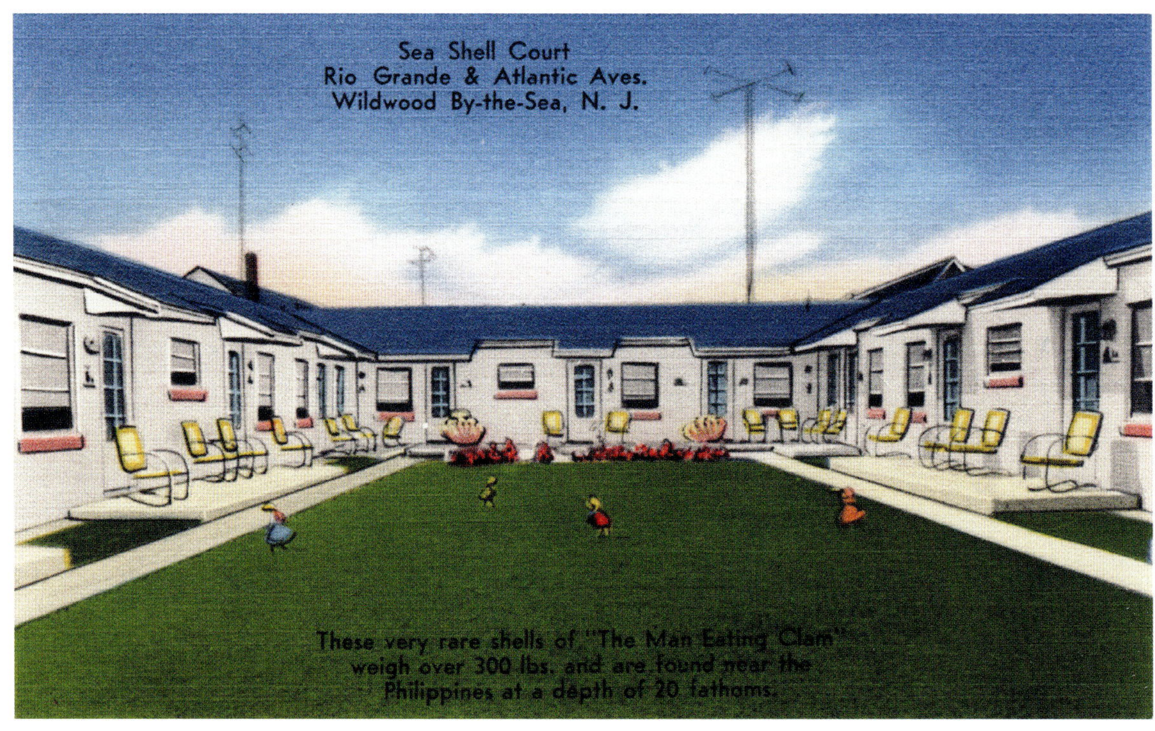

The Lantern Lane Cottage Colony's office building playfully borrows from Streamline Moderne. *Courtesy of Digital Commonwealth*

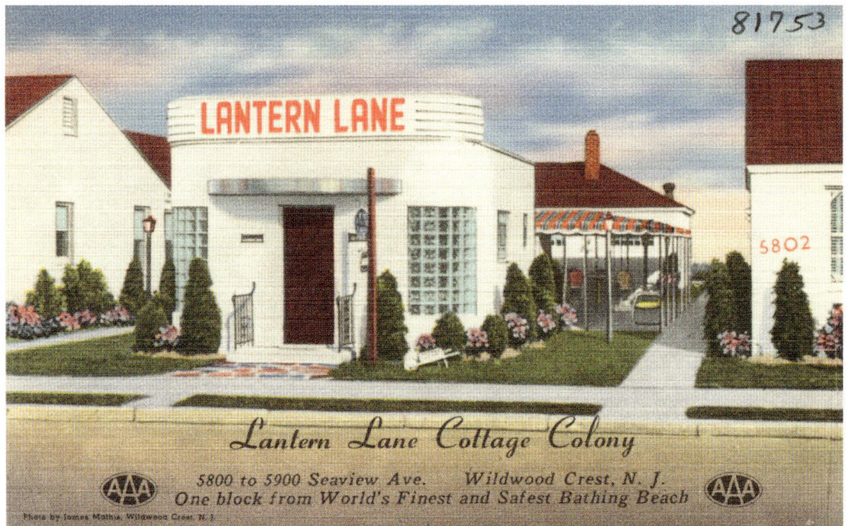

These courts mostly stuck to a tried-and-true formula: two long, inward-facing, single-story buildings divided into rooms and topped with a gable roof. Occasionally, an additional office building would be thrown into the mix (usually doubling as the owners' living quarters). Plenty of these buildings appeared throughout the Wildwoods, with names such as Holly Beach Court, Heather Court, and Maple Court that referred to their street locations. The initial response from Wildwoods locals was mixed—in the 1949 city directory, for instance, the few courts that existed were listed under apartment buildings. However, by 1954, some twenty "tourist courts" were listed, including several that had the word "motel" in their name. One court, the Lantern Lane Cottage Colony in the Crest, snuck in a sly reference to the grandeur of streamline moderne with a rounded stucco façade and glass block corners.

Meanwhile, local carpenter Ben Schlenzig constructed the Ship Ahoy Apartments at Taylor and Ocean Avenues in 1939, across the street from Wildwood's boardwalk. A year later, he constructed the Sun Deck, Sun Beam, and Sun Dial Apartments a block away at Ocean and Andrews

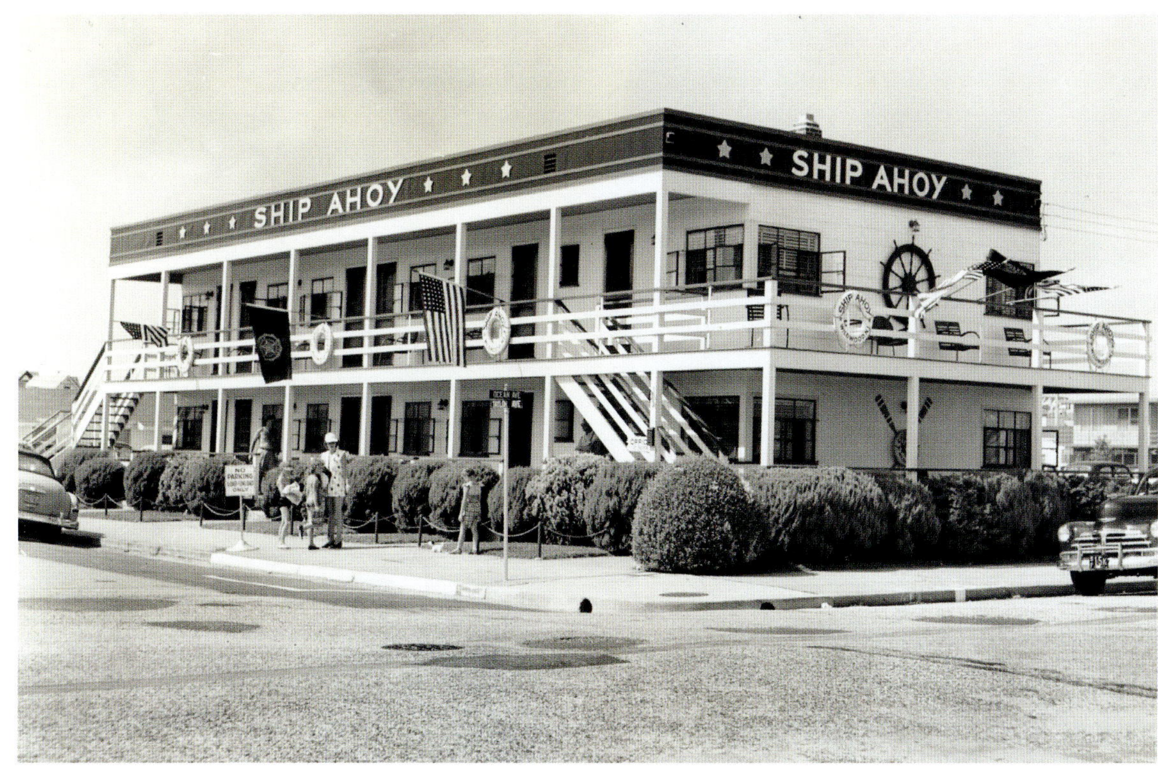

The Ship Ahoy Apartments expressed a cohesive theme and had an exterior common balcony; both of these elements became key features of motels. *Courtesy of Wildwood Historical Society*

Avenues. These buildings built on the tourist court form but had two stories, making more efficient use of what was fast becoming competitive beachfront real estate. They were nondescript except for the Sun Deck, which had streamline moderne rounded corners and a smokestack rising from its roof, a reference to vernacular roadside architecture. Schlenzig's constructions were innovative for their era, even though they catered to long-term residents rather than short-term guests. By the mid-1950s, the Sun Deck expanded with an additional building and a pool. The Wildwoods were coming around to the idea of motel-like architecture.

None of these early courts were advertised with the name "motel," though. The Wildwoods came somewhat late to the game of building motels: Arthur Heineman, a California entrepreneur, had opened the Milestone Mo-Tel in San Luis Obispo as early as 1925. He planned to copyright the word "motel," "like Kleenex," and open a syndicate of "motels dedicated primarily to the service of the motoring public." However, Heineman's plans did not come to fruition, and during the 1930s and 1940s a series of roadside motels began to pop up along America's highways.

The exact date the first "motel" opened in the Wildwoods is lost to history, but three important early motels opened for the 1952 season. The first was built by a family that would come to dominate the Wildwood economy. Raised in small bay community West Wildwood in a family of seven

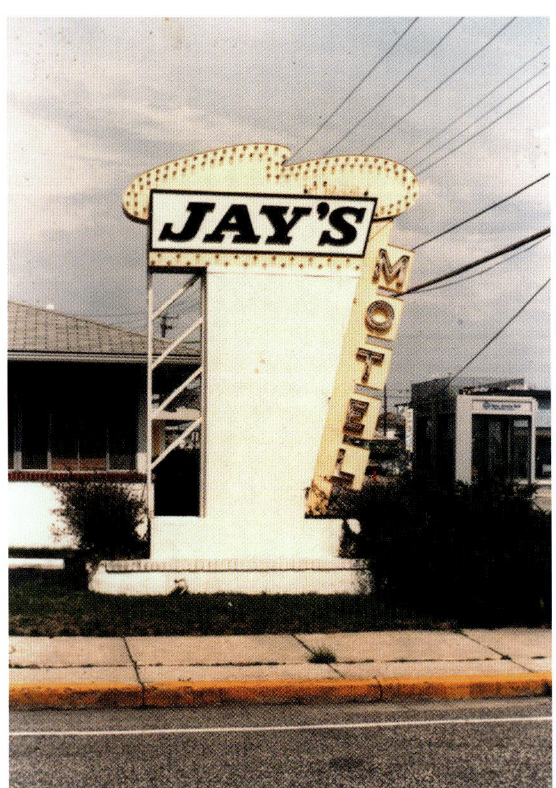

The Morey brothers' first motel, Jay's Motel, shown in the early 1990s, was architecturally plain but sported creative signage. *Courtesy of Fedele Musso*

children, Lewis and Wilbert Morey (better known as Lou and Will) vacationed in Miami Beach during the 1940s, getting an eyeful of the large-scale creations of Morris Lapidus and the small streamlined motels of the South Beach District. Their father, Lou Sr., had moved to Wildwood with his father, Samuel, in the 1920s. Drafted into World War II in a noncombat role as a carpenter, Lou Sr. died in 1944 from complications of asthma while serving the US Coast Guard. To make ends meet, Lou's sons took up construction in his footsteps. In 1947, Will bought a block in a residential area of Wildwood. Enlisting the help of his friend Fred Langford (then an architecture student at the University of Pennsylvania), Will built fifteen homes on speculation, then sold them, an easy feat in a healthy postwar housing market.

Jack Morey, Will's son, remembers, "There were five brothers and two sisters in the Morey family. They were all poor. They were born and raised in West Wildwood, and they all developed work in the trades. Basically, all carpenters. So at some point in time, they were all either a part owner or a carpenter with Morey Brothers. The company was based in Lou Morey's house." Several of these original Morey one-story beach houses survive today. The ones at 134 West Leaming Avenue, 5105 Arctic Avenue, and 135 and 137 West Bennett Avenue are remnants of an entire block once populated with Morey-built houses. The former two typify Wildwood summer houses of the era, with gable roofs and wide clapboard siding. The West Bennett Avenue houses reflect Will's exposure to South Florida architecture—they sport flat roofs, brick façades, jalousie windows, and, in the case of 135, a rounded front porch demarcated by a metal railing with an "M" insignia.

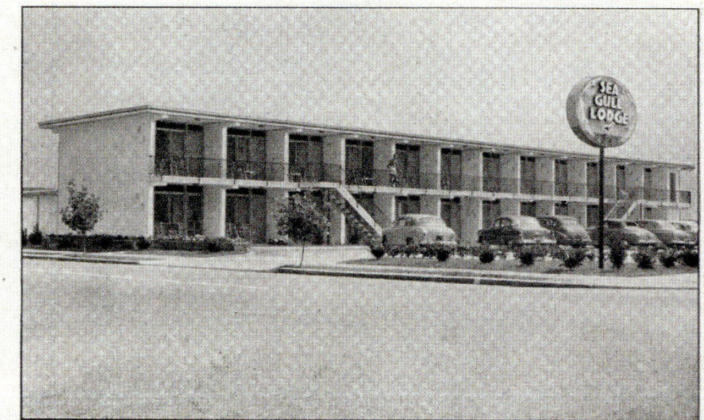

Since this 1952 advertisement, the Sea Gull Lodge (now Motel) has been greatly expanded. *Courtesy of Wildwood Historical Society*

After completing these houses between 1947 and 1949, Langford went back to school. Will, meanwhile, decided to delve into contracting, and his brother Lou, encouraged by Will's financial success, joined him in the family business. In the fall of 1951, Josephine Juvino contracted the Moreys to build a tourist court at Hildreth and Atlantic Avenues. Will and Lou Morey built an archetypical court: it had one story, was L shaped and clad in pink-painted stucco, and had an L-shaped parking lot that allowed guests to park at the door of their room. On the street corner, the Morey brothers built a single-story bungalow. With a hip roof and tall picture windows, this bungalow, like the rest of the motel, alluded to the Florida architecture that had inspired the Moreys. An upright stucco sign on the street corner completed the picture, spelling out "Jay's Motel" in Bauhaus-style chrome letters. Jay's Motel opened for the summer of 1952.

While Jay's was a tangible first step for the Morey brothers, its courtlike design was regressive. Also in 1952, at the intersection of Cresse and Atlantic Avenues in Wildwood, Harry Marin built a two-story motel called the Sea Gull Lodge (its use of the word "lodge" robbed it of the distinction of being one of Wildwood's first motels, though by 1956, Marin had changed "lodge" to "motel"). Though architecturally simple, its format influenced the Wildwoods' future motels. Both floors had exterior balconies running the length of the building; in a nod to court architecture, the Sea Gull sat behind a spacious grass courtyard.

Another 1952-vintage motel was the most significant for several reasons—not only did it eventually become a Wildwood institution, but it was also a harbinger of the imaginative motel architecture that would soon abound in the area. Ben Schlenzig, who had built the Ship Ahoy and its siblings a decade earlier, owned a lot at the corner of Rio Grande and Ocean Avenues. Sometime in the winter and spring of 1951–1952, he built a motel at this prominent intersection. Like the Sea Gull, Schlenzig's Rio Motel was two stories. Parking spaces sat at the door of each of the first-floor rooms, and each second-floor room had both a front private balcony and a rear common one. Each room's front wall was angled toward the ocean, allowing occupants a better beach view, and this gave the motel a strong sense of motion. Though Ben Schlenzig appears in period city directories only as a carpenter, he put the artistry of an architect into his design for the Rio. It was no mere tourist court.

Other motels and courts continued to open on the island. In 1953, the El-Ray Motel, a single-story court at Taylor and Atlantic Avenues, opened, as did a few long-gone courts such as Fowler's Motel on Poplar Avenue in Wildwood. The same year, well-known local resident Lewes D. Wingate, who owned a house next to the Rio Motel on Rio Grande Avenue, built his own motel to capitalize on the trend. The Wingate Motel was a single-story, L-shaped court next to his house; Wingate ran it from his living room. Farther north, Ruth Gall built the Flame Inn in North Wildwood, featuring the Wildwoods' most remarkable neon concoction yet, a rotating candle.

Meanwhile, a musical revolution was overtaking Wildwood. Singers arriving from Philadelphia began to workshop an emerging genre—rock and roll—in the resort town's bars and clubs. Rock-and-roll music combined the guitar-driven texture and Tin Pan Alley lyricism of country music with the stomping beat and sexual tension of doo wop and rhythm and blues. Pennsylvania rock singer Bill Haley played his soon-to-be hit record "Rock Around the Clock" for the first time at

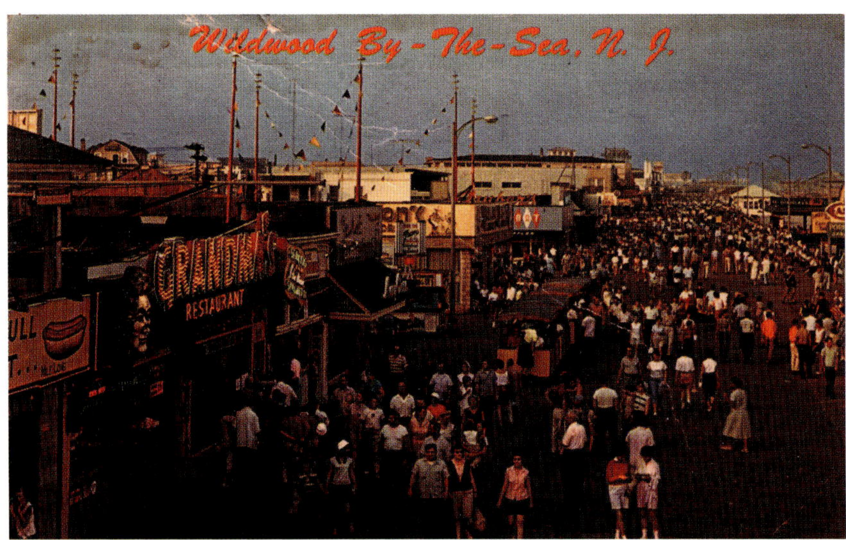

By the 1950s, brightly colored neon signage had made the Wildwoods' boardwalk a wonderland at night. *Author's collection*

Wildwood's Hof-Brau Hotel in 1954, and musicians from Philadelphia such as Chubby Checker and Charlie Gracie followed suit. Paul Russo, owner of the Cool Scoops Ice Cream Parlor in North Wildwood, remarks, "Chubby Checker did the Twist at the Rainbow, which was at Spicer and Pacific—now it's the Cattle and Clover. In the 1950s and 1960s you could go to a bar on Sundays and it was a jam. All the bands played together. It was called the Sunday Jam." Wildwood began to draw crowds to its nightclub scene as well as to its beach.

During the 1950s, the Wildwoods' amusement pier industry continued to blossom. W. C. Hunt had taken his time in rebuilding his Ocean Pier, which had burned in 1943. In 1957, he opened a new pier that took the lead from state-of-the-art piers in nearby Atlantic City. Rather than housing amusements under a roof, Hunt left them open to the sunshine and sea breezes. The year Hunt's Pier opened, Hunt premiered the Flyer, the island's second rollercoaster, which would leave a lasting imprint on vacationers. In succeeding years, Hunt expanded his pier and added rides such as Jungleland and the Golden Nugget, whose themes of a rainforest safari

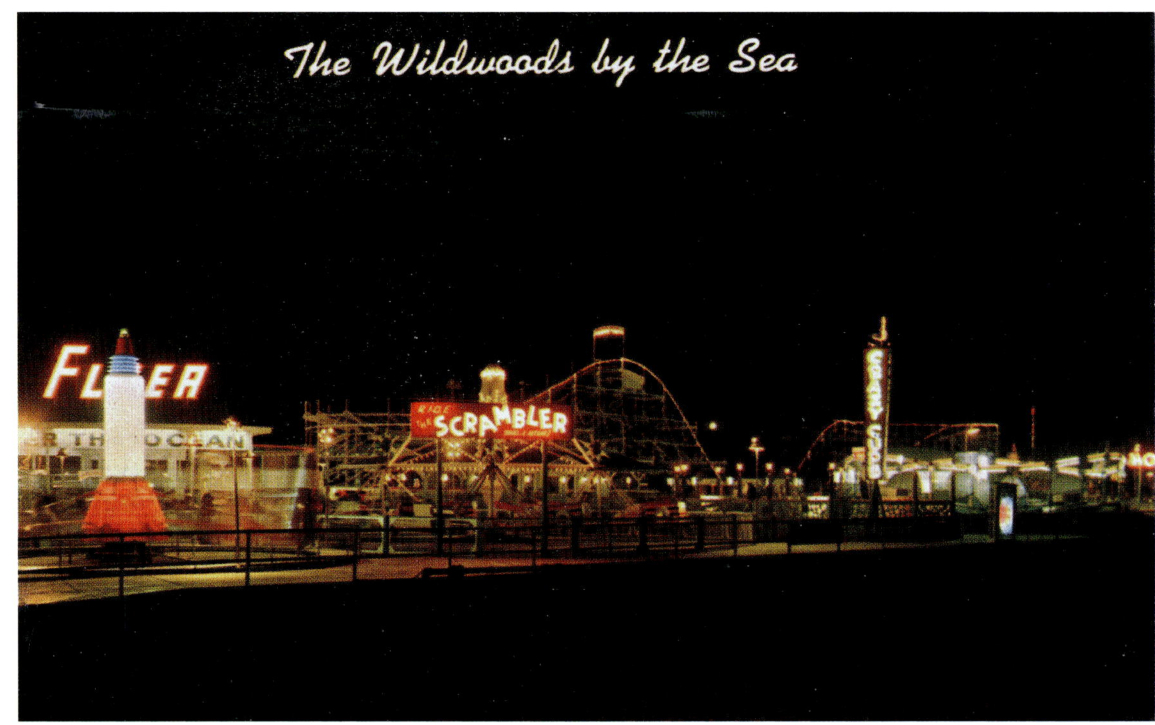

The vibrant Hunt's Pier in the mid-1960s. *Author's collection*

and a western mining town, respectively, transported riders to exotic locales, an idea that pervaded the island's motels as well. With this new pier, Hunt led the Wildwoods to prominence among beach resort towns. The same year, Joe Barnes bought the Wildwoods Convention Center Pier and transformed the aging building into a new amusement pier. Though Fun Pier borrowed from earlier ideas of pier design, it became a beloved Wildwood institution and reinforced the Wildwoods' postwar return to prosperity.

During the 1950s, visitors began to flock to the Wildwoods in increasing numbers. In 1955, the New Jersey Highway Authority opened the first stretch of a new highway, the Garden State Parkway, which hugged the Atlantic coast between Paterson and Cape May. For the first time, vacationers had a straightforward route to access New Jersey's southern shore points. Previous travelers had taken serpentine back roads to the Wildwoods, such as New Jersey Route 47 from Philadelphia and US Route 9 from New York. Pavement had made these roads navigable, but the publicity generated by the Garden State Parkway (which had two exits leading to the Wildwoods) brought a new influx of tourists. Estimates predicted that the parkway would bring 349,000 additional cars to the island each year, and accordingly, traffic lights and parking meters were installed to deal with increased traffic. This new access also created more demand for hotel and motel rooms.

Between 1953 and 1956, the island's lodging industry kept pace with its expanding tourism industry. Most of this era's motels, though, were relatively plain. In the 1955–56 Wildwood city directory, twenty-nine tourist courts are listed, most of which have "motel" in their names. These include pioneers such as Jay's and the Wingate as well as some new arrivals, such as the Skylark Motel, a large U-shaped motel at Spencer and Atlantic Avenues in downtown Wildwood that featured an attention-grabbing sign outfitted with flashing incandescent bulbs. The same era also saw a series of smaller motels appear in nooks and crannies of the Wildwoods' side streets. These motels, with such names as the Magnolia, San's, and the Lilly, were unremarkable save for dynamic neon signs.

For the first time, the 1955–56 directory lists motels in Wildwood Crest. The city of Wildwood, which already had plenty of gaudy bars, hotels, restaurants, and amusements, was receptive to motels, and certain districts of North Wildwood also welcomed them, though other parts of North Wildwood remained residential (by social norm rather than by ordinance). Wildwood Crest's planning board, though, forbade the construction of motels, which it believed would attract an undesirable element. In 1953, John Moyer challenged this mandate and built the small Breezy Corner Motel at the intersection of Louisville and Seaview Avenues, two blocks inland. The Breezy Corner was modest, with only four units, but its bright-green neon sign and large parking lot angered Wildwood Crest residents. Builders and developers in the borough tried to persuade the planning board to allow motels, but residents continued to oppose the motion. On August 27, 1953, the Wildwood Crest Planning Board convened a town meeting to hear both sides of the issue. Several local builders defended their motels as objects of "architectural beauty," and several residents spoke out against "undesirable" motel clientele. After the forum, the planning board moved to allow motels in the Crest.

Motel owners used pop-art-like brochure graphics to advertise their motels, often preferring stylized drawings to photos. *Courtesy of Wildwood Historical Society*

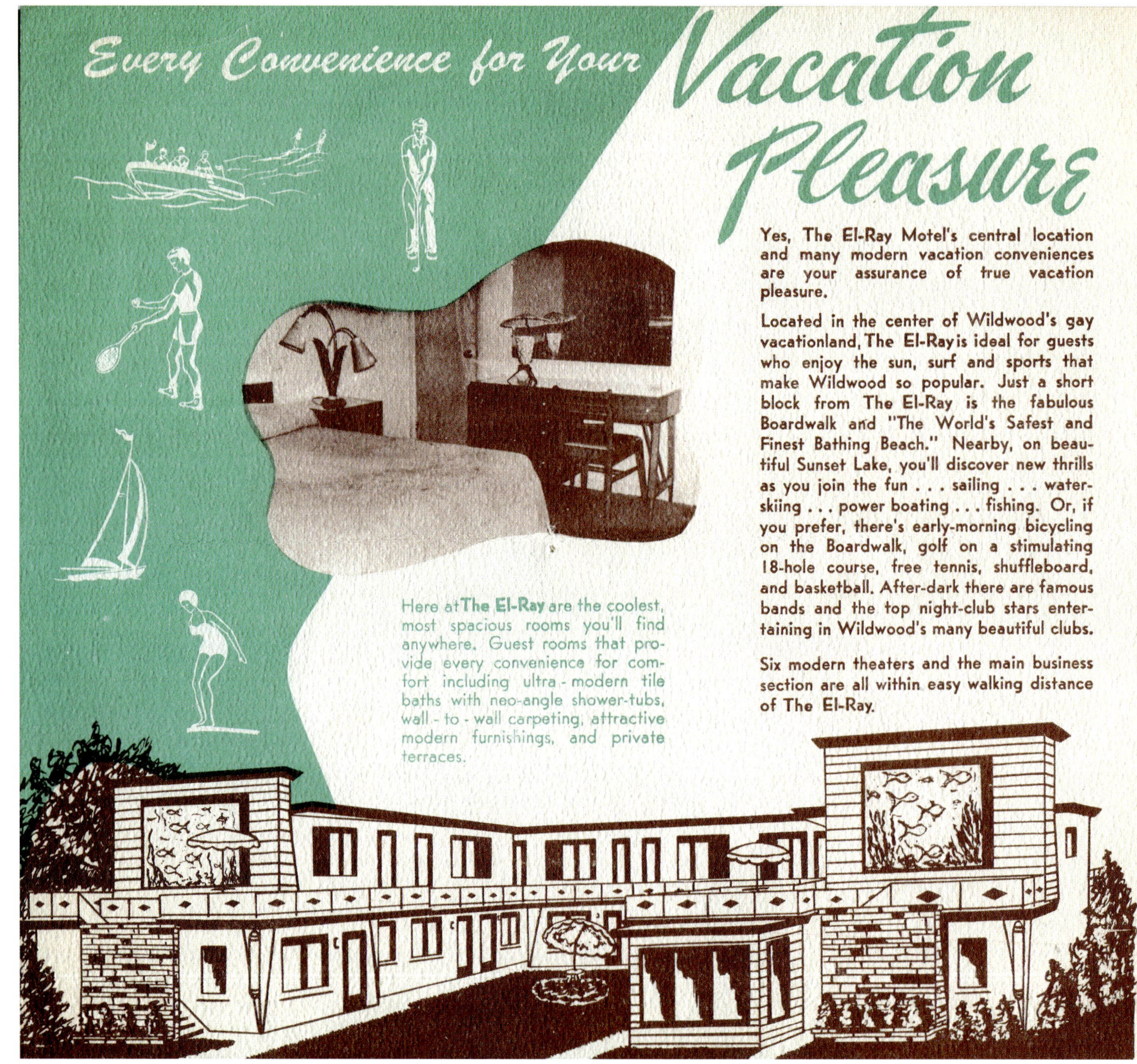

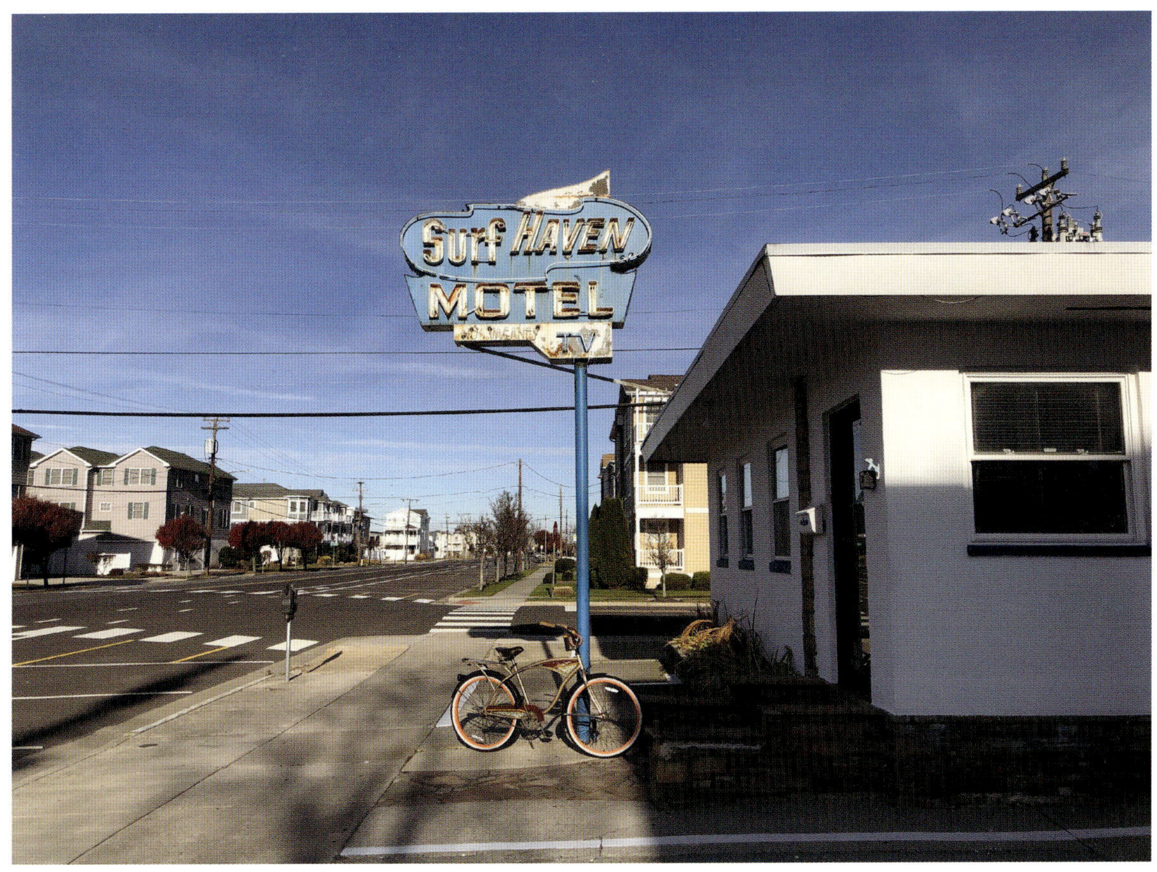

Neon signs got bigger over time. The modest sign for the Surf Haven, still standing on Surf Avenue in North Wildwood, exemplifies the minimalism of early 1950s advertising.

Jet-Age Enthusiasm

By the time the 1957–58 Wildwood city directory was published, a construction boom had produced two full pages' worth of motels. Owners of outdated tourist courts began to adapt their buildings to the demands of the island's growing lodging industry. Courts such as the Sea Shell, El Ray, and Del-Fon-Sea received updated neon signs emblazoned with the word "motel," often accompanied by the addition of a floor or two and a pool (an amenity that became popular in the Wildwoods in the late 1950s, baffling early motel owners, who believed that their guests would be content swimming in the ocean nearby). Many of these new motels explored the art of neon as advertising. "North Wildwood had many smaller signs that were almost like folk art," says local sign builder Fedele "Fred" Musso, who has repaired most of the Wildwoods' neon signs at one point or another (and who has designed and built many new ones). "They had a lot of animation and little motifs on them.

Neon designers in the Wildwoods created masterworks of "electronic persuasion," using arrows to beckon to travelers.

The Blue Jay Motel's sign combined neon lettering with a border of chasing incandescent lights, which added movement to the sign. *Courtesy of Kyle Weaver*

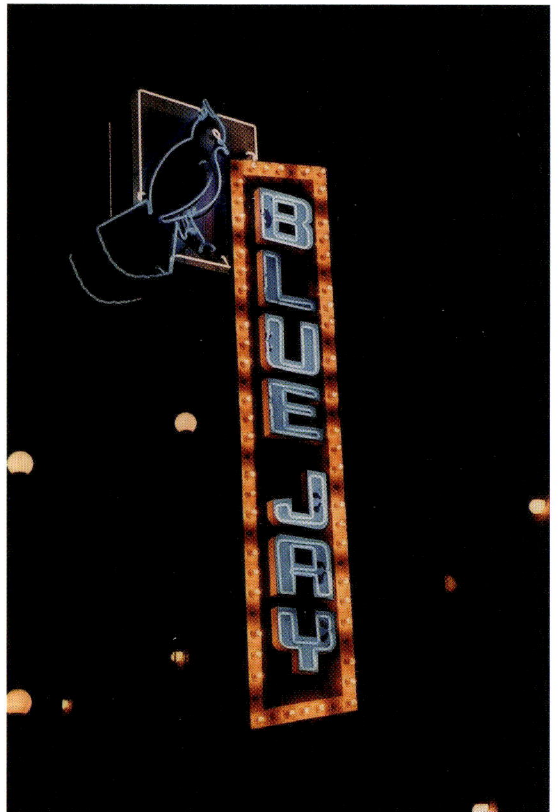

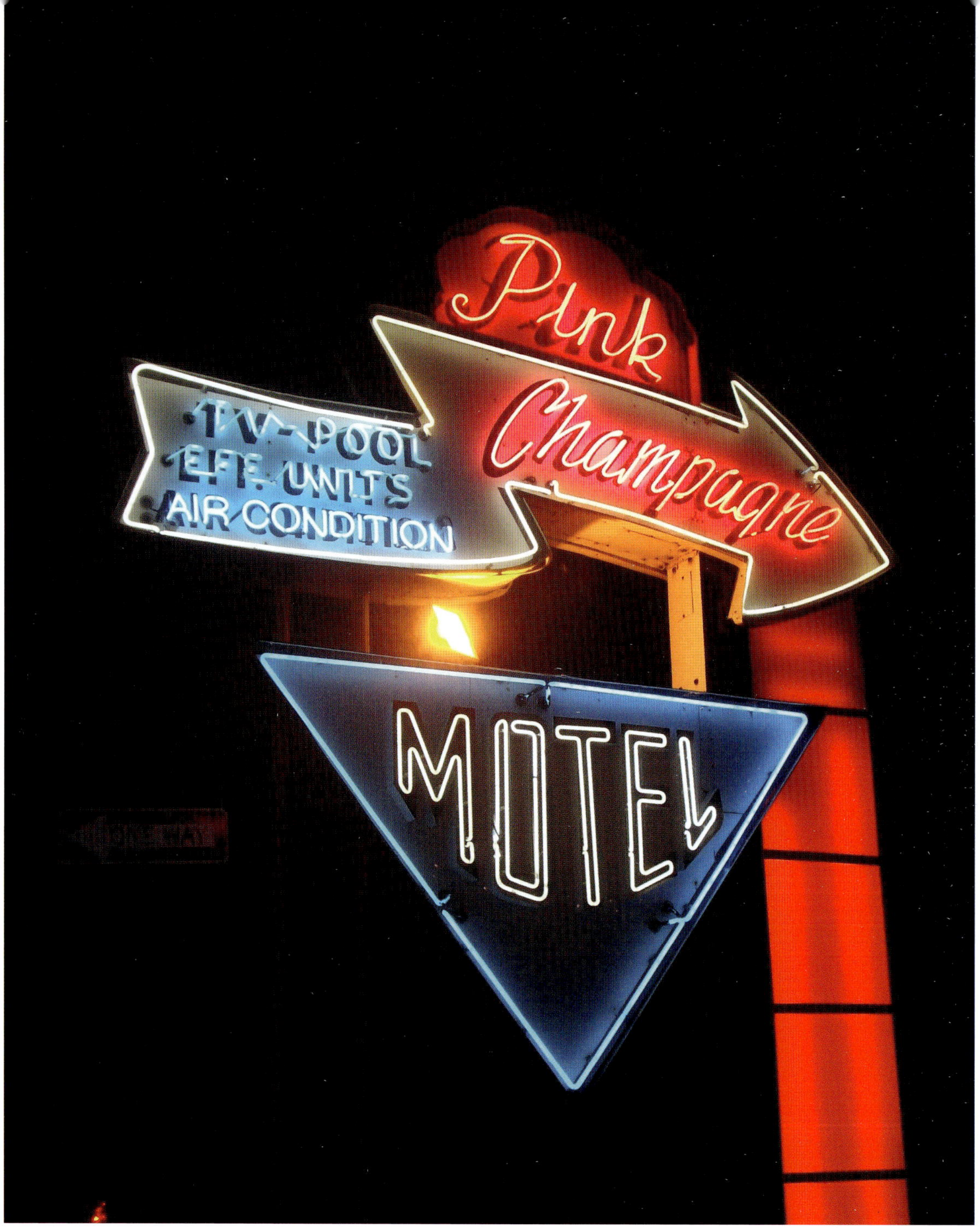

I think ABS did a lot of those. They have a lot of little things going on." Alas, most of the Wildwoods' 1950s neon signs do not survive.

During the 1950s, Allied Signs, a company owned by talented sign builder Ted Pollis, built most of the neon signs in town. Toward the end of the decade, employee Harry Lanza took over Allied, which existed for several decades afterward under Lanza's ownership (when Lanza died in 1993, another sign company, JT Signs, bought Allied but went out of business soon afterward). In 1955, another Allied employee, Charlie Szczur, left the company and started Ace Sign Company (Musso notes, "It seems like all of these guys worked together on and off in the late 1950s and early 1960s."). In 1964, Ace employee Bob Hentges left Ace and started ABS Signs (and then bought out Ace the next year). Randy Hentges, Bob's son and the current owner of ABS, says, "My dad actually worked for a sign company when he was in high school. Then he ended up buying them out over time, and that's how it started. The reason they named it ABS was because of the phone book. Now there's no phone book, but back then everything was in alphabetical order. So people would go through the yellow pages, and ABS was the first sign shop that would come up." Bob Hentges reverse-engineered ABS into Always Better Service.

Starting in the mid-1950s, designers such as Pollis, Lanza, Hentges, and a neon bender at Allied named John Fallone (Musso says, "He was known in neon circles as 'the legend.'") created a series of neon signs that combined modern typefaces, animation, and bright colors to make Wildwood a brightly lit wonderland at night. Earlier neon signs were smaller scale and less masterful than their later creations: the 1954 sign for the Flamingo Terrace Motel, for instance, featured a neon flamingo and a chunk of text: "Motel, Eff. Units, TV, Air Conditioning, Pool." Several neon signs from this era advertised amenities that were state of the industry in 1955 but are quaint today. As Musso notes, "Whenever you see 'TV,' 'Private Baths,' or 'Phones' on a sign, you know it's from the 1950s. And if you see 'Cable TV,' that's from the 1970s." Some signs in town have unique wording: "The White Caps is the only sign in town that says, 'Sorry, no vacancy.' Most of them just say 'No vacancy.' And over at the Florentine is the only neon sign that says 'elevator.'"

In 1956, Will Morey built the Fantasy Motel, a significant building on an unassuming block of West Rio Grande Avenue. The previous New Year's Eve, Will and Lou Morey had dissolved their building partnership. As Jack Morey, Will's son, remembers, "I don't think Lou was a formal architect. Lou was really creative. I think Lou, individually, probably had more creativity than any one of them and maybe anyone else on the island at the time. He would draft things himself. He didn't have quite the business savvy, but he had the creative architectural savvy. My father, on the other hand—to some, he was this big dreamer, but as you compare him to Lou, he was far more practical. The two of them ended up splitting because there was a rub between the creative dreamer and the practical dreamer. They were both dreamers, no question about that!" This friction led to good-natured competition between the two, who would construct several innovative motels on the island over the next decade.

The Fantasy Motel was the first of these creations. A canny land speculator, Will bought a small lot at 131 West Rio Grande Avenue. Although it was neither a beachfront nor a bayfront location, he made the best of the site's limitations. Opening for business on April 29, 1956, the Fantasy Motel

Will Morey's Fantasy Motel brought neofuturism to a street populated by American Foursquare houses. *Courtesy of Wildwood Historical Society*

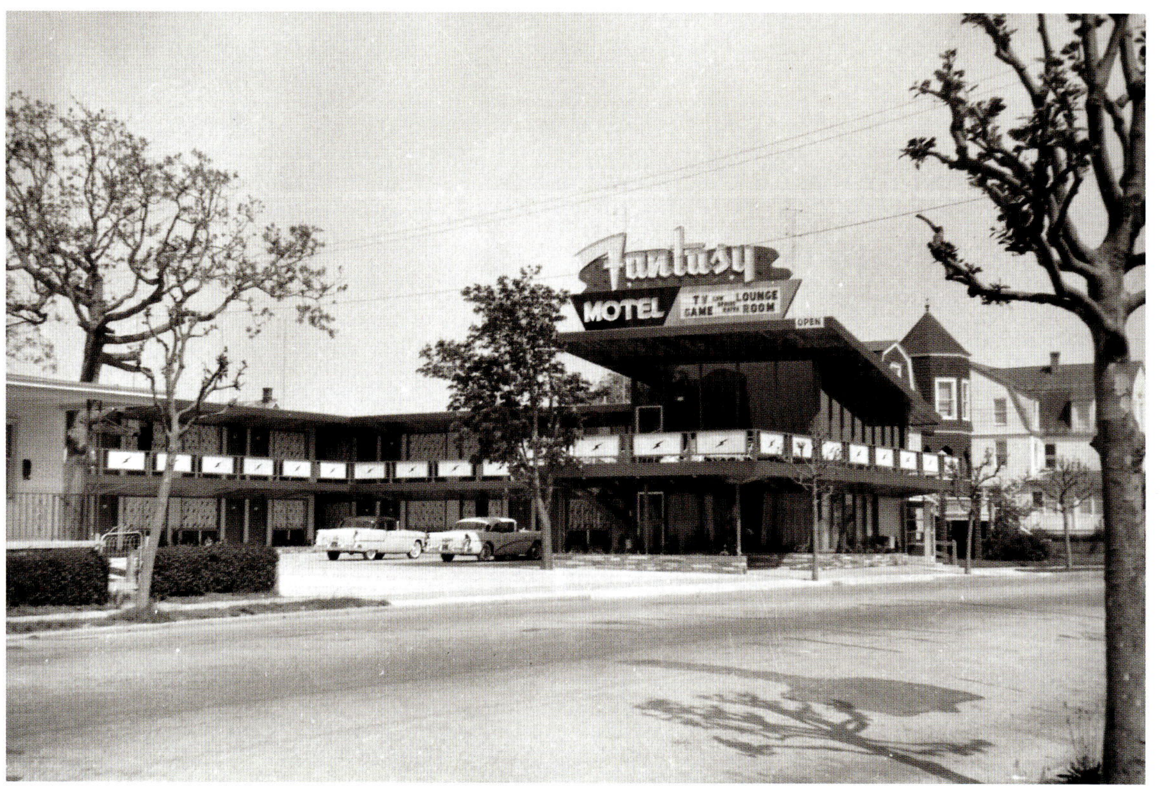

was unlike any building Wildwood had seen before. In the *Wildwood Leader* of April 26, Will took out an advertisement to announce his new creation as "the newest look in motels." With its asymmetrical glass-enclosed lounge, topped with a massive, sloping roof and an enormous Allied neon sign, the Fantasy created a stir. Jinny Wood, a local resident, remembers, "We didn't know how the thing stood up—it was all *windows*!" Local builders took notice and rushed to emulate its luxurious design. (In the Fantasy's early years, a banner hung above its office, reading, "We're not expensive, we just look that way." Will Morey had spent $125,000 on the Fantasy, an extravagance in 1956 but a small figure compared to later motels on the island.)

Also in 1956, Earl and Ralph Johnson built the Carousel Motel at Lavender and Ocean Avenues in the sparsely populated Crest. With a circular lounge and a Playbill neon sign, the Carousel expressed a unified circus theme that recalled the Hotel Seville of thirty years earlier. The same year, Will Morey built Schumann's Restaurant in Wildwood Crest. With its prowed roof and a largely glass façade, Schumann's introduced the design language of California-style coffee shops into the Wildwoods' vocabulary. It also heavily featured a masonry material called flagcrete, a tile-like mixture of flagstone and concrete that would proliferate in the next decade.

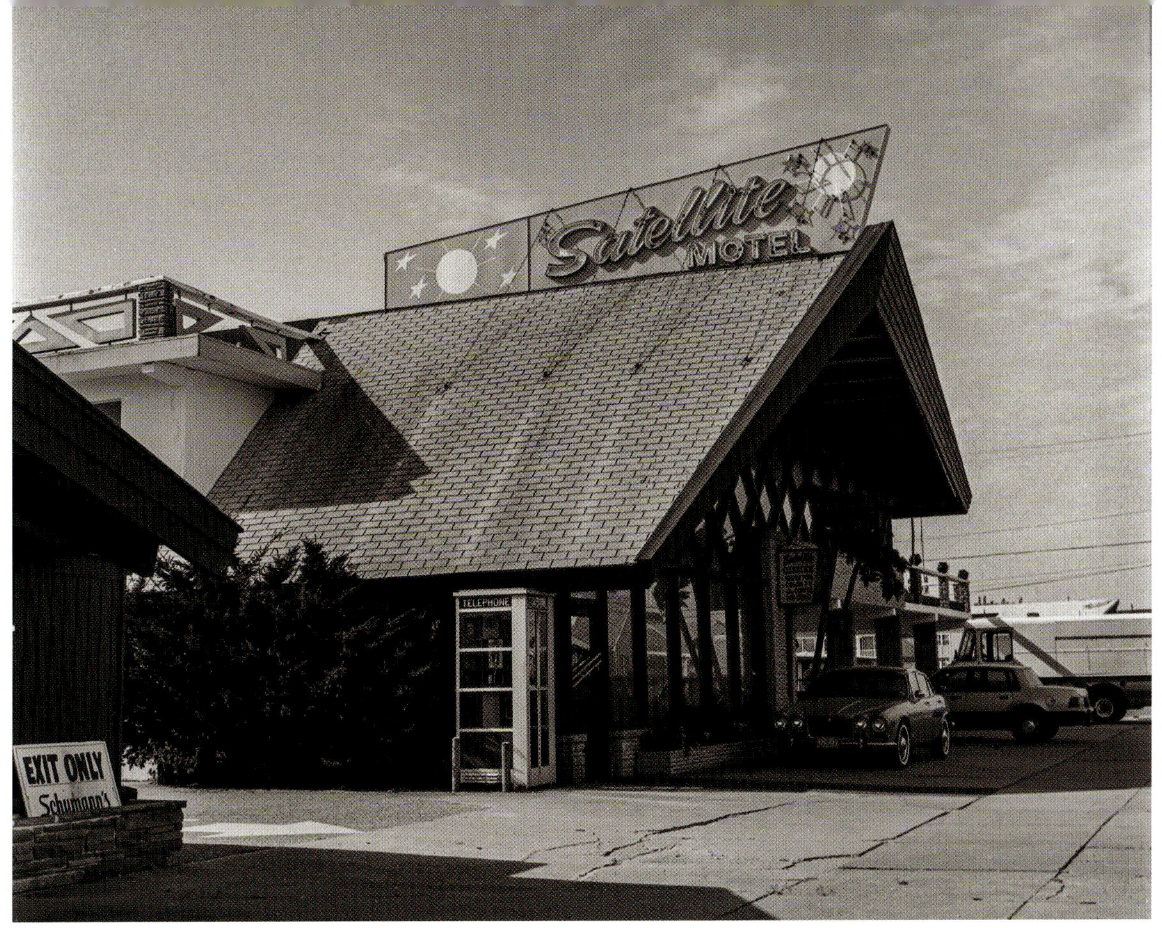

With his 1958 Satellite Motel, shown here in 1986, Will Morey raised the bar for the Wildwoods' motel builders. *Courtesy of Ed Steinerts*

Lou Morey, too, continued building novel buildings, such as the Crest's Ebb Tide and Markay Motels, which featured canted walls and bright-yellow color schemes. In 1957, he built the Eden Roc Motel, a remarkable design with a brick façade, a pool shaped like a jelly bean (known as "kidney shaped" in some circles), and two wall-hung neon signs that spelled out a name Lou had borrowed from Morris Lapidus's Eden Roc Hotel in Miami. (Lou also built the Sans Souci Motel on 21st Avenue in North Wildwood, which took its name from another Miami Lapidus building.) Inspired by this budget escapism, other local builders began turning out exotically themed motels. These contractors observed the Morey brothers' motels carefully and erected motels with similarly bold shapes and combinations of modern materials such as flagcrete, glass, and neon.

Despite this new abundance of motels and motel builders, the Morey brothers continued to be the stars of the island. In 1958, their friendly rivalry reached its peak, as Lou constructed the Caribbean and Tangiers Motels a few blocks apart in Wildwood Crest (as well as the less flashy El Reno farther south), and Will built the Satellite Motel. With their dynamic use of shapes, materials,

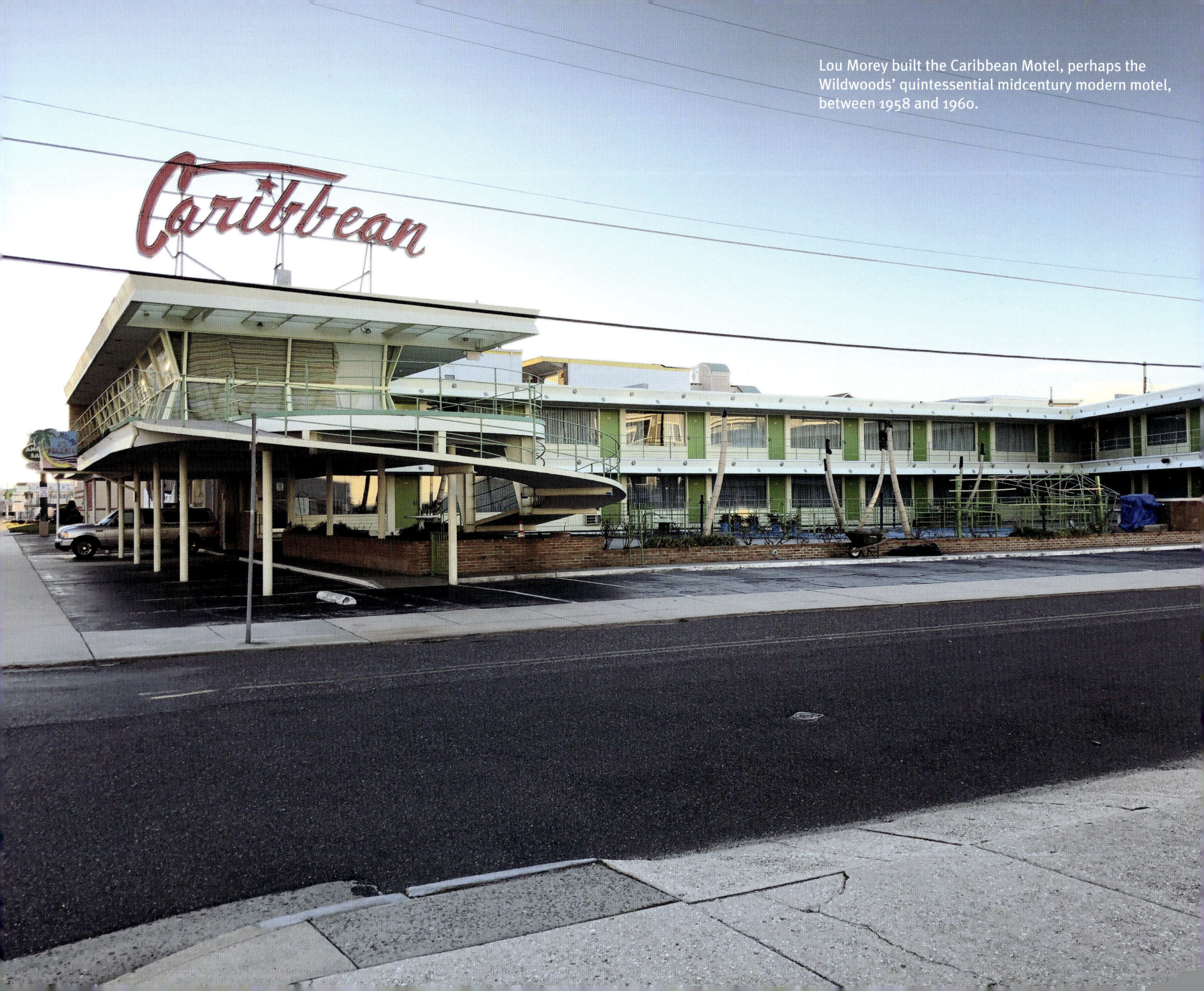

Lou Morey built the Caribbean Motel, perhaps the Wildwoods' quintessential midcentury modern motel, between 1958 and 1960.

and themes, these motels occupied a tier of their own. The Satellite showcased a cartoonishly asymmetrical gable roof, covered with X-paned glass and flagcrete and topped with a blue-script neon sign. A few blocks away, the Caribbean featured a circular ramp, canted glass walls, another script neon sign, and a chartreuse color scheme, and the Tangiers furthered the California coffee shop look with diagonal wood paneling, tan brick accents, and an asymmetrical lounge roof. These motels upped the ante for builders around the island. Jack Morey says that his father, Will, was "a builder before everything else. He would work with the sign guys, but he was basically a contractor and a carpenter. The sign became part of the architecture. I guess he was marginally successful as a contractor. My mom would joke that the only job that he actually made money for was the one where he accidentally figured the windows twice!"

Motels began filling up empty lots all over the island in the late 1950s. Several patterns are noticeable: The Fantasy Motel ignited a jet-age enthusiasm that peaked in 1963 with Lou Morey's Admiral Motel, whose asymmetrical lobby, large panes of glass, and sweeping lines recalled Eero Saarinen's 1962 TWA terminal. Also, the popularity of James Michener's 1947 novel *Tales of the South Pacific* and its 1960 musical adaptation *South Pacific* caused a tiki craze to strike the Wildwoods in the late 1950s and early 1960s, a decade after it had struck California. Several Polynesian-themed motels, such as Wildwood Crest's Casa Bahama and Tahiti, used vernacular architecture to evoke A-frame huts and bamboo trees. Builders mixed imagery from the Bahamas, Hawaii, and generic Hollywood ideals of tropical locations, making a uniquely American (but culturally confused) package.

The Wildwoods' motels transported their guests to a variety of eras and locales. The Saratoga, Gaslite, and Midtown Motels used lanterns, Old English typefaces, and brick façades to recall colonial America. The Crusader and Ivanhoe went even further back, evoking medieval times. The Astronaut, Apollo, and Galaxie looked beyond air travel to present a midcentury vision of the space age. The Bel Air, Caprice, and Skylark Motels took their names from futuristic automobiles of the 1950s and 1960s, while the Aztec, Singapore, and Safari Motels used signage and decorations to transport viewers to budget-friendly miniatures of exciting vacation spots. Other motels took their names from plants (Mango, Sunflower) or birds (Sandpiper, Blue Jay, Condor), while some merely offered escapism and high living (Pink Champagne, Hi-Lili) or a beachfront retreat (Surf Holiday, Sun Haven). Throughout this era, builders added similarly modern architectural elements to businesses, shops, movie theaters, and restaurants around the island.

In 1962, the Wildwoods suffered a setback. An Ash Wednesday nor'easter battered the Eastern Seaboard between March 6 and 8, dumping massive amounts of rain and tearing away beaches. The federal government declared the New Jersey coast a disaster area, and residents requested more than $2 million in assistance loans. When the waters receded in the Wildwoods, the island

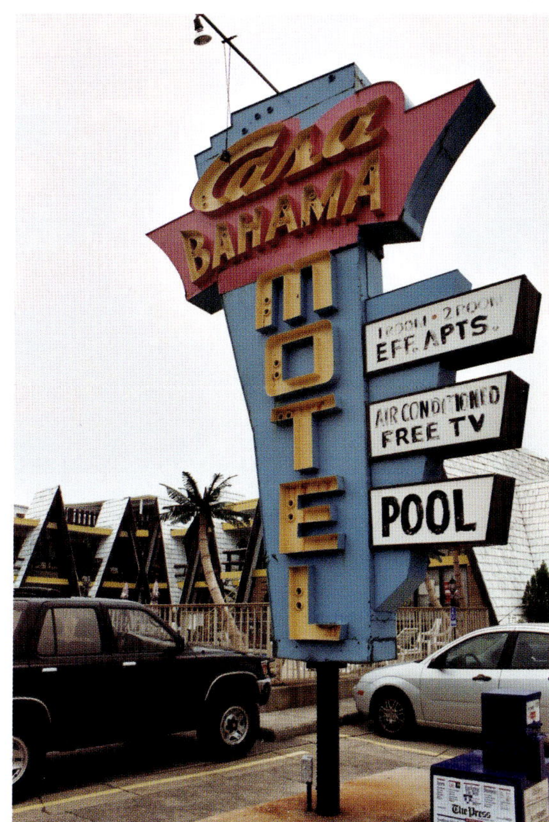

The Casa Bahama Motel inaugurated a Polynesian craze in the Wildwoods, even though, as shown here, it mixed elements from various cultures, including 1950s Americana. *Courtesy of Kyle Weaver*

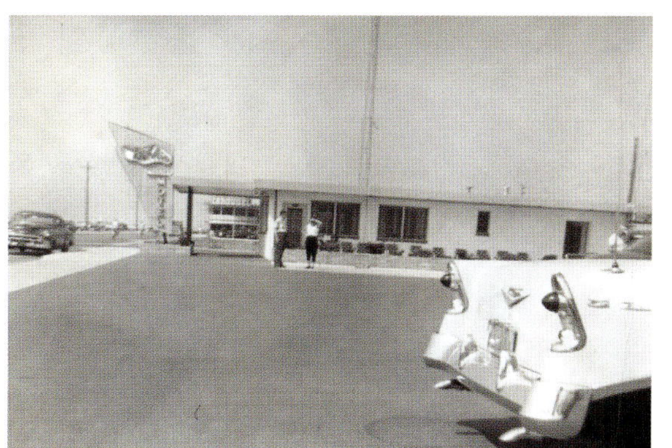

Many motels in the Wildwoods were named after cars, including the Bel Air, shown here as originally built in 1956 with one story. *Courtesy of Wildwood Historical Society*

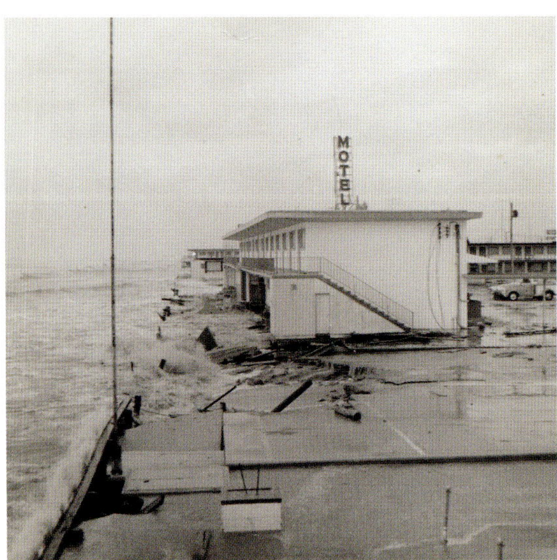

The Crest's Beach Waves Motel weathers the March 1962 nor'easter. *Courtesy of Wildwood Historical Society*

found itself in a unique predicament. Oddly, the storm had caused the beach to expand by a quarter mile. Wildwood city officials elected not to shift the boardwalk once again, a move that would have disrupted the local economy. Wildwood Crest, though, capitalized on the beach expansion, adding two new lengthwise streets along the beachfront. The new Ocean Avenue and Beach Avenue opened several new blocks of oceanfront real estate to development. This new development hampered motels that already existed, though. Melissa Roy, who owns the VIP Family Motel in Wildwood Crest, remembers that her family's motel had once advertised a beachfront view, but in the early 1970s the Armada Motel, built on one of the new blocks, obscured this view. "I remember my dad trying to purchase the new beachfront property with intentions of adding on, but he was told it was dedicated property [for a future park]. One spring, upon going to the shore to start opening, he saw where they started to build the Armada's foundation. My father was very upset and filed a petition to stop work. He was told that they made a mistake—the south-side property of Forget-Me-Not Road was the dedicated property. My father was extremely upset to lose our beachfront view!" Scenes like these played out throughout the Crest during the 1960s.

Before any of this new building could begin, several existing motels needed repairs, particularly in Wildwood Crest, where the absence of dunes and a boardwalk left oceanfront buildings vulnerable to storm damage. Photos show that the Crest's beachside motels suffered extensive damage. The Morey brothers (and several other building teams, such as the Buckingham Brothers Builders, the Johnson brothers, and the Bada Brothers Builders) began not only repairing existing motels but also building new ones. Lou Morey took particular advantage of the renewed interest in beachfront development and put up several new motels for the 1962 summer season, including the Cara Mara, the Astronaut, and the Nomad. Will Morey built the beachfront Flagship Motel and the boardwalk-front Shore Plaza that year.

Local Headwinds

After a boom between 1962 and 1964, motel construction began to wane in the last half of the 1960s. Most of the Wildwoods' beachfront land had been developed. A 1960 survey counted 3,238 motel rooms on the island, 1,309 of which had air-conditioning and 1,730 of which had a television. By 1963, about 2,000 more motel rooms had opened, which adroitly handled the 380,000 visitors who spent time on the island that summer. With this growth came conflict, however; in a country divided by civil rights, several motel owners refused admission to African American vacationers. After the NAACP staged protests in front of several motels in the summer of 1963, Wildwood's Hotel and Motel Association formed a biracial committee to address the matter. Period articles do not reveal how the issue was resolved.

In 1967, the Diamond Beach Lodge opened at the southern tip of Wildwood Crest. This resort-style building portended the next era of the Wildwoods' motel building. Several obtrusive high-rise hotels appeared during the 1970s: the Acropolis Oceanfront Resort opened in 1976 on John F. Kennedy Boulevard in North Wildwood, blocking ocean views of the buildings behind it; so did Wildwood Crest's Reges Oceanfront Resort and Bal Harbour Motor Inn (the latter displaced

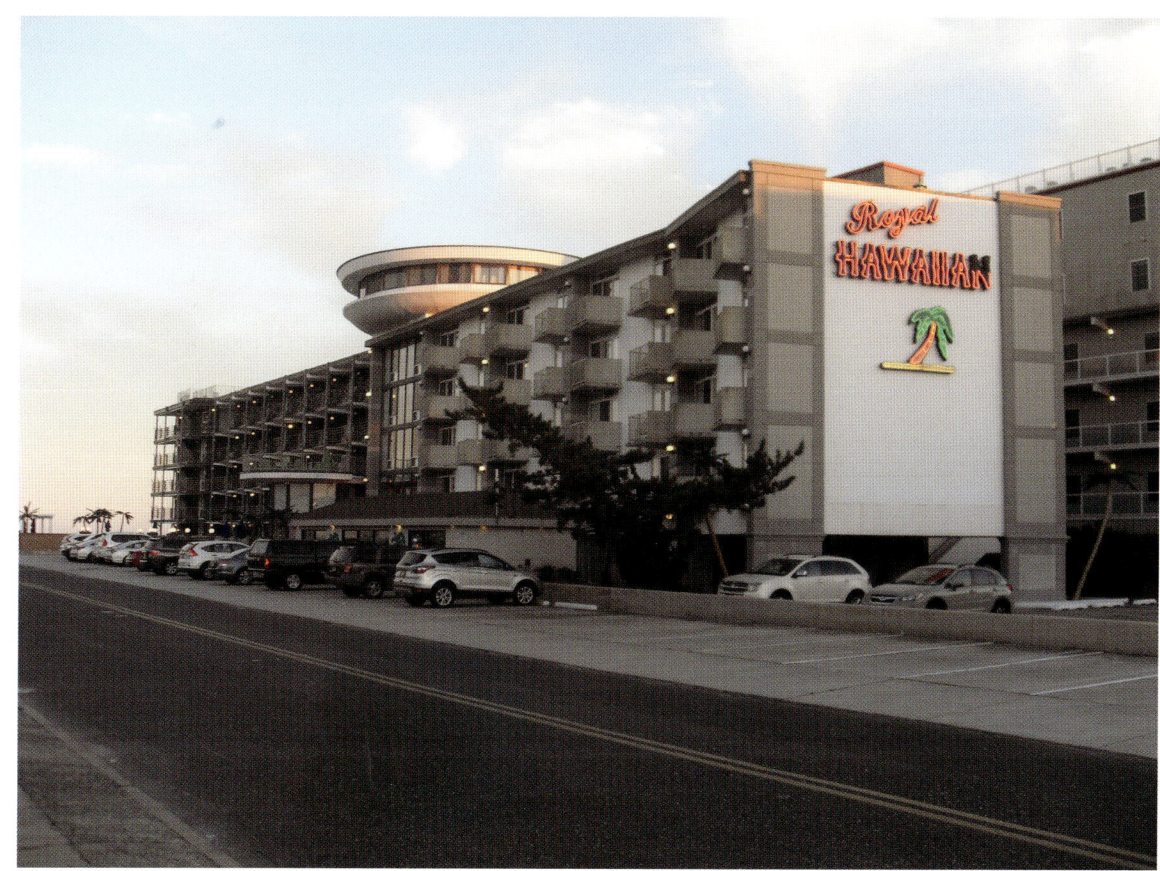

In the late 1960s, motels grew in size. Lou Morey's Royal Hawaiian, built in 1969 and expanded with a flying-saucer-like penthouse in 1978, translated the tiki aesthetic to a larger scale.

the Beach Waves Motel, bulldozed in 1972) and Wildwood's Ocean Towers. Most of the Wildwoods' two- and three-story motels stayed intact, but the new motels that opened in the 1970s were larger than those that had come before. Motels such as the Waikiki and the Bristol Plaza in Wildwood Crest had six or seven stories and mammoth street-side parking lots. Several of these latter-day motels featured stunning, but isolated, midcentury details (Lou Morey's Royal Hawaiian, opened in 1969 and expanded in 1978, had a flying-saucer-like penthouse on its roof), but the magic that had permeated the Caribbean, the Fantasy, and the Satellite was gone.

Lou Morey finished his last motel projects in the late 1970s (including the Royal Hawaiian, Sea Scape, and Pink Panther Motels in the Crest) and died in 1983. His brother Will, meanwhile, had built the Pan American and Port Royal Hotels in 1964 and 1972, respectively. The former translated a midcentury modern aesthetic to a unique hotel format, with a rotating rooftop sign that replicated a satellite out of plastic. The Port Royal, however, had few whimsical details and exemplified the Wildwoods' 1970s motels: functional, but devoid of the pizzazz that had adorned earlier motels.

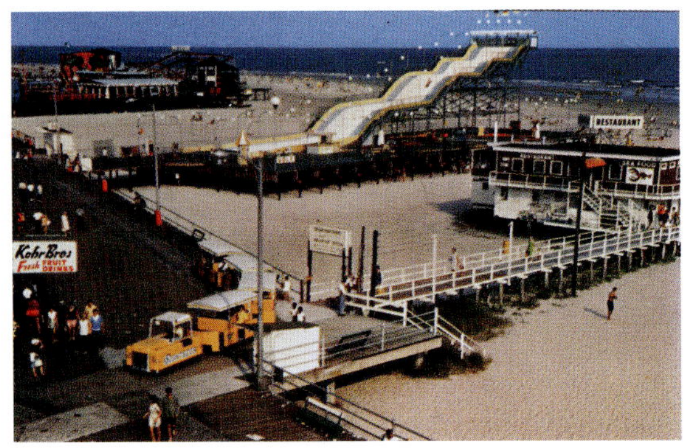

Will and Bill Morey opened Morey's Pier in 1969. *Author's collection*

In 1969, Will teamed up with another Morey brother, Bill, to buy a fairground slide. They built a pier at 25th Street to house the Wipe Out slide and named it Morey's Pier. Before long, Morey's Pier became a raging success, and Will and Bill Morey expanded by buying several other piers. Morey's Piers has become one of the Wildwoods' largest employers.

As the Moreys moved on from motel construction, the motel industry in the Wildwoods slackened, halting completely in the 1980s. The island's nightclub scene continued to thrive, though. Maria Enos, owner of the Pink Champagne Motel, remembers: "In the 1970s and 1980s, there was a bar and a restaurant on every corner, and you could walk home at four in the morning and it was as busy as it was in the middle of the afternoon." The popularity of bars and clubs threatened the wholesome image the Wildwoods had tried to cultivate in the 1950s and 1960s. As spilled oil washed ashore and New Jersey unemployment hit its highest levels in recent memory, the Wildwoods saw an economic decline that slashed beach attendance and subjected many motel owners to hard times. Steve Reeser, owner of the Bel Air Motel, remembers a stopgap solution many motel owners employed while maintaining their plastic palms—replacing fronds with branches from artificial Christmas trees. "Those Christmas tree branches were here when I got here. You had to take the branches out at the end of the season and store them inside. Fronds were pricey!"

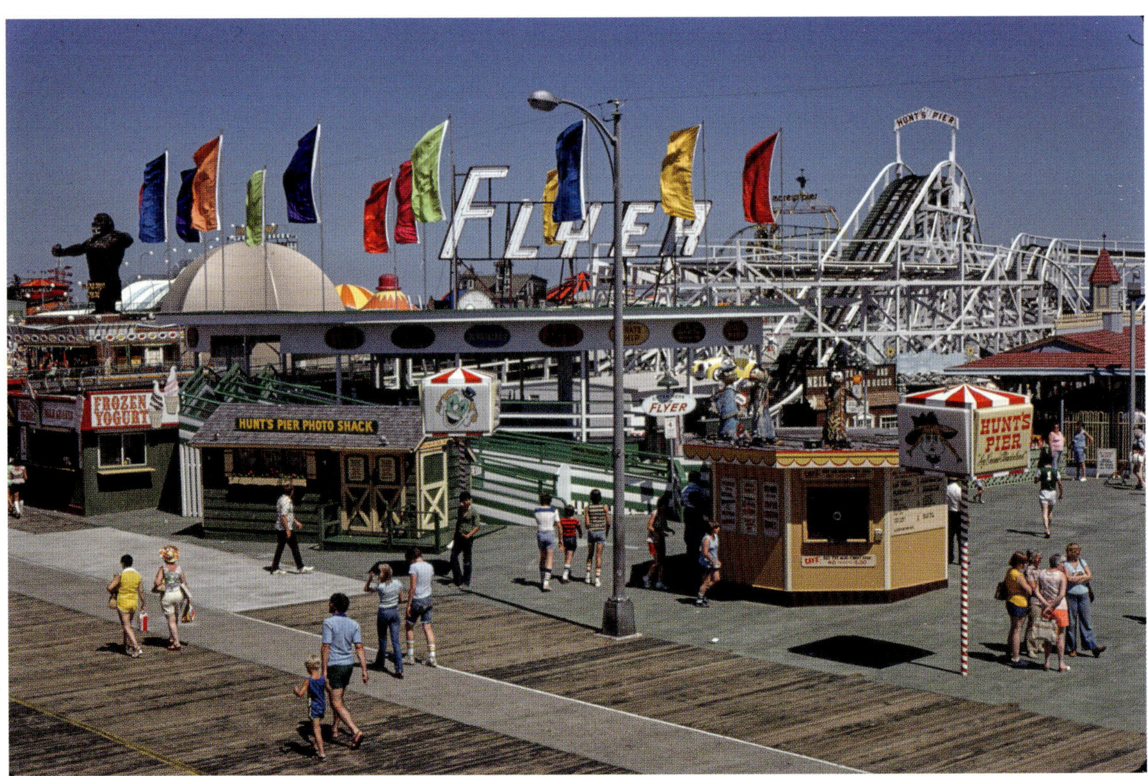

The 1970s and 1980s saw the island's fortunes sink, though its amusement piers continued to flourish, as seen in this 1978 photo of Hunt's Pier. *John Margolies photo*

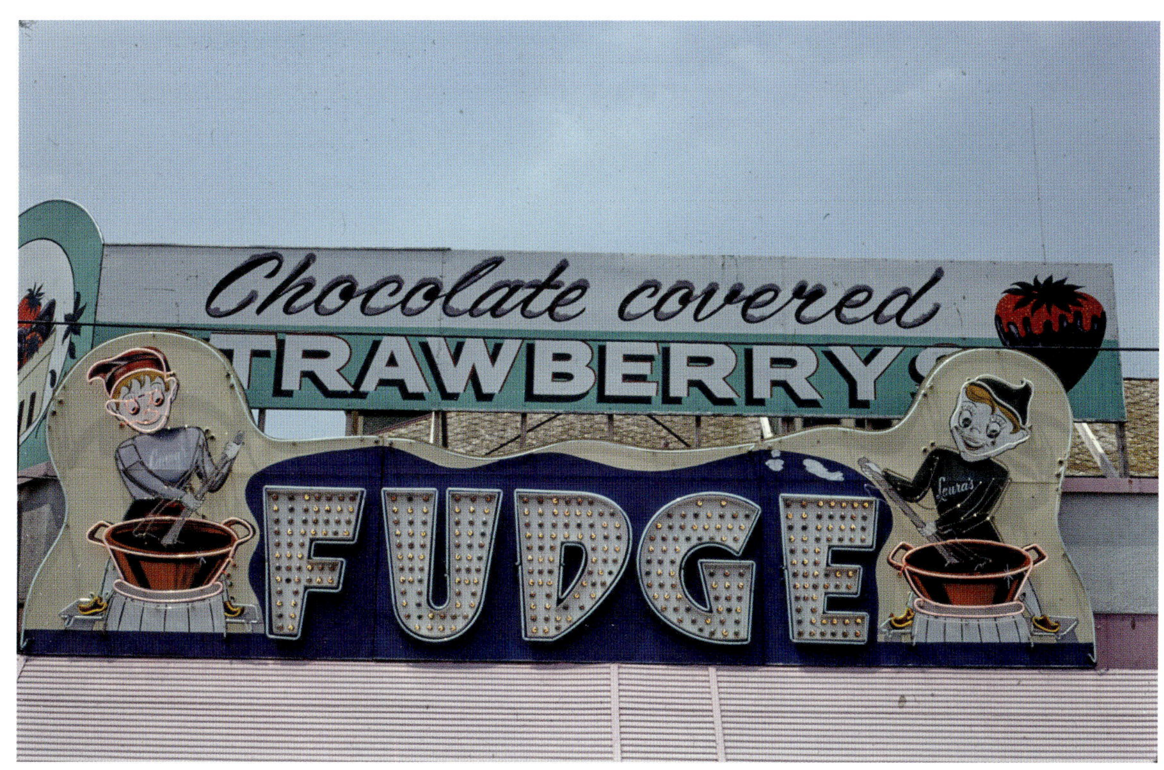

Neon lost favor in the 1970s and 1980s. As seen in this 1978 photo, the owners of Laura's Fudge augmented their neon signage with billboard-like wooden panels. *John Margolies photo*

As the local economy worsened, the extravagances that had characterized the Wildwoods' motels of the 1950s and 1960s became passé and were removed during renovations. Flagcrete gave way to stucco; neon disappeared in favor of plastic signs. Soon-to-be neon tube bender Fred Musso did not renew the lease for a game he operated on the boardwalk, opting to leave the Wildwoods and set up a surf shop in Jupiter, Florida. The era of the Wildwoods' midcentury magnificence was over.

The Wildwoods' economic downturn had one hidden benefit: while redevelopment was claiming midcentury architecture in many other parts of the country, the Wildwoods' motels stayed intact, if not always successful. "The motels were just contemporary culture at the time," observes Jack Morey. "It wasn't unique—it was everywhere! It was around on Route 66 and Miami and a lot of resort places. It survived here the longest because the economy here wasn't rich enough for them to change it over. It was preservation by poverty." The Wildwoods' sluggish economy dissuaded developers from coming to the island, and its vintage motels remained virtually unchanged for decades. Some were the worse for wear after years of deferred maintenance. The Fantasy, for instance, had seen its original neon sign replaced with a pale plastic replica and its pool surrounded by a utilitarian chain-link fence.

Steps toward Preservation

In 1970, preservation activity in its neighbor to the south inspired Wildwood's next steps. Carolyn Pitts had been hired as a historical consultant for a citywide urban renewal scheme in Cape May that would have seen several blocks of its historic downtown bulldozed. Pitts was an active preservationist, making her presence on an urban renewal project curious. She conducted a survey of Cape May's Victorian properties and submitted her findings to the city, but she met resistance when she suggested to city officials that the historic houses be preserved. Rather than lose a trove of nineteenth-century Victoriana, Pitts submitted her documentation to the National Trust, which surreptitiously listed the city (as a whole, in addition to several individual properties) on the National Register of Historic Places.

While this nomination enraged Cape May's commerce-oriented civic leaders, who were now barred from building a lucrative mall, the listing motivated Cape May residents. In 1970, concerned citizens founded the Mid-Atlantic Center for the Arts (MAC) to preserve Cape May's Emlen Physick house, an 1879 Frank Furness building that was close to collapse. After restoring the Physick house, MAC then took on several other historic Cape May properties, including its lighthouse and a World War II–era lookout tower. In the late 1980s, MAC's board of directors listened to a presentation from two Wildwood citizens who wanted to preserve the Wildwoods' equally significant collection of architecture.

One of these citizens was Chuck Schumann, who had earned local fame running popular "Sightseer" boat tours up and down the Wildwoods' beach. "We became very envious of Cape May," remembers Schumann. "It had a Victorian air that was very marketable—beautiful homes, trolley tours. But we knew that Wildwood had Victorian homes too. So one day, when we had time, we did a photo album of all the Victorian homes in Wildwood, as well as some of the fifties motels. We took that and presented it to Mid-Atlantic Center for the Arts' board of directors, suggesting that maybe they would like to do a Victorian tour in Wildwood also. When he called us back to talk to us, he said that we don't really have a critical mass of Victorian buildings, but they said that we have great fifties buildings. He said we should try to promote the midcentury architecture instead."

Schumann adjusted his focus, creating a new presentation showcasing the Wildwoods' midcentury motels. He followed the lead of the Society for Commercial Archaeology, a group of aficionados of midcentury modern architecture who had produced a pamphlet called *Wildwood Workbook* for a 1983 conference—the first work to examine the Wildwoods' commercial architecture in a serious way. That pamphlet had stated, "Common to most commercial architecture is the rapid change in design these properties undergo to meet business needs. . . . [The motels have] suffered a good deal of alteration, diminishing the architectural qualities of some permanent buildings."

Absorbing this preservationist mindset, Schumann organized a trolley tour to draw attention to the island's fifties-vintage architecture. The Moreys pitched in too, as Jack Morey remembers. "We had a trolley for the Seapointe Village project, and we said, go ahead, use the trolley." The 1991 season of trolley tours was a resounding success. "The first year, we received a state award for creative

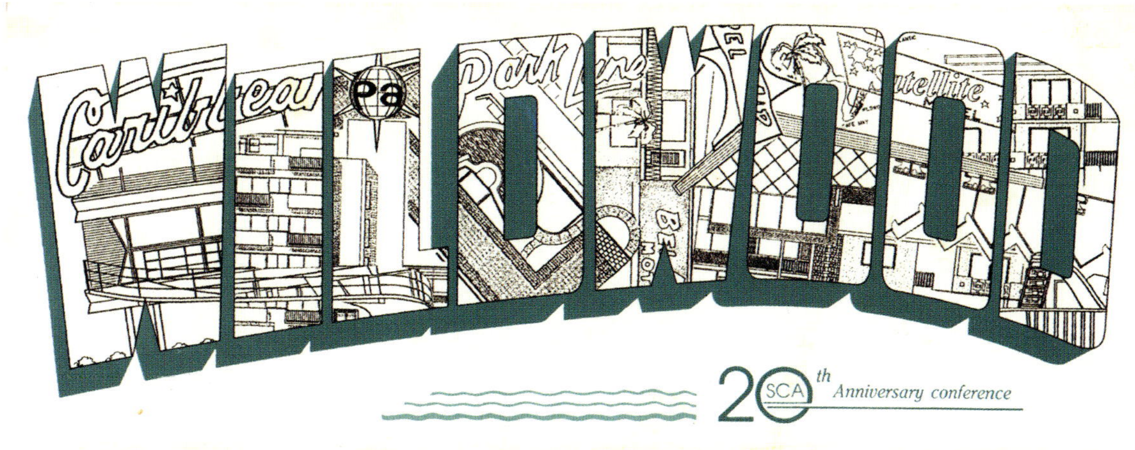

Academic interest in the Wildwoods peaked with a 1997 Society for Commercial Archaeology conference. *Courtesy of Fedele Musso*

tourism," Schumann says. "We did fairly well for two or three years. But then some other business-people wanted to be involved." The tours fizzled out after a couple of years, but they had inspired an enduring appreciation for the Wildwoods' collection of postwar architecture.

In 1997, Steven Izenour, a noted architect who had helped compile an innovative architectural study of the White Tower burger chain, worked with several of his architecture students at Yale and the University of Pennsylvania to publish a pamphlet called *Learning from the Wildwoods*. Izenour had also collaborated with architects Robert Venturi and Denise Scott Brown on their pivotal 1972 book *Learning from Las Vegas*, one of the earliest academic works to celebrate commercial architecture. He brought this same enthusiasm to the Wildwoods, which he'd gotten to know during a series of animated walk-and-talks with Jack Morey. Izenour preferred the Wildwood boardwalk a bit rough around the edges. "He said, 'Tacky can be good,'" Morey says. "Steve was a very special guy. I was walking with Steve on one of the piers, and I was about to pick up a piece of trash, but he said, 'Leave it! Leave it! Leave it!' I remember that like yesterday."

Izenour observed the Wildwoods' motels from an academic perspective, expounding on their architecture at length in an essay titled "What Is Popular Culture," which appeared in the *Learning from the Wildwoods* pamphlet:

> Because of its constant need to change, most resort architecture is transitory and eclectic; i.e., next year's ride, snack shop, t-shirt are built and/or sold next to or in place of last year's version of the same. . . . These pragmatic two[-] to three[-]story [motels] were the most efficient way to get a family into a room, their car parked right outside, on a city block, with a pool and a lounge deck. Since all these buildings were based on the same basic prototype, differentiation of the product was achieved by the use of flamboyant decoration in railings, signs, porte-cocheres, plastic palms and exotic names borrowed from far away resorts: the Caribbean, the Palm Beach, the Tropicana, etc. Since these motels were primarily built and are still owned by individual entrepreneurs, they have always been very individual in their expression. . . .

The goal is to develop these major assets, the boardwalk and the piers, and the motels in a way that allows for moderate growth, but responds to changing times and tastes while preserving and cultivating what works from the Wildwoods' rich seashore traditions of bright lights, great rides and flamboyant motels.

Izenour and his students studied the motels on the island, producing detailed notes and blueprints. Emboldened by this academic validation, enthusiasts of the Wildwoods' midcentury modern architecture formed a group to advocate for the motels. Jack Morey and Chuck Schumann led the charge, as did neon sign builder Fred Musso, who had returned to Wildwood in 1996 and ended up working at ABS Signs for a couple of months. "Jack Morey called me over the winter. I think Steven Izenour might have had something to do with that," says Musso. "He told Jack to get a lot of craftsmen and roadside historians on board to help with the revival."

The movement also found a supporter in Dan MacElrevey, owner of the Granada Motel in Wildwood Crest. "The people who started this movement were friends of mine. I wanted to be part of it!" says MacElrevey, who would eventually become president of the organization. The first order of business was to name the Wildwoods' architectural style. Two early contenders were "Googie," Alan Hess's name for California coffee shop architecture and the title of his 1985 book about that style, and "Populuxe," a term Thomas Hine had coined in a similar 1986 book dealing with the East Coast. Eventually, the Wildwoods' preservationists settled on "Doo Wop" because of its familiarity as a music genre and its relevance to the Wildwoods in the 1950s. Schumann remembers, "We wanted to name the architectural designs here different than the ones in California. We did not want to associate with that. We wanted to stand alone." The advocacy organization, then, became the Doo Wop Preservation League, and architect and preservationist Ellen Collins became its first president. This name got a mixed reception: as Patrick Davenport, the owner of the Biscayne Motel, says, "I know what Doo Wop music is, but what's a Doo Wop building?"

In 1997, the Doo Wop Preservation League set to work. Musso and fellow preservationist and Morey's Piers employee Rom Nardi began repairing and storing neon signs that sat unlit all over the island. Jack Morey, meanwhile, spearheaded an effort to hand out flyers to motel owners, advertising the Doo Wop Preservation League. Most motel owners wanted nothing to do with it. "I'd go in there and mention what it was, and it was nasty," Musso remembers. "I'd say, 'I'm not a salesman, but here's what's happening, if you want to take a look!' I think I went to North Wildwood. Rom Nardi and some other guy went up to the Crest, and they came back with really long faces."

Undeterred, Morey organized a town hall meeting and invited motel owners to attend. Musso remembers, "Jack got up to speak at the 1997 SCA conference and he said, 'How many actual motel owners are here?' One guy raised his hand, only one motel owner." The chilly reception forced Morey to reinvent the league's approach. "The future [of the Wildwoods] was not clear," he says. "I and others [had] formed the Doo Wop Preservation League to inspire and motivate a certain change. I started to realize that perhaps the answer was so close to our nose that we couldn't see it. It was Wildwood's wide beach, its amazing collection of rides, and its one-of-a-kind collection of motels. And then I went on a mission to foster a rebirth of the town based on those three things."

The Doo Wop Preservation League set up shop in a storefront on Pacific Avenue in downtown Wildwood. There, they created a museum featuring neon signs that Musso and Nardi had rescued, as well as vintage furniture and displays centered on the Wildwoods' Doo Wop music history. The music display was a later addition to the museum. "We never focused on the music until about three years later," says Schumann. "Someone said that it was the fortieth anniversary of Bill Haley and the Comets' 'Rock Around the Clock.' That began in Wildwood, and it was [one of] the first rock-and-roll record[s] to sell a million copies. I think that entitles us to be the home of rock and roll!"

The Doo Wop Preservation League spread the word about the island's vintage architecture. Despite most motel owners' trepidation, a few bright spots stood out. For one, new Doo Wop construction began to appear. In the early 1990s, the owners of the outdated Sherry Motel on 25th and Surf Avenues in North Wildwood had torn down the 1940s bungalow that served as their motel office, added a third story and an animated neon sign to their motel, and renamed it the Surf. In 1996, Peter Ferrerio bought the Crest's aging Georgeanna Motel and remade it with a Rolling Stones theme, with a guitar-shaped neon sign, rock memorabilia, and a pool slide that resembled the Stones' famous tongue logo, and named it the Memory Motel after a Stones song. These renovations were tame and tacky, respectively, but they represented a newfound appreciation for vintage architecture in the Wildwoods, and the Doo Wop Preservation League proudly posted pictures of this "Neo Doo Wop" architecture on its website. In 2000, the Moreys bought the 1953-vintage Wingate Motel at the busy intersection of Rio Grande and Atlantic Avenues and hired Philadelphia architect Richard Stokes, who had worked with Steven Izenour at the University of Pennsylvania, to redesign it as a twenty-first-century interpretation of the 1950s. Stokes's creation, named the Starlux, featured plastic palms, checkerboard tile surrounding a new pool, angular windows, and a lounge building with an asymmetrical roof that rose to a point that emulated Phillips 66 gas stations. With the Starlux, the Neo Doo Wop movement hit its stride, and the media took notice.

In August 2001, Izenour, one of the Doo Wop movement's founders, passed away unexpectedly. Inspired by his legacy and by the effervescent Starlux, business and motel owners around town began to remodel their businesses in a Neo Doo Wop style. A new Wildwood Convention Center, which opened in 2002, sported neon-lined circular orbs, a nod to midcentury designs; three years later, Maria and Aldo Tenaglia hired Richard Stokes to perform a Starlux-like renovation on their Shalimar Motel. Across the street from the convention center, the owners of the Newport Motel bought a sandwich shop next door and converted it into a Neo Doo Wop Subway franchise with a neon sign and an Astroturf-paved patio. The popular Philadelphia-area convenience store chain Wawa even agreed to break with corporate design guidelines and open a Doo Wop store on Rio Grande Avenue, including a neon marquee and stainless-steel columns. Acme, McDonald's, Walgreen's, and Commerce Bank also opened fifties-inspired branches around town.

While the Neo Doo Wop trend brought attention to the Wildwoods' vintage aesthetic, it also distracted from an alarming number of demolitions of original motels from the 1950s and 1960s.

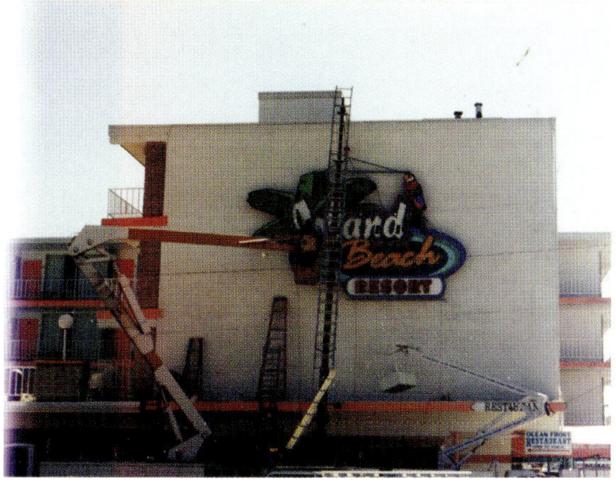

With the movement toward retro in the 1990s, motel owners began to embrace neon. Here, ABS Signs installs an elaborate sign at the Olympic Island Beach Motel. *Courtesy of ABS Sign Co., Inc.*

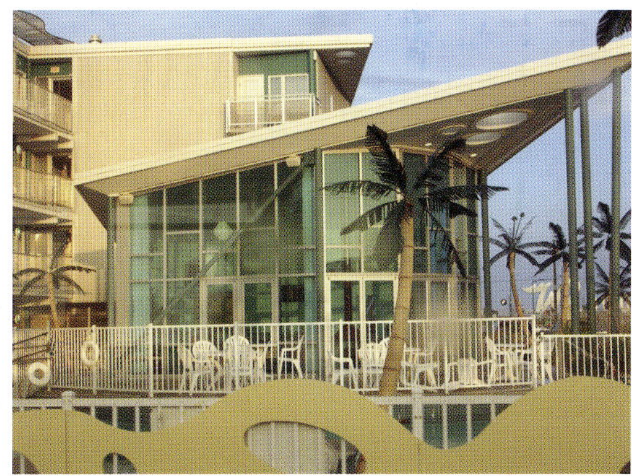

Richard Stokes's Starlux lounge features an asymmetrical roof, supported by bean poles, that recalls 1960s Phillips 66 gas stations.

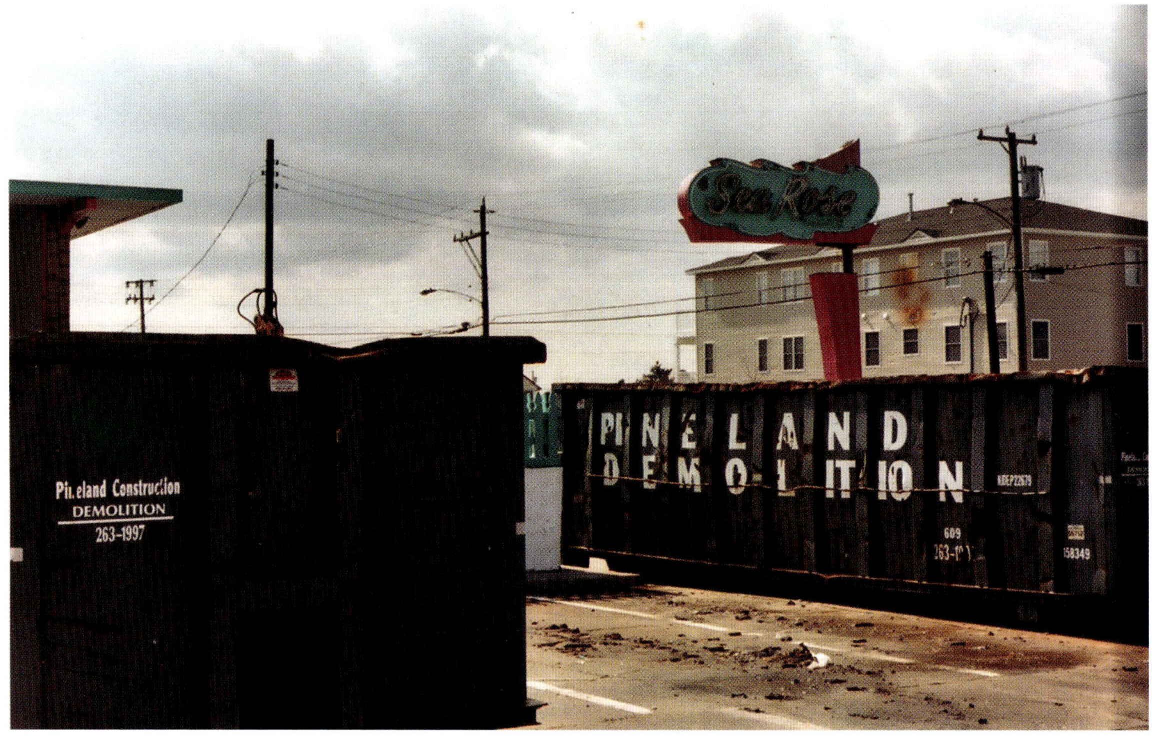

Between 2000 and 2005, developers demolished more than a hundred motels on the island. *Courtesy of Fedele Musso*

Condo Boom

By 2000, the Wildwoods had largely recovered from the slump of the 1980s and 1990s. Vacationers, deterred by the rising costs of room rentals and beach tags in neighboring Cape May and Stone Harbor, began to return to the Wildwoods. But what they found were motels badly in need of updates. Many were owned by the same families—even the same people—who had built them, and as the owners approached retirement age, they had lost interest in their properties.

A few development-related demolitions occurred in 2001, such as the Memory Motel in Wildwood Crest, the ill-advised Rolling Stones–themed motel that Peter Ferrerio had opened in 1996. The next year, about fifteen more motels met the wrecking ball. In the 2003 and 2004 off-seasons, developers tore down dozens of untouched vintage motels and replaced them with bland high-rise condominiums. "Some of the buildings needed to be torn down," says Jim Johnson, owner of the Imperial 500 Motel in Wildwood Crest. "But some buildings were in very good shape. The Palm Beach [a block away] was one of them—it's now condos. The steel was in great shape; the concrete was in great shape—to see something like that being torn down was a shame." Motel owners accepted attractive offers—many in the multiple millions—then happily retired. In a 2004 *Press of*

Atlantic City profile on the Wildwoods' motel demolitions, Wildwood Crest planning commissioner Mike Preston said, "If you have an old eighteen-unit motel [that] you think is worth $600,000 and someone offers you a million for it, you're going to say, 'Goodbye! Here's the key.'"

"Visit it quickly," warned a *Press of Atlantic City* article in 2005. "The Dunes. The Satellite. The Tally-Ho. The Tahiti. The Frontier. The Martinique. The Bonanza. The Casa Nova . . . These Wildwoods motels—and too many other examples of classic Doo Wop architecture to list here—are gone, demolished to make way for shorefront condos." Several motel owners defended their decisions. Ralph DiCicco, owner of the Kona Kai Motel in Wildwood Crest, said, "We feel like we're in the line of fire. For a small motel like us, it would be impossible to get back a return on our investment if you could renovate or add on. You can only change people so much." His next-door neighbor, Lisa Ferrante at the Hi-Lili Motel, agreed. "People want Hiltons. They want Mariotts. This is not what people want anymore. I think if Wildwood puts in the big motels, then the little motels will have to come down." Both motels disappeared after the 2005 season.

An outcry arose from Doo Wop architecture buffs across the country. "Lovably tacky and endangered," said a *Philadelphia Inquirer* headline on October 6, 2002. Joe Salerno, owner of the Imperial 500 motel (and father-in-law of Jim Johnson, now his co-owner), bemoaned the demolitions. "It's heartbreaking to see motels torn down that are still very workable. I don't like to see motels that shouldn't come down come down just for profit." Many motel owners opposed the preservation effort. Preservationist Stephanie Hoagland remembers: "Even after multiple attempts to educate motel owners regarding regulation, multiple statements made indicated a lack of understanding of what it meant to be listed on the state and national register. The owner of the Hialeah Motel even went so far as to say, 'I think I'm being raped of what I deserve.' Needless to say, the Hialeah met the fate of the wrecking ball later that year [2006]."

The Doo Wop Preservation League and several other advocates had attempted to quell the tide of demolition. Hoagland remembers: "Jack Morey was concerned about the recent demolitions and began working with the cultural-resource-management company ARCH² about the issue of historic preservation, and to see if the motels would be eligible for protection. They understood that the first step would be an inventory of the relevant properties." ARCH² hired Hoagland as an intern to help with the documentation, and she later joined the firm full-time to complete the project. She took pictures, filled out forms, and researched histories. On April 8, 2003, ARCH² and the Doo Wop Preservation League submitted a nomination to the New Jersey Historic Preservation Office for a forty-three-block historic district in Wildwood Crest, including ten blocks, between Rambler and Farragut Avenues, that were particularly rich with motels of all shapes, sizes, themes, and ages.

In July 2003, the New Jersey Historic Preservation Office determined that the district was eligible for a historic listing. As Hoagland remembers, it also determined that Wildwood Crest's famous Captain's Table Restaurant "was a contributing resource to the historic district, and that replacing the one-story restaurant with a seven-story condominium would have an adverse effect on the district." Yet that same month, Captain's Table Restaurant was demolished.

Following the outcry in Cape May in the 1970s, the National Trust for Historic Preservation had instituted new guidelines for listings that required the permission of building owners, but motel owners continued to be noncommittal.

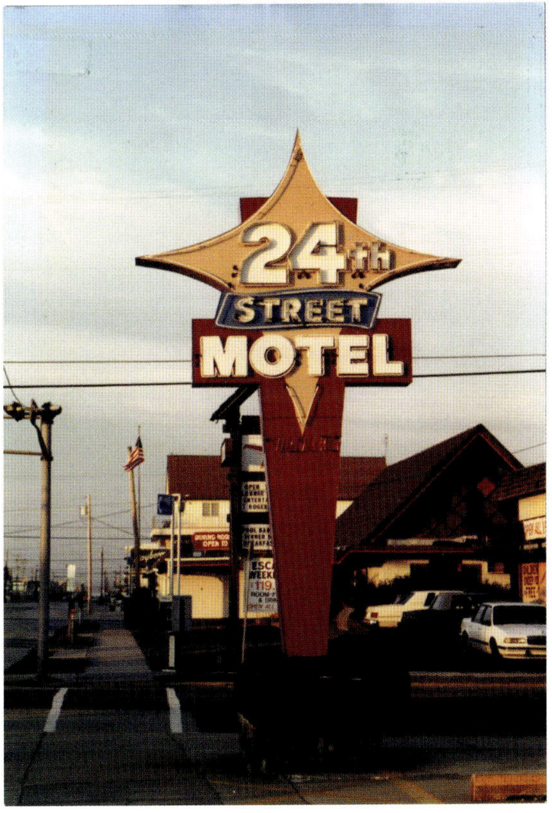

Before 2002, the "Surf Avenue strip" in North Wildwood, which included the 24th Street Motel, contained several uninterrupted blocks of neon signage and midcentury architecture. Today, most of the motels that made up the strip are gone. *Courtesy of ABS Sign Co., Inc.*

By this time, new condominiums built throughout the proposed motel district had irrevocably changed its character. "Unfortunately, the historic preservation office felt that the integrity of the area had fallen below the point of creating a cohesive historic district," recounts Hoagland. "Time moved forward, and the idea of creating a historic district had essentially been put to bed."

By 2006, 121 of the 319 historic motels Hoagland and ARCH[2] had surveyed were torn down. North Wildwood's Surf Avenue strip lost most of its classic motels, as did Wildwood Crest's motel district. "A lot of those North Wildwood Surf Avenue blocks had small motels on all four corners," Fred Musso remembers. "They started to come down in the late 1990s, and no one cared or barely noticed!" In 2006, the National Trust named the Wildwoods' Doo Wop motel population one of America's eleven most endangered historic attractions.

Ed Pangburn, who owns the Astronaut Motel at Stockton Road and the beach in Wildwood Crest, watched the demolitions with dismay. "Right across the street from us used to be the Swan Motel. Right behind us was the Bonanza. Right across from the Bonanza was the Hi-Lili. Next to that was the Kona Kai. Right across from the Kona Kai was the Waterways. When you would go walking around at night, and everything was here, everything was lit up with this blue glow. The Bonanza didn't have white lights outside—it was blue. At the Waterways, it was a sea green. The

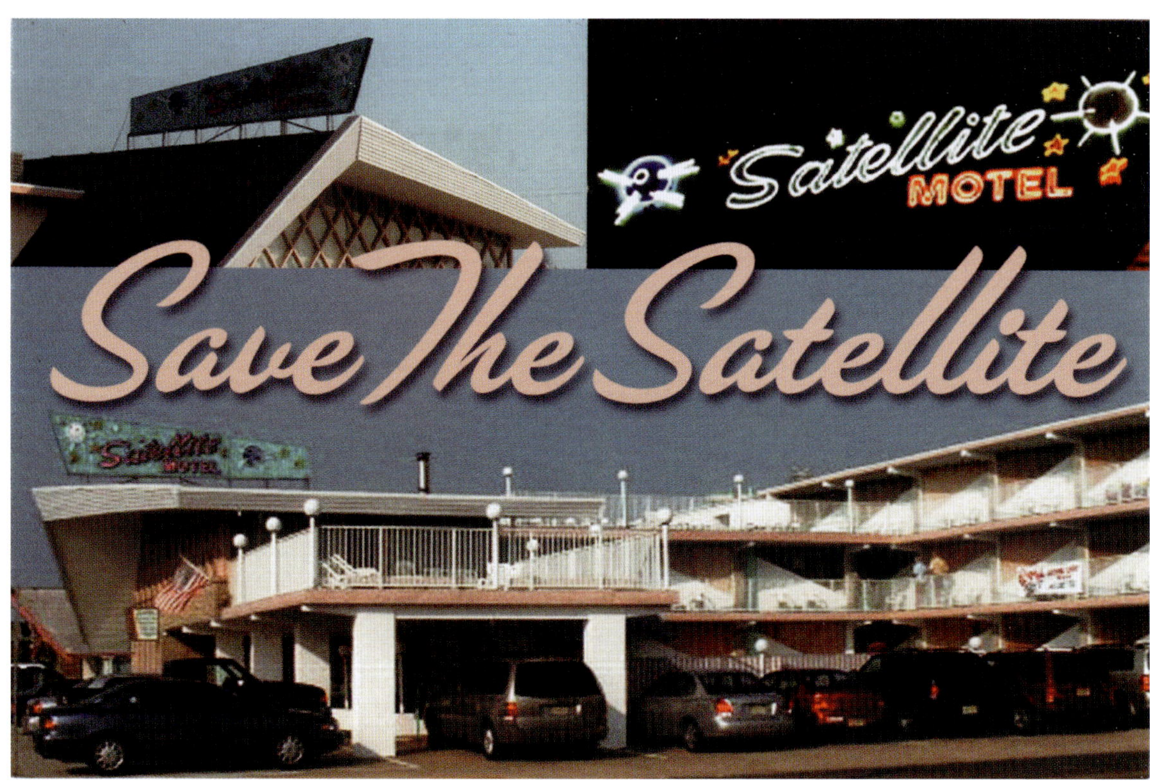

Michael Hirsch launched a postcard drive to preserve the historic Satellite Motel; unfortunately, it was torn down in 2004. *Courtesy of Michael Lorin Hirsch*

Kona Kai had these tiki torches out front. That was their thing. Every night they would light these two tiki torches, and it really had this Polynesian feel to it. There was also the Tahiti right around the corner. They had tiki face signage. It was neat." Many motel owners were persuaded to sell out, fearful of owning the last motel on their block. Pangburn noticed a changing dynamic in his neighborhood. "Motel people are different than condo people," he says. "You barely see condo people—they tend less to be at the pool; they're always down at the beach."

Concerned citizens launched their own preservation efforts. One was Michael Lorin Hirsch, a longtime Wildwoods vacationer and currently president of the Society for Commercial Archaeology, which had held the pivotal 1983 conference in Wildwood. In 2003, word circulated that Will Morey's iconic 1958 Satellite Motel would be torn down that winter. Hirsch made postcards preprinted with the address of Wildwood Crest mayor John Pantalone, urging the borough to intervene and save the motel. "Please consider incentive zoning to save the Satellite Motel and to protect the proposed Wildwood Crest National Historic District," read the back of the card. "Incentive zoning for historic preservation will safeguard our heritage. . . .We owe it to future generations of New Jerseyans and visitors to Wildwood Crest to consider designating this building as an official landmark and creating a historic district." The Satellite stayed open for another summer but came down in October 2004.

Other preservationists worked from different angles. Fred Musso had begun salvaging signs in 1997, and as demolitions continued, he rose to the challenge. "After I did the first few and I wasn't afraid of heights anymore, I saw how they came apart in sections." Alternatively, he would offer

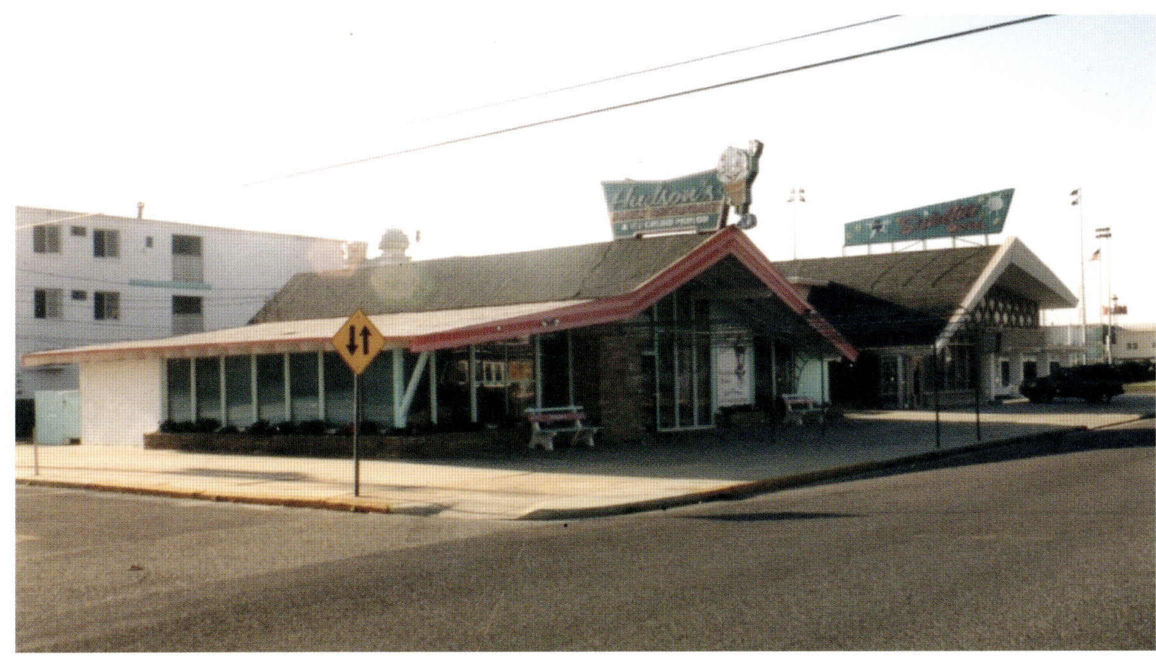

This 2002 photo shows Hudson's Restaurant (formerly Schumann's) and the Satellite Motel. Two years later, both would be gone. *Courtesy of Fedele Musso*

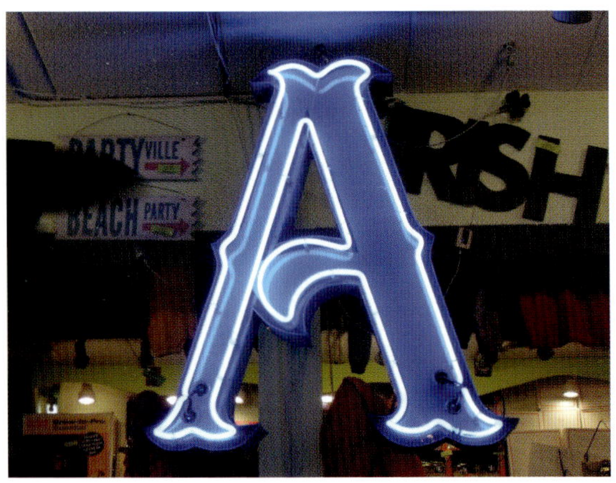

Preservationists such as Fred Musso have salvaged signs from many demolished motels. This "A" from the former Bonanza Motel lives on inside the Lime Ricky Arcade on the Wildwood boardwalk.

demolition crews $50 to save the signs for him. "Some of the owners were getting millions of dollars for their motel, but they still wanted $5,000 for their sign. I learned to wait—there was a narrow window when the owner was out of the picture and the motel was still standing," he says. "I got a couple dozen for the [Doo Wop Preservation] League and gave them some of my own. But then it just got too overwhelming, and I started selling some off."

Signs that Musso has saved have migrated across the country: "There's one guy in North Dakota who has over thirty signs from me and ABS!" Musso says. He continues to promote neon as an eye-catching mode of advertising in the Wildwoods, making and installing signs in boardwalk shops and restaurants.

Amid the demolitions, there were still some bright spots. Two motels' owners had the foresight to place their buildings on the National Register of Historic Places. In 2003, Pete and Betty Crossan listed their Chateau Bleu Motel, a 1959 Lou Morey gem with wishbone columns, a heart-shaped swimming pool, and boomerang-shaped lettering. Two years later, George Miller and Carolyn Emigh listed the historic Caribbean Motel both on the National Register of Historic Places and the Historic Hotels of America registry. Then, in 2007, the Doo Wop Preservation League carried out the movement's ultimate success story.

In 2002, Michael John had sold his Surfside Restaurant, a circular diner with a round pleated roof, to Jim Ranalli, the owner of the Water's Edge Motel next door. Ranalli planned to demolish the restaurant, but Jack Morey launched a fundraising drive to pay for the Surfside to be dismantled

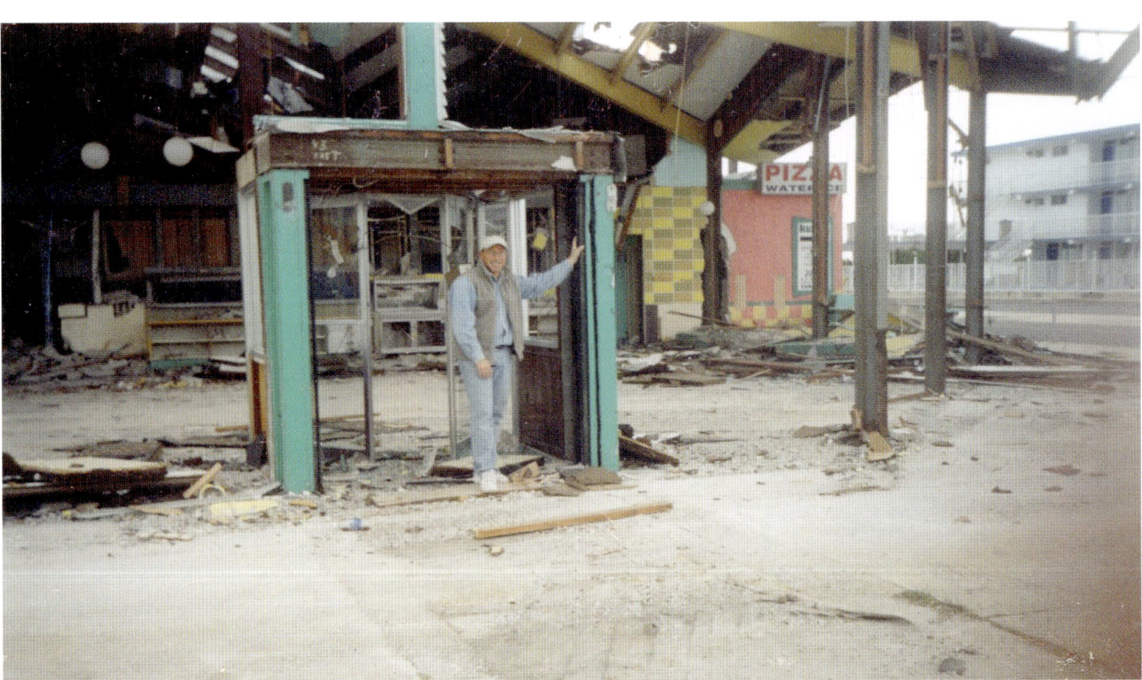

Jack Morey stands inside the skeleton of the Surfside Restaurant as it is being dismantled. *Courtesy of Wildwood Historical Society*

instead. On October 15, 2002, crews disassembled the Surfside, and the Doo Wop Preservation League publicized plans to rebuild the restaurant on Rambler Avenue in Wildwood Crest as an oceanfront welcome center. Those plans fell through, but the cause had generated enough publicity that the league found the necessary funding. "By that point, enough of the more progressive folks were engaged and we were able to approach Tom Byrne, whose father left a large sum of money to the city," says Morey. "They put a very good chunk of change into it."

In 2007, the former Surfside Restaurant reopened in Fox Park, on Ocean Avenue at Davis Avenue. "The city of Wildwood stepped up to the plate there," says Dan MacElrevey. "[Mayor] Ernie Troiano was very excited about it being here, and here it is." The Doo Wop Experience, as it was named, featured a Richard Stokes–designed interior that included pieces of fifties memorabilia that the Doo Wop Preservation League had accumulated. Musso installed several of the neon signs he had rescued inside the museum. Outside, Randy Hentges of ABS installed a "sign garden" of four other signs rescued from motels. "We decided it would be a neat display of signs," says Schumann. "Of course, our architect, Richard Stokes, suggested that we call it a sign garden. Bingo!"

Around 2007, the motel demolitions abated. As the US economy hit a downturn, the market for expensive beachfront condominium units waned, and lots where motels had been demolished began to sit empty. Many condominiums languished short of completion or occupancy. (A few Doo Wop buildings were demolished after 2007, such as the La Vita and Sand Castle Motels in Wildwood Crest and North Wildwood's Lamp Post Diner, but these are exceptions.) Around the same time, the Doo Wop advocacy movement began to diminish. While the league had saved the historic Surfside Restaurant, over a hundred historic Doo Wop properties had disappeared.

In 2000, Jack Morey had believed that building on the island's Doo Wop heritage was the way forward. But after a decade of demolitions and taxpayer resistance, he decided to push the Wildwoods in a new direction. "I was smart enough to change gears and have a backup plan," he says. "I was worried Doo Wop wasn't going make it. Maybe it'll make it, maybe it won't. But what's important is that Wildwood became quirky. Wildwood should be a bit tacky and proud of that. I think we're on our way."

The concept of "quirky" encompasses all of the town's historic motels but also includes less overtly vintage projects, such as Richard Stokes's 2007 "Wildwoods" sign on the boardwalk at Rio Grande Avenue and giant curly-fry-shaped signage on Morey's Piers. The Doo Wop Preservation League, meanwhile, kept the preservationist spirit alive by printing a pamphlet, *How to Doo Wop*, that displayed many of the Wildwoods' classic properties and listed dos and don'ts for preserving a motel or business.

The future of the island's historic architecture looks bright. Several motel owners have plans to preserve their motels for succeeding generations. The Morey family, in their role as owners of several lucrative amusement piers and prominent public spaces, continues to make the island quirky, one public-space project at a time. Recently they opened a baseball field in Wildwood Crest across the street from the Pan American Hotel and protected it from traffic with baseball-shaped bollards. But there is still work to be done to raise preservation awareness. In 2019, for instance, new owners renamed the Surf Motel and the Sea Shell Motel, removing their historic neon signs.

Continuing Appeal

Despite these losses, much of the town's midcentury modern architecture is well preserved and functional. The Society for Commercial Archaeology (SCA), founded in 1977 to focus on US midcentury modern architecture, has held several conferences in the Wildwoods over the decades. And popular road-guide author Beth Lennon, who maintains the Retro Roadmap website, hosts annual get-togethers for like-minded aficionados at the Caribbean Motel, of all places.

Why not in some other town? For one, the Wildwoods' motels remained largely unchanged between the early 1970s and the first years of the twenty-first century. The economic slump that consumed much of the 1980s and 1990s prevented extensive redevelopment from taking place, and as Astronaut Motel owner Ed Pangburn mentioned, a concentration of motel owners in a small area created a community unlike any other.

Contrary to some criticism, the buildings have enduring architectural interest. Gordon Clark, the general manager of Morey Resorts, says, "Motels in the Doo Wop era were very boring buildings with one iconic Doo Wop *thing*—the neon, the glass walls, the Phillips 66 highway gas station [shape]. That influenced the Starlux lounge." He's stating a popular misconception about the

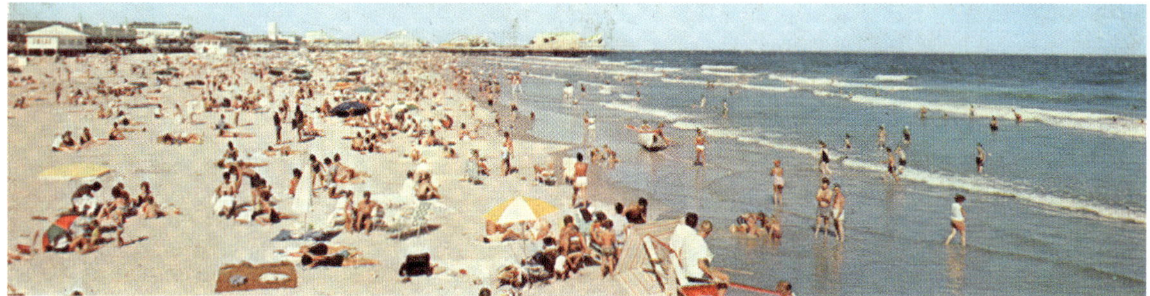

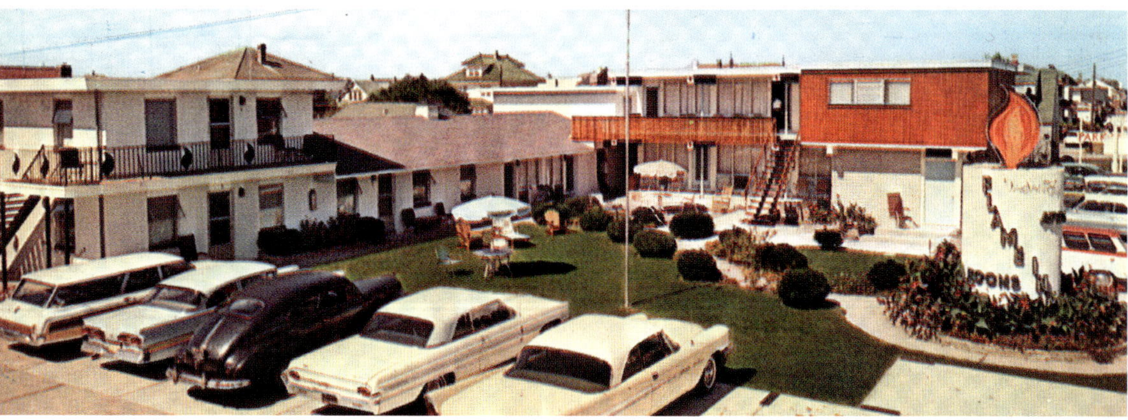

The loss of small motels such as the Flame Inn, shown here in an early 1960s postcard, deprived the Wildwoods' motel neighborhoods of the cohesion they needed to become historic districts. *Author's collection*

Wildwoods' cache of midcentury modern architecture: that Doo Wop is simply a pastiche.

In fact, the motels' minor design details should receive more credit than they do. As early as 1983, the SCA pamphlet *Wildwood Workbook* had identified balcony decorations and color schemes as among the motels' most crucial features. The builders of Wildwoods' motels used patterned railings, bright color schemes, geometrically shaped jalousie windows, fun landscaping, and numerous other subtle factors to make their motels pop, and these factors enhanced visitors' vacations as much as the larger elements. The unique chevron railings at the Jolly Roger Motel may not be as eye-catching as the 20-foot-tall, pop art neon sign at the Lollipop Motel, but as affordable and modern enhancements, these railings are just as important.

In the first few years of the 2000s, Philadelphia photographer Mark Havens began to document the island's motels, many of whose days were numbered. "We used to drive around and see all of the interesting signage and colors the way people would drive around and look at Christmas lights during the holidays," he says. Havens's view was different from many of his contemporaries: "I was always conscious that they were there as a sort of backdrop. But I don't think it was until they started getting

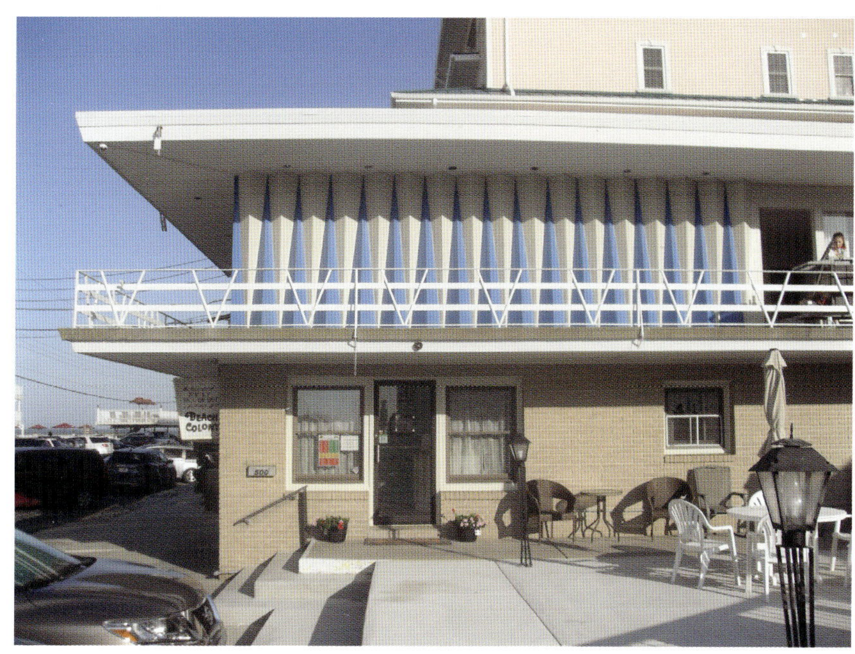

The faceted wall at the Beach Colony Motel (formerly the Golden Nugget) shows Wildwoods motel builders' attention to detail.

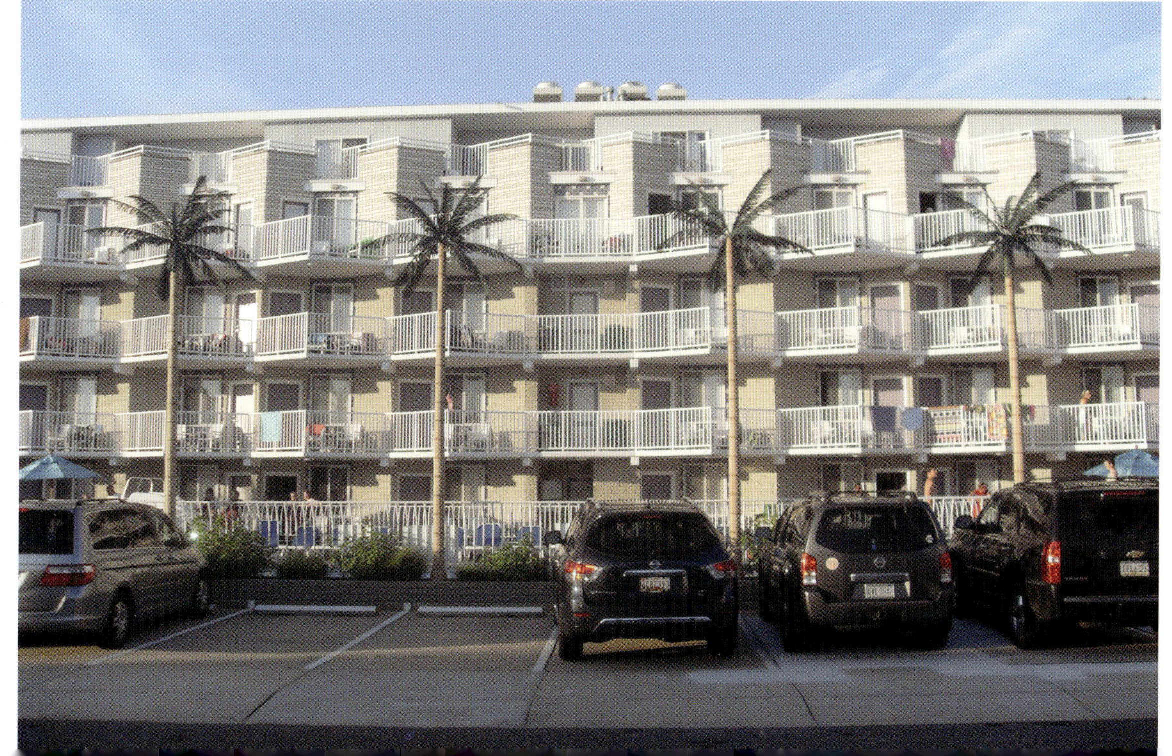

As shown by Richard Stokes's 2005 expansion of the Crest's Shalimar Motel and its sawtooth balconies, patterns are as important to the Wildwoods' motels' aesthetic as large, sweeping gestures.

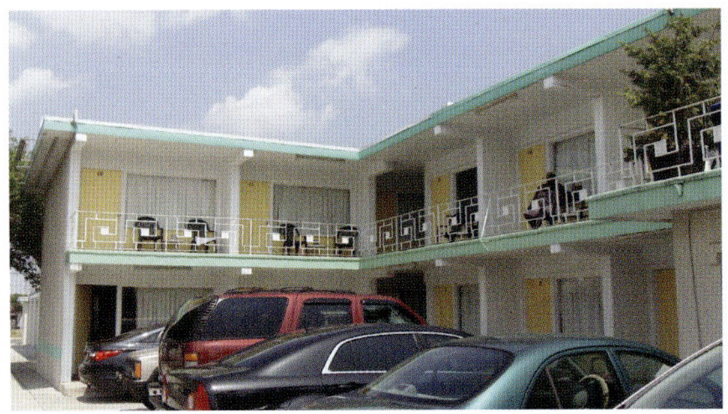

Several motels in the Wildwoods used "square spiral" railings, such as these at the former Knoll's Motel in Wildwood. Here, the railings are combined with a summery color scheme of sea green and pastel yellow.

demolished in favor of condominiums that I started to realize that they're not as removable as the landscape—that they may not be there in the future." The key word is "backdrop"—the Wildwoods' motels were built both to be flashy billboards and unobtrusive settings for family vacations, and these two concepts often coexisted within the same building. Rather than focusing on the attention-grabbing elements, Havens photographed large expanses of doors and windows and the interaction of colors across neon signs, poolside chaise lounges, and roofline trim.

In an introductory essay for *Out of Season*, Havens's 2016 folio of his Wildwoods photos, Parsons School of Design professor and MoMA curator Jamer Hunt muses, "If all that Wildwood showcased was luscious signs and kooky names, the style would be strictly superficial and forgettable—a boardwalk of empty calories. Instead, the motels reveal a depth of decorative minimalism that is both rigorous and whimsical. . . . The components of Wildwood's more subtle expressivity range from contrasting painted doors and poles and the judicious use of flagcrete to curvilinear balustrades, canted walls, ornamental brickwork, and strategically placed light fixtures." Hunt name-checks the Aztec, whose concrete parking barriers are spray-painted aqua blue to match the motel's roofline, and the Waikiki, whose orange night illumination "gives depth and theatrical punch to the otherwise identical cubicles." In another essay in the same book, eminent architecture critic Joseph Giovanni expands on Hunt's observations, noting that these subtleties, as novel then as now, added to these motels' escapism: "The goal was not to feel poor together but rich together."

Stephanie Hoagland dismisses the condominiums that have risen from the ashes of the motels. "With faux Victorian features and contemporary designs, they didn't fit in with the architectural style of the motels, and, stylistically, they could be anywhere," she says. Most advocates of Doo Wop architecture agree that the boxlike condominiums hardly match the cohesion, wit, and dynamism of the 1950s and 1960s motels. Describing a particularly potent example, Jamer Hunt notes, "There are few motels as visually coherent as the Mango Motel, and here we can see the full effect of an integrated compositional strategy. The colors themselves—swimming-pool blue and coral red—are an atypical combination that cleverly harmonizes to create a vivid, vivacious style." The rhythm of chairs, curtains, doors, and railings of the Wildwoods' vintage motels cultivates a unified aesthetic that the condominiums lack.

Another factor in the Wildwoods' motels' appeal is best described by Chuck Schumann: "Many of these were designed by the man who built them! He was not an architect. He was a builder. But he had to make the façade of that building attractive to the guy in his car who drove along and said, 'Wow, look at that sign!'" Elsewhere in the United States, a healthy percentage of midcentury modern architecture was designed by established architects. It is astonishing that builders such as the Moreys could progress from simple beach bungalows to groundbreaking designs in less than a decade. And more amazing is that this creativity spread across the entire island; even tiny mom-and-pop motels located off main streets sported detailed decorations, pop art color schemes, and bright neon signs.

Several observers of the Wildwoods' motel scene use the term "folk art" to describe the island's midcentury architecture. "Hot rods are American folk art," says Schumann. "Somebody makes something for a purpose, but it has artistic characteristics to it. He's not an artist. He's making something he needs, but there's an element of art in it. The American hot rod doesn't exist anywhere else." The Wildwoods' motel builders were carpenters and contractors who added elements that they believed would make their buildings more attractive to customers.

Most commentators agree that the motels should be considered serious architectural subjects, despite their origins as cheap objects of luxury. While the Wildwoods have not had a cohesive critical mass of historic motels since the early first decade of the 2000s, the ones that remain exemplify the detail and exuberance that once flourished on the island. Even in depleted, often-modified, and occasionally deteriorated states, the motels of the Wildwoods are still outstanding pieces of postwar opulence, manufactured for the working and middle classes.

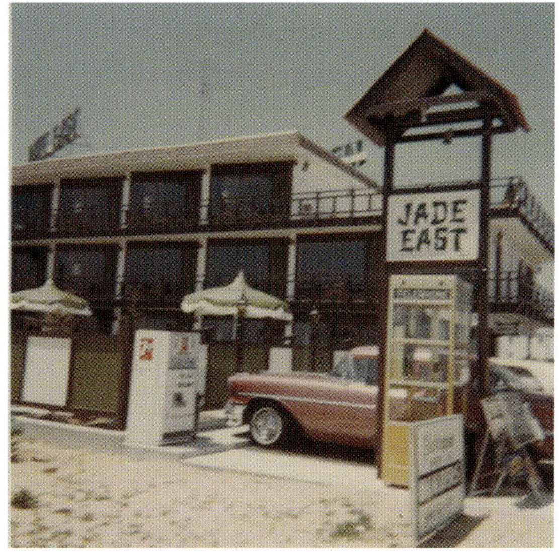

Harriet Bevans's homegrown approximation of Asian motifs at the Jade East Motel shows what many commentators describe as the "folk art" of the Wildwoods' motels. *Courtesy of Dorothy Kulisek collection*

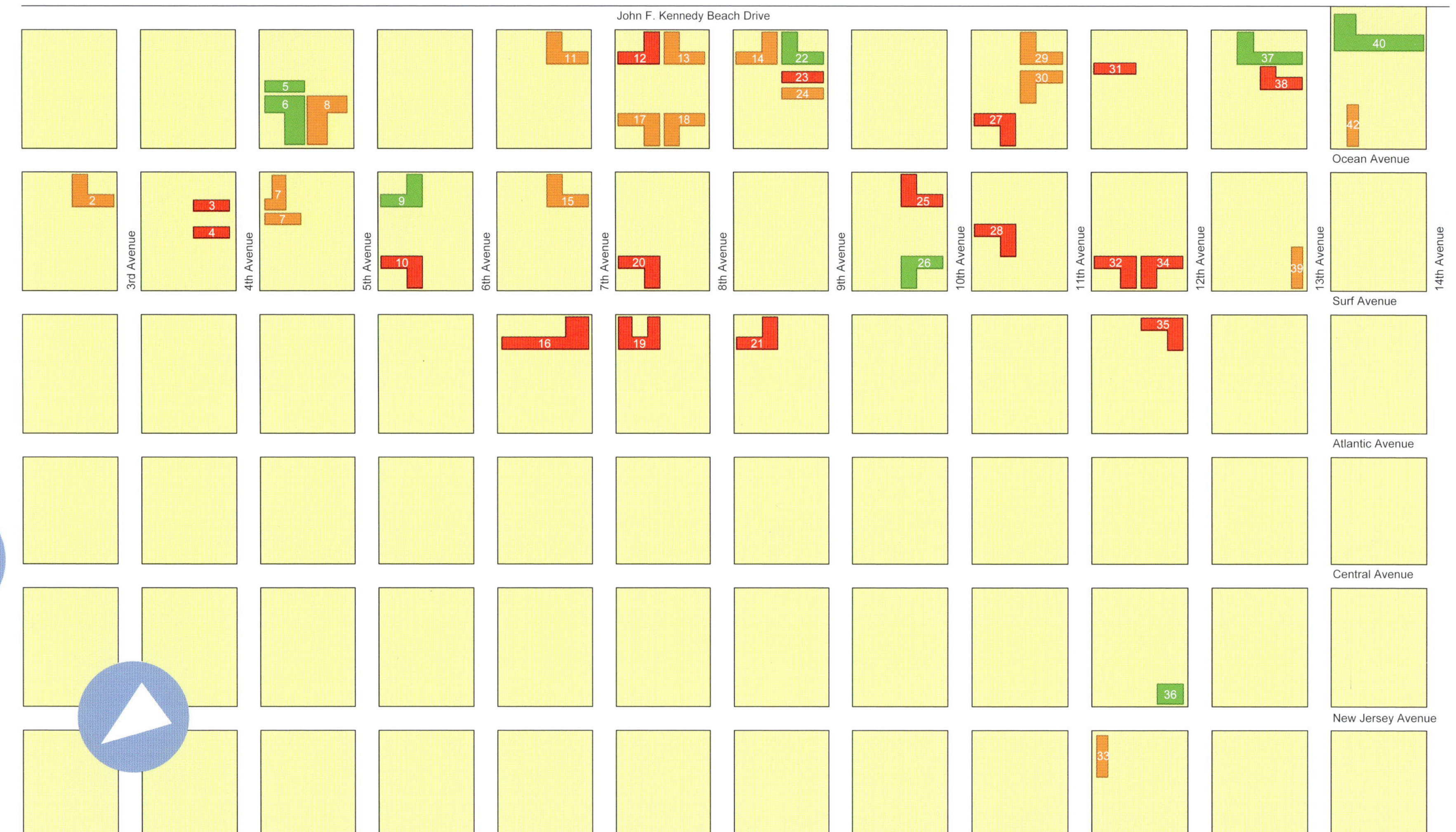

North Wildwood

MAPS AND PROPERTY LISTINGS

How to use the listings: Each building on the maps is identified with a number. That number correlates with a listing in the following pages, which describe the history of many motels, movie theaters, businesses, and restaurants. The umbrella term "motels" is often used to refer to Wildwoods' midcentury architecture in general, and the inclusion of several nonmotel buildings acknowledges the broad scope of modernism that once pervaded the Wildwoods.

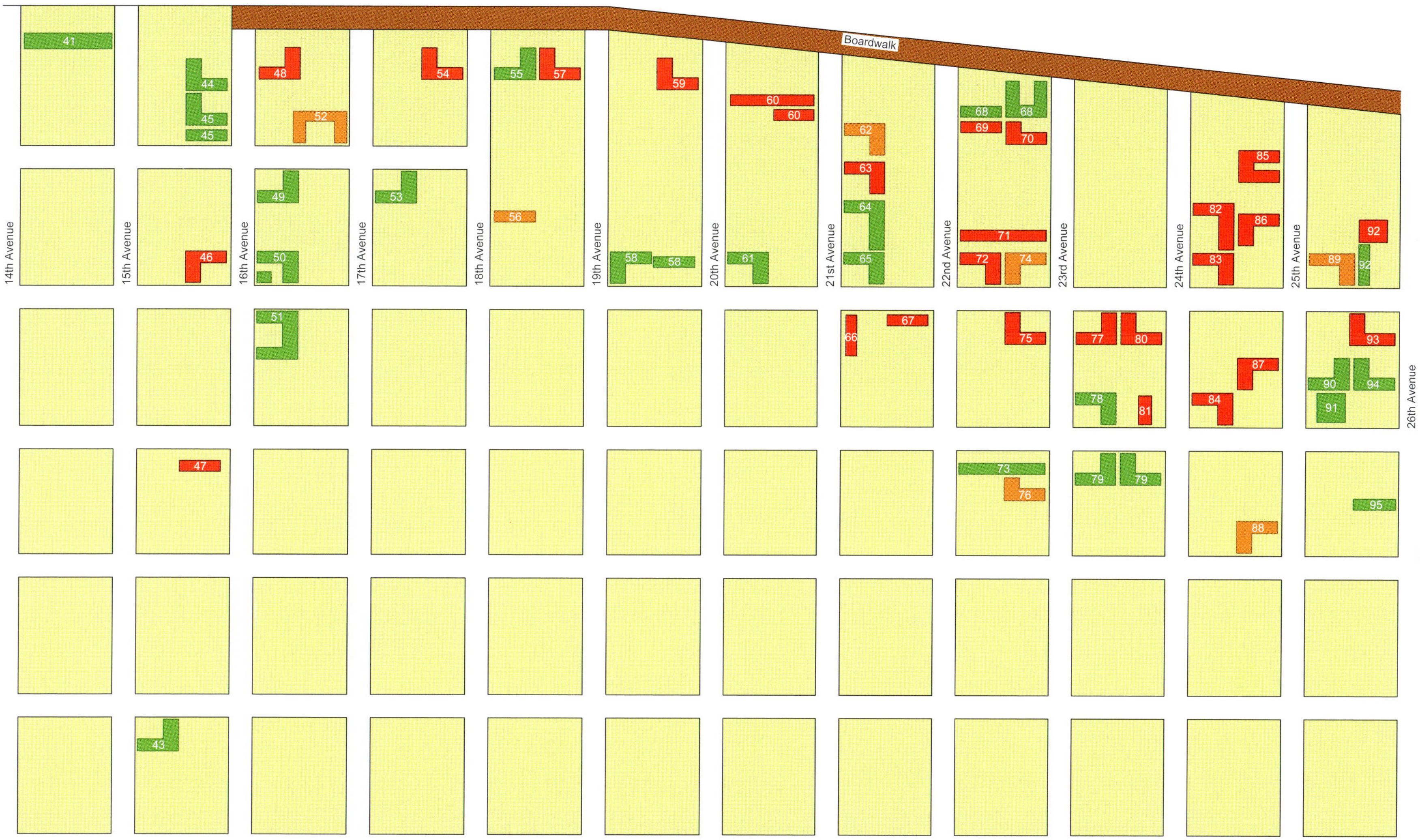

The map has been slightly distorted to better fit onto a rectangular page layout, but each building's address is listed for easy cross-reference with online maps.

The focus is on authentic midcentury properties; the only modern ones listed are expansions of older motels or restaurants (such as Cool Scoops and the Starlux). It is not complete, but rather a representative cross section of the extant and demolished midcentury modern architecture of the Wildwoods.

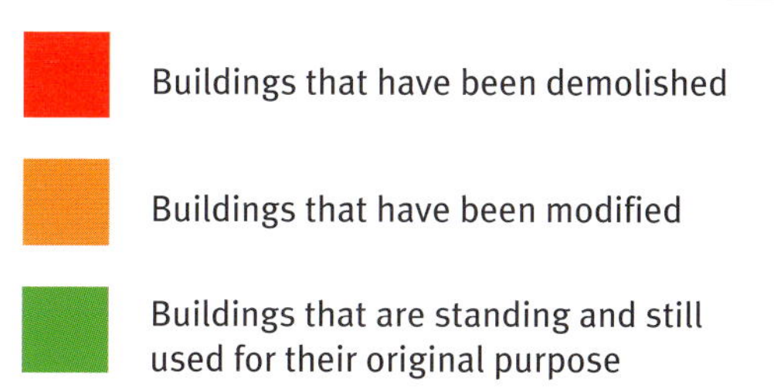

North Wildwood

BUILDING KEY (SEE MAP ON PREVIOUS SPREAD)

The most residential of the Wildwoods' three contiguous boroughs, North Wildwood once had a sizable motel population. Since 2000, demolitions and modifications for condominium ownership have decimated North Wildwood's midcentury architecture (especially its motels), though some prime specimens remain.

[1] Lamp Post Diner (6 Weeks Avenue, not shown on map)
One of the earliest of the Wildwoods' many diners came prefabricated from Paramount Diners in Oakland, New Jersey, in 1939. The North Star Diner had evocative, streamlined glass block corners and a rooftop neon star. In the mid-1960s, its owners faced the diner with American Colonial–style brick and added a gable roof, a dining room, and a new grid-light sign. By the 1970s, the diner had been renamed the Lamp Post, and all traces of its stainless-steel origins had vanished. The Lamp Post closed in the first decade of the 2000s and sat empty until 2015, when developers bulldozed it.

[2] Beach Hugger Motel (210 Ocean Avenue)
Al and Ann Codagnone opened Al Sann's Beach Hugger Motel for the 1972 season. Architecturally simple, it had a freestanding neon sign with Bauhaus lettering surrounded by chasing bulbs. The building survives today as condominiums (though without the sign).

[3] Fontaine Motel and Apartments (415 East 4th Avenue)
Charles Carullo built the small Fontaine in the late 1960s. With a concrete breeze-block fence around the pool, an ornamental fountain, and a red-and-blue freestanding neon sign in the middle of the parking lot, the Fontaine beguilingly combined modern and baroque aesthetics. It led a low-key existence until being demolished around 2002.

[4] Chateau Motel and Apartments (411 East 4th Avenue)
In the mid-1950s, Jack and Harriet Bevans built the single-story Chateau Apartments two blocks from the ocean, on 4th Avenue. It had a distinctive neon sign featuring a peanut-shaped orb, though with later decades came a variety of more up-to-date signage. After several additions, it fell to the wrecking ball in 2004.

[5] Jade East Motel (510 East 4th Avenue)
When Harriet Bevans decided in 1966 to sell her Chateau Motel and move closer to the ocean, the new motel she built reflected her appreciation for Asian architecture. The three-story Jade East had a red pagoda-like mansard roof, wooden post-and-rail balustrades, and a Japanese garden. "When we bought it, it did not have a pool—it just had a Japanese garden," says current co-owner Jane Lawrence. "People wanted a pool—they could[n't] care less about a Japanese garden!" Steve and Jane Lawrence bought the motel in 1979, added a pool in 1985, and replaced the cedar shake roof with shingles. That same decade, the Lawrences also installed a roadside neon sign that spelled the motel's name in a vaguely Asian font, replacing two original rooftop signs. "There was nothing here,"

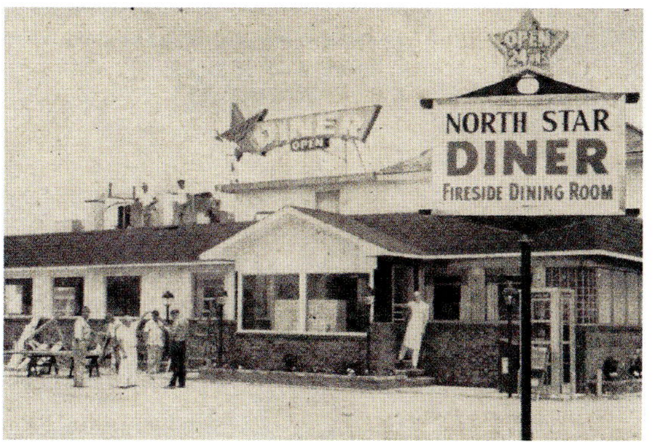

In this rare shot of the North Star Diner (before its transformation into the Lamp Post), an art deco glass block window peeks out on the right, bridging the diner's original streamlined façade with its later American Colonial identity. *Courtesy of Wildwood Historical Society*

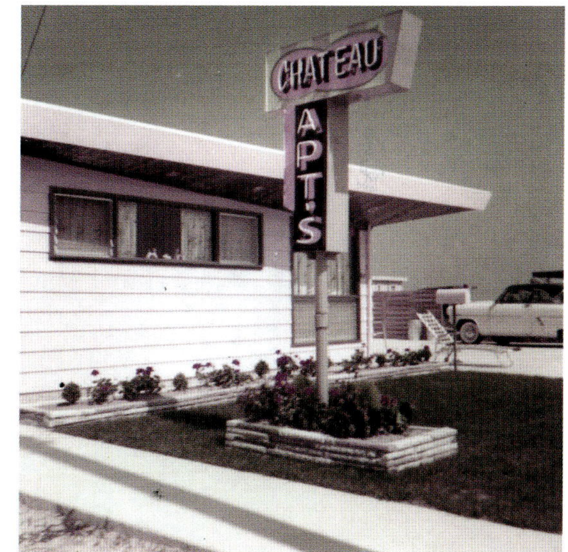

The Chateau Motel in its 1950s guise as a single-story courtlike motel with a candy-striped neon sign. *Courtesy of Dorothy Kulisek collection*

Steve and Jane Lawrence have updated the Jade East with modern amenities, but its original distinctive theme remains intact.

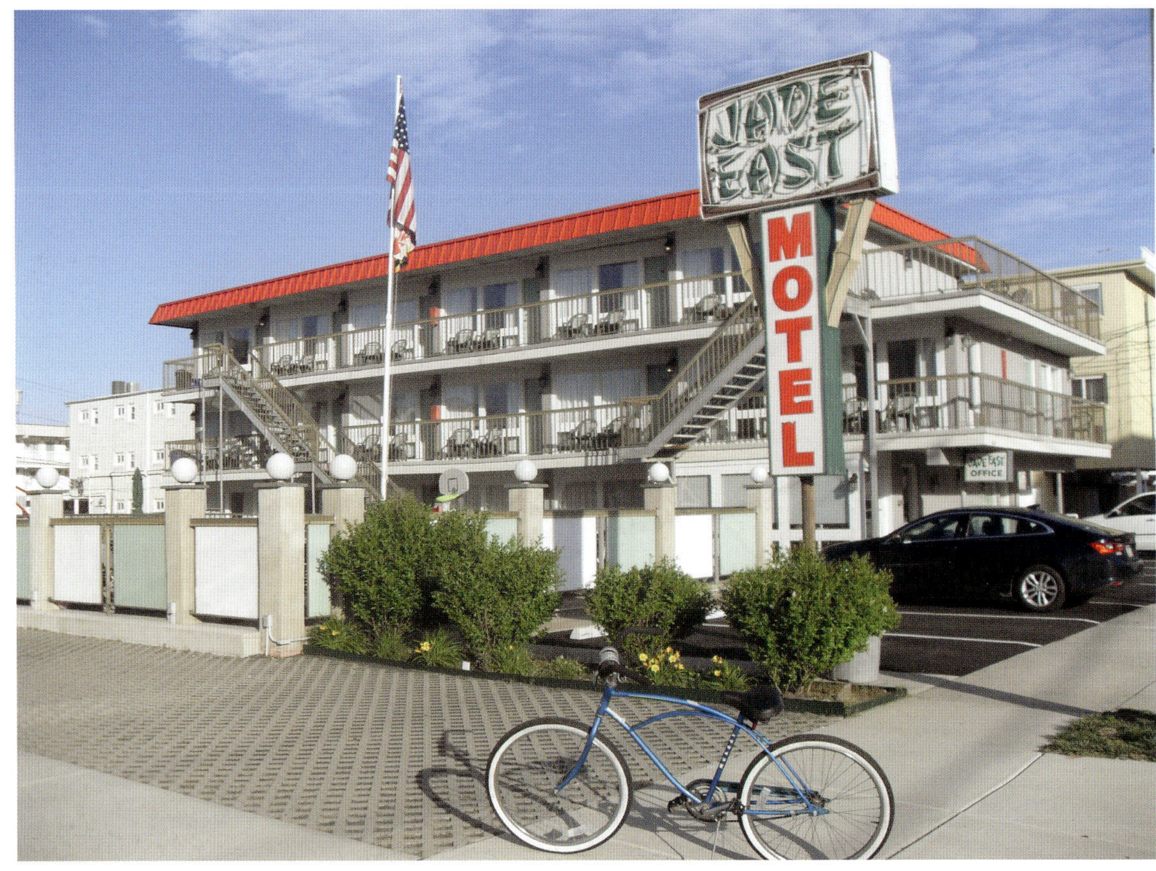

Steve remembers, "so when you came across the bridge from Stone Harbor, you could see the Jade East sign up on the roof." Originally, the Lawrences lived in a tiny apartment above the motel's office, accessible by a spiral staircase, but later their son Mark designed a modern house across the parking lot; this house won an award from *AIA Architectural Review*.

[6] North Wind Motel (401 Ocean Avenue)
In 1970, Anthony Profeto built the North Wind Motel at the undeveloped corner of 4th and Ocean Avenues. He commissioned a pair of distinctive neon signs (one roadside and one rooftop) with four-pointed stars. Today the motel remains, but both signs disappeared in the 1990s.

[7] Oceanaire Motel (424 East 4th Avenue)
Anthony and Marie Patrizi opened a small apartment building, the Patrizi Apartments, in 1964. A few years later, they renamed it the Telstar (after the Tornados' 1962 instrumental hit), built an

annex, and added a rooftop neon sign featuring a red lightning bolt. The motel later became the Oceanaire and remains today as the Oceanaire Condominiums.

[8] Mediterranean Motel (405 Ocean Avenue)
The Mediterranean, which opened in 1970, had diamond-patterned railings and a two-story, vertical, green neon sign with a red scroll across its top. The sign was removed around 2010; the building remains under condo ownership.

[9] Isle of Capri Motel (500 Ocean Avenue)
Recent owners Jim and Gail DeFeo said that Lou Morey built the motel's first story in 1959 and the second story in 1962; directories from the era show Anthony and Winifred Artur as the original

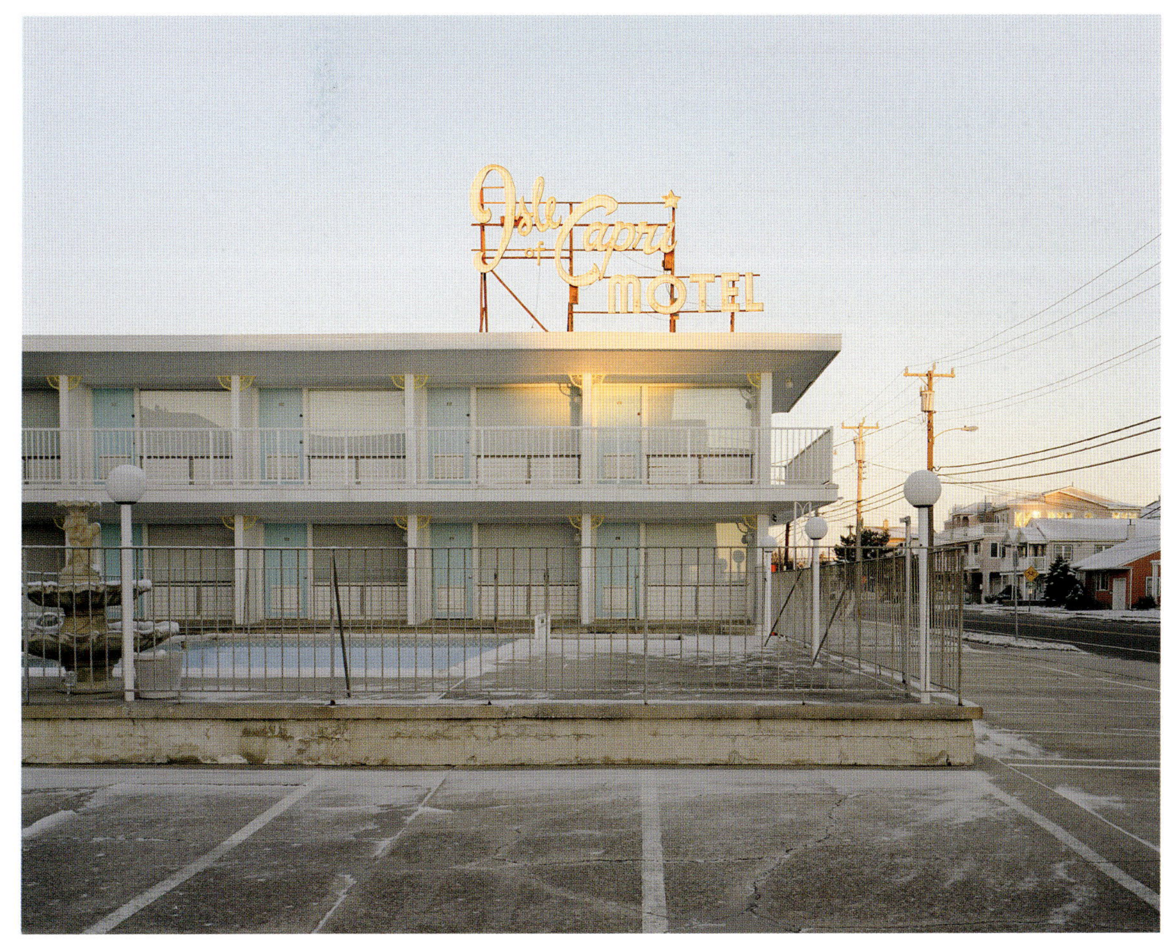

An early-morning wintertime shot of the Isle of Capri Motel shows its pop-art-style yellow gingerbread (since removed) and its neon sign, one of the oldest ones remaining on the island. *Courtesy of Tyler Haughey*

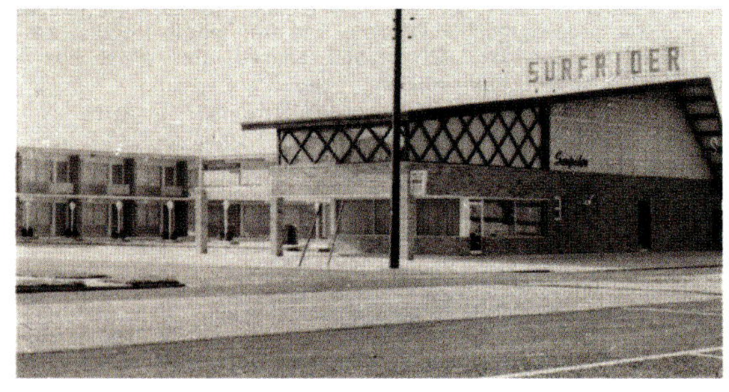

The Buckingham brothers borrowed heavily from the Crest's Satellite Motel to design the Surfrider Motel, shown here shortly after opening. *Author's collection*

owners. "You can see how the tile color changes in the bathrooms," said Jim. "It's all original." The motel claims one of the deepest pools on the island, at 10 feet. In addition, it has an original neon sign that is one of the oldest on the island. The DeFeos were proud of their sign. "Because it's the original, we just want to hold on to it as long as we can," Gail said. But Jim admitted, "Keeping that sign running is quite a chore. It's an old sign, and all the electrical connections are exposed to the elements. They're just hanging out there, and during the wintertime, when we get 40- or 50-mile-an-hour winds, the whole thing is rocking up there. It doesn't take much to break everything."

In 2019, when the Lerro family bought the Isle of Capri, one of their first items of business was to hire Fred Musso to restore the motel's neon sign.

[10] Caribbean Breeze Motel (501 Surf Avenue)

Wildwood's Buckingham Brothers Builders built the Surf Rider Motel in 1964. They borrowed its oversized lounge and asymmetrical cantilevered roof wholesale from Will Morey's famous Satellite Motel, but the Surf Rider added a distinctive window design, with muntins arranged in a chevron-like pattern like those of North Wildwood's Buccaneer Motel. The Surf Rider liberally featured beige flagstone, which gave it California-style Googie flavor. Around 2000, a later owner renamed this derivative but dynamic motel the Caribbean Breeze, but it was demolished in 2003.

[11] Coral Reef Motel (513 East 7th Avenue)

[12] Ocean Spray Motel (514 East 7th Avenue)

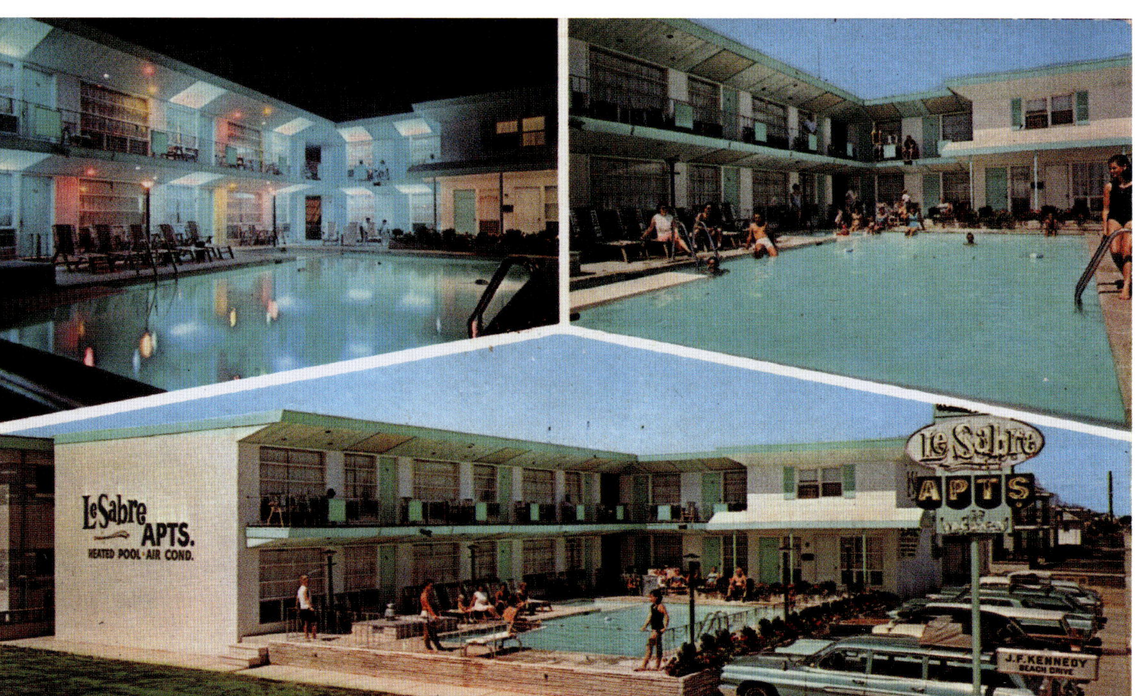

This early postcard of the Le Sabre Apartments (later Motel) emphasizes its pool, shown in day and night shots. *Author's collection*

[13] Alanté Oceanfront Motel (515 East 8th Avenue)

[14] Le Sabre Motel (512 East 8th Avenue)

These four motels spanned two oceanfront blocks on North Wildwood's Beach Drive. The Ocean Spray, built by Arthur DiAndrea around 1960, featured an endearing plastic sign with a yellow incandescent arrow and was demolished in the first few years of the 2000s. In the midsixties, George and Doris Seeger built the LeSabre Apartments, endowing them with a freestanding neon sign that touted "apartments" until the 1990s, despite the building itself being renamed a motel two decades earlier. The building survives today as condos, minus its sign.

In 1967, contractor James Smith built the On-the-Beach Apartments and Motel as an addition to a bungalow; a few years later he expanded and renamed the motel the Coral Reef. The Coral Reef survives today, painted pink but minus the sign, as condominiums. The previous year, Philadelphia comedian Cozy Morley, who owned the Club Avalon in Wildwood and was a popular presence on the island, had built Cozy Morley's Continental Motel a block away; the motel featured a revolving plastic rooftop sign (replaced in the early 1980s with script neon). Today, the motel is known as the Alanté; in 2015, a rotating rooftop "Alanté" neon sign disappeared.

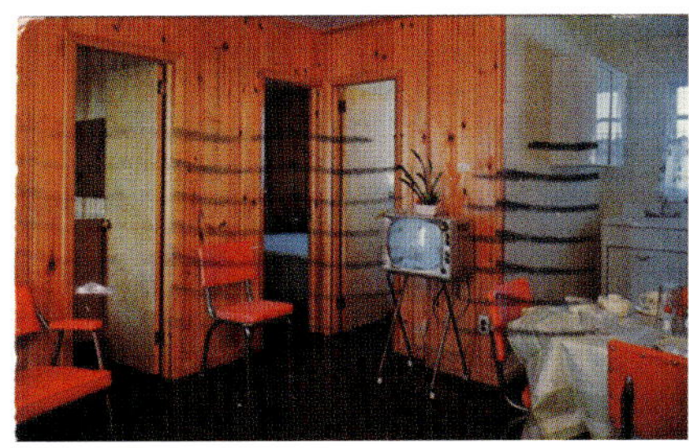

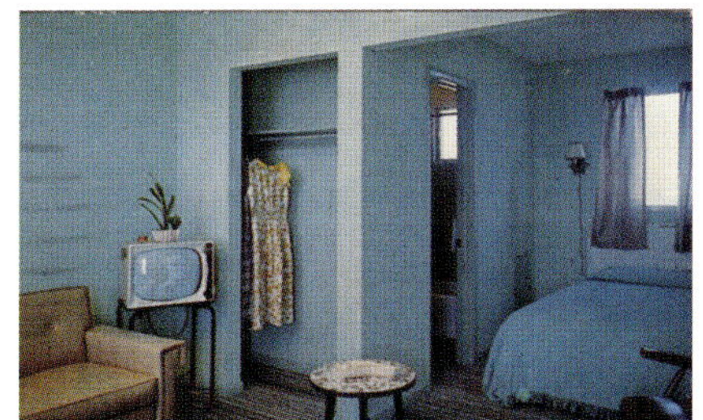

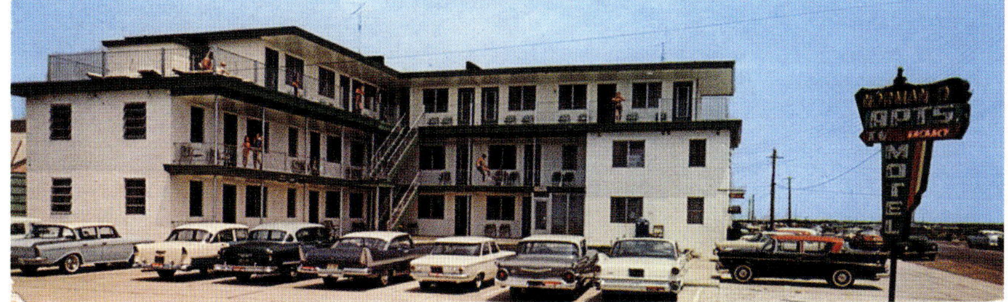

This postcard of the Norman-D Motel & Apartments shows the vivid primary colors that motel room designers often used in the early 1960s. *Courtesy of Fedele Musso*

[15] Atlantic Ocean Winds Motel (608 Ocean Avenue)

Norman Danella and Alfred Salvatore built this two-story (later three-story) apartment building in 1960, naming it the Norman-D after Danella. Beginning in the early 1980s, it went through several names, including the Amity Motel and Apartments, the King Neptune Motel and Apartments, and the Atlantic Ocean Winds. Around 2005, developers converted it to condominium ownership. "The [Atlantic Ocean Winds] sign was laying [*sic*] on the sidewalk, and they were supposedly going to reuse it on the condos, but of course it vanished," says Fred Musso. "It was in excellent shape."

[16] Lurae Motel (331 East 7th Avenue)

In the early 1950s, Louis Hasson built a motel court at the corner of 7th and Surf Avenues. A decade later, he and his wife, Mildred, bought the rest of the block, which had hitherto sat vacant, and expanded the court into an L-shaped motel with an additional wing. They also installed a carport and

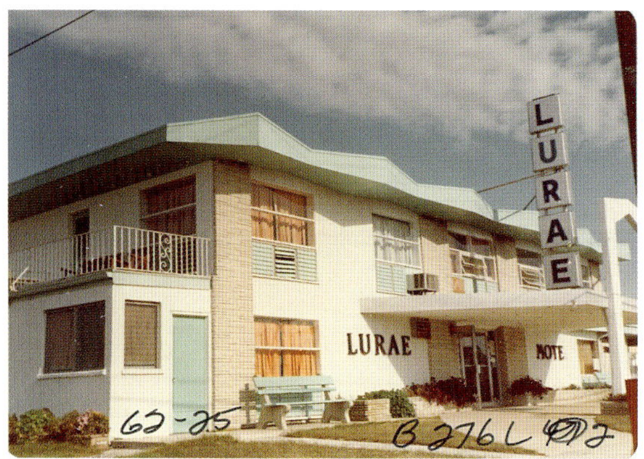

The arch on the far right disappeared not long after this 1982 photo of the Lurae Motel was taken. *Courtesy of Wildwood Historical Society*

an oversized Greek-style segmented arch, surmounted by a distinctive plastic sign with stacked block letters. Lou and Millie (as brochures list them) incorporated the motel in the late 1960s. A few years later, Lou passed away, leaving Millie to run the large motel herself, which she did for several years. A succession of later owners modified the motel, removing its elegant arch and painting the motel an incongruous green. In 2006, developers bulldozed the motel, an act that inspired public outcry.

[17] Friendship 7 Motel (701 Ocean Avenue)

[18] Flying Dutchman Motel (711 Ocean Avenue)

Ed and Irene Nesbitt built these adjacent and identical motels for the 1970 season. Both had bright-red doors and curtains adorned with a bright-blue geometric pattern. In 1972, the Nesbitts bought the Hialeah Motel in the Crest and sold the Flying Dutchman to new owners, who immediately tempered its bright color scheme. Still, the Nesbitts continued to make the Friendship 7 a midcentury showpiece, adding a neon and plastic rooftop sign. Both motels still exist, modified for condo ownership.

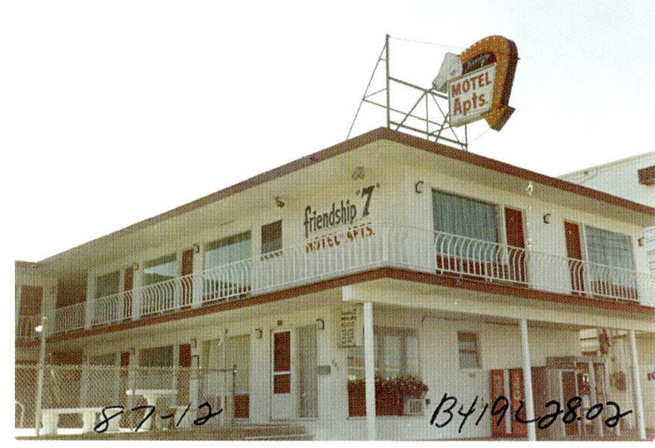

Many motels' signs featured arrows, but the Friendship 7 Motel's emerged from a neon-outlined flashlight. *Courtesy of Wildwood Historical Society*

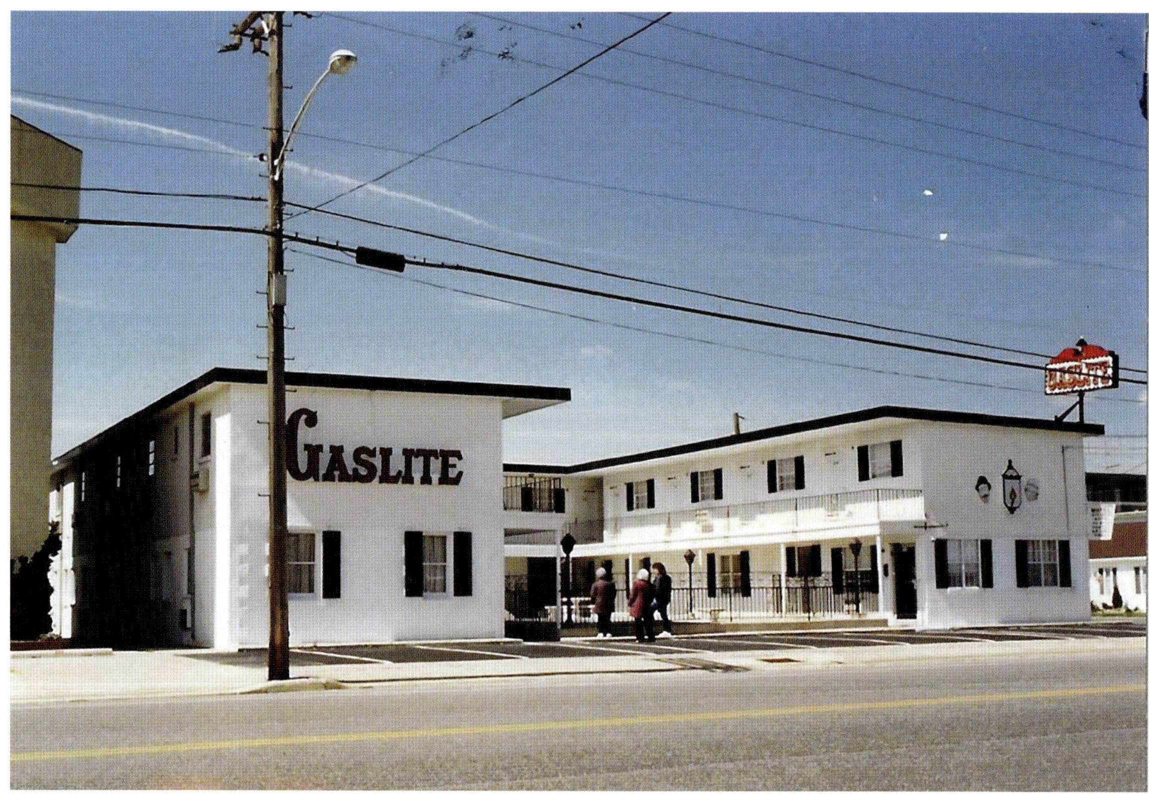

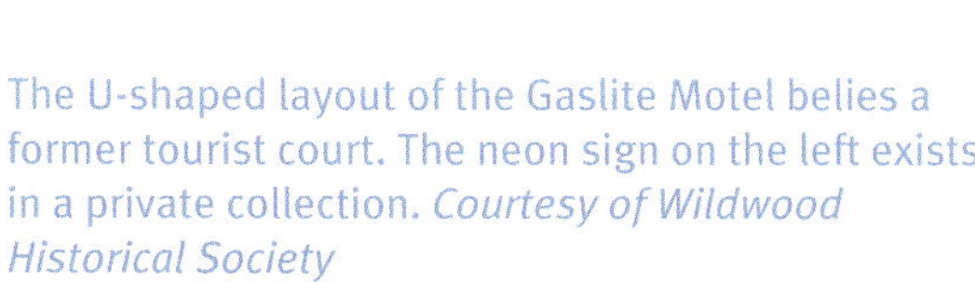

The U-shaped layout of the Gaslite Motel belies a former tourist court. The neon sign on the left exists in a private collection. *Courtesy of Wildwood Historical Society*

[19] Gaslite Motel (700 Surf Avenue)

[20] Surfside 7 Motel (701 Surf Avenue)

Across 7th Avenue from the Lurae, Eugene Sanguinetti built the U-shaped Lilly Court in the early 1950s. In 1957, he sold the court and built a new Lilly Court across Surf Avenue. The original Lilly Court's new owners, Stella and Casimir Brzyski, renamed it the LeCas Court Motel, which it remained until 1967, when it became the Gaslite. That year, the Brzyskis added a pair of neon signs (one wall-mounted, one rooftop) that spelled "Gaslite" in Playbill letters. The Gaslite, "North Wildwood's best-kept secret" according to its brochures, remained mostly unchanged until being demolished in 2002, whereupon ABS salvaged one of its neon signs.

Meanwhile, the new Lilly Court Motel and Apartments at 701 featured the best midcentury modern styling that builders of the era had to offer, including square spiral railings, a purple color scheme, and a massive, freestanding, mermaid-shaped neon sign in the motel parking lot. Photos from the early 1980s show that the neon sign's tubing had been removed, giving it an odd, shapeless appearance. Around 1985, the motel became the Surfside 7, a name it kept until being demolished in 2006.

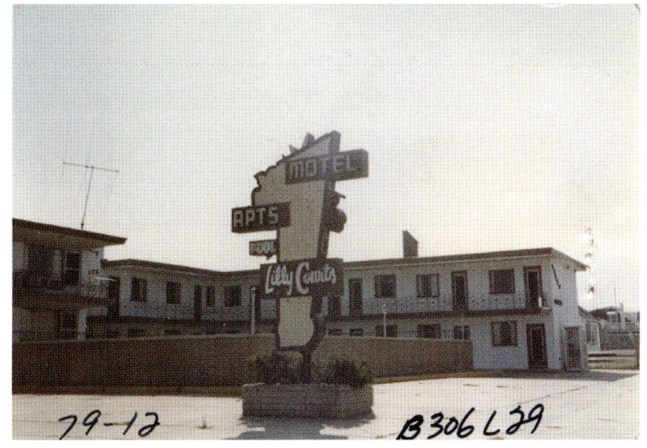

A few years after this 1982 photo, the Lilly Courts Motel & Apartments was renamed the Surfside 7. *Courtesy of Wildwood Historical Society*

[21] Surf Holiday Motel (802 Surf Avenue)

Opened in 1953, the Surf Holiday was one of the first motels in North Wildwood. Original owner Armand Rosati built a two-story rectangular motel addition to his bungalow and decked it out in bright-yellow clapboard siding and deep-red trim. For the street corner, Allied supplied a freestanding

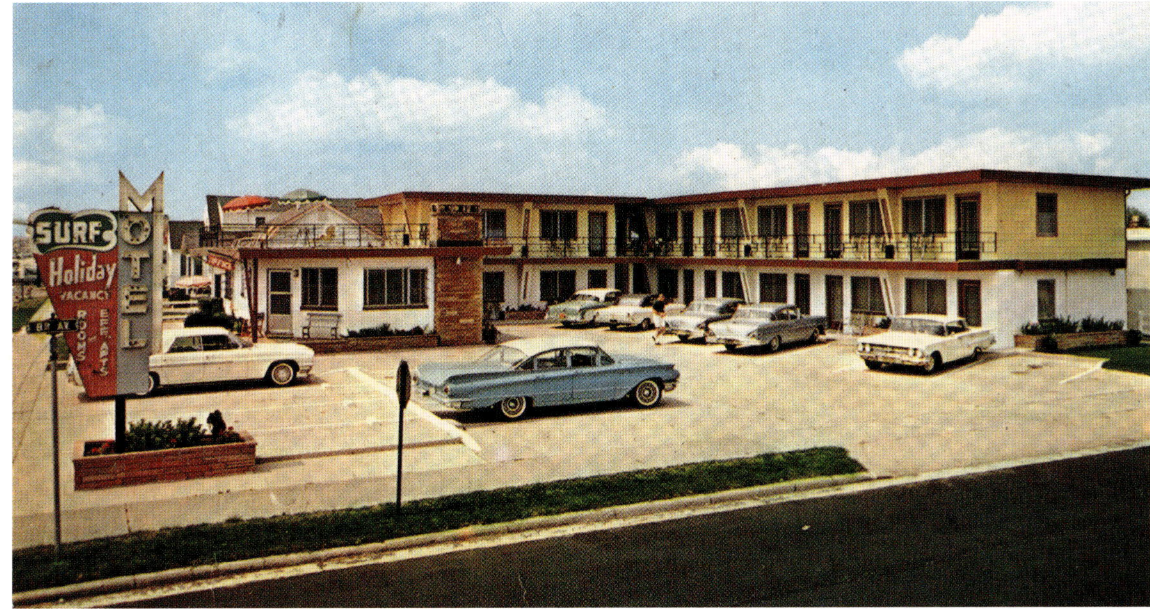

The Surf Holiday Motel had colorful midcentury modern style but no pool. *Author's collection*

neon sign, painted yellow and surmounted by a large red neon "M." Later owners painted the motel and sign different colors over the years, including eye-catching magenta in the 1960s. By the 1990s, the motel, which lacked a pool and was two blocks from the ocean, had fallen on difficult times. In 2003, it was demolished to make way for condominiums. ABS Signs salvaged the neon sign, one of the oldest motel signs on the island, on behalf of the Doo Wop Preservation League.

[22] Long Beach Lodge (539 East 9th Avenue)

George Lee built this motel in 1956 and surrounded it with a sandy lawn (less of an extravagance in the 1950s, when this neighborhood was relatively sparsely populated, than it would be today). A large, freestanding neon sign on the street corner advertised the "motel/lodge/apts." with beautiful Bauhaus lettering. Later owners expanded the motel and modified its sign. Today, the building survives as condominiums, but with all midcentury embellishments removed.

[23] Sea-Aire Motel (511 East 9th Avenue)

[24] Mermaid Motel (507 East 9th Avenue)

These two small, rectangular motels opened in the mid-1950s. Salvatore Russo built the Sea-Aire and Edward Kane built the Mermaid, and both sported freestanding neon signs, which disappeared

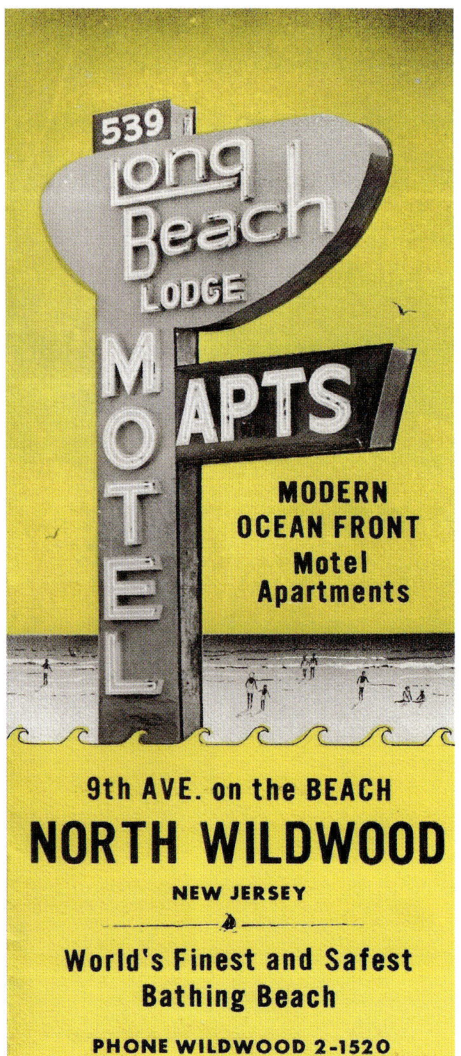

This brightly colored brochure for the Long Beach Lodge incorporated a photo of the motel's original neon sign. *Courtesy of Wildwood Historical Society*

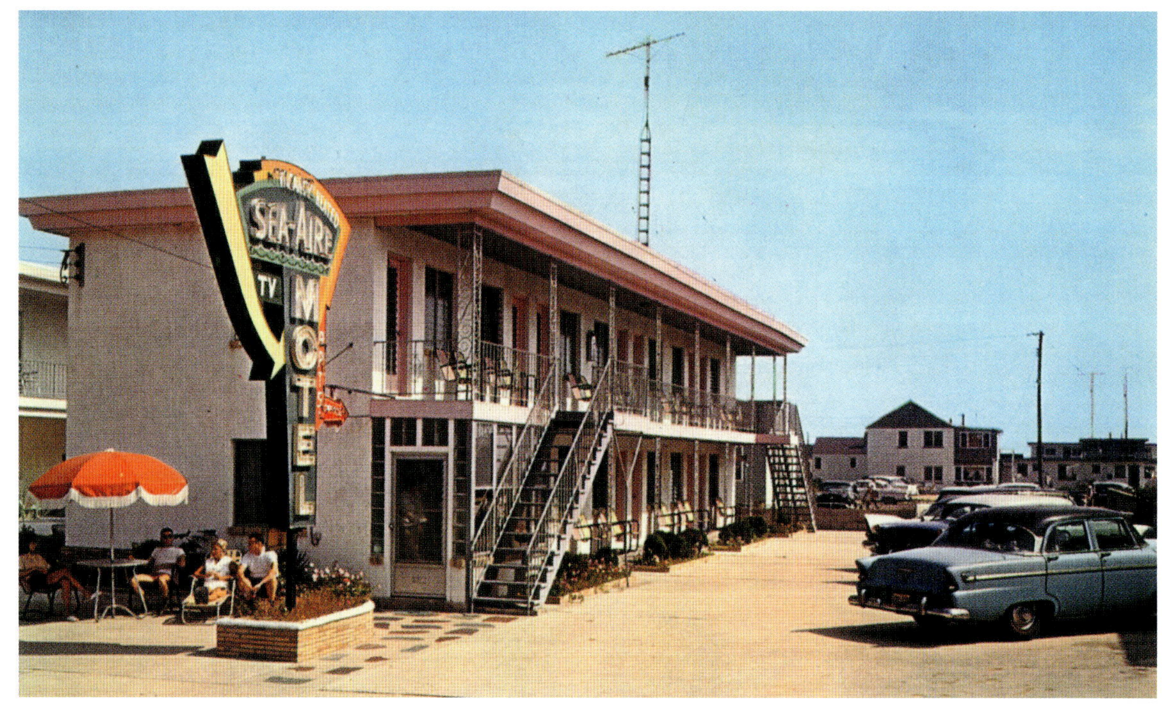

Though the Sea Aire was small, its owners raised its profile with an eye-catching neon sign. *Courtesy of anonymous collection*

in the 1980s. The Sea-Aire was demolished in about 2005, but the Mermaid building, stripped of all vintage detail, survives under condominium ownership.

[25] El Morro Motel (908 Ocean Avenue)

The El Morro, opened by Edward and Bertha Brick around 1960, offered a potpourri of memorable midcentury decoration, such as rustic post-and-rail wooden railings, red louvered doors, elaborate curtains, and a crenellated roadside sign with script neon letters. Later renovations gradually tempered these exuberant details, and the motel gave way to development in 2005.

[26] Chateau Bleu Resort Motel (911 Surf Avenue)

Lou Morey constructed the Chateau Bleu Motel in 1959. The motel's name was French, but its undulating carport canopy, supported by wishbone-shaped columns, was pure Miami Beach. On a blank wall behind the carport was a pair of light-blue neon signs that spelled the motel's name in boomerang-shaped letters. The Chateau Bleu was a cohesive unit, mixing the serious and the humorous in a way that radiated fifties Americana (especially the heart-shaped pool in the middle of the motel's expansive courtyard).

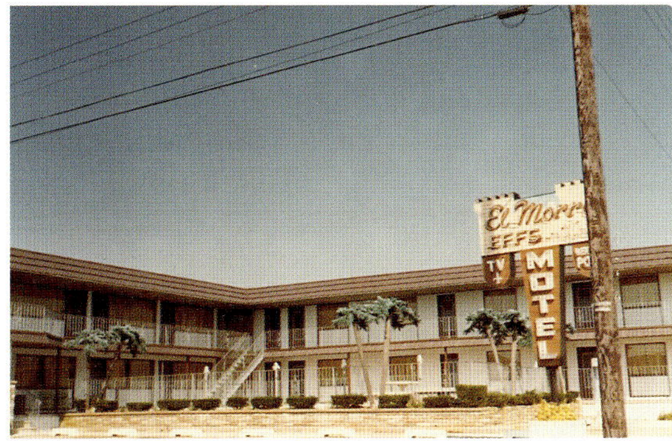

In this 1982 photo of the El Morro Motel, note that the motel's owners have stuffed artificial Christmas tree branches instead of palm fronds into its plastic palm trunks! *Courtesy of Wildwood Historical Society*

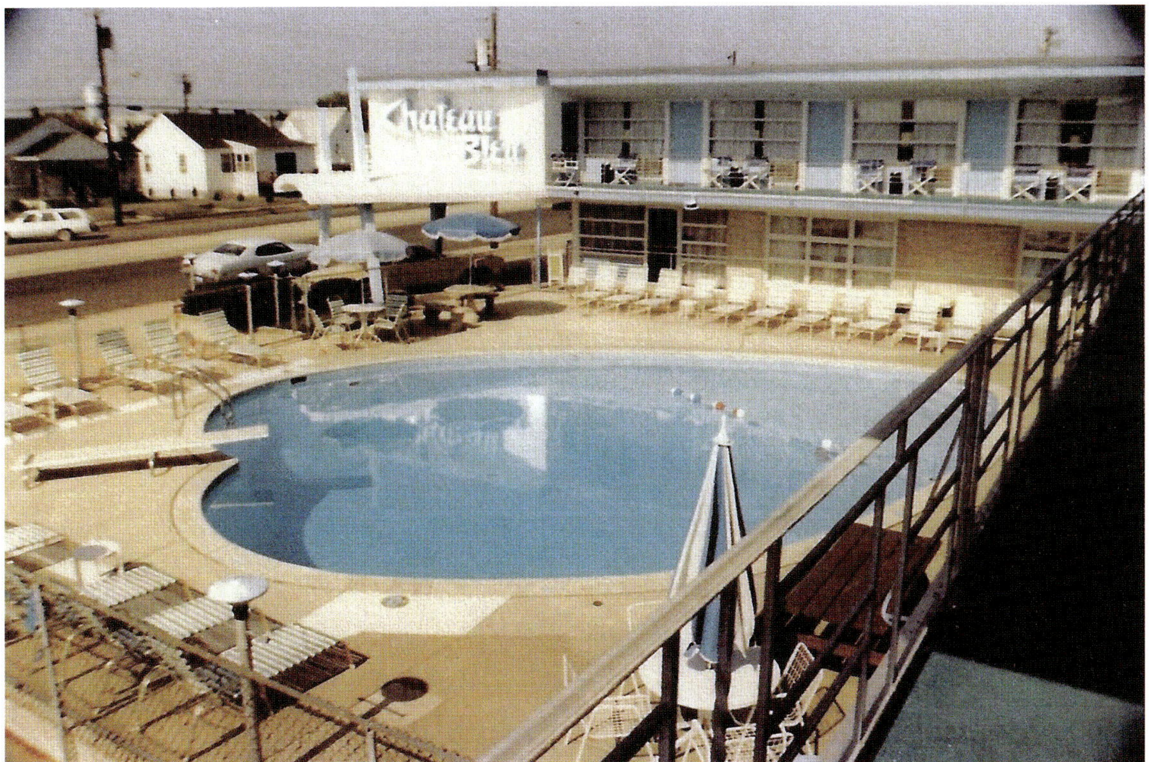

The Chateau Bleu combined artistic wishbone columns with a playful heart-shaped pool and undulating carport. The neon sign shown in this late 1970s photograph has since been replaced with plastic. *Courtesy of Wildwood Historical Society*

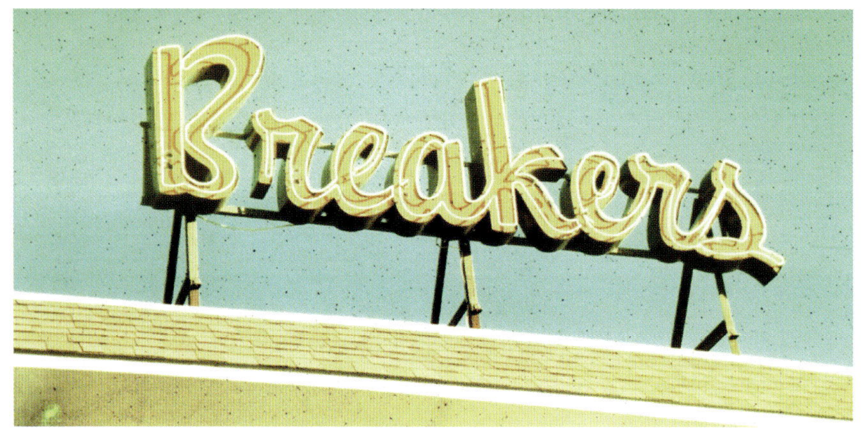

One of two identical neon signs at the Breakers Motel. *Courtesy of Fedele Musso*

By 1972, the motel's original owners, Leo and Florence Sacco, had sold out to Phyllis and Anthony Catanoso. Later that decade, the Catanosos painted the motel's original blue doors beige. In the 1990s, new owners Albert and Betty Crossan scrapped the original neon signs, replacing them with blue plastic backlit letters in the same shape. In 2003, however, the Crossan family took a step toward preservation and submitted their motel to the New Jersey Register of Historic Places and the National Register of Historic Places. These nominations were approved, and on January 16 and March 25, 2004, respectively, the Chateau Bleu joined the state and national registers, a historic development for the Wildwoods' Doo Wop preservation movement. "We're constantly maintaining it, and we've modernized the rooms with new furniture and microwaves," said Betty Crossan in an October 2003 article in the *Atlantic City Press*. "But we've never thought of changing it." The motel has remained in good condition since then.

[27] Breakers Motel (1001 Ocean Avenue)
The Breakers, which opened around 1955, graced the corner of 10th and Ocean Avenues with bright-yellow-and-orange trim, plastic palms, and two rooftop neon signs juxtaposing crashing blue waves with orange lettering. The motel was demolished in 2005. Fred Musso salvaged both neon signs; one now resides in local entrepreneur Randy Senna's collection.

[28] Ranch House Motel (408 East 10th Avenue)
The Ranch House, a sizable motel complex that was operated in conjunction with a miniature golf course, opened for the 1959 season. Its original owners, the McNulty family, instituted an elaborate western theme (wagon wheels, post-and-rail balustrades, and a tall plastic sign), but the motel was a bit too far from the beach to turn a profit, and it was demolished around 1985.

[29] Time and Tide Motel (515 East 11th Avenue)
Local contractors the McAlarnan Brothers built the Time and Tide in 1964. A freestanding neon sign sporting life preservers, red flags, and letters drew the attention of beachfront drivers. The sign vanished in the 1980s, but today the building survives as stucco-coated condominiums.

[30] Rest Cove Motel (511 East 11th Avenue)
Around 1960, Rocco Guzzone bought a four-year-old apartment building and expanded it into a motel, commissioning from Allied a huge rooftop neon sign to draw guests. This sign, which featured large script lettering and a multistroke yellow arrow, was joined in the 1970s by a fondly remembered banner that said, "If you were staying here, you'd be home by now!" Today, the building survives, minus the sign, as condominiums.

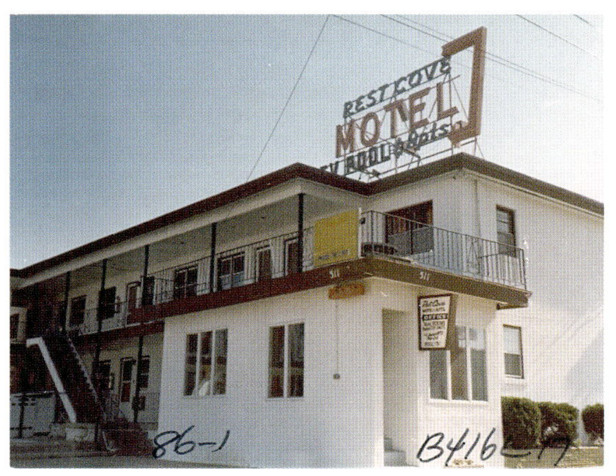

The Rest Cove still stands today as condominiums, but this huge rooftop neon sign has vanished. *Courtesy of Wildwood Historical Society*

[31] Galaxie Motel (510 East 11th Avenue)

Unlike many of the Wildwoods' most dynamic motels, the Galaxie languished in relative obscurity. The Galaxie first shows up in city directories in 1964, owned by Rocco and Mary Guzzone, who may have built it. It featured an atom-shaped neon sign and a pair of A-frames that enveloped the parking lot, deck, and entrance to the office. These were white when the motel was built, but by the 1980s they had become bright Crayola shades of yellow and blue. In the 1990s, the hard-to-maintain A-frames were removed, but the animated sign remained. When developers tore down the motel in the first few years of the 2000s, Fred Musso saved the sign, which exists today in a private collection in Minot, North Dakota.

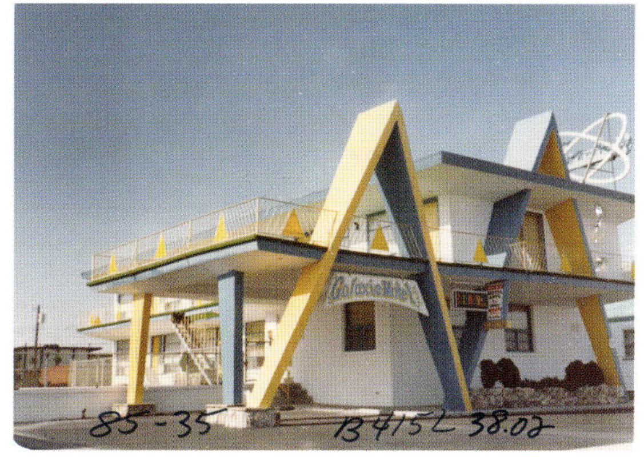

The Galaxie Motel's vivid color scheme, distinctive A-frames, funky railings, and atom-shaped neon sign (visible in the upper right corner) made it a hidden gem. *Courtesy of Wildwood Historical Society*

[32] Sea Rose Motel (1103 Surf Avenue)

In 1958, Florence Artur cashed in on the Wildwoods' tourist trend and purchased the single-story Sand Dollar Motel at 9th and Surf Avenues. Five years later, she and her husband upgraded to new construction: they hired Lou Morey to build the Sea Rose two blocks away, which opened for the 1963 season. Morey incorporated an array of midcentury modern details, including multicolored flagcrete wall accents, railings punctuated by pillars and blue keystones (later replaced with generic metal railings), and a green freestanding neon sign with pink letters.

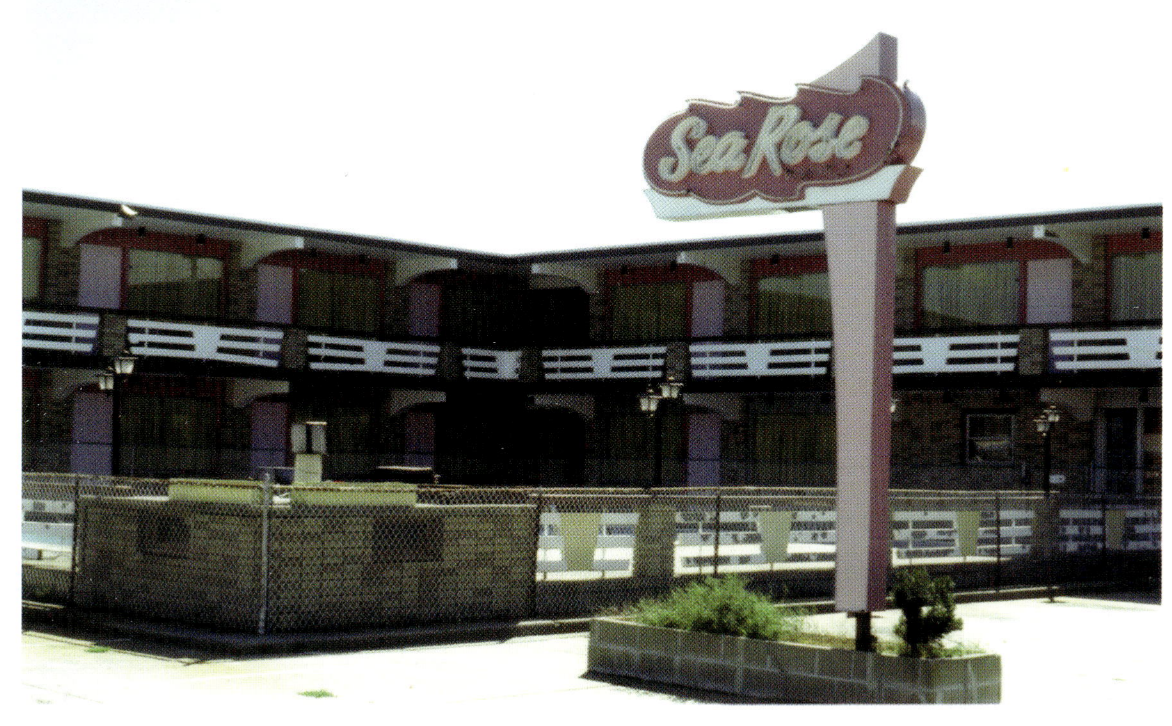

The Sea Rose Motel's neon sign catches the eye, and its railings, made from brick pillars and wooden slats, continue its theme. *Courtesy of Fedele Musso*

In 2004, the Artur family sold the motel to developers. "I bet they had a hard time knocking it down," remembers Fred Artur, Florence's son. "The Morey family built a good one!" Fred Musso saved the neon sign, which resided for several years in a Philadelphia collector's kitchen.

[33] New England Motel (104 West 11th Avenue)

This early 1970s-vintage motel along New Jersey Avenue combined American Colonial and modern aesthetics: zigzag balconies and bright colors were incongruously juxtaposed with strap-hinged doors and a neon sign with Playbill lettering. The building survives as condominiums.

[34] Bel Aire Motel (401 East 12th Avenue)

The Bel Aire opened around 1957 (the first year it shows up in city directories), a year after the more famous Wildwood Crest motel with a similar name. It sported a folksy neon sign starring an animated bell. "I built that one in the early 1960s," ABS founder Bob Hentges told Len Davidson in the late 1990s. "I had an artist working for me at the time. That was his drawing; he was very creative. His name was Jack Driscoll, probably one of the finest sign designers that ever lived in Wildwood. I would go out and see the customers, find out basically what they wanted. Then I'd come back to

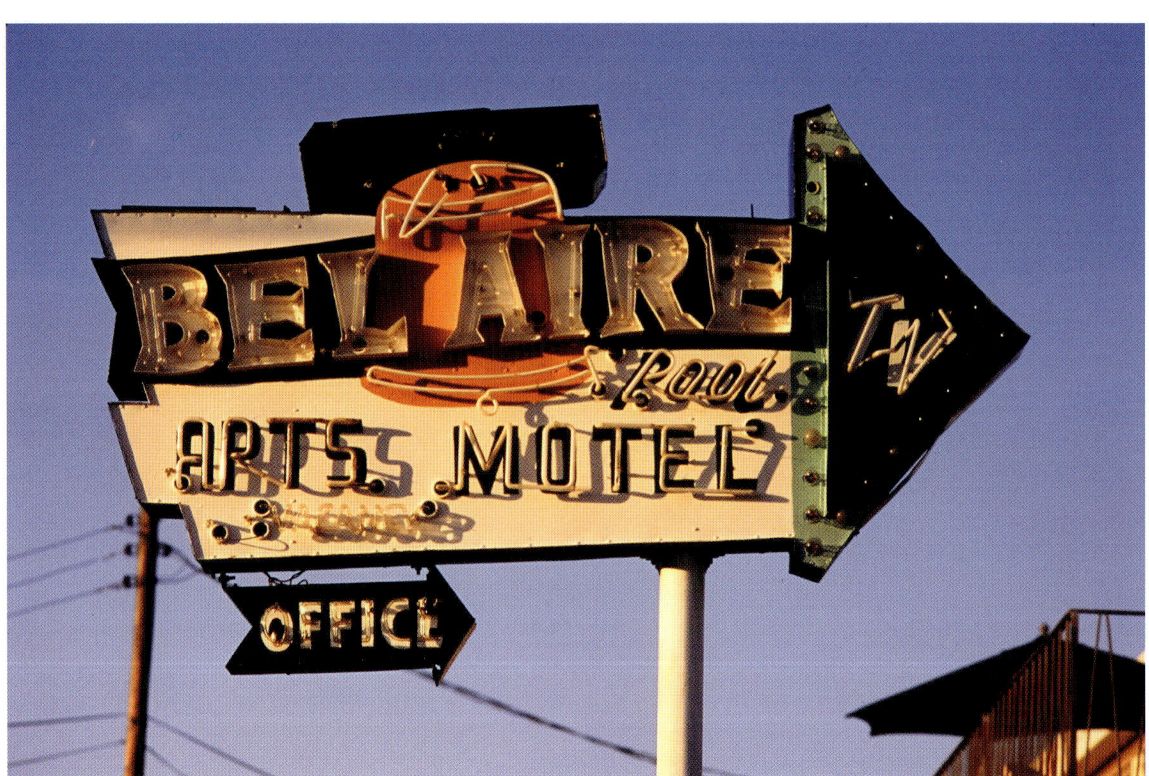

The Bel Aire Motel, not to be confused with Wildwood Crest's more famous Bel Air, had one of North Wildwood's most distinctive animated neon signs. *Courtesy of Steve Weir*

my sign shop and have Jack come up with the design." When the motel was demolished in 2004, Fred Musso saved the sign and later sold it to a collector in Minot, North Dakota.

[35] Sun 'N' Sand Motel (1108 Surf Avenue)

Nazareno Regalbuto, who later built several notable motels on the island, built this nondescript apartment building in the late 1940s. In the 1950s, it gained an addition and a freestanding neon sign. The complex came down in 2002.

[36] Cool Scoops Ice Cream Parlor (1111 New Jersey Avenue)

In 1956, Alta Kogl constructed the tiny K's Motel at 12th and New Jersey Avenues. Kogl lived in a bungalow on the property and rented out the four motel units to guests. A few years later, she decided to diversify her business and opened Rachel Salon de Beautie in her living room. The early seventies owners, the Capua family, expanded the bungalow to two stories and renamed the motel the Golden Way, but they kept the salon in business in the motel's lobby. Located four blocks from the ocean, the Golden Way did a sluggish business. When New York cabinetmaker Paul Russo first saw the motel, it was named the Abree. "It's not somebody's name or anything," says Russo. "But they wanted to be in the phone book in the A section."

Russo left the interior design business in 2001. "I designed fifty-eight floors of World Trade Tower One for Goldman Sachs—the architectural layout for the furniture. I saw the firemen carrying out some of my product [on September 11, 2001]. I lost people there that I knew. It hit me so hard that I said I have to come down to Wildwood. My wife's family was down here; they owned motels like the Florentine and a mini-golf course." When Russo arrived, he saw potential in the Abree Motel, which was dilapidated. "[It] had no ceilings and no floors. I think the owners had birds or something."

Russo bought the Abree in October 2001 and converted it into Cool Scoops, an ice cream parlor. He commissioned a new neon sign from ABS Signs, spent $14,000 to buy two 1957 Chevrolet Bel

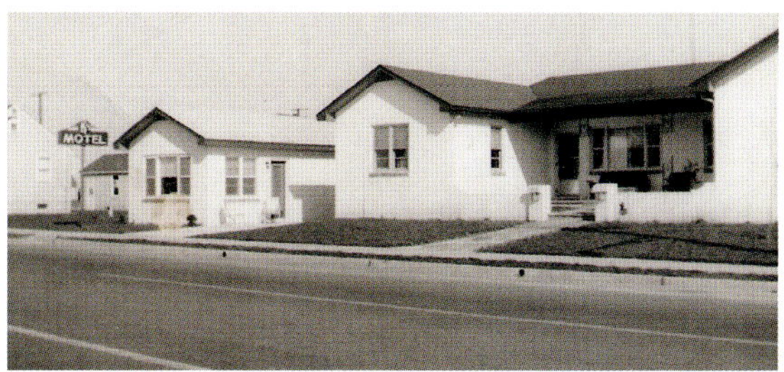

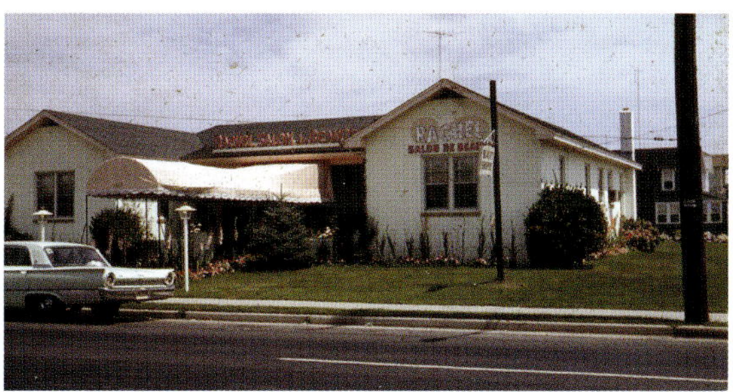

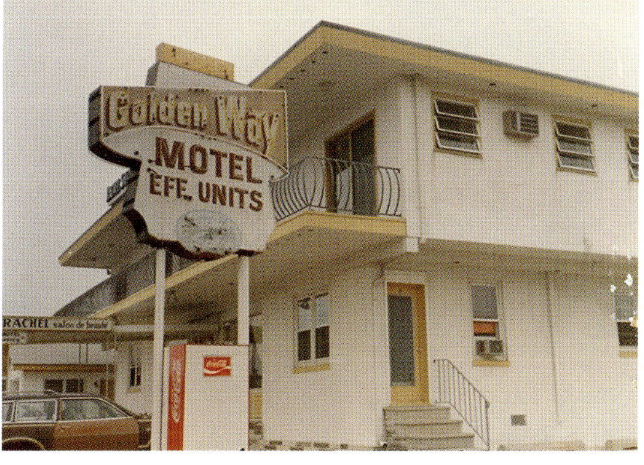

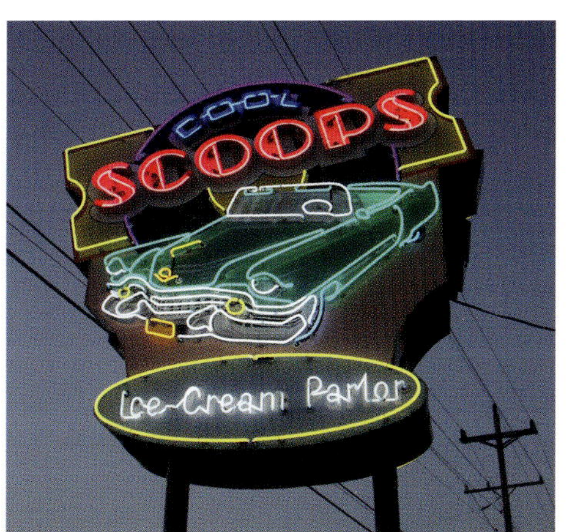

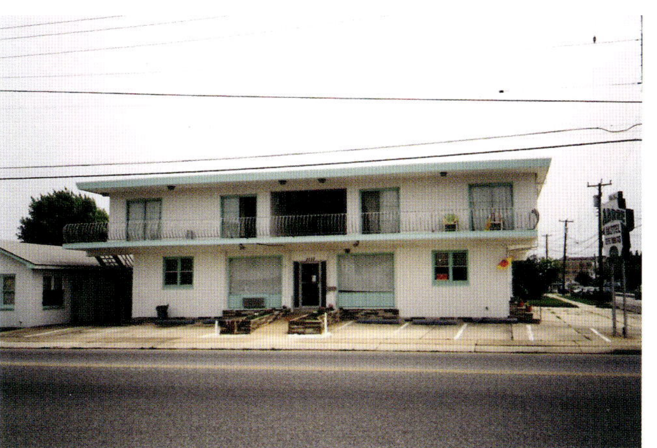

Evolution of a Neo Doo Wop renovation. The original K's motel was plain but functional (*courtesy of Paul Russo*); original owner Anita Kogl later installed a beauty salon in the motel's lobby (*courtesy of Paul Russo*), which remained in place when the motel was renamed the Golden Way (*courtesy of Wildwood Historical Society*). Paul Russo bought the motel, now named the Abree, in 2002 (*courtesy of Paul Russo*) and transformed it into thriving retro ice cream parlor, Cool Scoops.

Airs that had been damaged in accidents and cut them into pieces to use as booths, and opened in the summer of 2002. "That first season we opened in July, so we missed half the season. But we did very well the first year because we were on HGTV's *Trading Spaces*." Russo furnished the four ground-floor rooms of the ice cream parlor with items from his extensive collection of pop culture memorabilia from the 1950s and 1960s. "This is a destination location," he says. "This is where Doo Wop meets dessert. It's a museum! I should charge you to come in and give you free stuff to eat. It's genuinely a learning experience to come here." Russo has turned the weary shell of a fifties motel into a thriving retro ice cream parlor, and today, Cool Scoops is among the Wildwoods' Doo Wop preservation success stories.

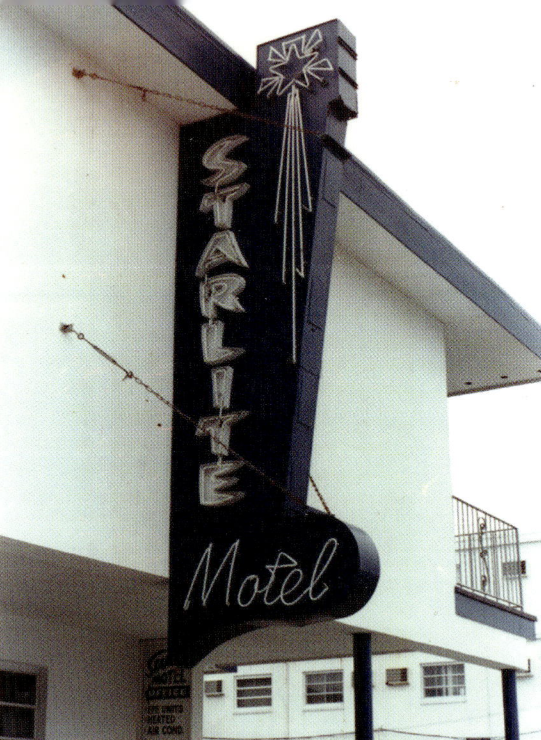

The Starlite's neon sign called attention to an otherwise plain motel. *Courtesy of Fedele Musso*

[37] Trylon Beach Resort (1200 Beach Drive)

In 1959, Theodore Gaitka opened a new motel on North Wildwood's sparsely developed Beach Drive. Despite being named after a futuristic sculpture designed by Wallace Harrison and J. Andre Fouilhoux for the 1939 World's Fair, the building had Mediterranean influences, with heavy vertical columns, a rakishly tilted roof, and a flagstone finish. It still exists and has been expanded several times.

[38] Starlite Motel (505 East 13th Avenue)

The Starlite Motel was built one lot away from Beach Drive in the late 1960s, sporting a wall-hung neon sign with Googie lettering and an animated shooting star. After ceding its beach view in 1972 to a new wing of the Trylon, the Starlite lost its competitive edge and led a quiet existence until it was torn down in 2002.

[39] Sunnyside Apartments (401 East 13th Avenue)

Bruce Evanoff built this building, originally the "Modern Apartments," around 1958. In the early sixties, Evanoff commissioned Ace Signs to install a detailed freestanding neon sign with a new name. The building stands today as condominiums (without the sign).

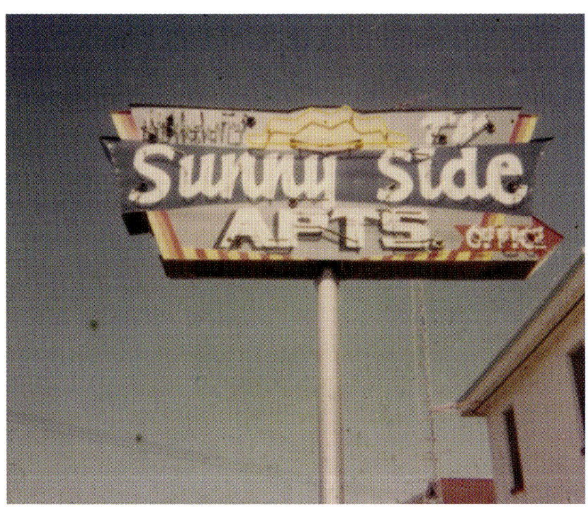

The Sunnyside Apartments' neon sign was a late product of Ace Signs. *Courtesy of ABS Sign Co., Inc.*

[40] American Inn Motel (510 East 13th Avenue)

[41] Le Boot Oceanfront Suites (510 East 114th Avenue)

Louise "Lou" Booth was a legendary presence in the Wildwoods' nightclub scene, and in 1970, she decided to branch out and open a motel. The Lou Booth Motel, on the beachfront at 14th Avenue, opened that season (an architect's rendering in a 1970 accommodations guide does not look much like the motel that was eventually built). A year later, Booth built a second motel (the Lou Booth Motel II) a block south. In the 1990s, Booth sold both motels to new owners on the condition that they change the motels' names. They survive as Le Boot and the American Inn, respectively; the Le Boot still has its original rooftop neon sign, modified with the new name (and without the neon tubing).

[42] Clipper Motel and Apartments (500 East 13th Avenue)
The Clipper was an early arrival on the North Wildwood motel scene, opening around 1955. Though a plain building, it sported a freestanding neon sign depicting a clipper ship and advertising efficiency units. Today the building remains, expanded and modified for condominium ownership.

[43] Suitcase Motel and Travel (1500 New Jersey Avenue)
Around 1966, Frank and Teresa Panzine built a small L-shaped motel on the corner of 15th and New Jersey Avenues. According to Randy Hentges at ABS Signs, the Panzines had trouble naming their motel. ABS founder Bob Hentges suggested the name "Suitcase" and made an amusing plastic and neon sign to match. This sign still stands, depicting a scantily clad couple waving hello from inside a neon-lined suitcase.

Today, Majura Dalpiaz owns the motel and operates a travel agency from its office. "I get a lot of good comments on the sign," Dalpiaz told author Len Davidson for his book *Vintage Neon*. "When

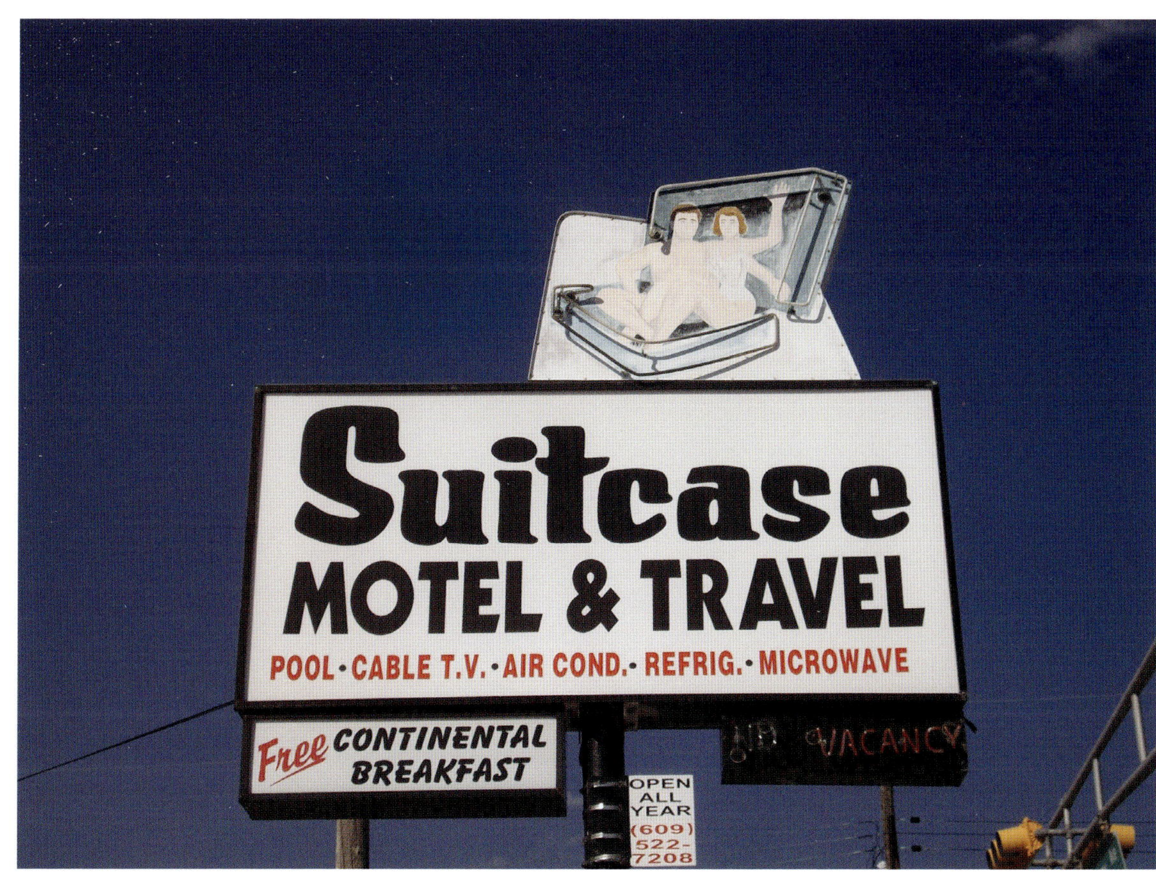

Bob Hentges named the Suitcase Motel while designing its charming but slightly risqué sign.

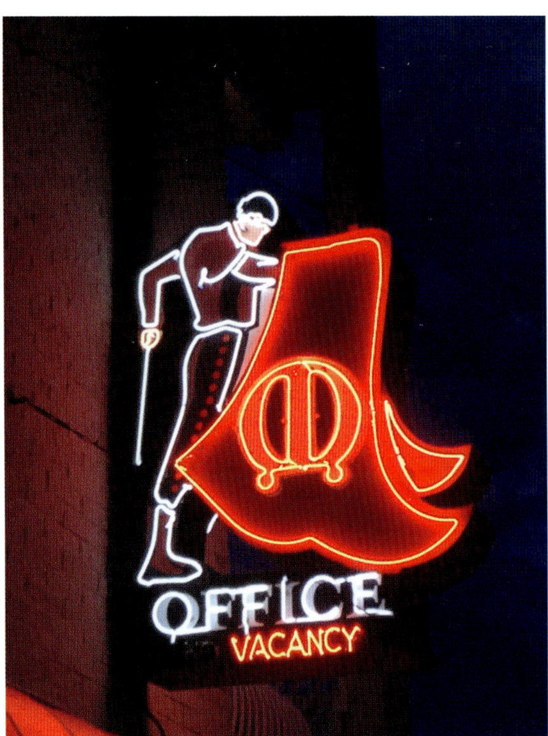

ABS continues to turn out works of neon artwork, such as this "office" sign at the Matador.

I had it repainted, I went to the original shop that made it and they looked it up in their book. It's a very unique sign. I love the name itself—there's hundreds of motels, but it's a name people can remember." The Suitcase still features its original herringbone wood trimming and diamond-patterned doors, as well as a garden with a variety of evergreen life.

[44] Matador Oceanfront Resort (16th Avenue and the Beach)
The Matador opened in 1971, sporting a pair of ABS neon signs (including a particularly vivid rooftop one), a novel Spanish theme, and a bright-red paint job. The motel remains today, and its original rooftop sign and a newer wall-mounted one continue to shine brightly.

[45] Condor Motel (1507 Ocean Avenue)
In 1957, George A. Hogg built the Melody Court Apartments at 16th and Ocean Avenues, near the northern end of the boardwalk. This plain apartment building sported a neon sign featuring a music note. In the 1980s, a new owner joined the Melody Court with the generic early seventies El Condor Motel next door. The enlarged El Condor spent the next couple of decades as a party destination, but current owners Frank and Kathy Sorrentino have commissioned a beautiful wall-hung neon sign from ABS and turned the newly renamed Condor into a family motel.

[46] Fran-Celia Motel (1504 Surf Avenue)
Myrtle Adams opened the one-story Myrtle Court for the 1954 season. Around 1966, new owners Frank and Celia Miserendino expanded the motel, renamed it the Fran-Celia, and added a freestanding neon sign encrusted with metal gingerbread. The late 1970s saw the motel's original watermelon-like color scheme of red and green changed to a more modern orange one. Developers leveled the Fran-Celia in 2004.

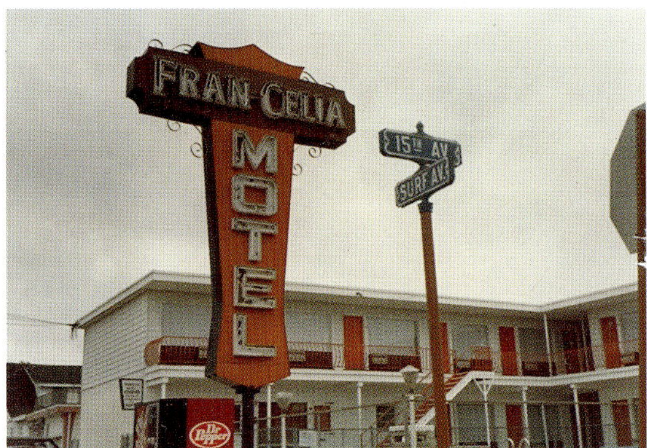

In this 1982 photo, the Fran-Celia Motel sports an unmistakably seventies color scheme. *Courtesy of Wildwood Historical Society*

The owners of the Driftwood Motel made up for its inland location with an eye-catching neon sign. *Courtesy of Wildwood Historical Society*

[47] Driftwood Motel (1504 Atlantic Avenue)
Raymond and Rita McAlarnan built the Driftwood Motel in 1956 as an addition to a rooming house next door. The small motel sported a freestanding neon sign that took on several colors over the years. When the Driftwood went condo in the first few years of the 2000s, Fred Musso saved its sign. The motel building still stands today.

[48] Tiki Motel (510 East 16th Avenue)
The Tiki Motel was deposited by a wave of enthusiasm for Polynesian culture that swept through the Wildwoods. Wally Zeug built it for the 1960 season and installed a giant wall-mounted

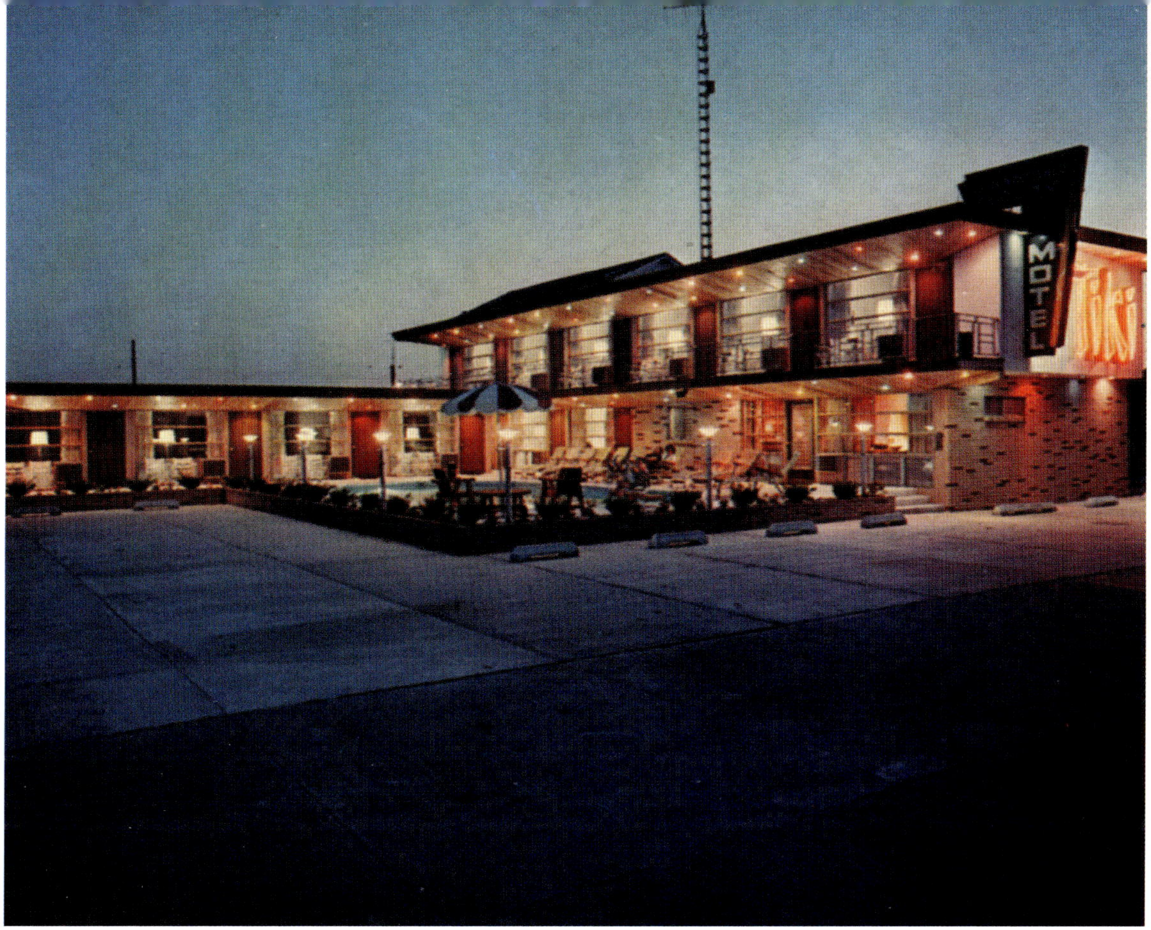

This detail from a 1964 postcard of the Tiki Motel shows its Googie-style spotlights and tan-brick walls. The orange "Tiki" wall-mounted neon sign would later migrate to the motel's roof. *Author's collection*

neon sign spelling out the motel's name in orange, wedge-shaped letters, which migrated to the motel's rooftop after a couple of years. After losing its beach view to a tall beachfront condo, the Tiki was demolished in the first few years of the 2000s.

[49] Shore House Residences (1600 Ocean Avenue)

Frank Zadlo and his son Richard tore down a three-story rooming house in 1970 and built the Sandpiper in its place. According to Rosemary Lawrence, Richard's daughter, "[My parents] were walking on the beach, and they were trying to think of a name for their new motel, and my mom saw all the sandpipers at the water's edge. The Sandpiper Motel was born." The family ordered a neon sign from ABS that featured a novel rotating sandpiper: "The spinning sandpiper on top of the motel sign was big stuff for the late sixties." In 2021, new owners renamed the motel the Shore House Residences; fortunately, Randy Hentges of ABS signs persuaded the new owners to retain the rotating neon sandpiper on top of a new plastic sign.

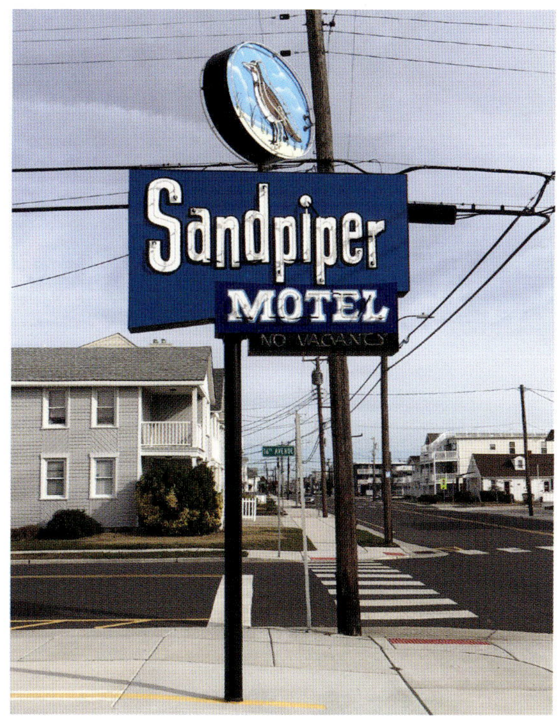

The Sandpiper Motel's neon sign has since been modified to read "Shore House," but the rotating neon sandpiper remains.

Note the grass courtyard in the foreground of this early 1950s photo of the Garden Manor Motel, now the site of a pool. *Courtesy of Wildwood Historical Society*

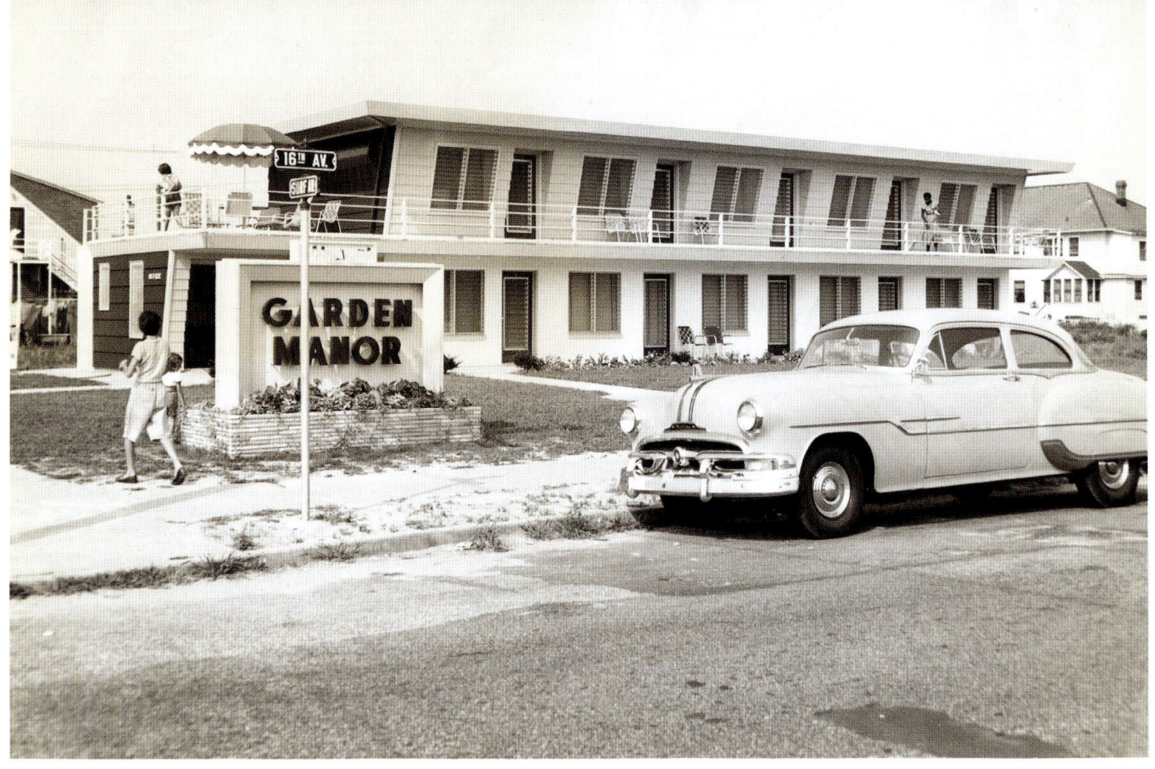

[50] Surf Haven Motel (1601 Surf Avenue)

Umberto Rosadi lived in a small, flagstone-trimmed bungalow on the corner of 16th and Surf Avenues, and in 1954 he built an L-shaped series of motel units around it. A small Allied neon sign with the name "Surf Haven Motel" stood on the street corner, and the whole building was painted bright yellow. Aside from the later addition of a pool and a new white-and-blue paint scheme, the motel remains mostly original, including the original neon sign, one of the oldest remaining on the island.

[51] Surf 16 Motel (1600 Surf Avenue)

Today's Surf 16 Motel opened in 1952, making it one of the earliest motels on the island, though its owners did not advertise it as a motel until a few years later. The original Garden Manor Apartments had a wide grass lawn, a billboard-like sign with chrome letters, and outward-leaning walls. Looking at an early picture of the motel, recent owner Rick Geers remarks, "That's a 1952 or 1953 Pontiac Chieftain. And there's a dirt street there—no curbs or anything."

Sixties owner Irving Carroll expanded the motel to the footprint it has today, but the next owner let the motel deteriorate, as Geers found when his family bought the motel in 1993. In 2018, Geers sold to developers, who converted the motel to condominium ownership. "It's a hard business to put a lot of money into," Geers said in 2017. "If we were geographically located more south, and we could stay open for longer, a lot of things could be done with this place."

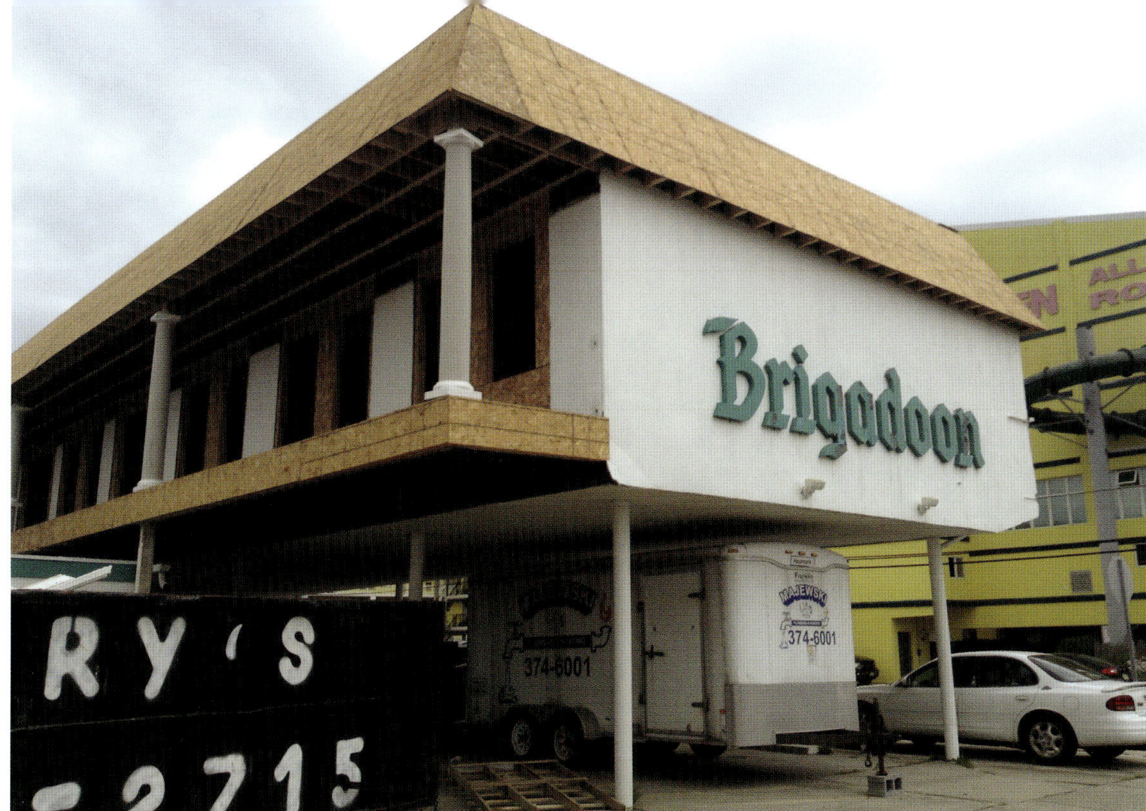

This 2014 photo shows the Brigadoon Motel being modified for condominium ownership with the addition of a mansard roof.

[52] Brigadoon Motel and Apartments (1605 Ocean Avenue)
George and Grace Hogg built the Brigadoon Apartments in 1963, naming it after a popular Scottish-themed musical. The L-shaped motel had a pool and a small, green,wall-hung neon sign; a later expansion added a futuristic wing that floated above the motel's parking lot. The building survives as condos and retains little trace of its midcentury origin. According to Fred Musso (who heard from the then owner of the motel), firemen salvaged the neon sign during a convention but later junked it.

[53] Golden Rail Motel (1702 Ocean Ave)
The Golden Rail's appeal relies on patterns, rather than sweeping gestures. Sawtooth-shaped balconies lined with yellow ship's-prow railings create a memorable cohesion. The Sittineri family built the motel in 1969, naming it the Beechwood Apartments. A few years later, they renamed the motel the Golden Rail. Neon signs have come and gone over the years, but the Golden Rail remains an evocative relic of sixties design.

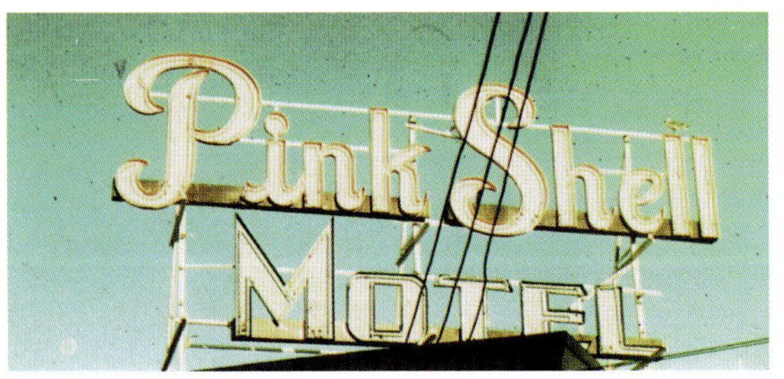

The Pink Shell rooftop sign replaced an earlier one that stood in the middle of the motel's parking lot. *Courtesy of Fedele Musso*

[54] Pink Shell Motel (507 East 18th Avenue)
Jerry and Adeline Mouchka built the Pink Shell Motel in 1957, installing railings with curlicue embellishments and commissioning an eye-catching, freestanding, shell-shaped neon sign starring a yellow arrow. A decade later, they added a rooftop sign, but when an expansion to the motel in the early 1970s demanded extra parking, they tore down the original freestanding sign. After the high-rise Montego Bay Resort blocked the Pink Shell's beachfront view, its days were numbered, and it fell to the wrecking ball in 2004.

[55] Sahara Motel (510 East 18th Avenue)
Carl Konopka built the two-story Sahara in 1968 next to the boardwalk, and later owners expanded it to three stories. The motel hangs on to its original neon sign (which includes a green cactus), but the neon tubes have vanished and the sign is illuminated at night by spotlights.

[56] Sea Star Motel (406 East 18th Avenue)
Built in 1957 by Francis Bella, the Sea Star had a neon sign featuring five yellow stars flashing on a bright-blue-and-red-painted background. During the 1970s, the motel sprouted a tropical garden

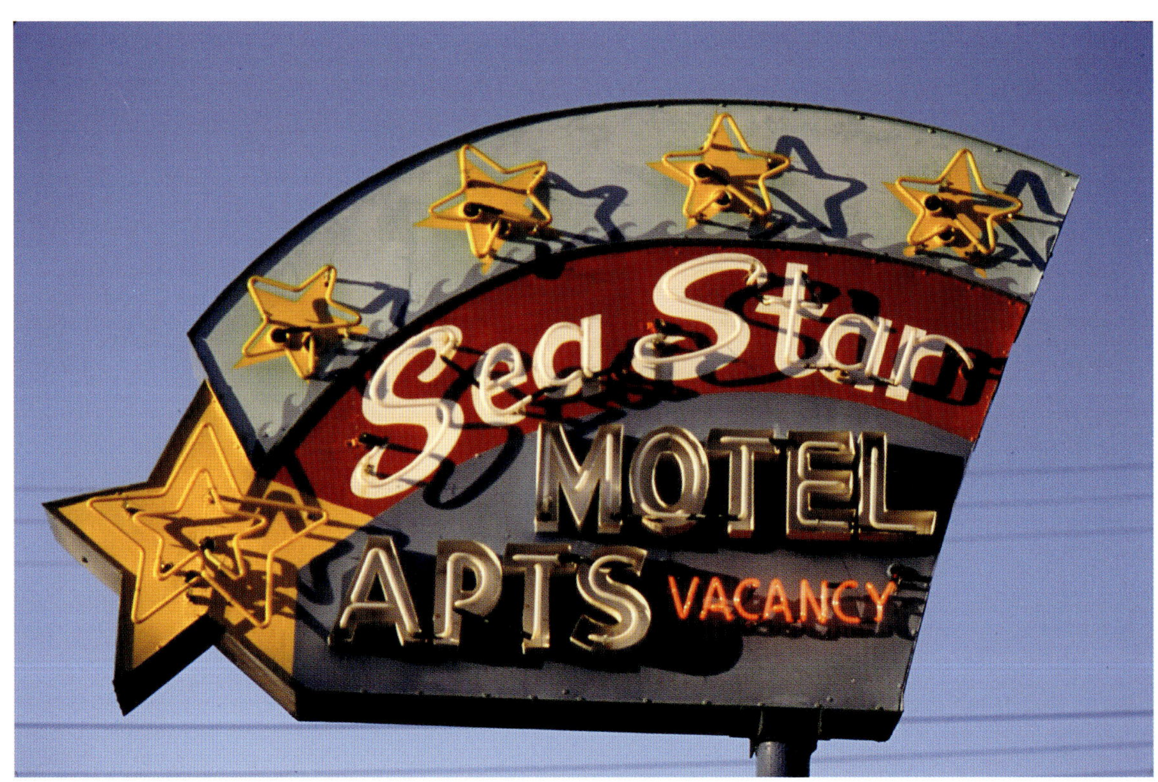

Several neon signs in North Wildwood had unique animations, such as the flashing stars at the Sea Star Motel. *Courtesy of Steve Weir*

on its second-floor balcony, complete with plastic palms, but this small urban oasis later vanished. Fred Musso saved the neon sign when the motel was converted to condominium ownership in 2004. "It was a wonderful sign," he says. "The stars were animated on a sequencer. I'm sorry I sold it!"

[57] Buccaneer Motel (503 East 19th Avenue)

Chester and Genevieve Kosloski constructed the Buccaneer in 1965 and coordinated a medieval theme in several architectural patterns. Doors were positioned on alternating sides of adjacent rooms, breaking up the motel's façade into porch-like localities of windows and doors. The doors themselves were painted brown with yellow diamond motifs, and the jalousie windows were broken up by V-shaped sashes. In the center of the parking lot stood a neon sign.

Developers bought the Buccaneer in 2004 and began demolishing it. However, due to logistical difficulties, they demolished only half of the motel. The rest sat vacant until 2007, when it was torn down and replaced with condominiums.

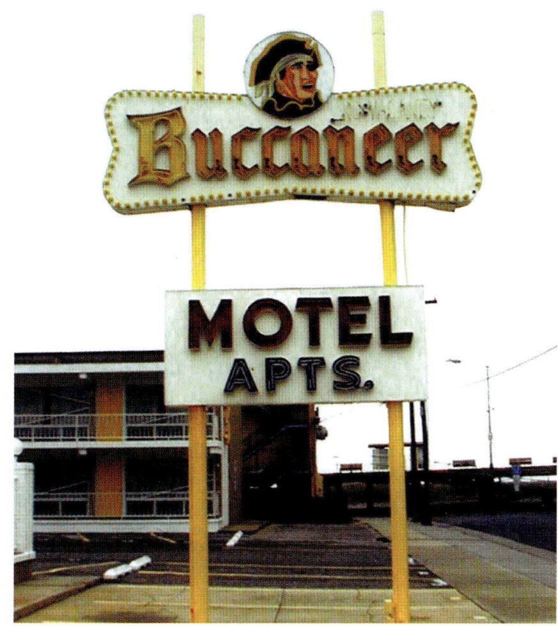

Throughout its life, the Buccaneer Motel held on to its original 1965 neon sign, shown here forty years later. *Courtesy of David and Theresa Williams*

[58] Florentine Family Motel (1901 Surf Avenue)

Alfred and Ruth Kleeman originally built the Sunrise Motel, which makes up half of the present-day Florentine, at this site in 1956. "It was owned by a guy named Al who weighed 500 pounds," current owner George Capua says. "He built an elevator because he couldn't walk up the steps. We're one of the few motels in the area to have an elevator." This original portion of the motel had an Italianate, outward-projecting, beige-brick façade and railings whose design mimicked the catenary arch of hanging ropes (the same railings appear at the Aruba Motel across 20th Avenue).

The Kleemans owned the Sunrise until the 1970s, by which time they had added a neon sign and a pool to bring the motel up to date. In 1977 the Kleemans sold to Marie Hess, who had recently built the Tuscany Motel across Surf Avenue. Her first move was to build an L-shaped addition that expanded the Florentine's capacity. Then, around 1984, according to Capua, Hess "changed the name to Florentine because in Italy, Tuscany and Florence are on opposite sides of the same river. She considered the street to be the river." The motel acquired a new neon sign, which continues to shine today. The fifties wing of the motel still has its original bird's-eye maple doors.

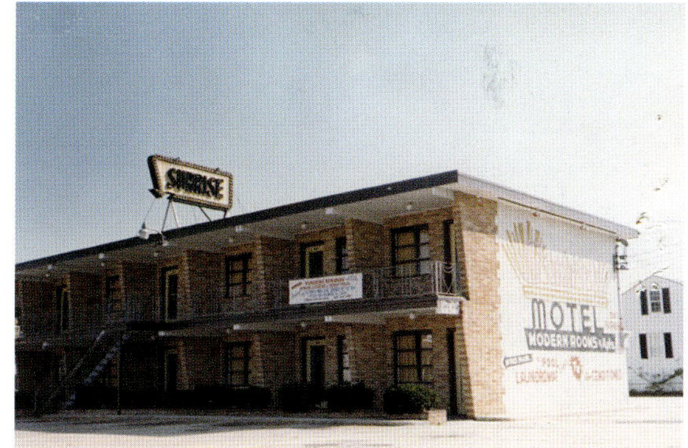

The Sunrise Motel was a couple of years away from being renamed the Florentine when this 1982 photo was taken; note the motel's upscale brick façade. *Courtesy of Wildwood Historical Society*

[59] Beach Cove Motel (429 East 20th Avenue)

In 1953, Michael Delfonce built the one-story Del-Fon-Sea Motel on the beach along 20th Avenue. It was never expanded, despite its sought-after site (though the construction of the high-rise 1900 Boardwalk condominium in front of it in the late 1970s marginalized the motel). Later owners renamed it the Lemon Drop and then the Beach Cove before selling to developers around 2004.

[60] Sans Souci Motel (421–423 East 21st Avenue)

Lou Morey built the Sans Souci Motel in 1956 for original owner Ethel Dodson. The name, which means "without worries" in French, referenced the Morris Lapidus hotel of the same name in Miami. In a nod to 1940s courts, two bar-shaped buildings faced each other over a parking lot. One of these wings was surmounted by a white Allied neon sign. When Dodson brought Morey back in 1962 to

One of two script neon signs that graced the Sans Souci Motel. *Courtesy of Steve Weir*

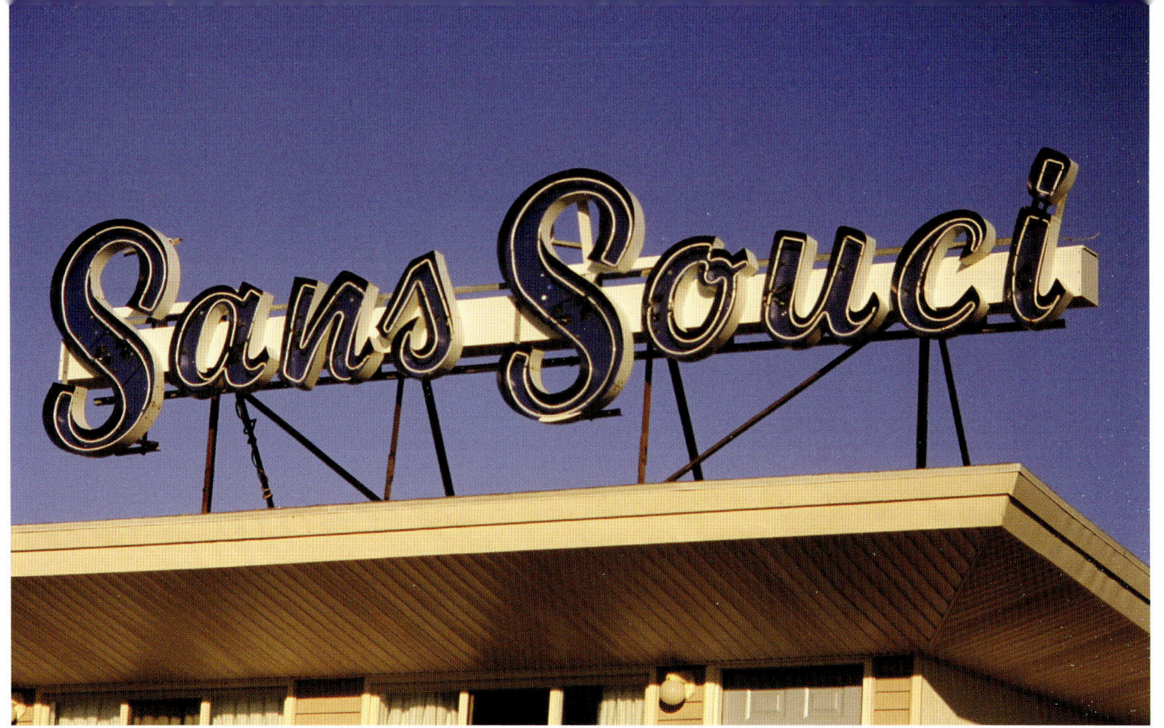

expand the motel, she commissioned a second neon sign on its new 20th Street façade. Both signs were replaced with newer ones in the 1970s, and Fred Musso rescued one of these seventies-vintage signs when the motel was demolished in 2005. That sign survives in the hands of a collector in Lancaster, Pennsylvania.

[61] Aruba Motel (2001 Surf Avenue)
In 1957, Julian Romolo sold his bungalow on Surf Avenue to Samuel Garfinkle, who tore it down and built a two-story, L-shaped motel. The Marquee was a subtle classic of midcentury detailing, featuring ropelike railings and a pop art color scheme of white, cream, and bright red. Later owners expanded it and changed its name to Le Marquee (in the 1990s) and then the Aruba (in the first decade of the 2000s). Today, its color scheme of bright-yellow brick trim with green railings and red doors, along with several plastic palms, makes it one of North Wildwood's hidden gems (although its ground-floor coffee shop is now closed).

[62] Lampost Beach Motel (442 East 21st Avenue)
In 1960, Frank Quirus built a three-story apartment building one lot away from the boardwalk on 21st Avenue. A few years later, new owner Cipolla Pasquale named the motel the Lampost Beach and installed a plastic sign with this new name, which ABS replaced with neon in the 1990s. When the Lampost went condo in 2005 or so, the sign survived for a couple years but then disappeared.

[63] Donaraile Motel (438 East 21st Avenue)

In 1956, Walter Pleasanton built a motel addition onto his 21st Avenue bungalow and added a small neon sign to match. Later owners expanded the motel and replaced that neon sign with a larger one. In 2005, the aging motel met the wrecking ball.

[64] Ivanhoe Motel and Apartments (430 East 21st Avenue)

[65] Panoramic Motel and Apartments (2101 Surf Avenue)

Both of these motels, still standing today, opened for the 1966 season. Norman and Thelma Danella, who had built the Norman-D Apartments earlier in the decade, commissioned the Panoramic to have a bright, beachy theme, with an aqua roofline, flagcrete walls, and a plastic sign spelling out the name of the motel in multicolored tilted blocks. The motel's current owners have painted the roofline brown and the doors aqua, a paint job that plays on the motel's midsixties vintage.

Also in 1966, Anthony and Marguerite Bianchi, who had recently sold their Silver Beach Motel in Wildwood Crest, built the Ivanhoe Motel and Apartments next door to the Panoramic. The

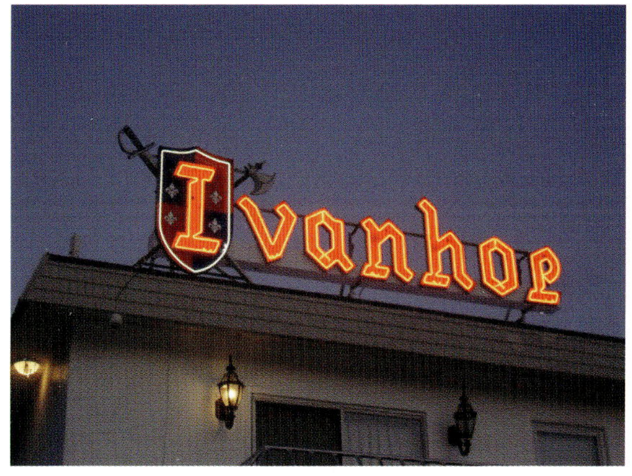

The Ivanhoe Motel's neon sign expresses its medieval theme.

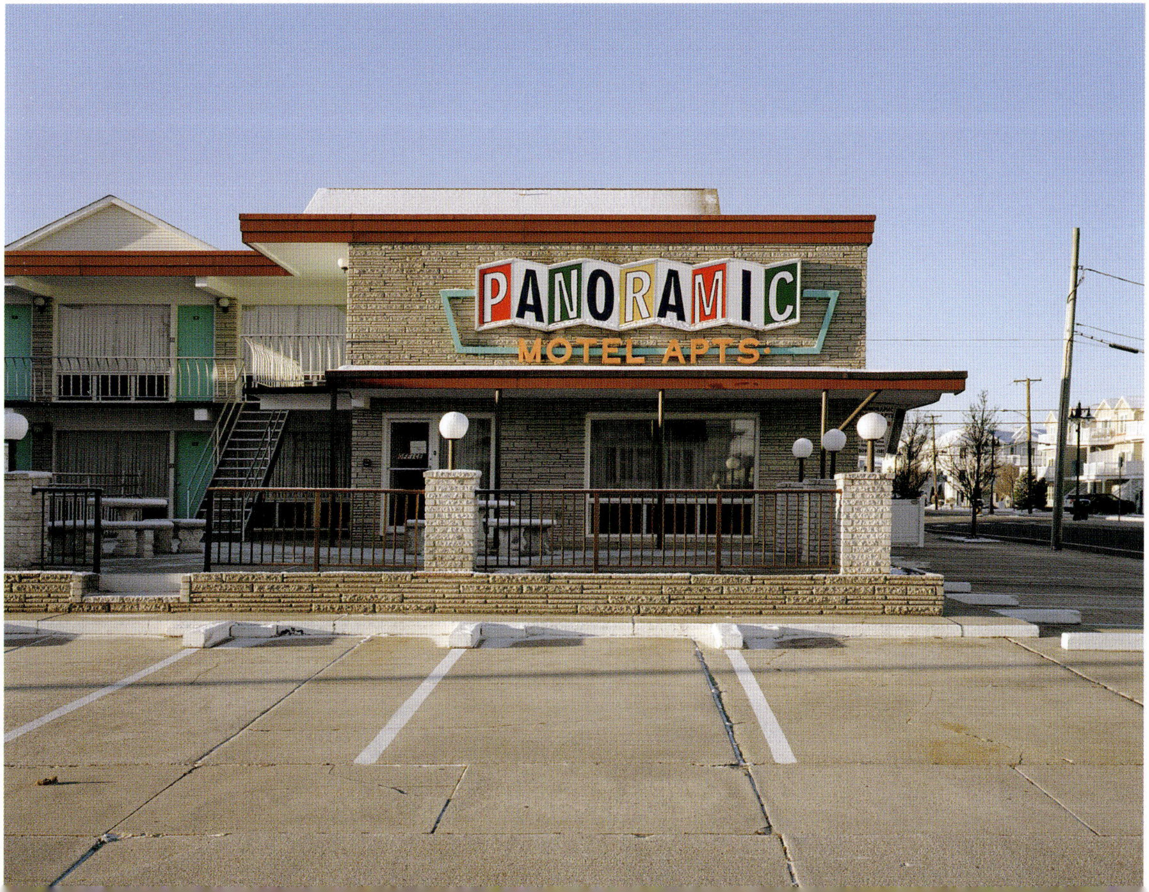

Though it doesn't use neon, the Panoramic Motel's colorful plastic sign and distinctive flagcrete façade express a fun midcentury theme. *Courtesy of Tyler Haughey*

In this early 1970s postcard of the Grey Manor Motel, note the original neon sign, later replaced with a much-smaller version. *Author's collection*

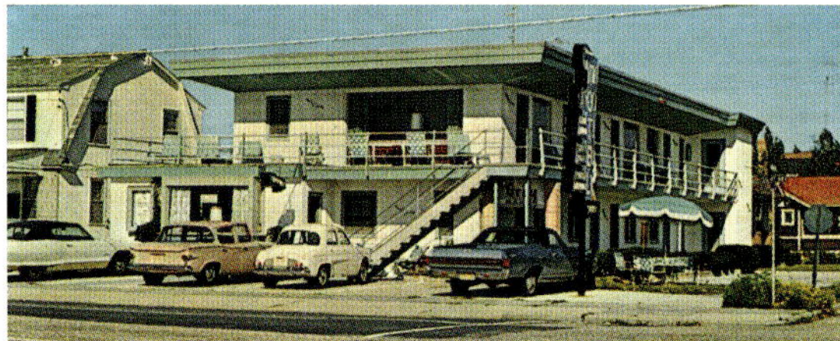

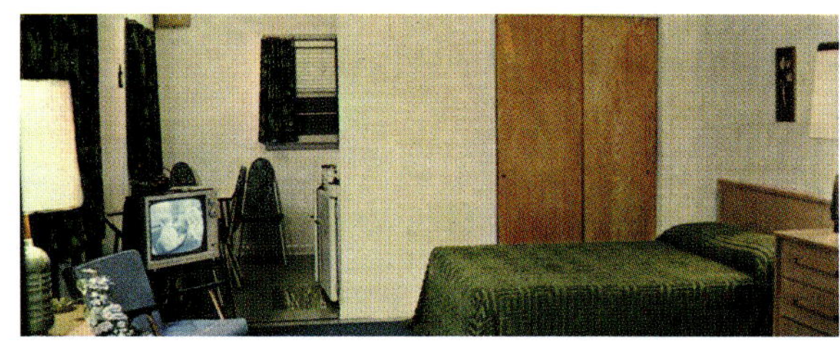

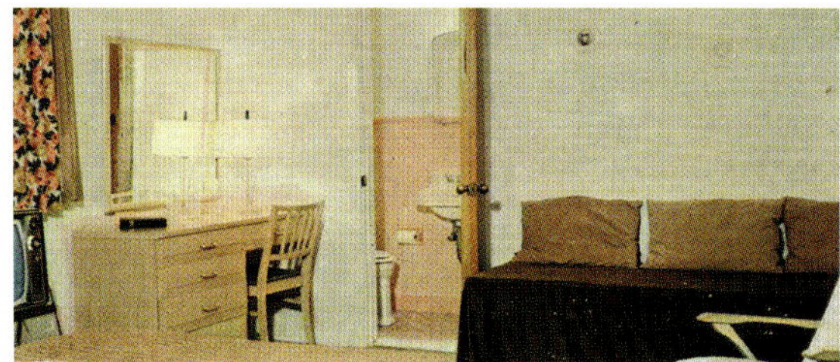

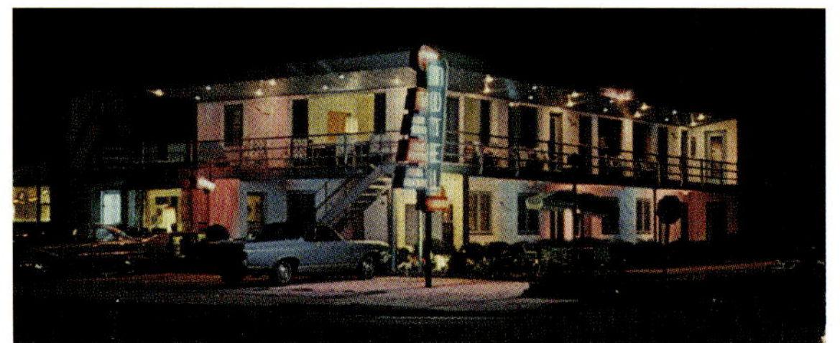

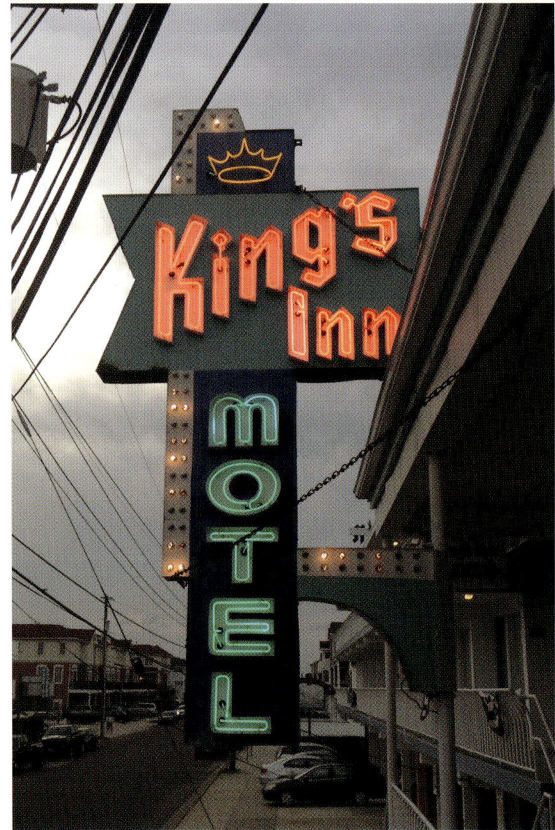

This neon sign beckoned visitors to the King's Inn until the mid-2010s, when the motel became part of a chain.

Ivanhoe expressed a medieval theme with lanterns and a red Old English neon sign. In 1984, Anthony and Marguerite's son, Chris, and his wife, Sue, bought the Panoramic. The Bianchis have kept both motels in original condition. Recently, they renovated the Panoramic's sign "because the panels had faded," Sue says. "We said that we had to keep it the same, because that's what makes it stand out. But we did replace the colors of the panels." The Ivanhoe's neon sign, though, is a bit more troublesome. "We have to change the neon every so often. ABS Signs, they're the only game in town!"

[66] Grey Manor Motel (2100 Surf Avenue)

[67] Lisa's Family Motel (2110 Surf Avenue)
These two small motels and their freestanding neon signs brought midcentury flavor to the 2100 block of Surf Avenue. Neil and Bernice Greydanus built the Grey Manor in 1955, and shortly afterward, William Jackson built an apartment building next door, which Fritz Flach renamed the Anchorage around 1965. The Anchorage Motel was briefly renamed Lisa's Family Motel in the early 2000s, but both motels came down in 2005.

[68] Boardwalk Hammock Inn and Suites (423 East 23rd Avenue)
The King's Inn, one of the Wildwoods' few motels to front the boardwalk, was built in 1966, according to city records. Its first owners, Vito and Edith Abessinio, built a motel that foreshadowed the utilitarian motels that would spring up around the island in the 1970s, though they did commission rooftop and wall-mounted neon signs from ABS. In 2017, the King's Inn and the neighboring Supreme Motel (formerly Court, at 422 East 22nd Avenue), an early fifties apartment building that the King's Inn had absorbed, became part of the hotel chain Howard Johnson's. Today the motel is a Hammock Inn and Suites.

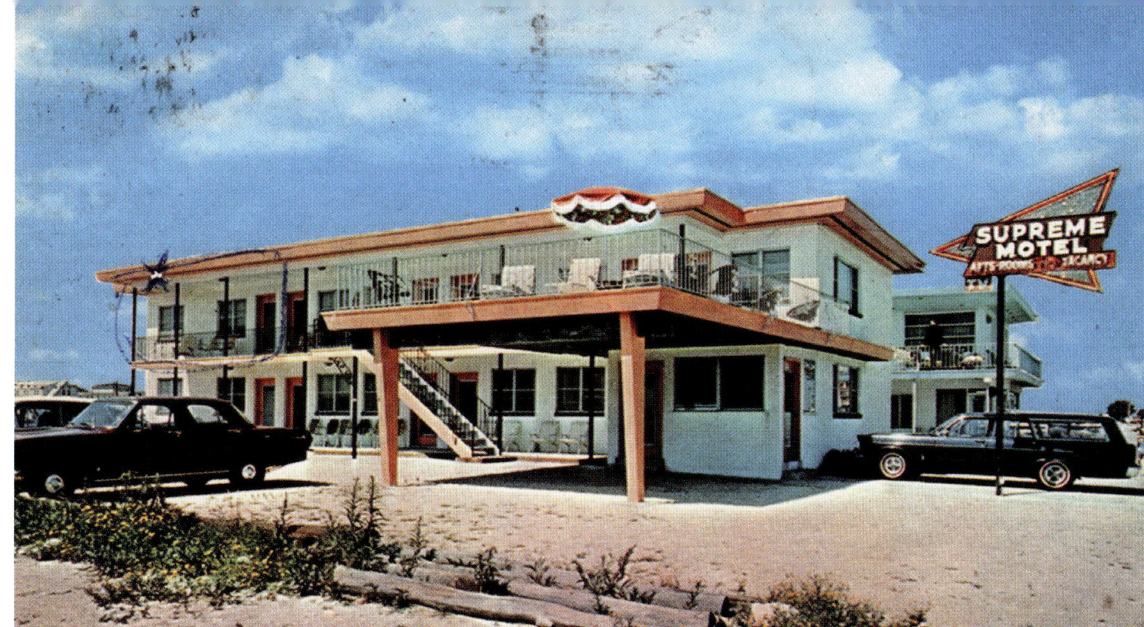

The Supreme Motel, shown here in the late 1960s, was previously the Supreme Court. Later, it became part of the King's Inn. *Courtesy of Fedele Musso*

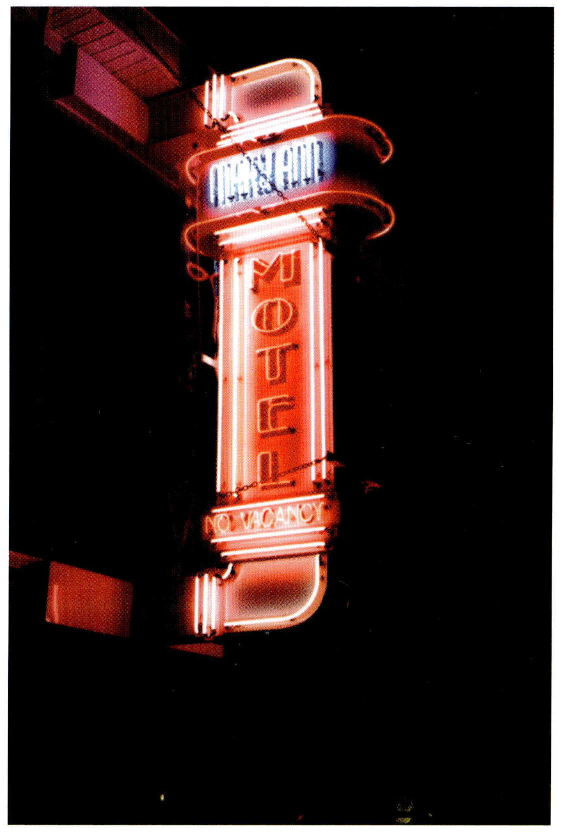

ABS Signs built this beautiful art deco neon sign for the Mary Ann Motel in 2000, replacing an earlier one. *Courtesy of Fedele Musso*

[69] Sea 'N' Surf Motel (420 East 22nd Avenue)

[70] Mary Ann Motel (421 East 23rd Avenue)
Elmer Whitehead built the Mary Ann around 1959 and commissioned two neon signs (rooftop and wall-mounted) for it. In 2000, ABS replaced the latter with a beautiful art deco–styled sign. Frank Penico, meanwhile, had built the Sea 'N' Surf Court in 1954, and it sported another elaborate neon pole sign. The two motels briefly merged in the first few years of the 2000s under the name Sea 'N' Surf, but both were torn down in 2005. A Sea 'N' Surf sign remained for a few years, advertising an empty lot, but today condominiums stand on the site.

[71] Sunrest Motel (411 East 23rd Avenue)

[72] Notre Dame Motel (2201 Surf Avenue)
Guido Carideo built the Notre Dame as a small court in 1953 or 1954, advertising it with a modest, freestanding, red neon sign (which later gained a giant yellow arrow). By 1963, Carideo had expanded the court into a U shape and added a pool. Later that decade, Carideo bought the 1957-vintage Sunrest Motel around the corner, expanded it, installed a neon sign on the roof, and operated the two motels in tandem. In the

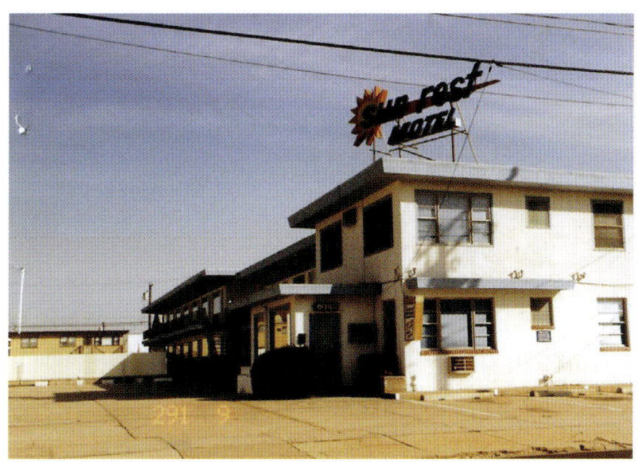

The Sunrest Motel in its later years. *Courtesy of Wildwood Historical Society*

1970s, the Carideos moved on to build the Carideon Motel a block west, and the Notre Dame and Sunrest carried on until being demolished in 2005.

[73] Carideon Motel (2200 Atlantic Avenue)

The Carideo and O'Brien families built the Carideon in the early 1970s; the Carideos had built the Notre Dame a block east two decades earlier. The Carideon was a distinctly seventies interpretation of the Wildwoods' brightly colored modernism, complete with script plastic signs and sawtooth-shaped balconies, and it continues to welcome guests today.

[74] Bayberry Motel (401 East 23rd Avenue)

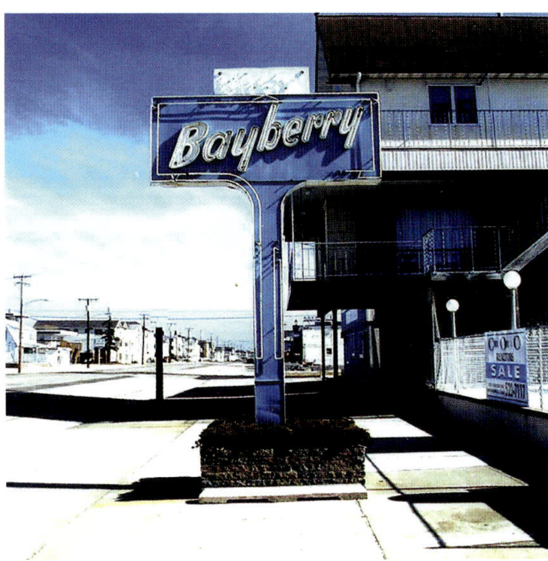

The Bayberry Motel stands today, modified for condominium ownership. This neon sign, added in the 1990s, was removed as part of the conversion. *Courtesy of David and Theresa Williams*

[75] Flame Inn (2206 Surf Avenue)

In 1953, when Jack and Ruth Gall built the Flame Inn, the Wildwoods' motel scene was in its infancy. Their choice of signage for the modest motel, a massive concrete cylinder covered in neon lettering and topped by an Allied-manufactured, rotating neon flame, was a massive leap forward in an architectural scene that had yet to move beyond small neon signage. "The original owner, Jack Gall, thought up the name," Bill Williams, a later manager of the motel, told Len Davidson. "He even built the 15-foot candle himself. The candle is masonry; you can go inside it to change the transformers. ABS Signs takes care of it. Everybody notices the candle!"

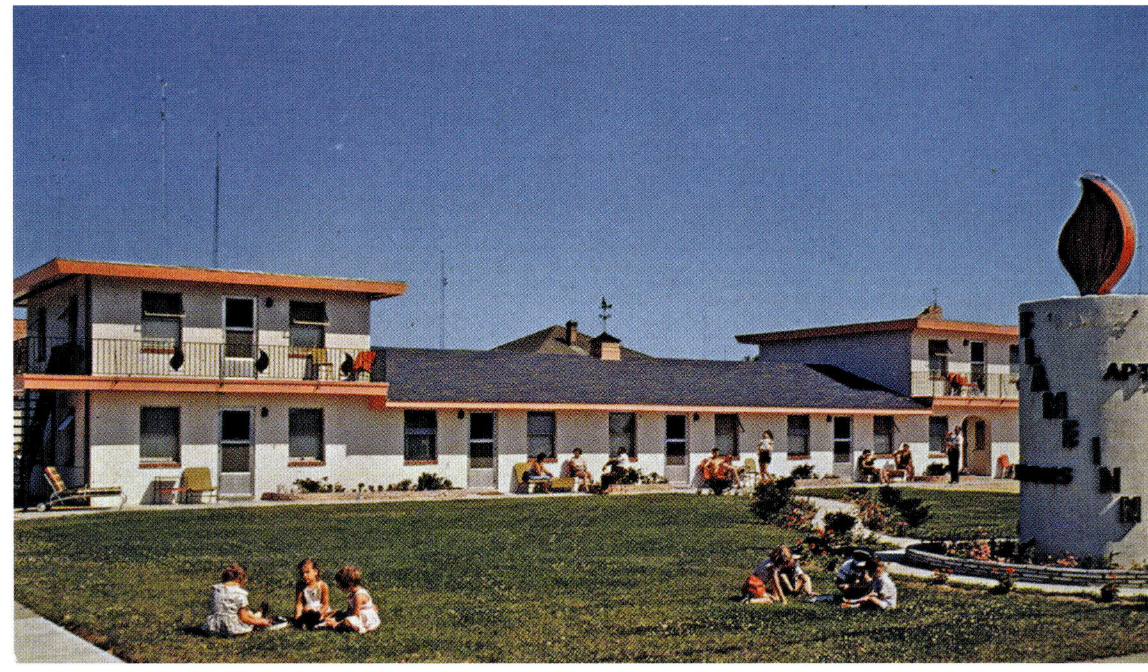

This early postcard of the Flame Inn shows the motel's original courtyard, later replaced with a pool, and its distinctive sign. *Author's collection*

The Gall family expanded the Flame Inn several times, but its original sign remained a Surf Avenue landmark until the motel's demolition in 2005. (An advertisement from the late 1980s uses reverse psychology to sell the Flame: "Do you notice anything different about this motel? Of course not! All motels look similar." This claim is odd, given the motel's arresting neon sign.) Fred Musso restored the neon flame, which now resides in a private collection. In the 1970s, the Gall family also bought the Bayberry Motel across the street, which Thomas Burns had built in 1957. The Bayberry survives today as condos without its neon sign (the motel's second).

[76] San's Motel (217 East 23rd Avenue)

Albert and Ina Neill built this small, L-shaped motel in 1953 as a trendy addition to their rooming house. An original grass courtyard later became a parking lot and pool, and seventies owners replaced the original small, pole-mounted sign with a huge rooftop neon sign reading "the SANS." Today, the building is covered with vinyl siding and a gable roof.

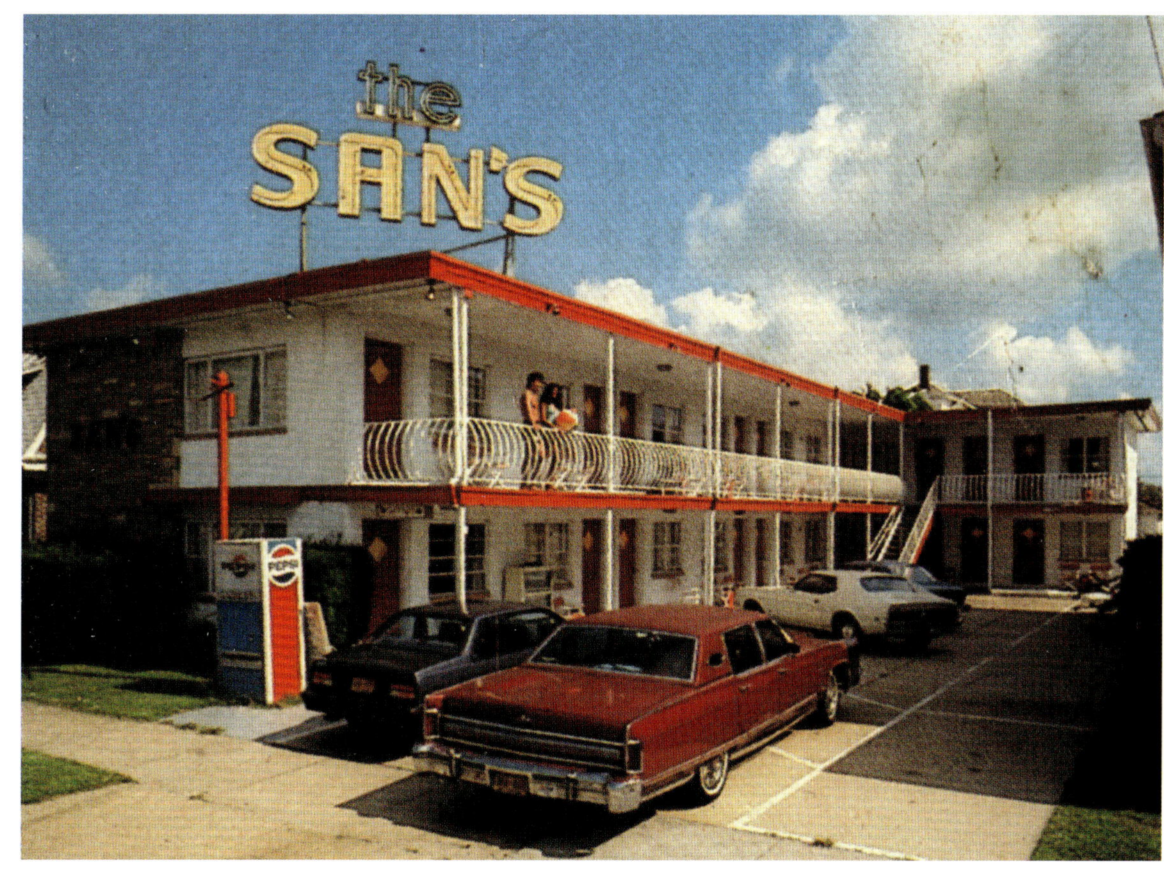

The San's Motel is shown in a 1980s Doug Hunsberger postcard. Notice the classic Pepsi vending machine. *Courtesy of Fedele Musso*

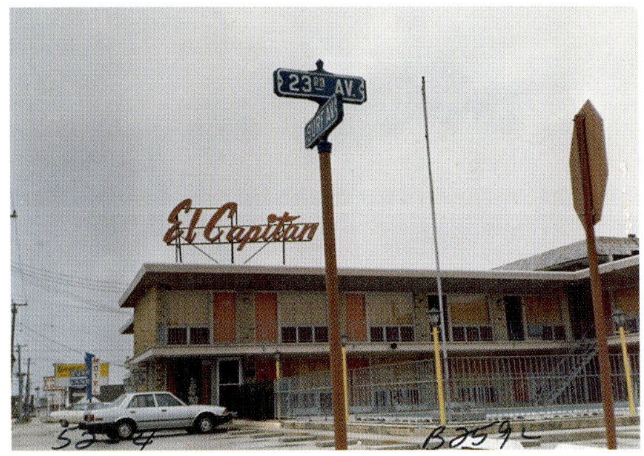

The El Capitan Motel and its neon sign in 1982.
Courtesy of Wildwood Historical Society

[77] El Capitan Motel (2300 Surf Avenue)
In 1966, Ernest and Mary Steubner sold their Surf Lane Motel, bought a lot next door, razed the house there, and built a new motel. On the roof they had Allied install an orange-script neon sign that had a hidden distinction: the capital "C" from the sign (now on display at Wildwood's Doo Wop Experience) is made from a single lengthy neon tube. "There are certain sign companies that seem to me to want to make gigantic tubes instead of making a tube in different sections," says Fred Musso. "The C from the El Capitan is the biggest [single] tube I've ever seen! That was the only sign that had neo-ruby glass, which they only made for one year." Musso salvaged the sign (an early 1990s replica of the original sign) when the motel was demolished in 2002 and replaced with condominiums.

[78] Lollipop Motel (2301 Atlantic Ave)
Often assumed to be an authentic product of 1950s culture, the Lollipop was built in 1970, according to municipal records, which situates it in a postmodern context. When built, it was an exemplary early seventies reinterpretation of classic fifties themes, with a candy-striped paint scheme and outward-bowing railings. Bizarrely, vintage postcards play down the motel's most notable aspect: its roadside sign, midway between iconic and passé in the early 1970s. Harry Lanza of Allied designed a striking roadside, pole-mounted sign that stood over 20 feet tall, with two smiling cherubic faces and a lollipop head made of swirling purple neon (later replaced with yellow plastic).

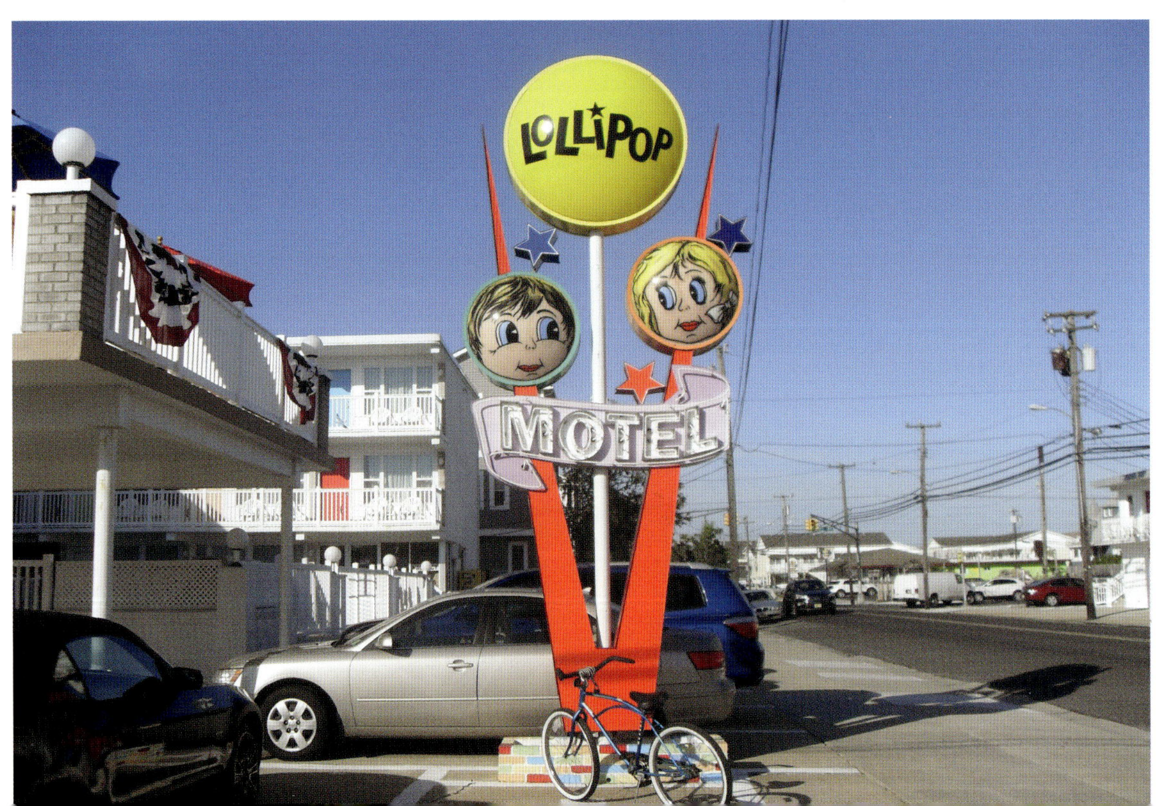

In 2012, ABS Signs refurbished the Lollipop Motel's amusing sign.

In 2004 the motel was converted to condominium ownership, but its owners have made few changes to the exterior of this North Wildwood landmark. In 2012, ABS Signs rehabilitated the neon sign, reconstructing every part except for the children's faces, which would have been too costly to replace. "It was all rotted apart," says ABS owner Randy Hentges. "We brought the whole sign in and traced it all on paper and made new [parts]. It has the kids' faces on it. Those were the only original things we kept. We cleaned them all up. They're all back-sprayed, and they're really cool. We made new Lollipop faces, but they didn't work." The Lollipop's sign remains one of the Wildwoods' most outstanding works of folk art.

[79] Cardinal Motel (2300 Atlantic Avenue)

The Cardinal Motel opened in 1967 on a corner formerly occupied by a boardinghouse. William and Jane Piotrowski and Adam and Stella Wisniewski, the motel's first owners, built an L-shaped, two-story motel with a central pool and perimeter parking. In the motel's early years, a pole-mounted neon sign featured a neon cardinal and an arrow outlined in chasing lights. A later expansion to the motel added an annex on the corner of 24th Avenue.

[80] Surf Lane Motel (349 East 24th Avenue)

Ernest Steubner built this small motel in 1954. Later owners expanded it, added a pool, and replaced the evocative bullnose, striped black neon sign, first with a larger neon version featuring a large arrow and then with a plastic one. Condominiums replaced the Surf Lane in 2005.

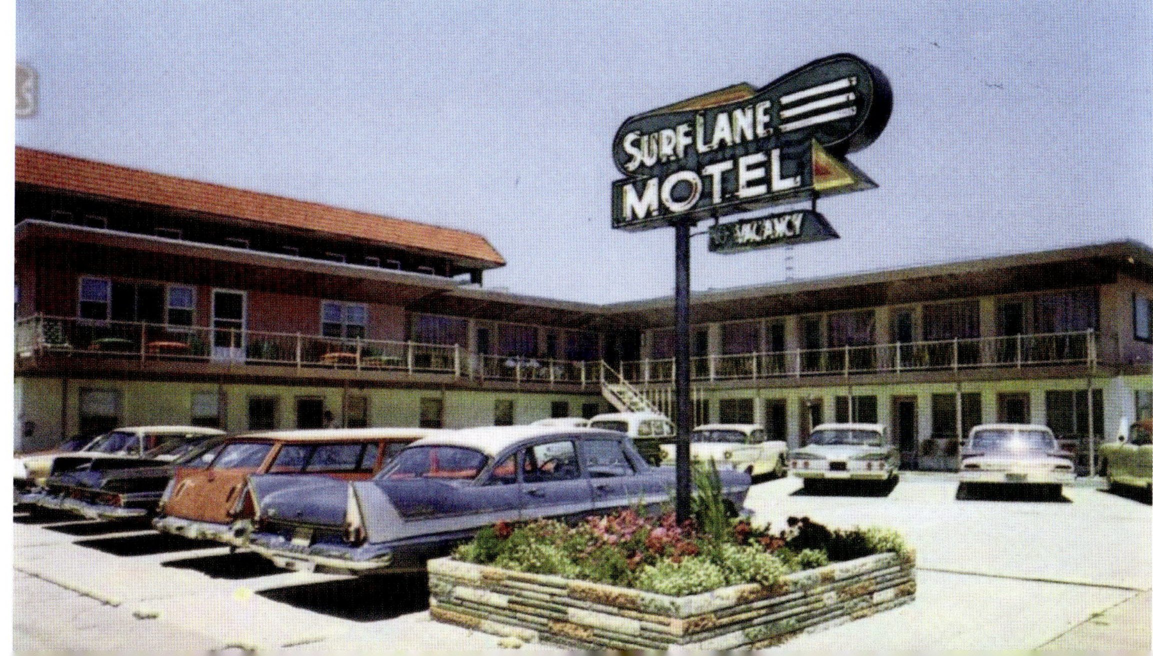

Sign companies and contractors often surrounded freestanding signs such as the Surf Lane Motel's with small gardens to prevent car collisions. *Author's collection*

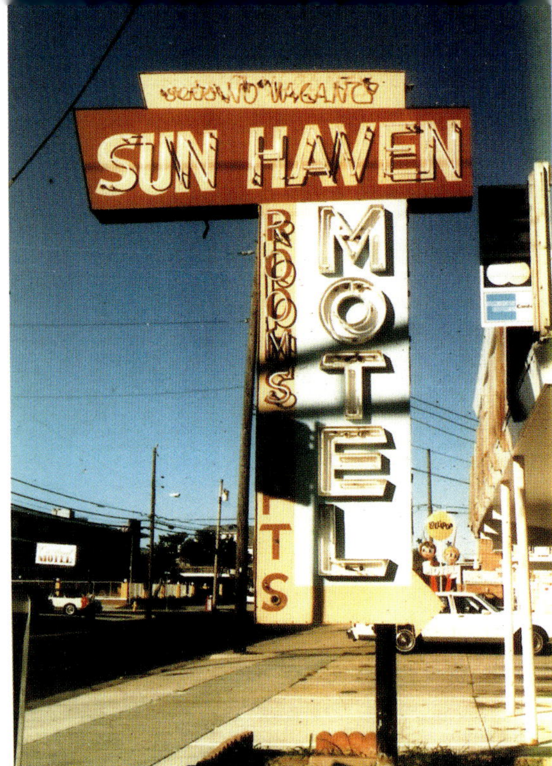

Even in its later years, the Sun Haven Motel's sign had barely changed from its 1960s heyday. *Courtesy of Fedele Musso*

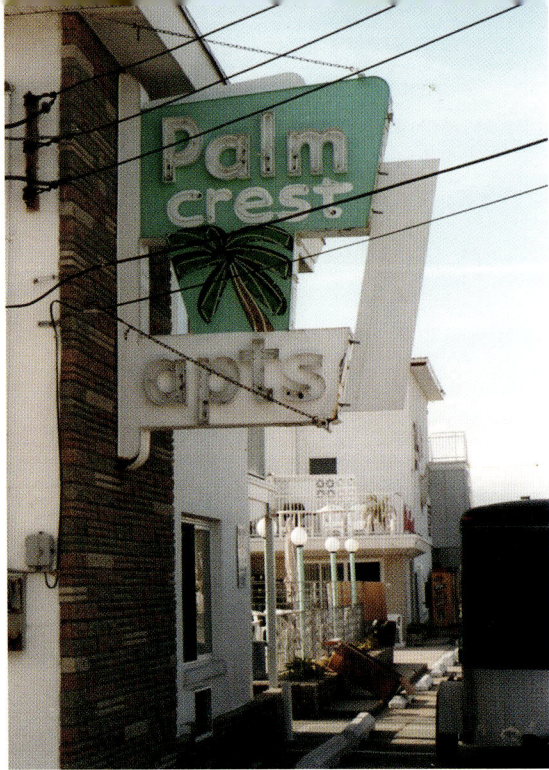

The small Palmcrest sported a colorful neon sign that alluded to the motel's past role as apartments. *Courtesy of Fedele Musso*

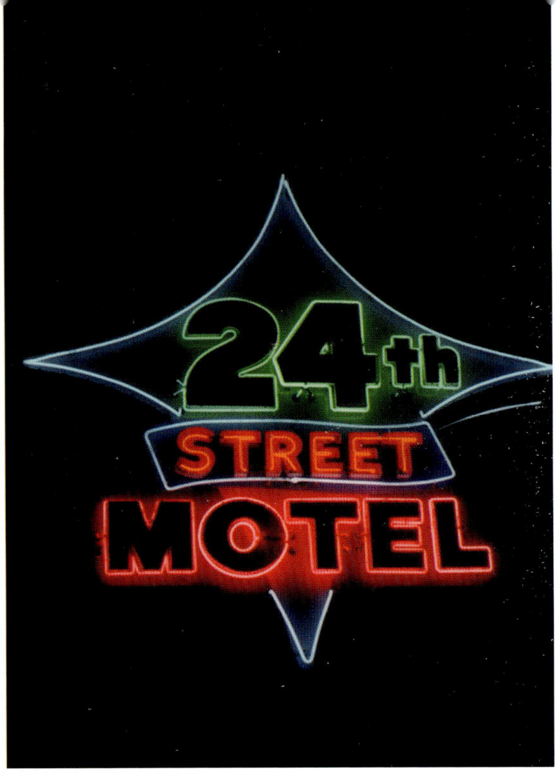

The 24th Street Motel sign's sheet metal background was painted red and yellow, but its neon tubes glowed blue and green at night. *Courtesy of Fedele Musso*

[81] Sun Haven Motel (301 East 24th Avenue)
Raymond Rakowski built the Sun Haven in the early 1950s and commissioned a freestanding neon sign from Allied, surrounded by a small garden. Despite later expansions, the motel never lost its original grass courtyard. "I'm not sure I ever saw the sign fully lighted," says a Wildwood traveler who stayed at the Sun Haven in the early 1990s. "The owner was a bit of a miser and would only light the 'Vacancy' tubing, complaining how expensive it was to light!" In 2003, developers leveled the Sun Haven.

[82] Palmcrest Motel (416–418 East 24th Avenue)
Curt and Ella Fisher tore down a bungalow and built this tiny midblock apartment building, which later operated solely as a motel, in 1957. With tan flagstone and brick trim and a modest green-painted, wall-hung neon sign, the Palmcrest radiated California cool. Unfortunately, it did not weather the Wildwoods' condominium craze.

[83] 24th Street Motel (2401 Surf Avenue)

The Baldassari family built the California-style 24th Street Motel in 1956 and commissioned a sign from Allied that spelled out the motel's amenities around an unfurled, neon-lined banner. In 1960, Bob Luglio, owner of the Sonata Motel a few blocks away, bought the motel. Ten years later, ABS replaced the sign with a new red-and-yellow, starburst-shaped one. At night, the neon tubing glowed an unexpected blue and green, a classic sign maker's sleight of hand that lent an element of surprise to several neon signs on the island, such as those of the Pyramid and Earle Motels.

In 1963, a brochure advertised that "the refreshing 24th Street Motel's rooms are large and breeze-swept." By 2006, development in the neighborhood surrounded the motel with traffic, and it was demolished that year and replaced with condominiums.

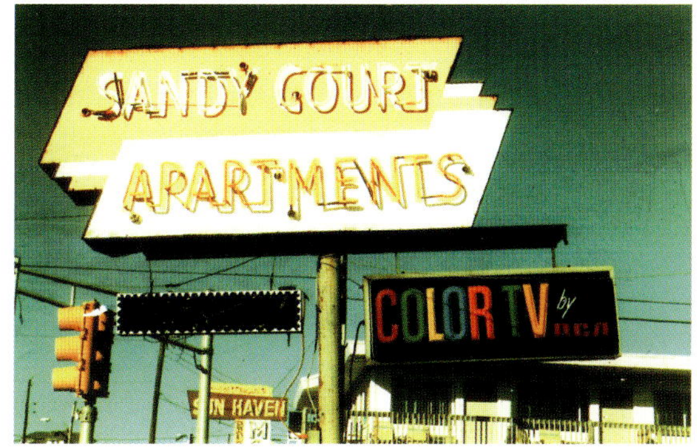

The Sandy Court Apartments' neon sign had a rare porcelain backing. *Courtesy of Fedele Musso*

[84] Sandy Court Apartments (2401 Atlantic Avenue)

During the 1950s, the Sandy Court evolved from a 1940s rooming house into a motel. The Sandy Court survived various additions over the years (including a rare porcelain and neon sign, installed around 1955 by then owner Samuel Sima) until being demolished in 2003. Fred Musso saved the sign, refurbished it, and sold it to an artist in Manhattan.

[85] Beach Rest Motel (425 East 25th Avenue)

In 1957, Salui Belfi and David Deola opened the L-shaped Beach Rest along 25th Avenue. A decade later, new owners built an addition that, oddly, faced away from the motel's courtyard and pool and

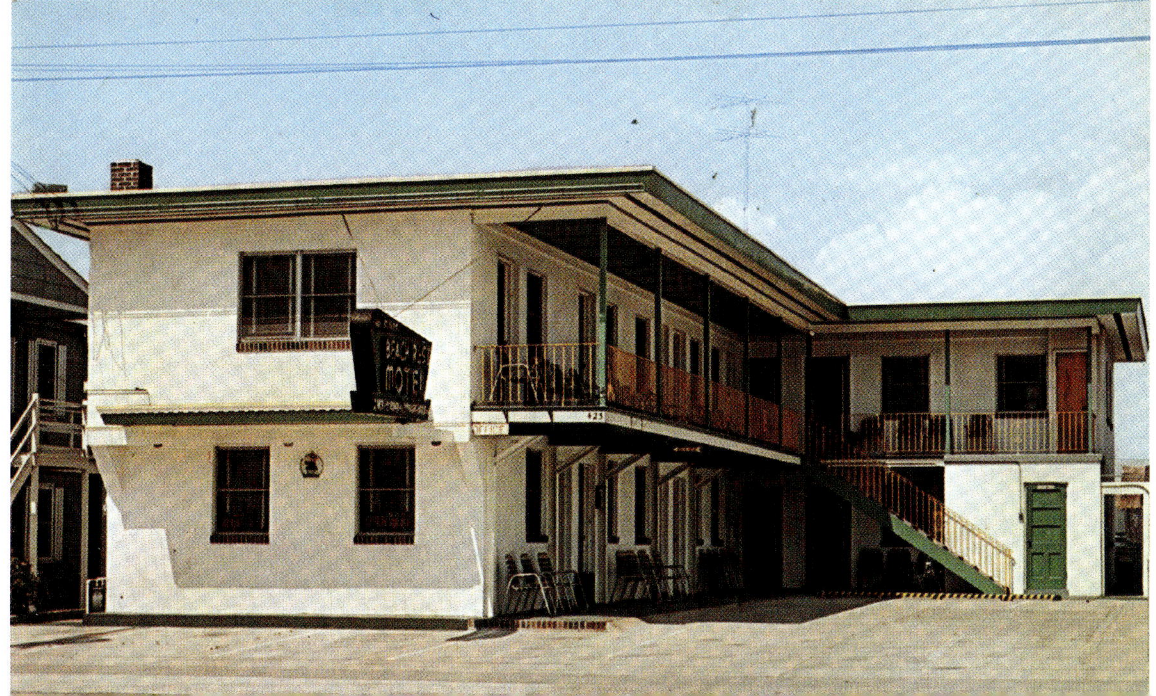

The Beach Rest Motel is seen in a postcard from the mid-1960s. Later expansions included a new pool, a new wing, and the replacement of this neon sign with a plastic one. *Author' s collection*

toward the boardwalk. The motel had trendy outward-bowing railings and a plastic wall-mounted sign with a yellow arrow-like accent but did not survive the Wildwoods' condominium boom.

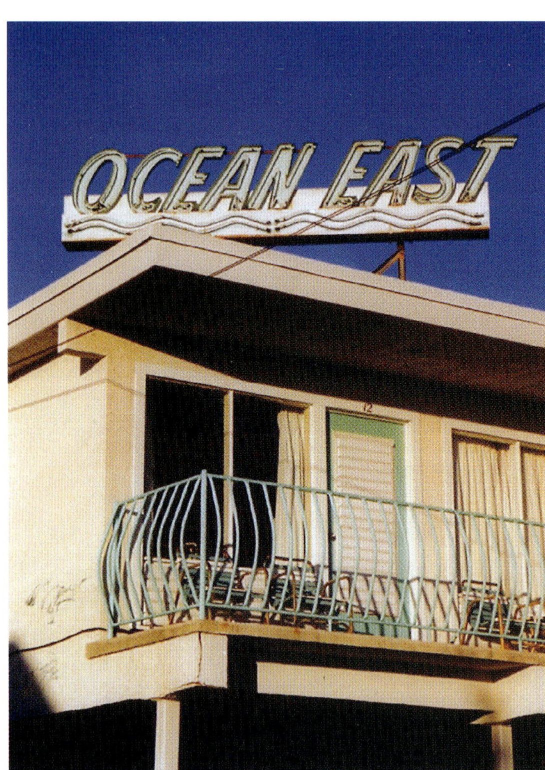

The Ocean East Motel united buildings of two eras under a classic 1960s neon sign. *Courtesy of Wildwood Historical Society*

[86] Ocean East Motel and Apartments (413 East 25th Avenue)

In 1968, Hildegard Lotz expanded her thirties-vintage rooming house, the Aletta Apartments, with a new motel wing. She renamed the motel the Ocean East and commissioned ABS to design a rooftop neon sign with green italic letters above crashing waves. It led a quiet existence until 2005, when developers tore it down and replaced it with condos. Fred Musso salvaged its neon sign, which now resides in Minot, North Dakota.

[87] Palms Motel (317 East 25th Avenue)

Opened by Rose and Bill Messerschmidt in 1957, this low-profile, L-shaped motel sported a trendy driftwood façade and a neon sign depicting a setting sun. Developers replaced it with houses in the first few years of the 2000s.

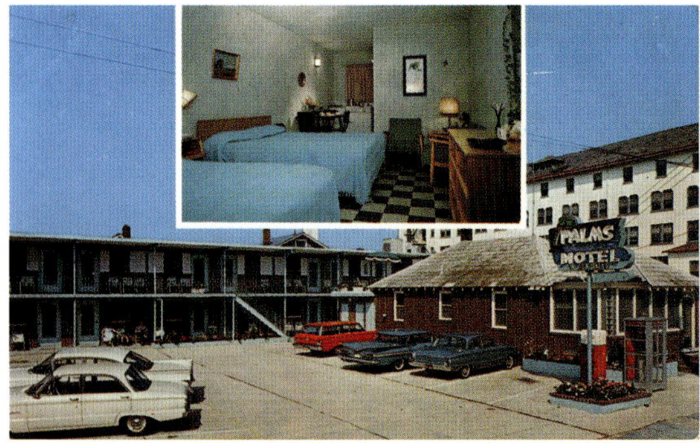

The Palms Motel, shown in an early postcard, was an addition to the bungalow at right. *Author' s collection*

[88] Central Motor Inn (2409 Central Avenue)

This brick-faced motel, located in a residential neighborhood three blocks from the ocean, once sported a prime seventies-vintage neon sign advertising motel and efficiency units, topped by a lantern that hinted at an American Colonial theme. The building survives today as condominiums.

[89] Surf Motel (402 East 25th Avenue)

The Surf Motel originated from the Sherry Motel and Efficiencies, two stories of motel units wrapped around a bungalow. An early nineties renovation demolished the bungalow, expanded the units to three stories, and renamed the motel the Surf. A new neon sign (featuring a blue animated crashing wave) was the only concession to a vintage aesthetic, unlike later Doo Wop renovations such as Richard Stokes's Starlux, which exuded retro modernism in every detail. Still, the Wildwoods of the 1990s shunned the past, and for a motel owner to install a new neon sign in that decade pointed the way toward Neo Doo Wop. In 2020, a new owner bought the motel and removed the neon sign as part of a renovation of the motel for condominium purposes.

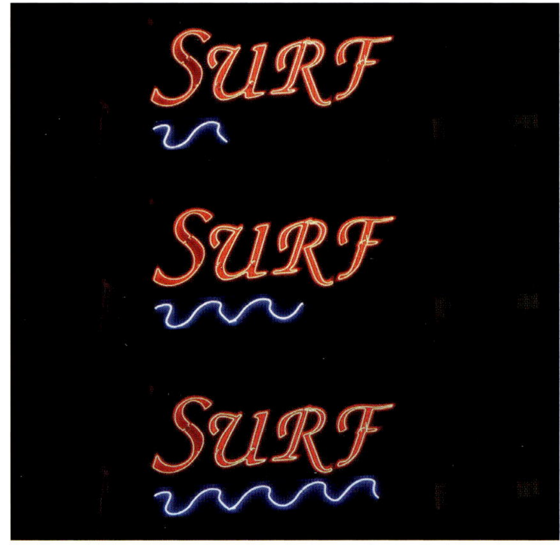

This sequence shows the 1990s-vintage animated sign of the Surf Motel.

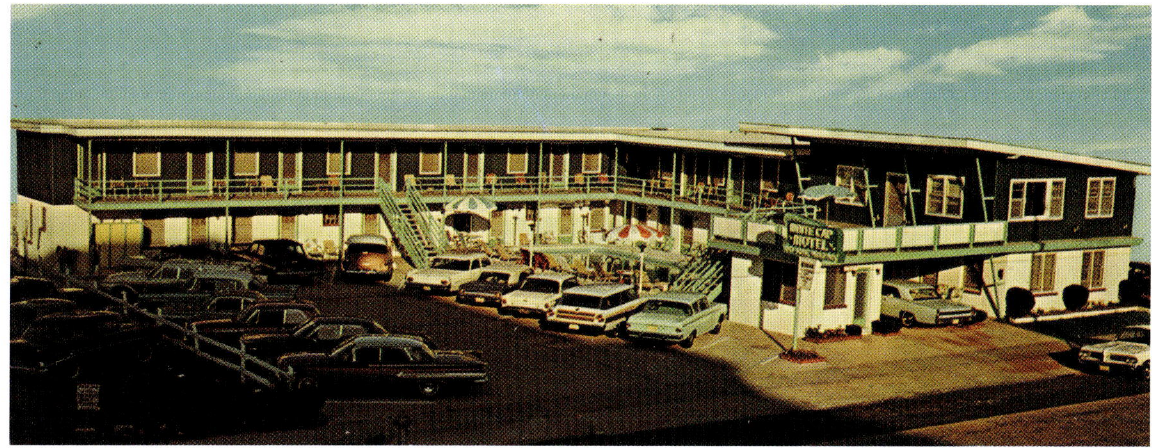

This 1960s postcard photo of the White Cap Motel shows the motel's original neon sign, its distinctive cantilevered sundeck roof, and a shadow creeping over the parking lot cast by the Manor Hotel, which was destroyed by fire in 1968. *Author's collection*

[90] White Caps Motel (310 East 25th Avenue)
Fritz and Clara Krause built the White Cap, its original name, in 1954. Aside from a cantilevered roof over a sundeck, most of its original midcentury detail has been modified, but more-recent owners have installed a neon-and-plastic sign with the unique phrasing "Sorry, no vacancy." According to Fred Musso, they plan to keep the neon lit.

[91] Sandy Shores Resort (2511 Atlantic Avenue)
Elmer and Willard Marshall built the Sandy Shores Motel in the early 1950s and borrowed elements from Miami's streamlined hotels of the 1930s, including flagstone accents, deep cornices for each balcony, and a tower in the center of the motel's façade adorned with iron letters. Later owners expanded the motel, and it stands today in this modified state.

[92] Island Breeze Motel (411 East 26th Avenue)
The Island Breeze Motel began its life as a 1920s-vintage rooming house called the Avalon Apartments, an unexceptional three-story hostel to which Leonard Mele added a motel wing in 1966. Mele also added a flashy new neon sign, a pool, and a giant "A" on the side of his new motel that doubled as two pillars. The Avalon Motel fell on hard times when, in 2013, its owner demolished the rooming house, leaving only the motel wing, then sold it to a new owner, who renamed the motel the Island Breeze. Fred Musso recalls that a neon sign that had hung from the porch of the rooming house disappeared when the building was demolished. "I knew the guy who bought it, and I had talked to him about redoing the pole sign [on the corner] to the new name. He told me, 'Go to this room over here—open the door—I want you to see something in there.' I went up there and the Avalon sign was in the room!" Musso expertly modified the original pole sign to read "Island Breeze," and the rooming house sign now graces a collection in Austin, Texas.

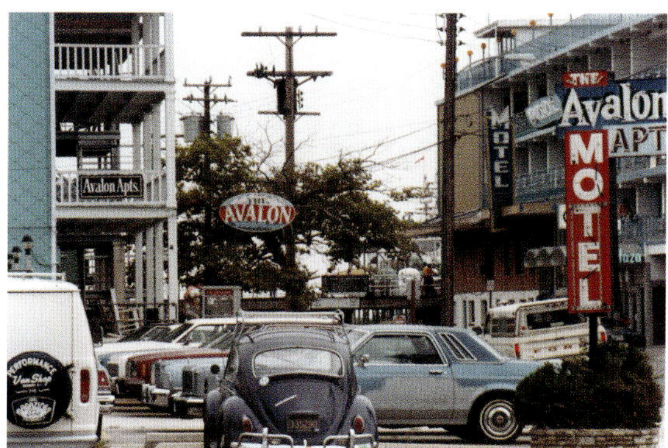

Note the assortment of vintage cars and signage in this 1987 photo of the Avalon, now known as the Island Breeze. The rooming house on the left was torn down in 2013. *Courtesy of Wildwood Historical Society*

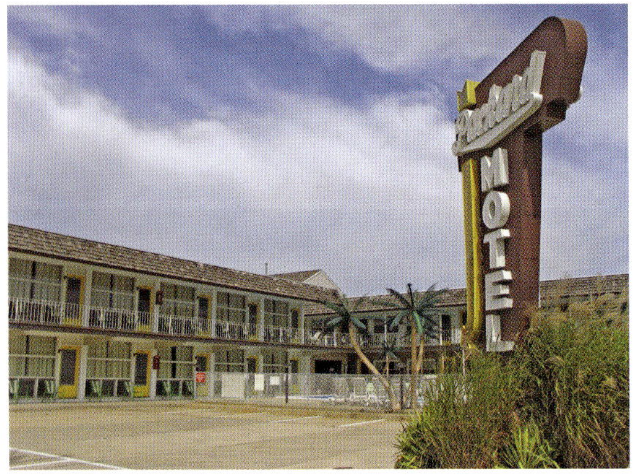

The Packard Motel once marked the southern end of the famous "Surf Avenue strip." *Courtesy of Dorothy Kulisek collection*

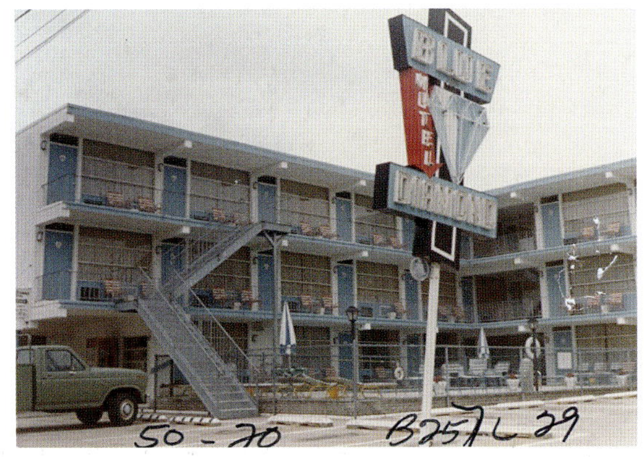

This 1982 view of the Blue Diamond Motel shows its stunning neon sign. Today the motel operates as the Bird of Paradise. *Courtesy of Wildwood Historical Society*

[93] Packard Motel (337 East 26th Avenue)

Located at the southern end of the onetime Surf Avenue strip, the Packard was once a North Wildwood landmark. Frank and Mary Greico built a simple bar-shaped motel in 1956, with a prominent garage door that might indicate that the motel was an expansion of a bungalow. Around 1960, the Greicos expanded their motel with an additional wing (making the motel an L shape) and a pool. Plastic palm trees, then a novelty in the Wildwoods, dotted the pool area (one leaning at a precarious 45-degree angle), a mansard roof approximated tiki architecture, and a freestanding neon sign, painted in red, white, and green candy stripes, attracted customers. (A rotosphere that initially sat atop the neon sign survived the harsh salt air only for a decade or so.)

Both the motel and sign underwent several changes in paint color throughout the years, but in 2005 developers tore down both. Fred Musso saved a small "office" neon sign, and a sign collector in (fittingly) Detroit bought it.

[94] Bird of Paradise Motel (333 East 26th Avenue)

In 1965, Joe Rossi tore down his outdated Victorian-era edifice, the Hotel Savoy, and built the three-story Blue Diamond Motel in its place. ABS made Rossi a sign with a glistening blue neon diamond, which stood in the motel's parking lot. In the 1980s, a new owner renamed the motel the Bird of Paradise and commissioned from ABS a new pole-mounted sign with Bauhaus lettering. The motel still stands, a little worse for wear.

[95] Lau-Ray Motel (221 East 26th Avenue)

Frederick Schillinger built this small, midblock motel in 1948 as the Lau-Ray Court. It originally had one story but was expanded in 1956 to two; a few years later, the neon sign was modified to reflect a name change to Lau-Ray Motel. Its small neon sign, originally black, saw a number of paint colors over the years, most recently pink, to capitalize on Doo Wop enthusiasm. Around 2005 the motel was demolished; its lot remains empty.

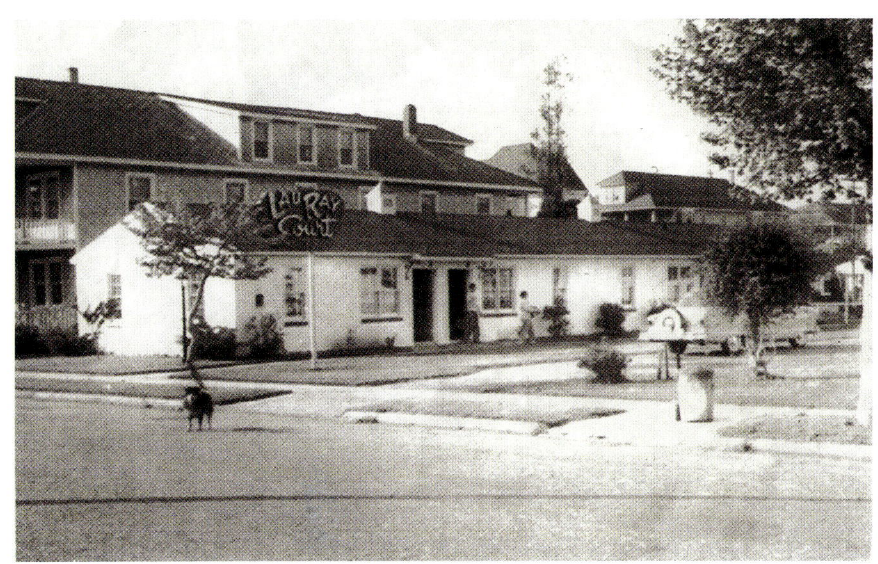

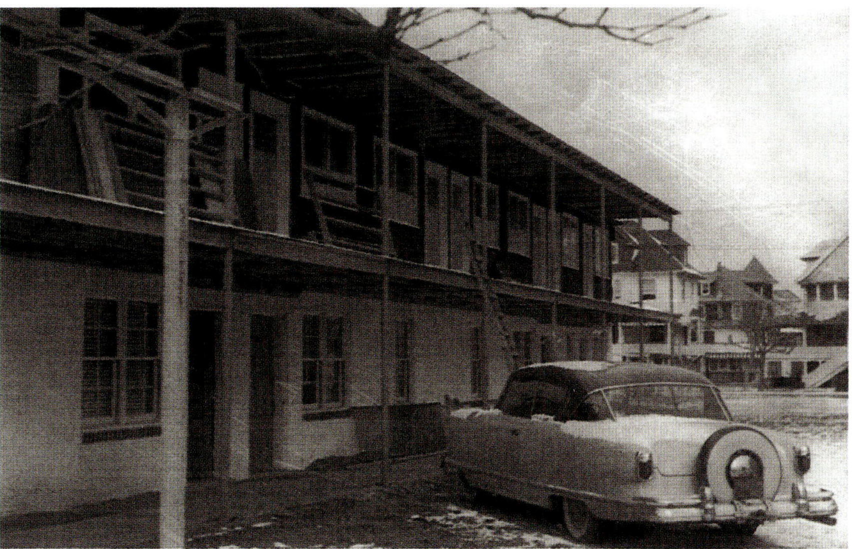

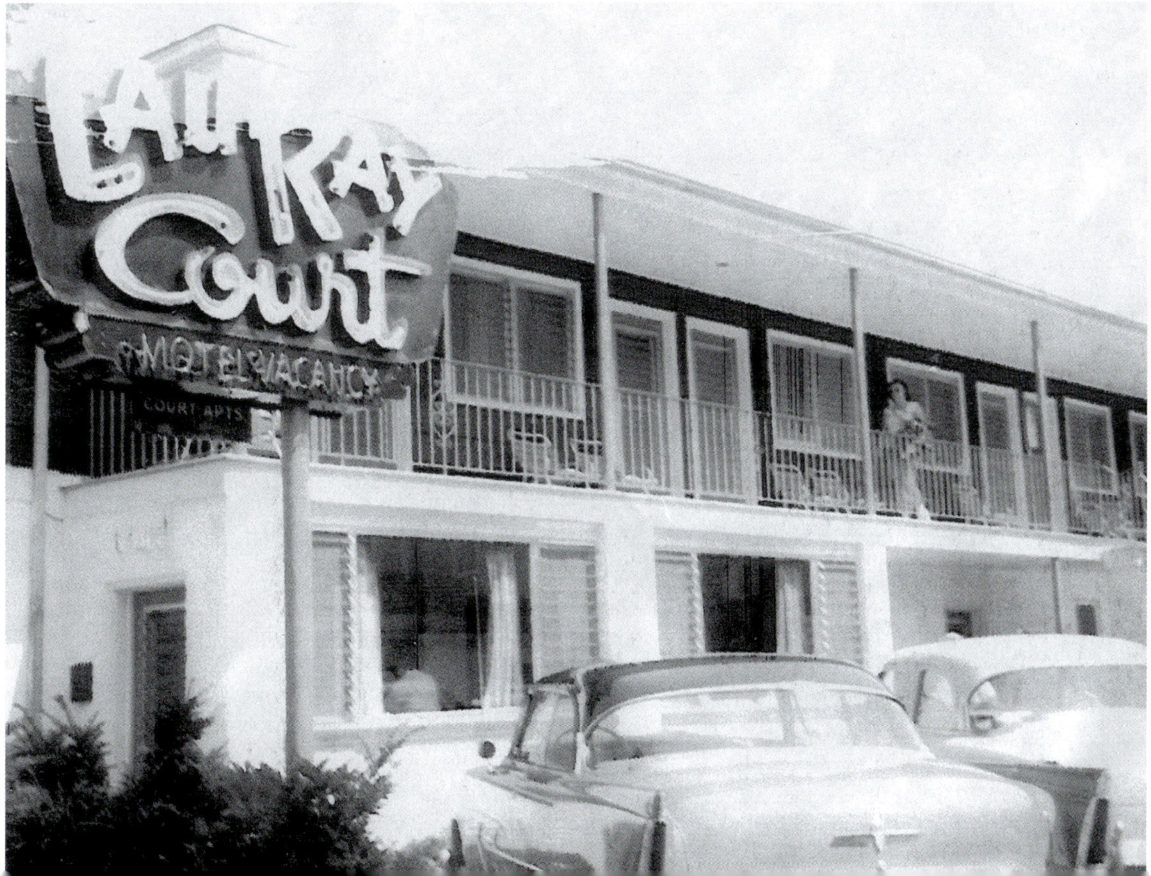

Three stages in the construction of the Lau-Ray Court (later Motel), a hidden gem on 26th Avenue. *Top*: The motel as built in 1948, with one story and a grassy courtyard. *Middle*: In 1956, the motel's neon sign has been removed from its pole (*left*) while a second story is constructed. *Bottom*: The completed court in the late 1950s. Aside from the modification of the neon sign to read "Motel," the Lau-Ray remained in this form until its demolition. *Courtesy of Al Alven*

96
101
Ocean Avenue
26th Avenue
Juniper Avenue
Poplar Avenue
Magnolia Avenue
Glenwood Avenue
Maple Avenue
Pine Avenue
Wildwood Avenue
Oak Avenue
Schellenger Avenue
Lincoln Avenue
Garfield Avenue
Spicer Avenue
Spencer Avenue
97
98
100
105
106
107
102
103
109
110
112
113
115
117
118
99
104
108
111
114
116
119
119
120

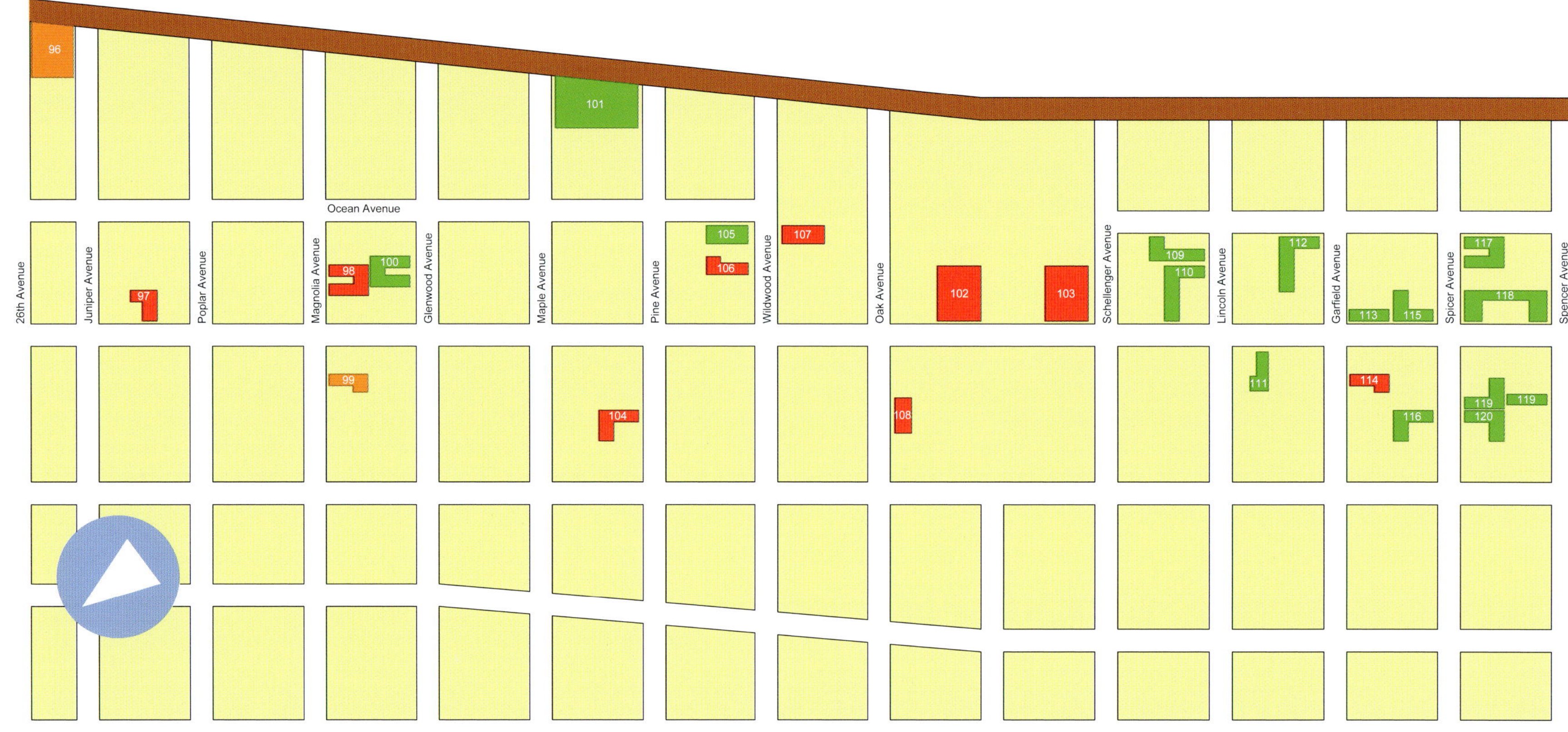

Wildwood

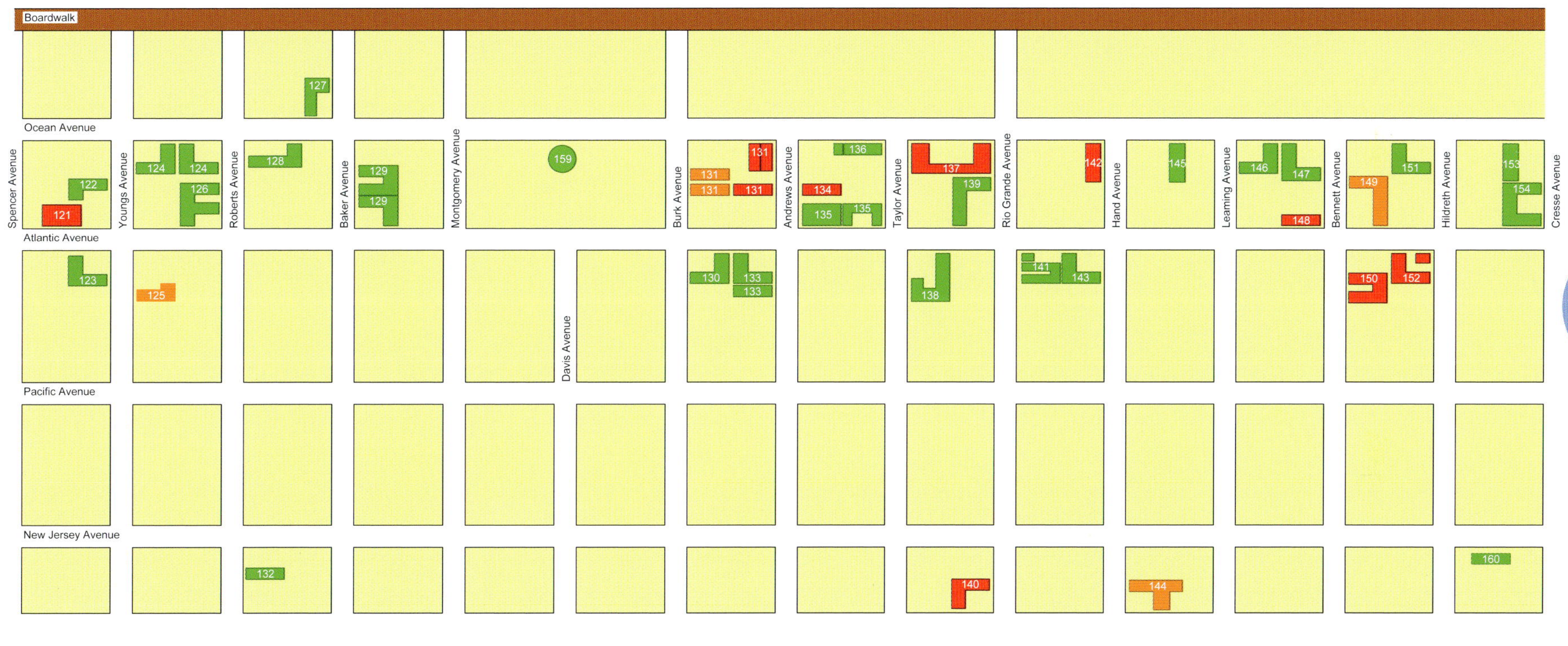

Buildings that have been demolished

Buildings that have been modified

Buildings that are standing and still used for their original purpose

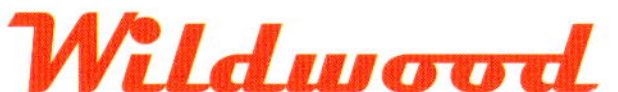

BUILDING KEY (SEE MAP ON PREVIOUS SPREAD)

Some of the earliest development on the island took place in what is now the city of Wildwood. Today, the city is the island's rowdy amusement hub. From motels to restaurants to piers to nightclubs, many businesses in Wildwood proper were designed with eye-catching midcentury elements. Because the condominium craze did not overtake Wildwood as extensively as it did North Wildwood and Wildwood Crest, Wildwood retains a higher percentage of its original midcentury architecture than do its neighbors.

[96] Shore Plaza Beach Resort (2600 Boardwalk)

Will Morey built the Shore Plaza Motel for the 1962 season (while also building the Flagship Beach Motel in the Crest). The Shore Plaza fronted the boardwalk; in fact, Morey built the motel around an existing boardwalk store, today the site of perennial boardwalk favorite Sam's Pizza.

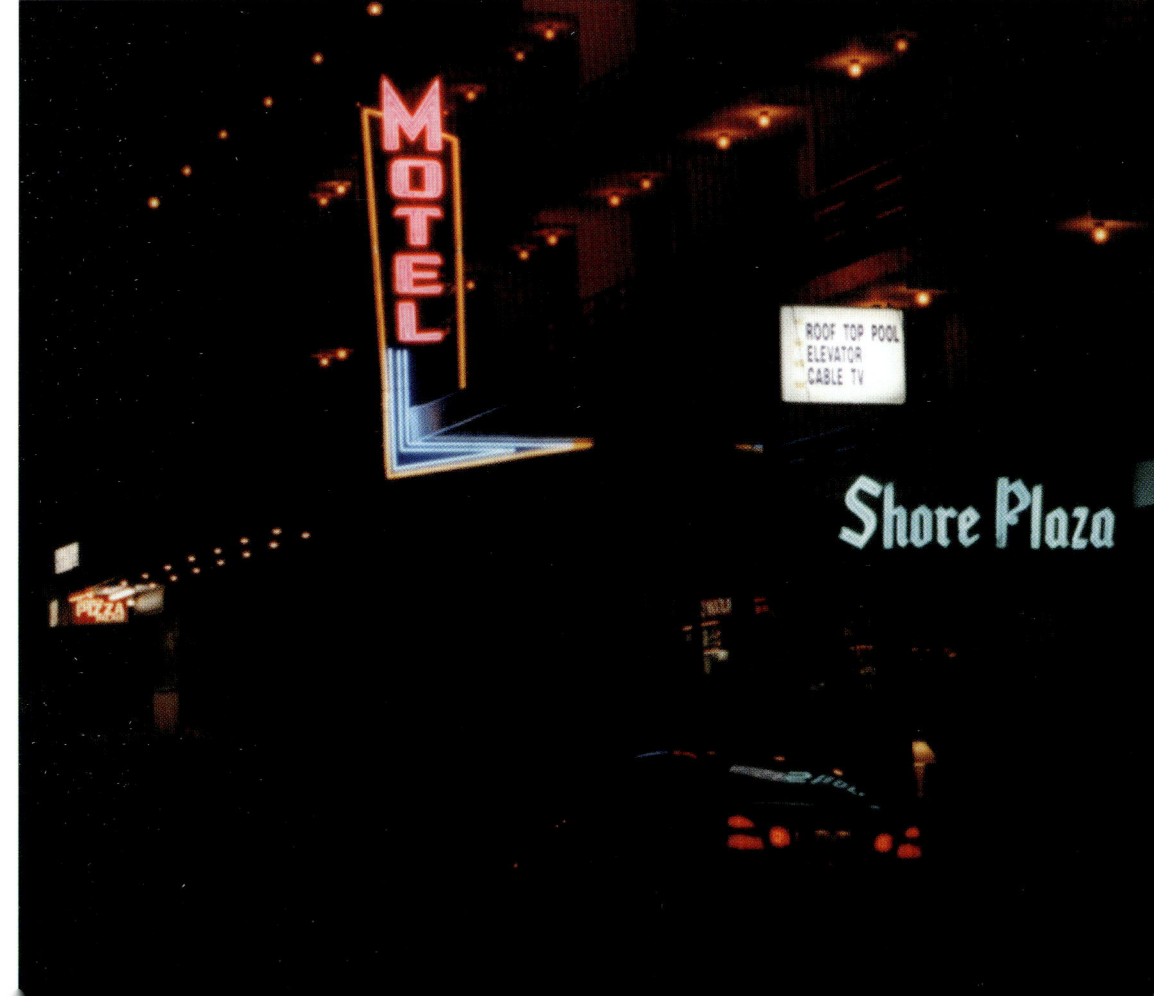

The Shore Plaza, one of the few motels on the island to front the boardwalk, had an array of neon signage above its lobby entrance. *Courtesy of Fedele Musso*

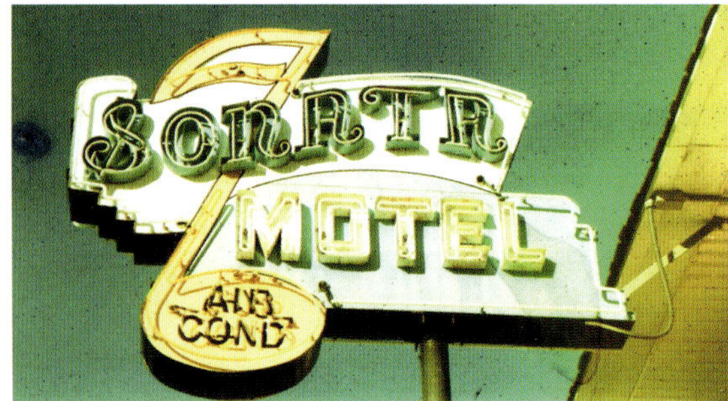

In addition to the musical-note background of this sign, the "S" in "Sonata" resembles a treble clef. *Courtesy of Fedele Musso*

The original Shore Plaza had two stories, only its second floor rising above the boardwalk storefront. It had two wall-hung neon signs with flashing arrows and railings with a diamond pattern. In 1965, Will Morey added a third story, including a novel rooftop pool and sundeck. The motel survived with many original features (as well as some later additions, such as a four-stroke Old English marquee neon sign above the lobby entrance along 26th Avenue) for several decades until being damaged by fire on December 9, 2005. After a firefighting effort that lasted through the night, the fire was extinguished, though not before critically damaging the motel and pizza shop.

Sam's Pizza's owners rebuilt for the 2006 season, but the Spera and Zuccarello families, who owned the motel, took their time, finally reopening in 2012. While less modernist than the original, the new Shore Plaza did feature a wall-hung neon sign designed by ABS, a nod to its former incarnation. The Zuccarello family, who had bought the motel in 1977, jumped at the opportunity to install modern HVAC equipment. "Each room now controls its own heat and air," Rosemary Zuccarello said in a 2012 *Atlantic City Press* piece. "We used to do it by vote. Some people were too cold and some too hot, so we had to ask them, 'Do you want air or heat?'"

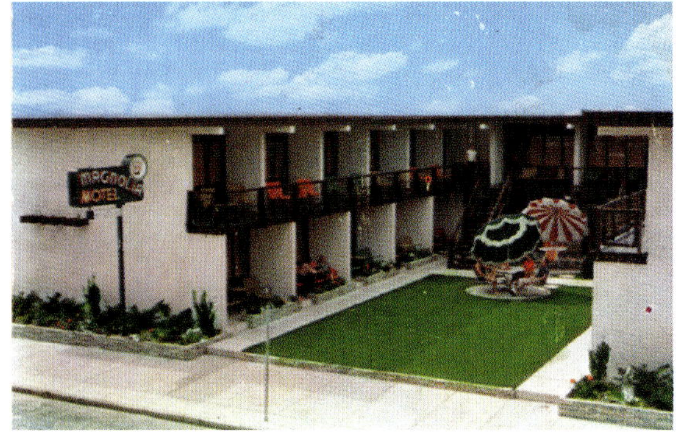

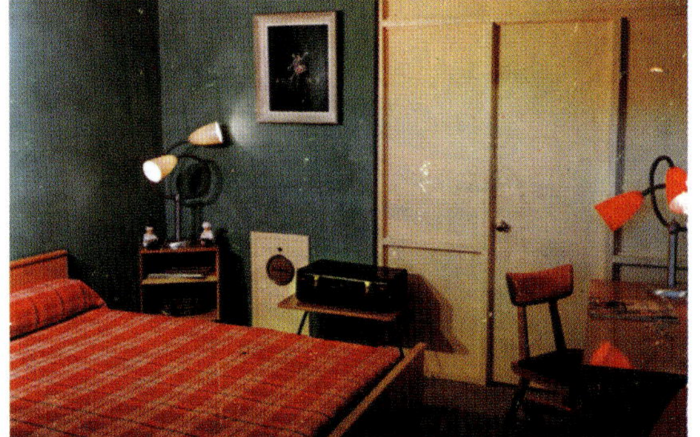

This 1950s postcard of the Magnolia Motel shows its modern rooms and grass courtyard. *Courtesy of Fedele Musso*

[97] Sonata Motel (2703 Atlantic Avenue)
Bob Luglio built the Sonata Motel for the 1954 season and decorated it in bright-red and white candy stripes. A small but dynamic freestanding neon sign underlined the motel's musical theme with the outline of a music note. Despite several expansions over the years, the motel vanished in the first few years of the 2000s.

[98] Deco Resort Motel (320 East Magnolia Avenue)
Before building the 24th Street and Shalimar Motels, the Baldassari family opened this unimposing two-story court, originally named the Magnolia Motel, in 1954. The Magnolia had a small neon sign and a grass courtyard that was never replaced with a pool, unlike many motel courtyards in the area. In the 1980s, the motel was covered in brightly colored stucco and rebranded as the Deco Resort, a nod to the Wildwoods' past. It was razed in the first few years of the 2000s.

[99] Luther Inn Retreat Center (228 East Magnolia Avenue)
The Lilly Motel, which opened in 1954, was among the earliest motels in Wildwood. The modest two-story structure looked out over a small parking lot and beckoned to visitors with a small green neon sign (later augmented with a yellow arrow and reinstalled backward on its pole). In the 1980s, it was converted into the Luther Inn, a religious retreat center, with little modification other than the removal of the sign. It still stands, very well preserved.

[100] Sunflower Motel (313 East Glenwood Avenue)
The Sunflower began as a 1920s rooming house called the York Apartments. In the 1970s, it gained a motel addition and a neon sign featuring an animated sunflower. Both wings of the motel operate today, as does the neon sign, a hidden gem for neon aficionados.

[101] Hunt's Strand Theater (3100 Boardwalk)

[102] Hunt's Casino Theater (Cedar and Atlantic Avenues)

[103] Hunt's Shore Theater (3511 Atlantic Avenue)
Among William C. Hunt's legendary entrepreneurial adventures in the Wildwoods were six theaters; these three were the most architecturally notable.

Hunt tore down several rooming houses at the corner of Schellenger and Atlantic Avenues and built the Shore Theater in 1939. With porthole doors, a stainless-steel-lined ticket booth, and a towering neon marquee, the Shore represented Hunt's intent to bring the industry standard in theaters to the Wildwoods. Just as work on the Shore was finishing, another of Hunt's properties, the Casino Theater, a block away at Atlantic and Cedar Avenues, burned down. Undeterred, Hunt

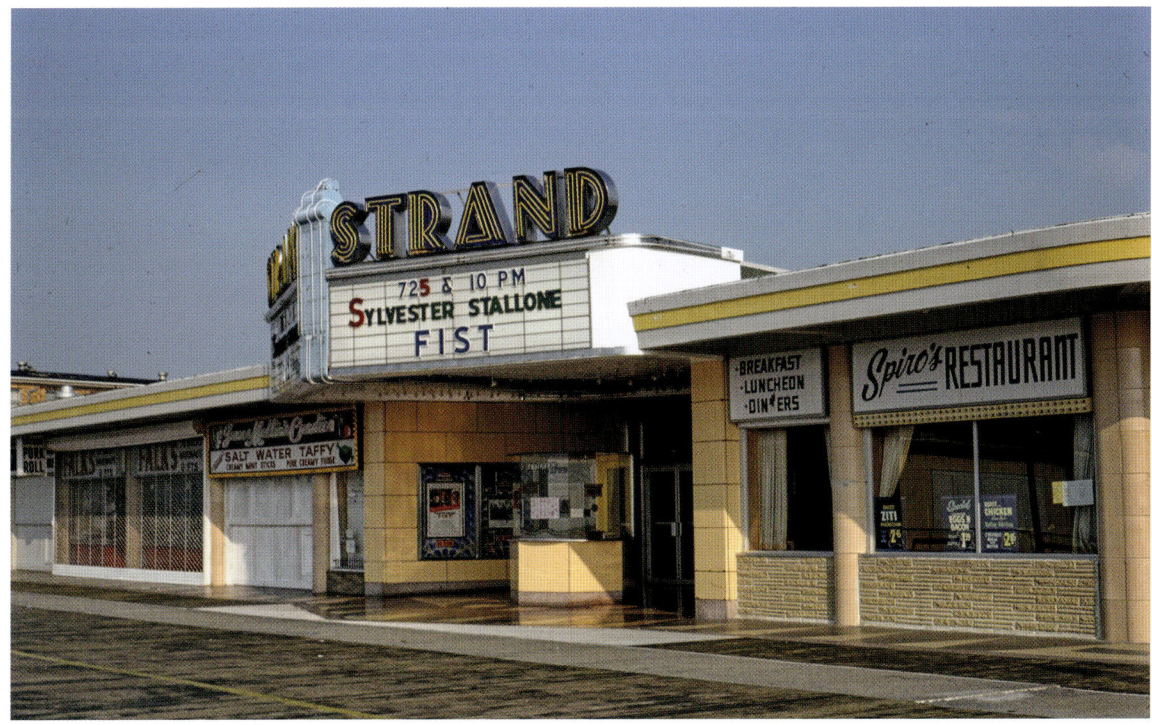

When John Margolies took this photo of the Strand Theater in 1978, it still had its breathtaking original terrazzo and porcelain tile lobby. *John Margolies photo*

contracted Joseph Scully, a noted theater architect, who devised an exceptional streamline moderne design for a new Casino Theater, with a glowing porcelain tile exterior and a stainless-steel marquee. "The Shore was Hunt's flagship theater," says Hunt's Theaters aficionado Scott Hand. "The Casino was part of Casino Pier, which was predominantly owned by [amusement pier mogul Gil] Ramagosa. So they were more like partners with Ramagosa on the Casino. [Hunt] built the Shore so he could have the Hunt's offices there." Between the Casino, Shore, and Blaker (a former vaudeville theater at Cedar Avenue), Hunt controlled two solid blocks of theaters.

Meanwhile, another Hunt theater, the Strand, on the boardwalk at Maple Avenue, burned down in 1944. Three years later, Hunt opened a flashy new, streamlined Strand with a punchy neon marquee and a roofline that encompassed a whole block of boardwalk shops. "W. C. Hunt and Walt Disney himself were really close," says Hand. "At the end of the summer of 1947, Walt Disney visited the Strand." Disney later tapped the Strand to hold the world premiere of *At What Price Glory* in 1952, and with good reason: "They had a big stage in front of the screen at the Strand," Hand says. "And the screen at the Strand Theater was 145 feet wide and over 50 feet tall. It had the big maroon curtains. When the movie would open, the curtains would part. Everything was red—the ceiling was painted red and they had gold wallpaper on the walls."

After these initial glories, Hunt's empire began a long decline. He died in 1970, and in 1985 his only living son sold out to local theater mogul Al Frank. Eager to turn a profit, Frank hastily divided all of Hunt's theaters into multiplexes (Hand recalls that at the Ocean Theater at Juniper Avenue, "the walls didn't match—the one wall was all deco with seashells, and the other was green board"). As for the Strand, "They tore the entrance out to put a T-shirt shop there!"

In 1979, amusement pier owner Gil Ramagosa had painted the Casino Theater an incongruous yellow and converted it into an arcade, and beginning in 1987 it housed a laser game called Photon. The Casino building was torn down in 1999, and the Shore and Blaker Theaters came down in late 2005 after sitting closed for eight years. The last remaining Hunt Theater, the Strand, hangs on to its neon marquee, but parts of its terrazzo entryway have been paved over, and parts of its roofline have been hidden by signage. The Strand has not operated as a theater since 2010, but perhaps a boardwalk entrepreneur can save it from oblivion.

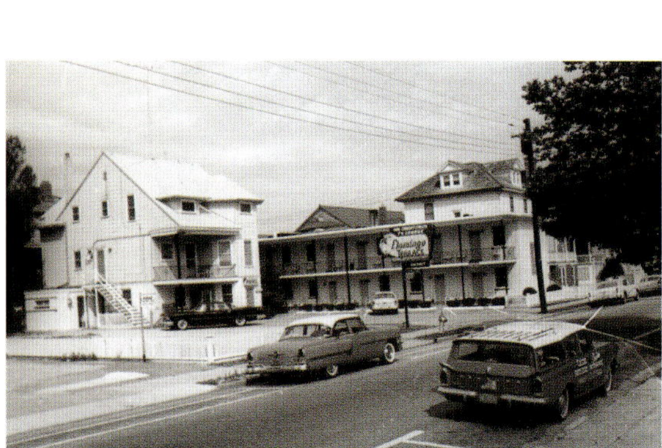

The Flamingo Motel initially combined a vintage rooming house (*left*) with a modern wing (*right*). Later the rooming house was torn down to make room for more motel units. *Courtesy of Wildwood Historical Society*

[104] Flamingo Terrace Motel (229 East Pine Avenue)

Richard Samuel built this small, two-story motel on quiet Pine Avenue in 1954, then boosted its profile by adding a pole-mounted neon sign listing the motel's amenities and depicting a pink flamingo. Despite the 1960s demolition of a neighboring rooming house and its replacement with another motel wing, the midblock Flamingo Terrace maintained a low profile. In the 1990s, the neon sign was replaced with a tame plastic version, and the whole motel was demolished and replaced with new houses in 2004.

[105] Laura's Fudge (357 East Wildwood Avenue)

In 1926, Kate Laura opened a boardwalk game and made homemade fudge to give away as prizes, and the fudge quickly became popular on its own. Two years later, when the concession stand burned

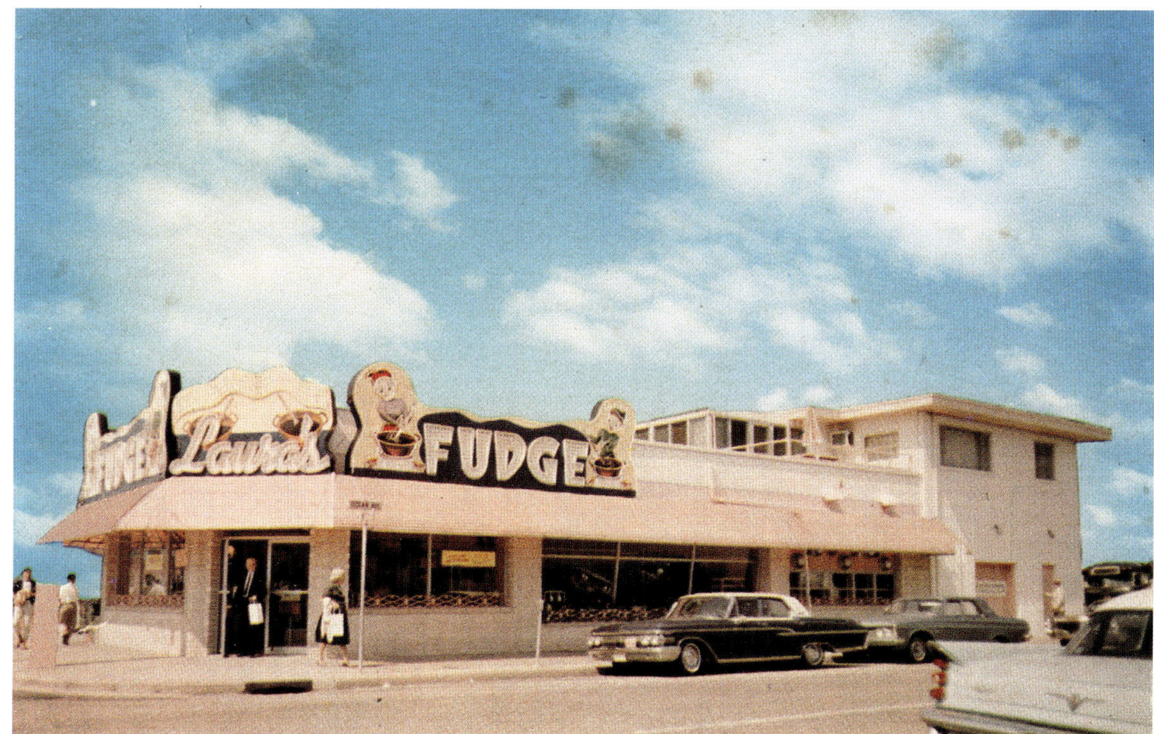

Laura's Fudge in its 1960s heyday. *Author's collection*

down, Kate and her husband, Joe, decided to sell the fudge in a new storefront in the Hotel Dayton. Laura's Fudge occupied several spaces around town for the next several decades.

Around 1960, Jack and Laura Gunn bought the business and moved it to a newly constructed building at the corner of Wildwood and Ocean Avenues, a stone's throw from the boardwalk (and, not coincidentally, from Laura's primary competitors, Douglass Fudge, a boardwalk fixture since 1919). The Gunns built a quintessential "decorated shed"—a term coined by Robert Venturi and Denise Scott Brown to describe a simple rectangular building decorated with signage. They covered the new Laura's Fudge with a façade of pink flagcrete, candy-striped red-and-white awnings, and several gigantic neon signs manufactured by Ace, which employed a young Bob Hentges at the time. Laura's neon signs were a tour de force, with animated images of elves stirring giant pots of fudge and the word "fudge" studded in grid lights. In the 1970s, the Gunns added wooden billboards to this tableau, and in the 1980s these were replaced with additional neon. "To me, the epitome of a great Wildwood sign would be Laura's Fudge," says Philadelphia neon designer Len Davidson.

After a painstaking 1998 renovation by ABS Signs, various owners have modified the original neon signs. "It was restored in kind of a poor way," says Davidson. "It doesn't work that well. From the look of it, I think it was originally porcelain, and I think they had somebody make painted panels." In recent years, much of the sign's neon tubing has been replaced with LED rope lights. The

The Sea Cove Motel is shown in an early 1950s postcard. Note the courtyard enclosed by an iron fence, an artifact of postwar decorum that was replaced with a pool a decade later. *Author's collection*

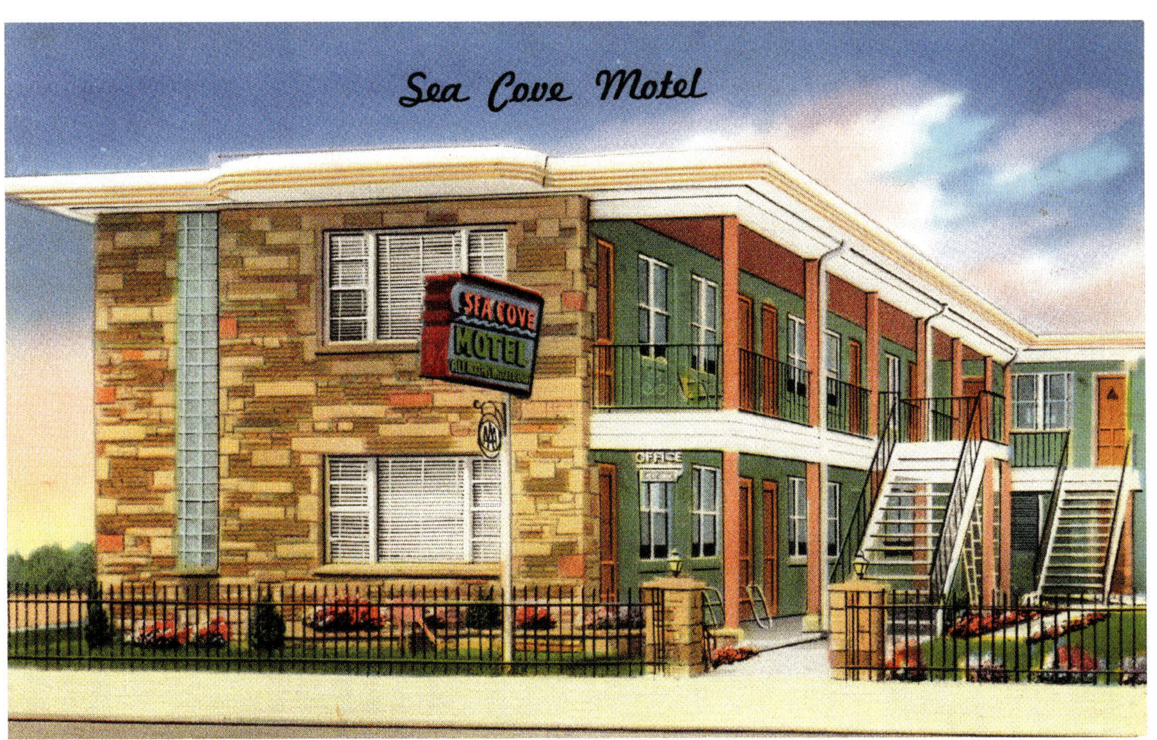

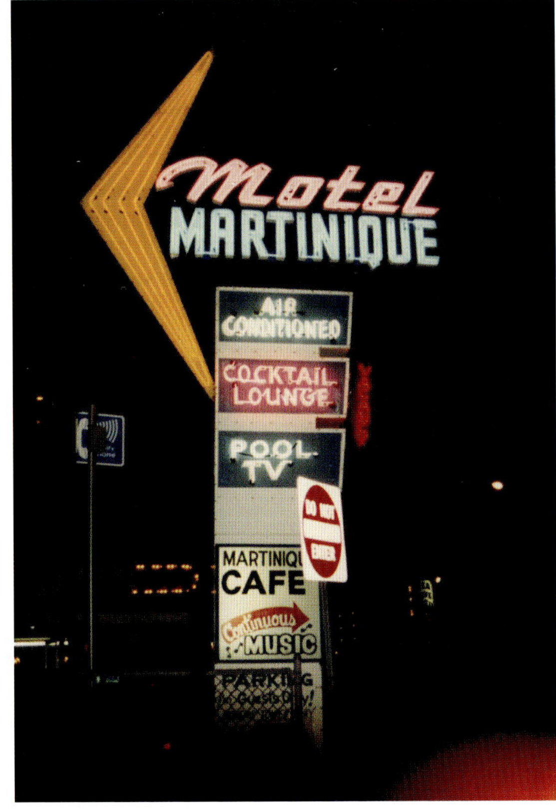

The Martinique complex included not just a motel, but also a cocktail lounge and package store. *Courtesy of ABS Sign Co., Inc.*

bones of the signs (including the metal channel letters) are extant, though, and perhaps they can be restored to their midcentury glory. Laura's remains a Wildwood institution, its fudge well loved by generations.

[106] Sea Cove Motel (323–325 East Wildwood Avenue)
This small motel, shoehorned sideways between two older hotels, popped up in 1955, sporting a flagstone façade and a freestanding neon sign. Charles Masciarella, a future Wildwood mayor who was involved with numerous motels on the island, built it, and a 1960s owner added a modernist glass-enclosed office cubicle. It remained mostly intact, albeit undermaintained, until being demolished around 2001.

[107] Motel Martinique (329 East Oak Avenue)
During the mid-twentieth century, entrepreneurs operated several ventures under the name Martinique on this block, across from Wildwood's now-gone bus terminal, including a package store and a bar. The motel, which opened in 1954, had a wild atmosphere and a distinctive neon sign. Since 2005, when the motel was demolished, the lot has sat empty. Large neon signs that once advertised the neighboring Martinique nightclub now reside in Philadelphia and Lancaster, Pennsylvania.

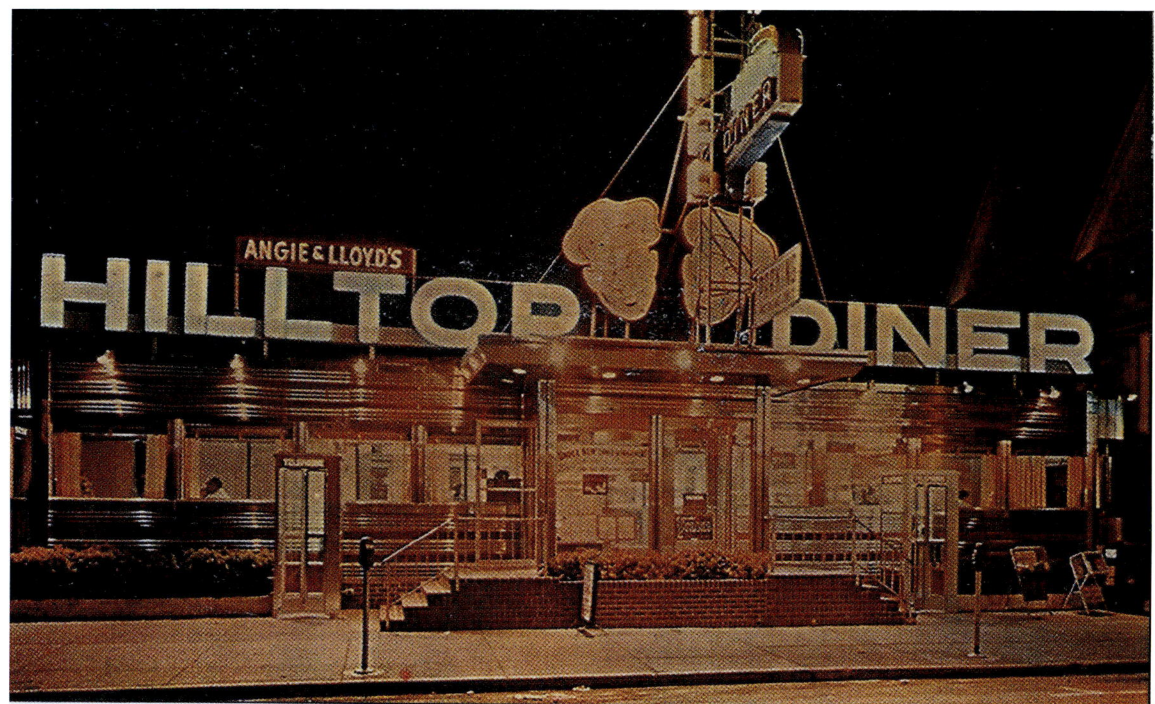

The owners of the Hilltop Diner drew in patrons with a wall of neon signage. *Courtesy of Wildwood Historical Society*

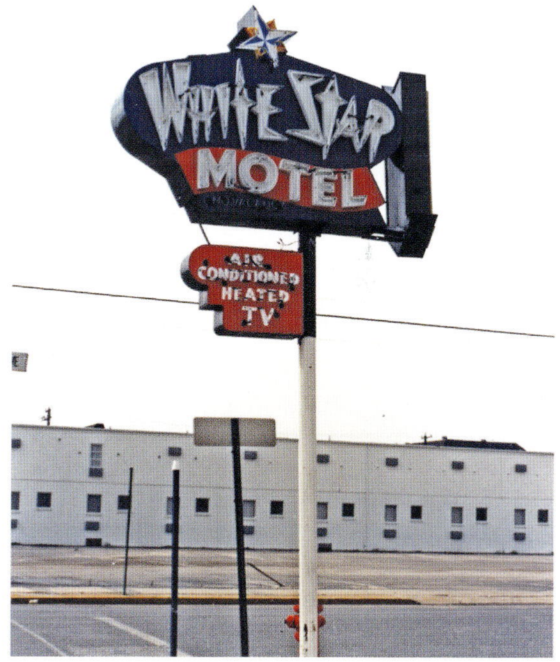

The White Star Motel's 1960-vintage neon sign in the early 1990s, a few years before it was replaced with a newer one. *Courtesy of Fedele Musso*

[108] Hilltop Diner (220 East Oak Avenue)
Manufactured in 1958 by the Kullman Dining Car Company of Newark, New Jersey, the Hilltop operated as a diner for only a decade. With its midblock location, it languished in the shadow of the more famous Atlantic and Wildwood Diners nearby. To combat this issue, owners Angie and Lloyd Hess installed a billboard-like array of neon signage, including renditions of their faces. Even this striking façade failed to draw enough business, and around 1969 the Hesses sold the diner to new owners, who covered it with stone and stucco and reopened it as Oak Avenue Seafood. In 2003, the owners of the neighboring Bolero Motel demolished it for a parking lot.

[109] Boardwalk Bungalow (3620 Ocean Avenue)
In 1960, Helmuth and Elizabeth Christensen built the two-story, L-shaped White Star Motel on the corner of Ocean and Lincoln Avenues, across the street from the boardwalk. Though the motel had an eye-catching pole-mounted sign with a neon-outlined star, it did not have a pool, an absence that put it behind the times (as did its odd marriage of American Colonial and jet-age aesthetics). In the 1990s, the motel got a new plastic-and-neon sign, which now resides outside the Doo Wop Experience. The motel now operates as Boardwalk Bungalow, part of the Morey Organization's Blue Palms Resort next door.

The Castaways Motel, one of Lou Morey's smaller motels, shortly after opening. *Courtesy of Fedele Musso*

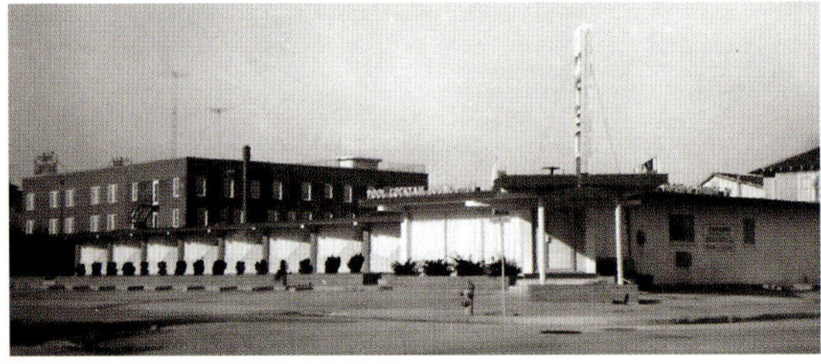

Shown here in 1961, the Lincoln Motel was built as an annex to the larger Hotel Lincoln, visible in the background. *Courtesy of Wildwood Historical Society*

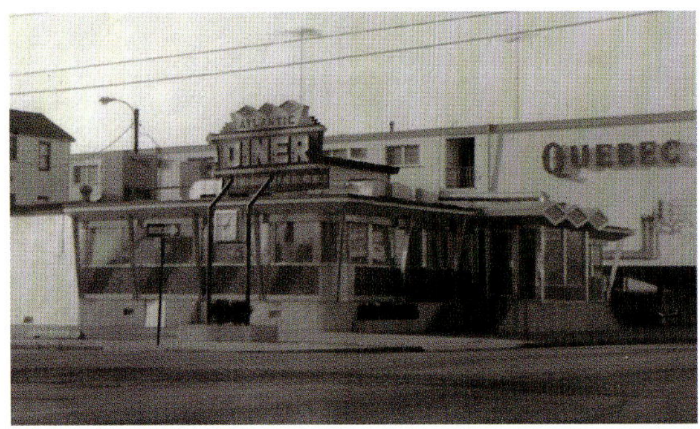

In the early 1970s, the Atlantic Diner still had its original flared roofline, supported by flying buttresses. *Courtesy of Wildwood Historical Society*

[110] Blue Palms Resort (3601 Atlantic Avenue)

The Midtown Motel, the Blue Palms' original incarnation, opened in 1967 at a prime location a block from the Jack Rabbit coaster and the Shore Theater. Don Twist, who built the motel, gave it an American Colonial theme, with Old English neon lettering and several lanterns. In 2005, Morey Resorts bought the Midtown and hired Richard Stokes to remodel it into the Blue Palms Resort. Encrusted with neon and populated with plenty of blue plastic palm trees, the Blue Palms exemplifies Neo Doo Wop.

[111] Beachside Resort (3700 Atlantic Avenue)

In 1958, Lou Morey built a modest motel two blocks from the ocean and commissioned a flashy neon sign reading "Castaways Motel." Aside from a new neon sign (and later a plastic one), the motel did not change much over the decades until 2017, when a new owner renovated its rooms and renamed it the Beachside Resort.

[112] Ocean Sands Motel (3302 Atlantic Avenue)

The Ocean Sands was built in 1961 as an addition to former Wildwood mayor Harry Steele's imposing Hotel Lincoln. The Lincoln, a venerable forties hotel that made headlines as one of the first hotels on the island to use fireproof materials, gained popularity because of its Mirror Bar. In 1960, Steele noticed the ever-increasing number of motels appearing on the island and updated his property with a motel annex. The one-story Lincoln Motel featured diagonal window sashes and a neon sign mounted atop a carport.

By 1978, Steele had his hands full with the aging Lincoln Hotel and sold the motel annex to a new owner, who renamed it the Ocean Sands and built a second floor whose windows matched those of the first floor surprisingly well. The motel stands today in mostly original condition.

[113] Pink Cadillac Diner (3801 Atlantic Avenue)

The Atlantic Diner opened on July 12, 1963. The diner was manufactured by the Kullman Dining Car Company of Newark, New Jersey, which had built the nearby Hilltop Diner five years earlier. It featured a wide, stainless-steel overhang and façade (later covered with pebbles in a late sixties remodel), as well as a diamond motif over its vestibule that was an early sixties Kullman trademark.

The diner's first owners—John Bickel, Bertram Mears, and Robert Fairlamb—had competition two blocks away in the Wildwood Diner, whose business was strong enough to support a 1961 addition. The Atlantic held its own, however. In 1982, the original owners sold to Ernie Dieterle, who covered the diner's exterior with checkered tiles in a nod to fifties nostalgia and renamed the place Big Ernie's. In a profile of Big Ernie's in Peter Genovese's 1996 book *Jersey Diners*, Ernie Jr., who had assumed ownership that year, said, "I plan to kill the drop ceiling, hide the air-conditioning and heating units, glass-block the vestibule, expose the Formica. I don't feel we need a major restoration, just a little makeover. A little elbow grease and a hammer and we'll get her back to normal."

In 2004, the diner was sold and renamed the Pink Cadillac. It remains today with much of the interior original but with the exterior restored in a postmodern style. Fred Musso has installed several custom neon signs inside and outside the diner, which add to its nostalgic vibe. As a side note, according to diner expert Larry Cultrera, the Mountain View–brand manufacturing tag visible above the front door actually comes from the former Centennial Diner in Atlantic City.

[114] Emandee Motel (220 East Garfield Avenue)
In 1960, Anthony Scheps, who owned a rooming house on Garfield Avenue, built a tiny motel addition next door with an appealing small neon sign, which remained intact for the next four decades. Both buildings were razed in 2004.

[115] Quebec Motel (3811 Atlantic Avenue)
In 1966, James Dare built a new motel on a former parking lot in downtown Wildwood; he outfitted it with outward-bowing railings, periwinkle trim and doors, and a striped picket fence surrounding the pool. A year or so later, he commissioned ABS to build a neon rooftop sign starring a yellow-outlined crown. The motel and sign are still resplendent today.

[116] Mango Motel (211 East Spicer Avenue)
Emmanuel Mangos today owns an early-twentieth-century bed-and-breakfast at 209 East Spicer Avenue, but in the early sixties he owned a small, two-story beach bungalow, lined by square spiral railings, next door at 211. The rest of his lot was empty, and in 1964 Mangos built the L-shaped

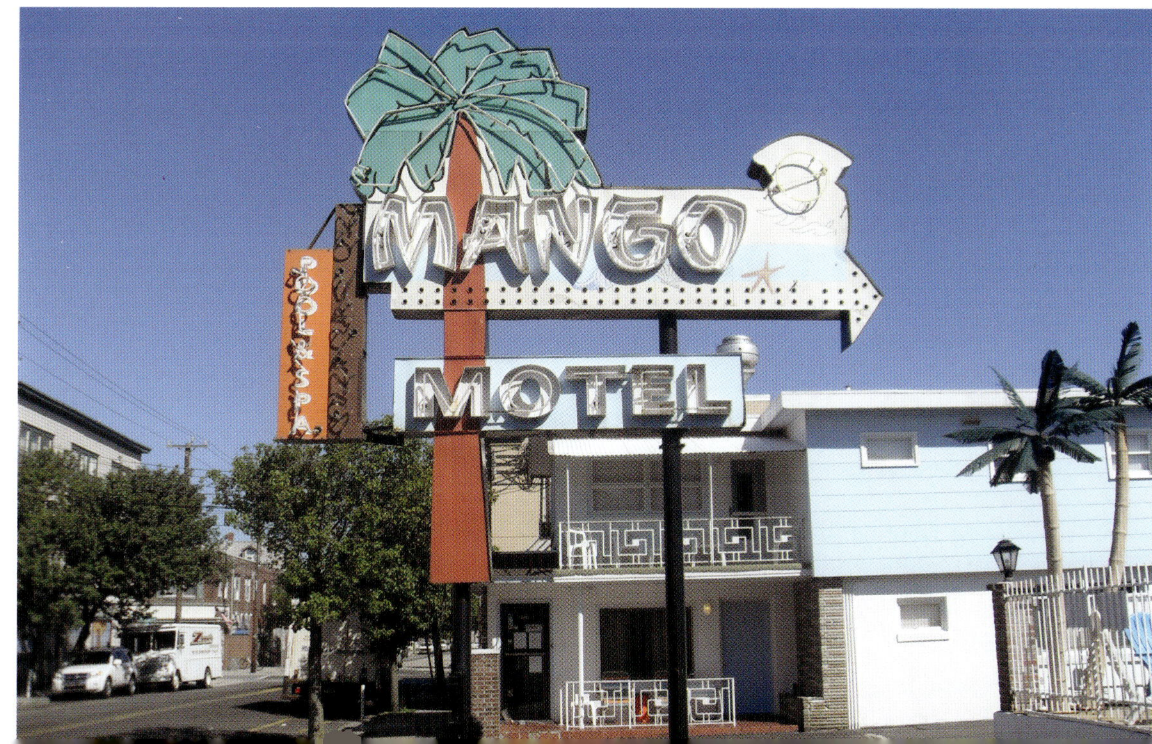

Emmanuel Mangos built the Mango Motel as an addition to the bungalow shown in the background.

Thomas Motel and Apartments, with his bungalow serving as the office. In the early 1970s, Mangos renamed the motel after himself, giving it a distinctive citrus theme in the process. He installed outward-bowing railings, a vivid coral-and-blue color scheme, and a detailed freestanding neon sign that included a whimsical typeface and the image of a palm tree.

In the 1980s, Mangos sold the motel and bought the bed-and-breakfast next door. Later owners of the Mango Motel added a pool but otherwise preserved its iconic vintage fixtures. The motel survives today, a treasure of the Wildwoods' midcentury architecture, and a joyful discovery on a tree-lined street.

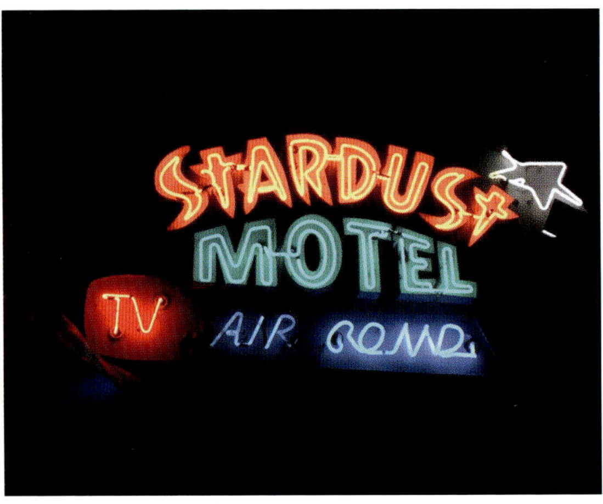

The Stardust Motel's neon sign shines as brightly today as it did in the late 1960s.

[117] Stardust Motel (3900 Ocean Avenue)

In 1960, Frank Accardi built a U-shaped motel at Ocean and Spicer Avenues and named it the Jackson Apartments. A few years later, he renamed it the Stardust Motel and expanded. ABS Signs made a wall-hung neon sign that spelled the motel's name in a font similar to that of the famous 1958 sign of Las Vegas's Stardust resort and casino. The motel and sign remain largely intact today.

[118] Skylark Motel (3901 Atlantic Avenue)

In 1955, Madge Tyler and May McGarry bought a corner lot on Atlantic Avenue, tore down the service station there, and opened a new U-shaped motel the next year. Probably named after the

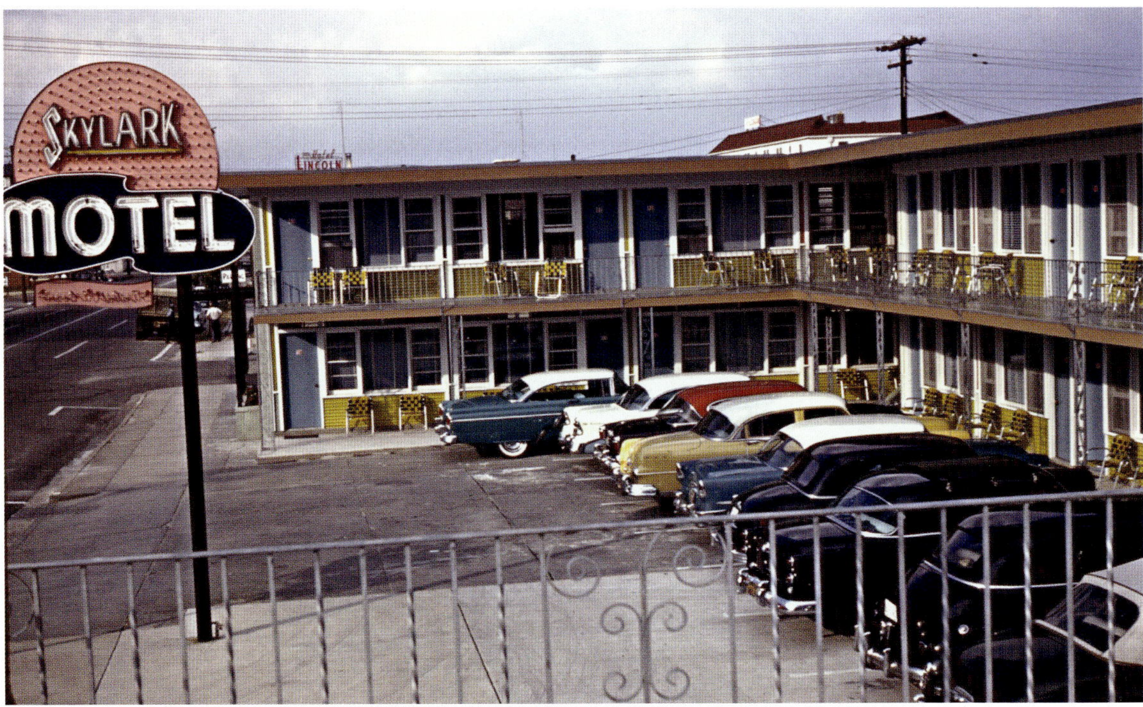

This 1956 photo from the balcony of the Skylark Motel offers a rare glimpse of the motel's original sign, replaced with a new one in the 1970s. *Courtesy of Ann Longmore-Etheridge collection*

popular sedan that Buick had introduced in 1953 (rather than the bird), the Skylark sported a fashionable neon sign studded with incandescent bulbs. Later additions included a pool, a full second story, and (in the 1970s) a new neon sign featuring a plastic back-sprayed bird that perhaps misrepresented the motel's roots. The motel and its newer sign survive today, despite a December 15, 2008 fire that necessitated a partial rebuild but did not cause any injuries.

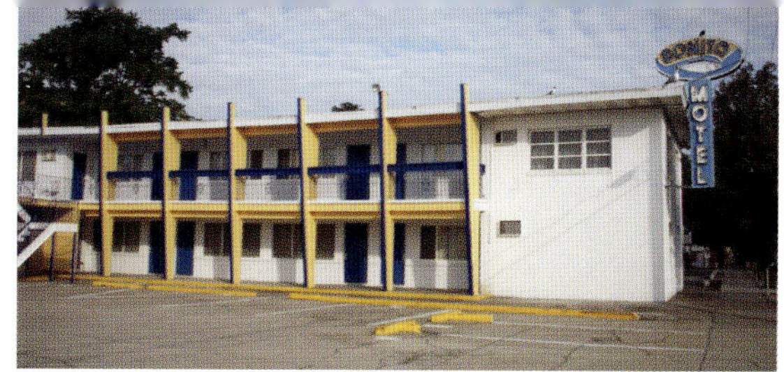

The Bonito Motel's brightly painted fins exemplify its 1950s vintage.

[119] Bonito Motel (236 East Spicer Avenue)
Anthony and Inez DeGrassa built the Bonito Motel in 1956 in two separate sections. An L-shaped motel overlooked Spicer Avenue, and the other half was slotted in sideways to neighboring Spencer Avenue. The Spicer Avenue wing had vertical fins that defined the motel's façade. While the motel originally had no pool (one was installed around 1970), it did have a beautiful pole-mounted neon sign featuring a yellow arrow outlined in incandescent lights. Today a new wall-hung neon sign has replaced the original one, but the motel is otherwise mostly well preserved.

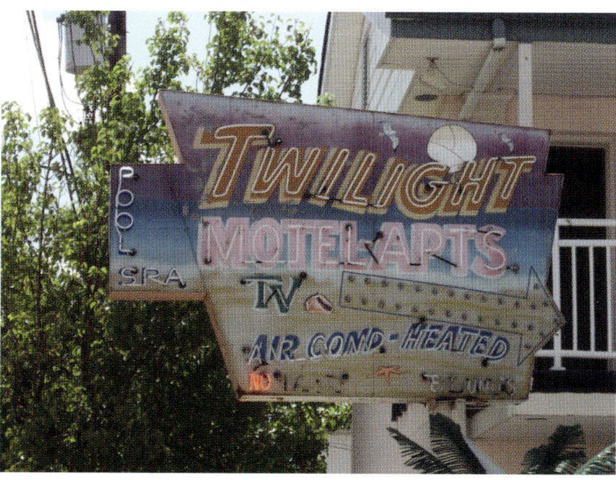

The Twilight Motel's elaborate 1970s-vintage neon sign, replaced in 2015.

[120] Twilight Motel (210 East Spicer Avenue)
Dom Randazzo spent the 1950s and 1960s renovating a small rooming house into a motel with several incremental additions. At first, he installed a small red neon sign with a white star, but in the 1970s he commissioned from ABS a remarkable freestanding sign that combined undulating letters, a sheet metal background painted to resemble a sunset, and text advertising several amenities. In 2015, the motel's owners replaced that exemplary neon sign with a plastic one.

[121] Wildwood Diner (4005 Atlantic Avenue)
Charles Masciarella, twelve years away from a term as Wildwood mayor, and Dominick Rossi opened the Wildwood Diner on May 27, 1956. Masciarella and Rossi had purchased a brand-new stainless-steel Jerry O'Mahony diner from Bayonne, New Jersey. After the diner was delivered, its owners installed landscaping and a rooftop neon sign (presumably built by Allied, Wildwood's preeminent sign company of the time).

The diner was immediately successful, but Masciarella and Rossi sold it in 1957 (Rossi opened the Caribbean Motel in the Crest the next year), and new owners Guy Muziani (another future Wildwood mayor) and Joseph Scrocca capitalized on the diner's popularity by expanding. In 1961, they contracted Superior Dining Car Company of Berlin, New Jersey, to build an addition. Superior built a new entrance and dining room, clad in stainless steel and aqua-blue porcelain tile, in front of the original O'Mahony diner and added a flashy pylon that held a new double-sided neon sign (which coexisted with the original neon sign for a few years; the latter was later usurped by two pole-hung signs on the corners of the diner's lot).

The Wildwood Diner's unique combination of segments from different eras, combined with its distinctive blue façade, made it a crucial part of Wildwood's Atlantic Avenue strip. Despite competition from the nearby Atlantic Diner and another Wildwood Diner that briefly operated on 17th Street before the Scroccas threatened legal action, the Wildwood Diner continued to run a successful business until the first few years of the 2000s, when the Scroccas sold. By 2005, the diner, which

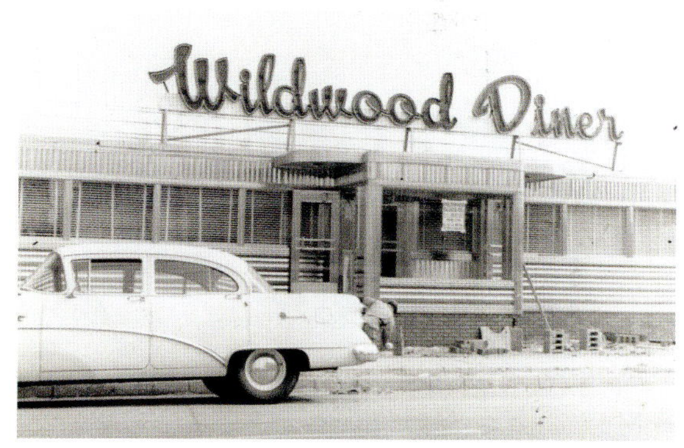

In this 1956 photo, the O'Mahony-built Wildwood Diner has arrived and crews are working on completing its landscaping before opening day. *Courtesy of Wildwood Historical Society*

A 1983 view of the Wildwood Diner, expanded in 1961 with a front dining room and distinctive corner pylon. *Courtesy of Larry Cultrera*

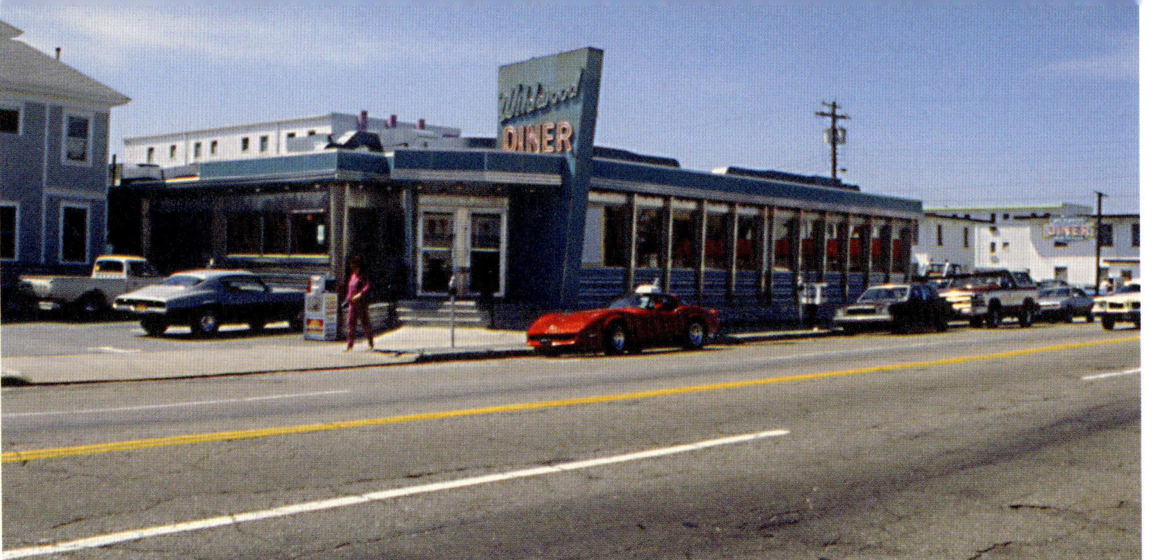

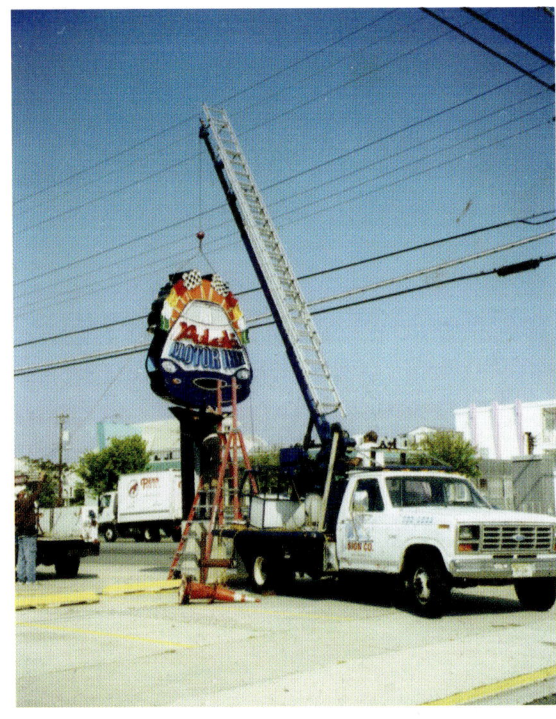

ABS installs a vivid new neon sign at the Pulaski Motor Inn. The sign survives today, with the word "Pulaski" amended to "Daytona." *Courtesy of ABS Sign Co., Inc.*

had often brought in capacity crowds over the decades, often sat empty. In December 2005, the diner was sold to developers, who tore it down early the next year. Fred Musso saved the "Diner Parking" pole sign, which had been badly damaged when firemen, in town for a convention, cut it down from its pole and let it crash onto the ground.

[122] Tropicana Motel (305 East Youngs Avenue)
In 1967, Hazel Aldridge razed her rooming house behind the Wildwood Diner and built a motel in its place. Perched on piles over parking spaces, the Bywood Gardens Motel used every inch of its tiny lot. Brightly colored fins mounted on the motel's end walls (painted a variety of colors over the years) called attention to the motel from a distance, as did a purple neon sign. In the mid-1980s, it was renamed the Tropicana, its name today; it now operates in tandem with the Waves Hotel, which stands on the diner's former lot.

[123] Daytona Inn and Suites (4010 Atlantic Avenue)
Before the motel era, the Pulaski Hotel, a 1920s rooming house, stood at the corner of Atlantic and Youngs Avenues. In the early 1970s, owners Edward and Catherine Namiotka sold the hotel to a developer, who tore it down and built the Pulaski Motor Inn on its site. Twenty years later, the motel's owners commissioned ABS to design a beautiful freestanding neon sign featuring a race car flanked by flags. The sign stands today and was updated when the motel's name was changed to Daytona just after the turn of the twenty-first century. Current owner John Donio has taken exemplary care of the motel and is active in local preservationist circles.

[124] Nantucket Inn and Suites (4100 Ocean Avenue)

In 1961, Bob and Elinor Thiel tore down one-third of their motel court, the Toywood Apartments, on the corner of Ocean and Youngs Avenues, and converted the rest into a new motel, the Nantucket. Painted bright blue, adorned with fake weather vanes and brick corners, and advertised by a free-standing neon sign, the Nantucket took a decent stab at translating the Cape Cod suburban aesthetic for the Jersey shore. Painted yellow, expanded, and sporting a newer neon and plastic sign, the motel continues to host vacationers.

[125] Pan-A-Lu Motel (242 East Youngs Avenue)

In the late 1950s, Daniel and Margaret Magni built the L-shaped M&M Motel around their bungalow (which they later demolished to make room for parking). Around 1967, new owners renamed the motel the Pan-A-Lu and installed a new neon sign, which was removed in 2015 and rescued by Fred Musso in 2020. The motel spent many years as budget apartments, but in 2020, new owners refurbished its rooms for condominium ownership, giving the Pan-A-Lu a new lease on life.

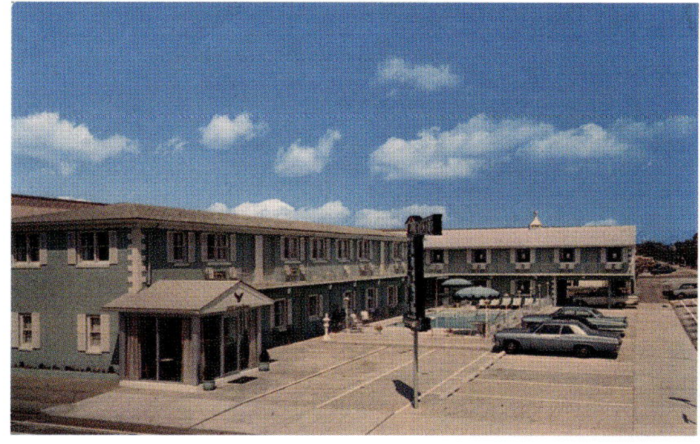

Since this early 1960s postcard was printed, the Nantucket Motel has been repainted yellow. *Author's collection*

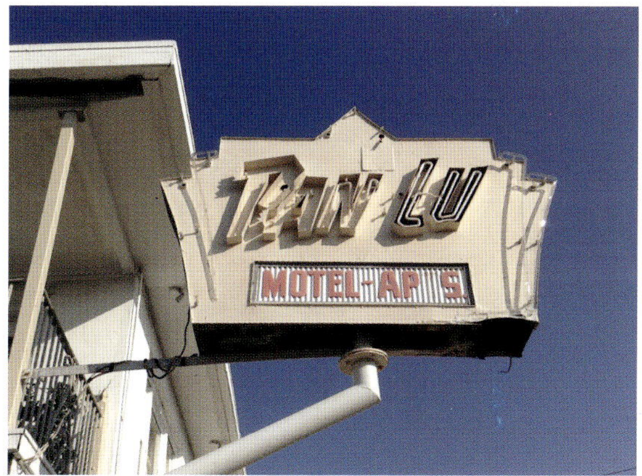

Several motel names in the Wildwoods were created by combining the names of two co-owners, as shown here at the Pan-A-Lu Motel.

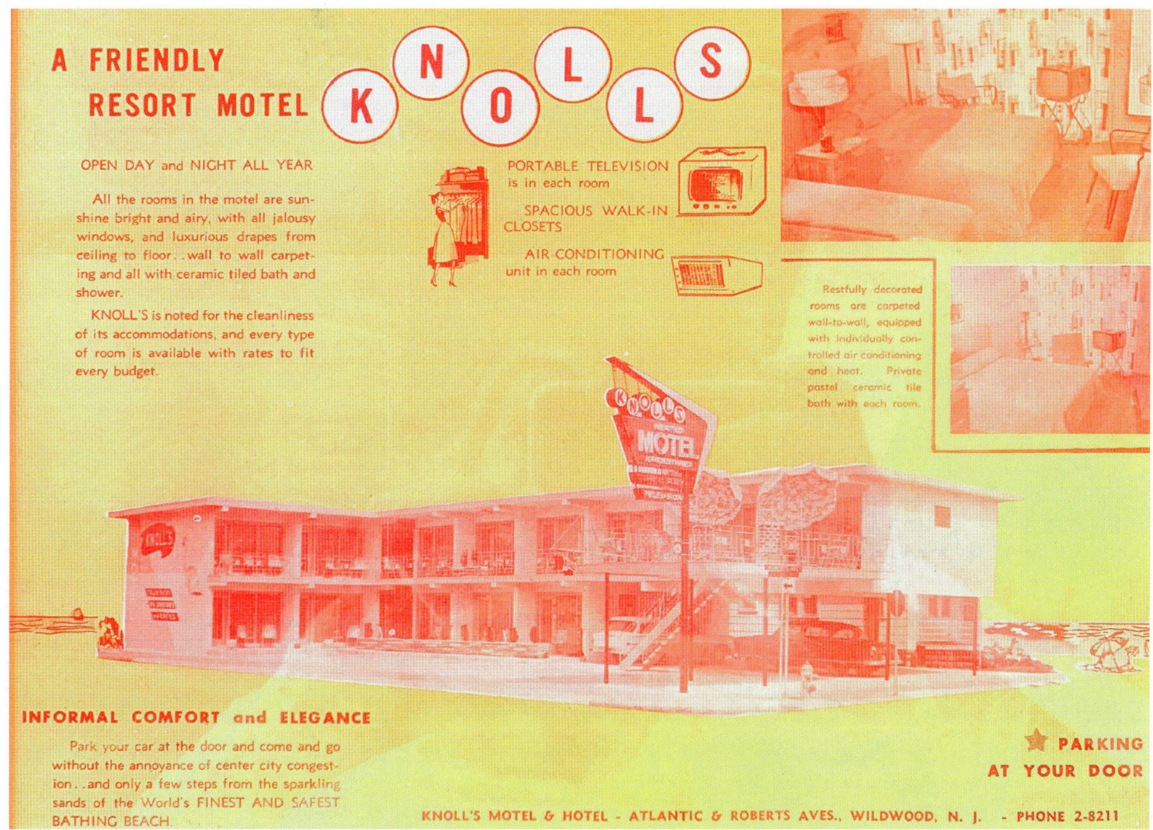

This 1957 brochure for Knoll's Motel shows the motel's original neon sign. *Courtesy of Dorothy Kulisek collection*

[126] Seahorse Inn (4111 Atlantic Avenue)

In the early 1950s, Effie Knoll and her husband, Bill, built a small rooming house (their second in town) on Roberts Avenue, one lot away from Atlantic Avenue. In 1953, Bill passed away, leaving his wife to run the family business on her own. Her granddaughter Agnes Knoll says, "My grandmother was a force to be reckoned with, and she was a very good businesswoman. After her husband died, she built up a very successful business from nothing!"

In 1957, Effie hired Lou Morey to build a modern motel on the adjacent corner lot. Knoll's Motel, which had square spiral railings and a pole-mounted neon sign with a flashing yellow arrow, met immediate success, and two years later she expanded with a second wing. She involved her family in the motel operation, and Agnes has many fond recollections of summers at Knoll's: "There was an empty lot across the street, and one year the Clydesdale horses were there, and I remember running over there to see the horses and watching them braid the horses' manes and put ribbons in. Also, the American Legion and VFW would take over the motel during their weekends down there, and we would sit on the curb and watch parades go by."

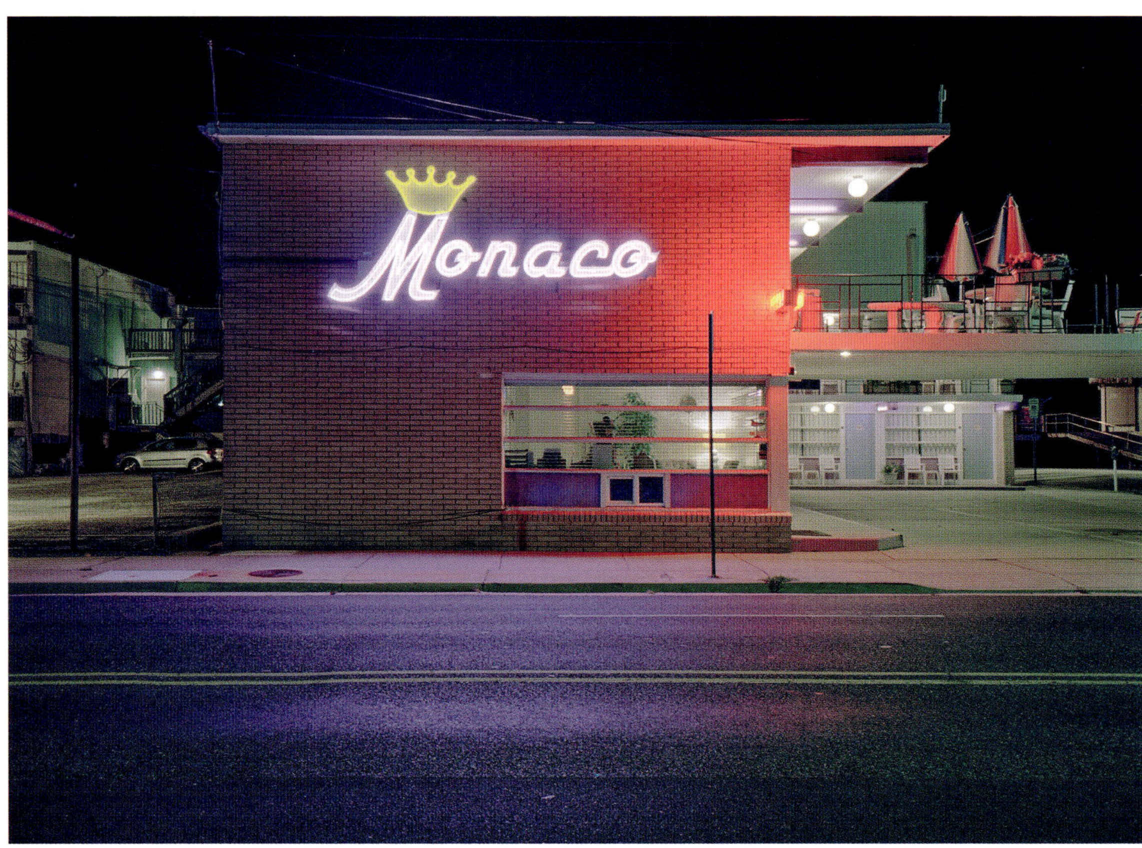

The color purple appears infrequently in the Wildwoods' neon landscape, but the Monaco Motel's 1970s wall-mounted sign is a sterling example. *Courtesy of Tyler Haughey*

One summer, Frankie Valli and the Four Seasons, performing on the island, stayed at Knoll's Motel. In 1978, the Knoll family sold to Hans and Karin Heumer, who painted the motel white and replaced its original neon sign with another (but kept its original railings). By 1990, this neon sign had been replaced with a plastic one.

In 2016, new owners installed vinyl railings, painted the motel beige and brown (more muted than its previous sea foam green and yellow), and renamed the motel the Seahorse Inn. "I wish the people who currently own the property at Roberts and Atlantic the best of luck," says Agnes Knoll. "It was like a tropical paradise."

[127] Monaco Motel (4211 Ocean Avenue)

[128] Caprice Motel (4200 Ocean Avenue)

In 1957, Anthony and Margaret Monaco opened the tiny Monaco Motel, inserted sideways into a lot at 4302 Ocean Avenue. A few years later, they deemed that motel inadequate for their needs, and in 1960 they built a new Monaco Motel diagonally across the street, at Baker and Ocean Avenues. This new building featured a neon pole sign and jalousie windows. In 1964, the Monacos sold to their son Anthony and his wife, Julia, who continued to maintain both motel buildings until the 1980s, when they sold the 1957 Monaco building (which became the Nova Motel and today is part of the Sunset Beach Resort). The 1960 Monaco is still open, missing its original pole sign but with a beautiful purple wall-mounted sign, added in the 1970s, which Fred Musso restored in 2010. Meanwhile, Anthony and Margaret built the Caprice Motel across the street around 1966; it still stands and is well known for its blue night illumination.

[129] Royal Court Motel (4301 Atlantic Avenue)

Opened in the mid-1950s as a one-story, L-shaped motel in the middle of a block on Baker Avenue, the Royal Court grew to encompass two more buildings over the next decade (including a three-story one on the corner of Atlantic Avenue). Over the years, the Royal Court has had a variety of neon signs, but a renovation around 2010 removed the last of them. One section of the Royal Court still hangs on to sixties-vintage square spiral railings, and the motel has a commendably family-oriented atmosphere in Wildwood's rowdy downtown.

[130] Bagel Time Café (4600 Atlantic Avenue)

In 1955, Ernest DiDonato demolished his house at Atlantic and Burk Avenues and built a two-story, brick-faced motel called the Ann Tina. A motel without a pool was hardly competitive in the Wildwoods, and the motel went through several names and owners over the years. In the 1970s, Veronica and Charles Thomas added a ground-floor café and renamed the complex the Atlantic Motel and Restaurant, complete with a gigantic rooftop neon sign featuring an incandescent-bulb-studded arrow and a rotating plastic clock. Later, the restaurant was renamed the Oceans Café, then Bob's Atlantic Café. Today the motel serves as budget apartments, but the restaurant space operates as Bagel Time Café, part of a regional breakfast chain.

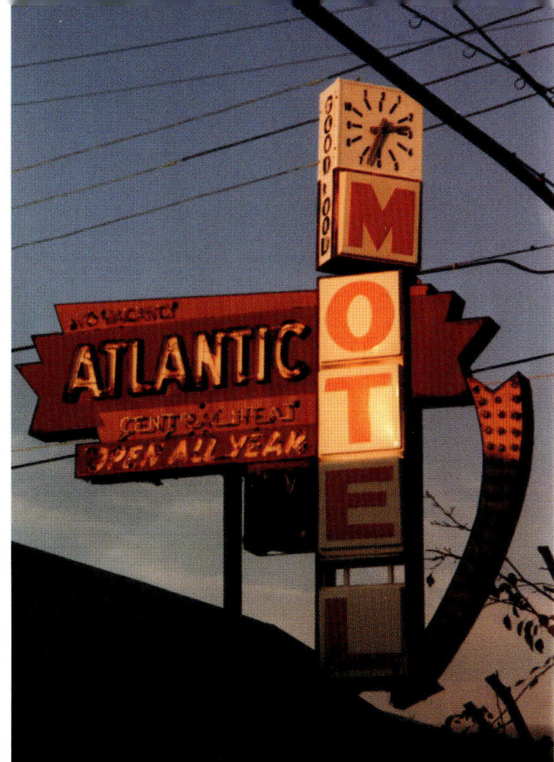

This building at Burk and Atlantic Avenues has had many names over the years; Atlantic Motel and Restaurant was one of the more enduring ones. *Courtesy of Fedele Musso*

The Sun Deck Apartments building had shed its vernacular smokestack by the late 1950s, but its streamlined shape remained. *Courtesy of Wildwood Historical Society*

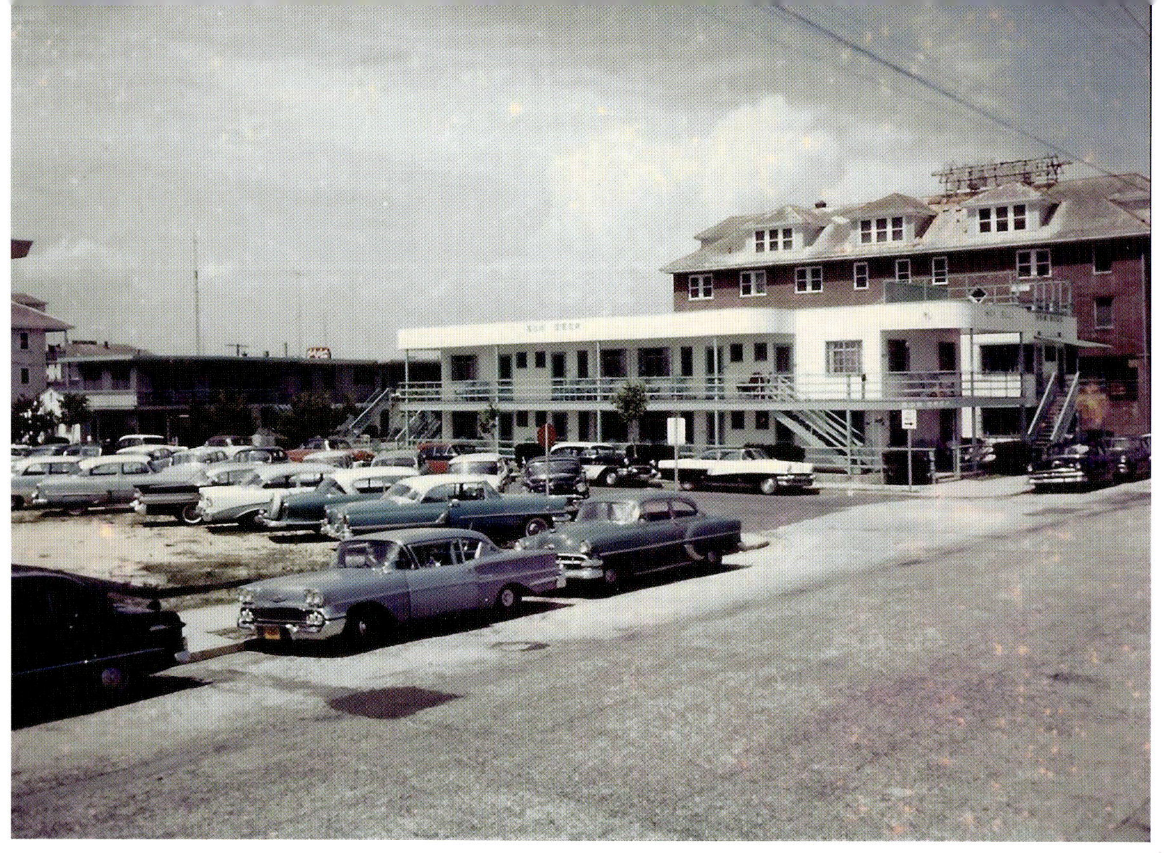

[131] Sun Deck Apartments (4610 Ocean Avenue)

[132] Ship Ahoy Apartments (formerly 4712 Ocean Avenue, now 118 West Baker Avenue)
These apartment buildings, part of a complex of five, were the earliest motel-type buildings in Wildwood. In 1939, Blanche Brown hired local builder Ben Schlenzig to build an apartment building, the Ship Ahoy, which had a rooftop neon sign and a nautical theme. A year later, Harry Rulon, who owned land a block away at Ocean and Andrews Avenues, hired Schlenzig to build three more apartment buildings: the Sun Dial, Sun Beam, and Sun Deck.

The Sun Dial and Sun Beam were plain clapboard-sided buildings, but the Sun Deck took inspiration from Depression-era vernacular architecture with a streamlined roofline (complete with rounded corners) and a faux smokestack emerging from the roof. A couple of years after Schlenzig built these apartments, Rulon rehired him to build an annex to the Sun Deck.

The Sun Deck flourished and evolved over the years, eventually growing to encompass the former Sun Deck and Sun Beam and a neighboring late forties motel court. Despite an attractive pole-mounted neon sign featuring a silhouetted woman, most of the Sun Deck complex came down in 1986 to make room for a Days Inn, except for the motel court, which still operates as part of the neighboring Hotel Oceanic (but is rumored to be scheduled for demolition). Meanwhile, Blanche Brown passed the Ship Ahoy down to her son Berthold and his wife, Anna, who operated it as a motel. In 1966, they received a generous offer for their oceanfront lot (which now holds the Aquarius Motor Inn) and moved the Ship Ahoy several blocks inland to Baker and Washington Avenues, where it still stands today, with a neon sign that ABS restored in 2017.

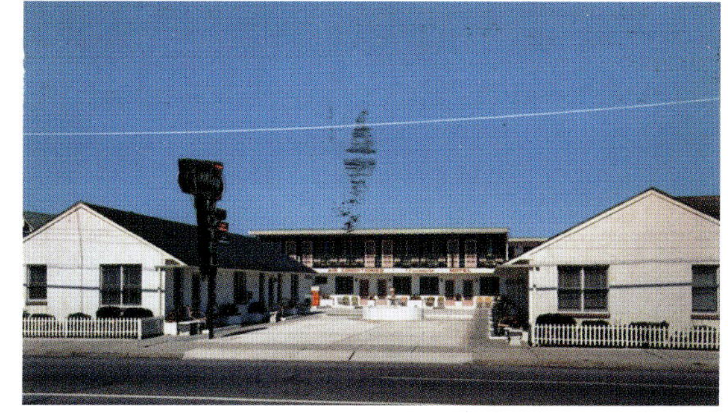

A few years after this early 1950s photo was taken, Leonard Jackson tore down the left third of the Fountain Motel and replaced its eponymous fountain with a pool. *Author's collection*

[133] Fountain Motel (4616 Atlantic Avenue)
After originating as a motel court in the 1940s, the Fountain grew a decade later into a motel with the amputation of one of its two inward-facing wings (changing its original U shape to an L) and the eventual addition of a pool. Today the motel survives (minus an early fifties freestanding neon sign) and encompasses its former neighbor, the Capri Court.

[134] Mir-A-Mar Motel and Apartments (307 East Taylor Avenue)
Helmuth Christensen opened this apartment building in 1946 with one story, then expanded it with another story a few years later. It stood out with a freestanding neon sign (which read "Motel," still an uncommon word on the island at the half-century mark), which Fred Musso saved when the motel was demolished in the first few years of the 2000s.

[135] El Ray Motel (4715 Atlantic Avenue)
Raymond Day built the El Ray for the 1954 season, a single-story, U-shaped court with a grass courtyard. Later in the decade, new owners expanded it, first with a second story with angled windows and diamond-patterned railings, then with an additional wing. Today the motel is in good condition, though various neon signs that once embellished the motel have disappeared, and its once-spacious courtyard now seems cramped when occupied by a pool.

[136] Aquarius Motor Inn (4712 Ocean Avenue)
Pasquale Di Stasio and Joyce Blumenschein built a new high-rise motel in 1969 on the former site of the Ship Ahoy Apartments. Three years later, Di Stasio commissioned Harry Lanza to build a spectacular, 45-foot-tall, freestanding sign, which juxtaposed vertically stacked plastic letters spelling "Aquarius" with an oval-shaped neon panel depicting a water bearer pouring water out of a jug. "They passed an ordinance so you can't make them that big anymore," Di Stasio's daughter Nancy Dinella said in Len Davidson's 1999 book, *Vintage Neon*. "It's a solidly built sign; we've had all kinds of storms but it's never been damaged. It just sways in the wind a little bit. The guests all love it. They say, 'I had to stay here because I'm an Aquarius. That's my sign.'" ABS replaced the sign with a more modern

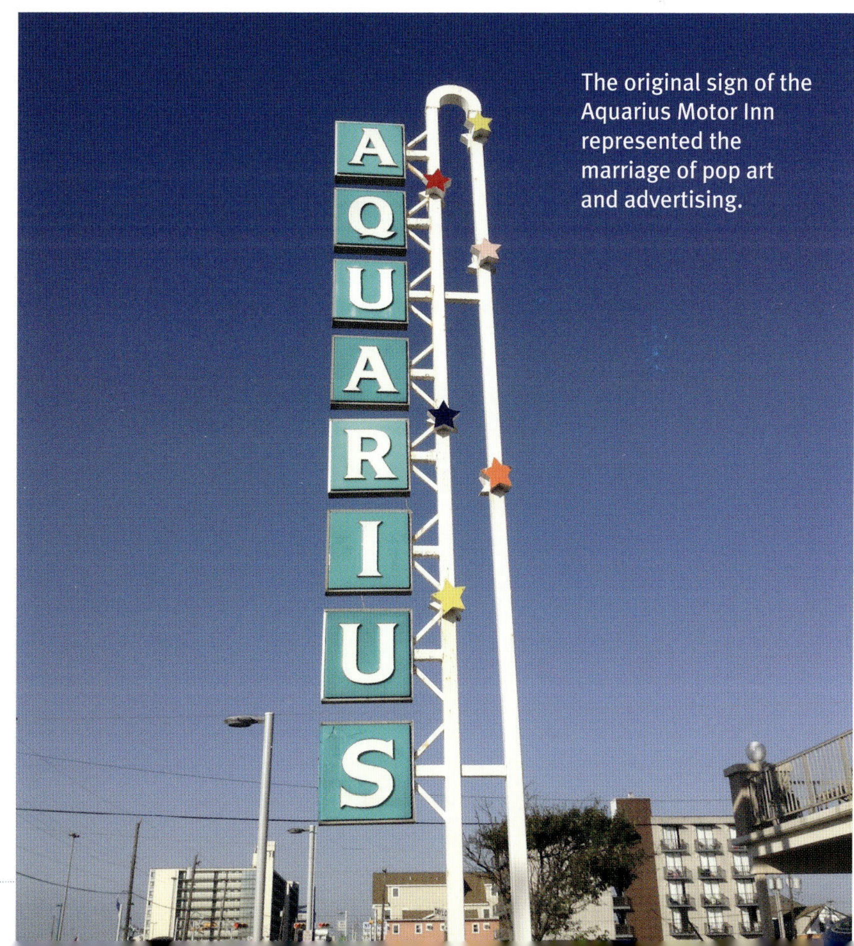

The original sign of the Aquarius Motor Inn represented the marriage of pop art and advertising.

plastic replica after the original was finally damaged in a storm in 2016. (In the 2010s, the owners of the Aquarius acquired the next-door Sea Mist Apartments at 4702, removing its small forties-era neon sign in the process.)

[137] Rio Motel (4806 Ocean Avenue)

In 1952, Ben Schlenzig, who had built the Ship Ahoy and its ilk a block north, built a two-story motel at Rio Grande and Ocean Avenues. The Rio was not the first motel in the Wildwoods, but while earlier motels had borrowed from tourist courts' layouts, the Rio brought a bold new twist to the Wildwoods' car culture. Schlenzig built a motel with a sawtooth footprint: each room was sharply angled toward the ocean and featured a front balcony for optimal ocean views. Louvered doors and windows, flagstone walls, and white-painted bean poles lent the Rio a California-style Googie aesthetic.

In 1956, new owners Carl and Adele Camp bought an adjacent lot along Rio Grande Avenue and expanded the Rio. The addition featured a second-story lounge framed by canted glass walls and a rooftop neon sign with a pink-outlined cactus. In the late 1950s, the Camps expanded the motel further, with a U-shaped addition that, while architecturally simple, boosted the Rio's profile and lodging capacity. The Camps also bought the neighboring Sun and Surf Bungalows on Taylor Avenue, adding them to the Rio complex.

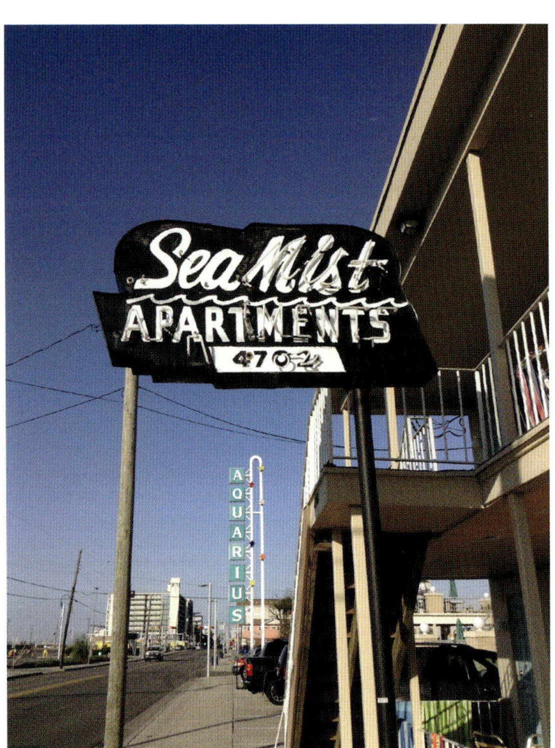

This 1940s neon sign disappeared after the Aquarius Motor Inn acquired the next-door Sea Mist Apartments in 2015.

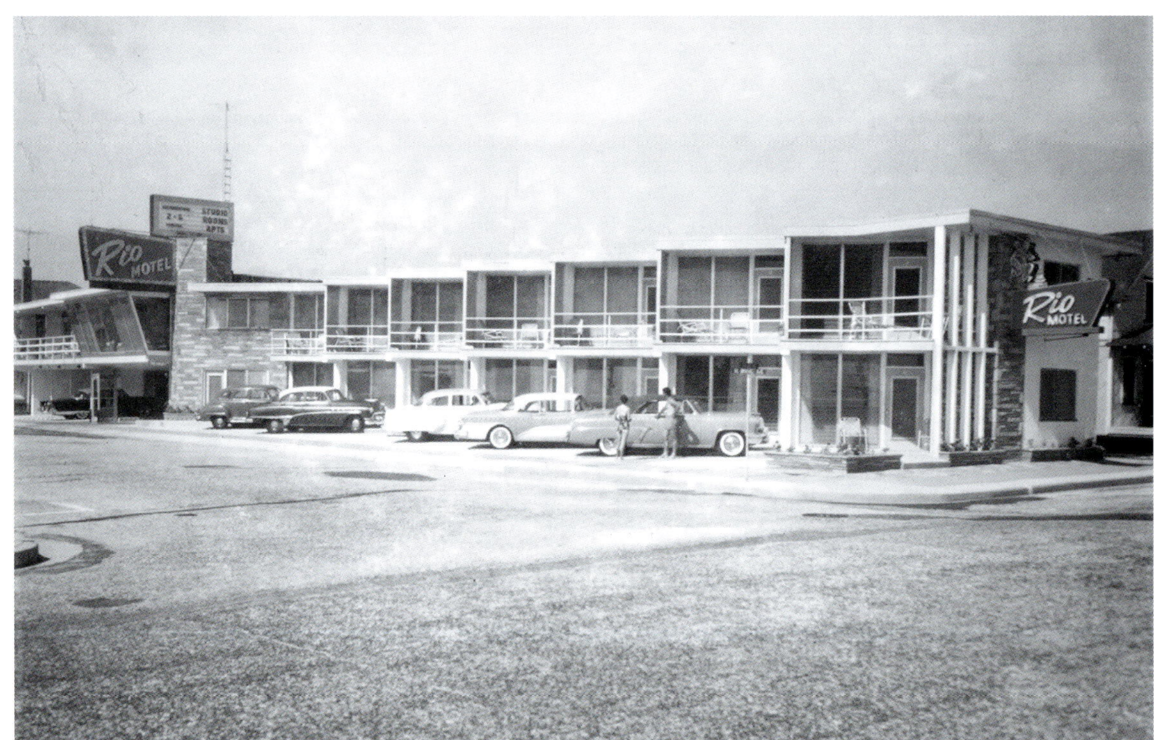

The Rio Motel's pioneering offset balconies are visible in this late 1950s photo. *Courtesy of Wildwood Historical Society*

Around 1966, Carl Aspenburg bought the Rio and maintained it for several decades. Aspenburg placed a sculpture of a sombrero-hatted man, Pedro, and his burro on the corner of Rio Grande and Ocean Avenues, where it became a well-loved photo opportunity. After the 2006 season, the Rio was sold to developers, who bulldozed the motel that fall. "I remember when I first came here, I was getting my hair cut and the barber was almost crying," says Gordon Clark, who manages Morey Resorts, including the Starlux next door. "She was remembering the Rio Motel." Fred Musso restored one of the motel's neon signs, which now resides in Golden Beach, Florida. Pedro and his burro can be seen today at the George Boyer Museum in downtown Wildwood. The lot on which the Rio stood, which contained some remnants of the motel foundations, was empty until 2015, when Starlux Mini Golf opened there.

[138] Surf Comber Motel (4800 Atlantic Avenue)

Margaret Thame built the Surf Comber at Taylor and Atlantic Avenues in 1956, incorporating jet-age flavor with a rounded office window. Except for the addition of a pool and the replacement of the original pole-mounted neon sign with a new wall-mounted plastic one, little about the Surf Comber has changed since its heyday. It is still a popular vacation spot.

[139] Starlux Boutique Hotel (305 East Rio Grande Avenue)

In 1953, Lewes Wingate constructed a one-story, L-shaped motel next to his family home at the prominent corner of Rio Grande and Atlantic Avenues; later in the decade, he expanded it to three stories and added a rotating neon sign shaped like a piece of wood. Postcards from the 1960s show a full parking lot, but by the end of the twentieth century the Wingate had fallen on hard times (the Wingate family had never installed a pool, an essential amenity).

In 2000, as motel demolitions around the island were beginning, the Morey Brothers bought the Wingate. Jack Morey met architect Richard Stokes, who was lecturing at the University of Pennsylvania. "He had a thick marker. And he scribbled all over a drawing of the Wingate, and I fell in love. It was so beautiful; I loved it." With significant assistance from Mike Hill and several architecture students from Kent State, Stokes drew a design that removed the Wingate's owners' house and several original rooms, adding a new glass-enclosed lounge with an asymmetrical roof that came to a dramatic point high above the entrance. Stokes also inserted a new pool (kidney shaped, of course) in place of the original parking lot (which he moved across the street, a seeming lapse of functionality). The new motel opened in 2001, and New Jersey governor Christine Todd Whitman visited the opening ceremony to speak about the Wildwoods' preservation movement.

A year after the Starlux opened, the Moreys added a fourth story and a new wing, which Stokes had originally drawn but which had been delayed due to budget issues. Since 2002, the Moreys have made the Starlux a centerpiece of their hospitality branch, Morey Resorts. In 2005 or so, they added a pair of sixties-vintage Airstream trailers and a transplanted beach bungalow to serve as additional units. Then, in 2015, they expanded the Starlux complex with a miniature golf course and Kohr Brothers ice cream stand. The Moreys have more plans for the Starlux, some more ambitious than others (including underground parking, one hundred additional rooms, and a banquet space). "We're

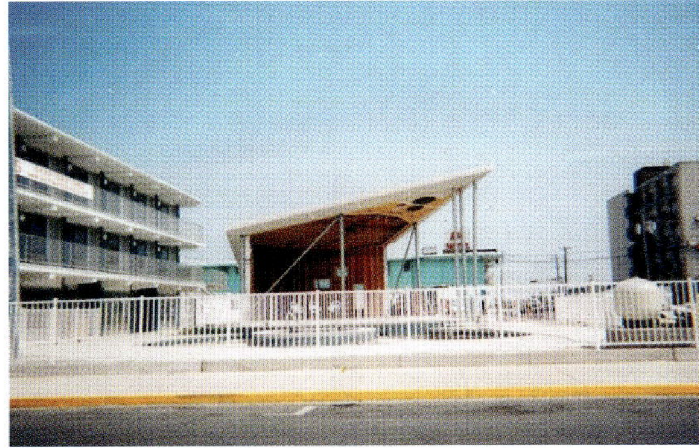

Building the Starlux, 2000. *Courtesy of Morey Family Archives*

dying to build the Starlux phase 3!" Jack Morey says. Although it is a modern reinterpretation of vintage elements rather than an original design, the Starlux drew crucial attention to the Doo Wop preservation movement.

[140] Fantasy Motel (131 West Rio Grande Avenue)

On April 29, 1956, Will Morey opened his new Fantasy Motel, and the island's architecture scene changed. "That was his first motel," says his son Jack. "He borrowed $15,000 from a car dealership." Morey had chosen a tiny lot on then-sleepy Rio Grande Avenue, blocks away from the beach and the bay; he made up for the cramped quarters and lack of a view with sheer individuality. With a second-floor glass-enclosed lounge, a lime-green paint scheme, a huge cantilevered roof overhang, a futuristic rooftop neon sign designed by Allied Signs, and small jet-age details such as lightning-bolt railings and curtains, the Fantasy made manifest Will Morey's new philosophy of bringing cheap luxury to the masses.

A couple of years after building the motel, Morey added a swimming pool. After he sold the Fantasy around 1962, old age was unkind to the motel: owners in the 1990s painted it white and replaced its exuberant railings and neon sign with pale plastic versions (a storm had damaged the original sign,

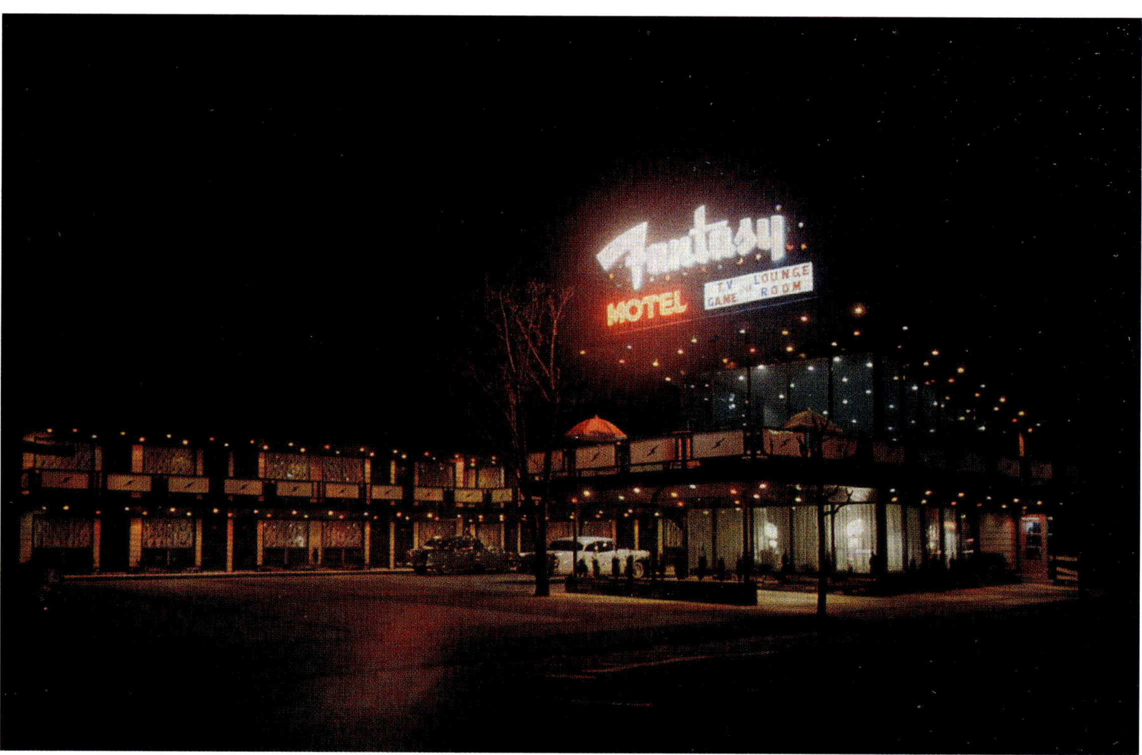

The Fantasy Motel did not have an oceanfront location, but it exuded neon modernism that was unmatched in the Wildwoods in 1956. *Courtesy of Fedele Musso*

making replacement the easiest option). By 2006, years of deferred maintenance had reduced the motel to a dilapidated shadow of its former self. When, that year, the owners of a Harley-Davidson dealership next door bulldozed the Fantasy to build a parking lot, the end was welcome.

[141] Motel Sun Shine (246 East Rio Grande Avenue)

The Sea Shell Motel, the Sun Shine's former guise, was built in 1950 by Lawrence and Anna Manning and expanded with a second story in 1952. With its two inward-facing wings overlooking a grass courtyard, it fell squarely into the category of a tourist court, though its original shell-shaped neon sign, reading "Sea Shell Court," was replaced in the late 1960s with a newer one that read "Motel," reflecting the changing times. "Neon is an inordinate amount of maintenance, with the wind and elements, and being near the beach," notes former manager Bob Van Eman. "I suppose it's worth it. There are so many people passing by around here who stop and take pictures with what appear to be very expensive cameras. You don't see signs like that anymore."

In 2019, new owners renamed the motel the Sun Shine and repainted it orange. Fortunately, Fred Musso salvaged the Sea Shell's neon sign.

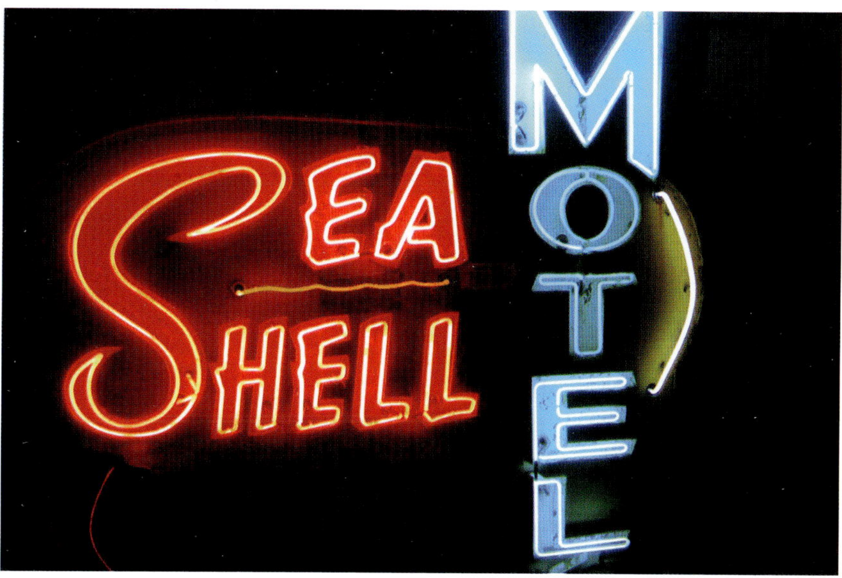

Fred Musso rescued the late sixties Sea Shell Motel neon sign when the motel was renamed the Sun Shine in 2019. *Courtesy of Fedele Musso*

[142] Gulfstream Motel (4910 Ocean Avenue)

Ruth Bethel built this small, metal gingerbread–adorned apartment building along Hand Avenue in 1949, then upgraded it to motel status about a decade later and added a freestanding neon sign announcing this transformation. The motel survived mostly intact until its 2005 demolition.

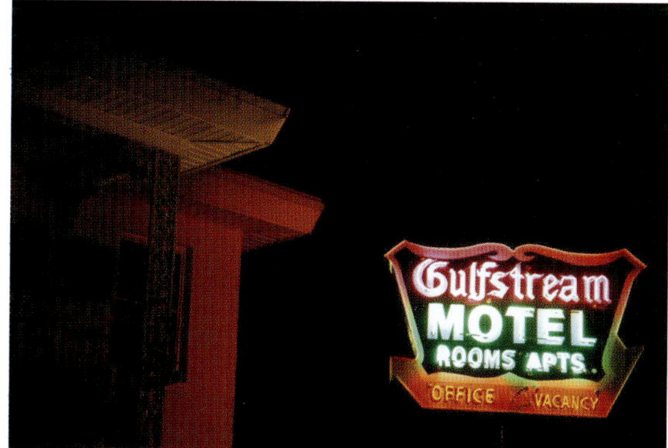

The Gulfstream Motel was plain, but its multicolored neon sign elevated it to a minor midcentury classic. *Courtesy of Dorothy Kresz*

[143] Pink Champagne Motel (249 East Hand Avenue)

The Pink Champagne has become one of the Wildwoods' most-photographed motels due to its effervescent neon sign. Rose and Angelo Graiff built the motel in 1959 on the former site of a summer house. In 1966, after adding a third story, the Graiffs sold the motel; a variety of owners since then have hardly changed the motel (down to its nostalgic Pepto-Bismol-colored trim). The neon sign, which features an arrow pointing to the motel

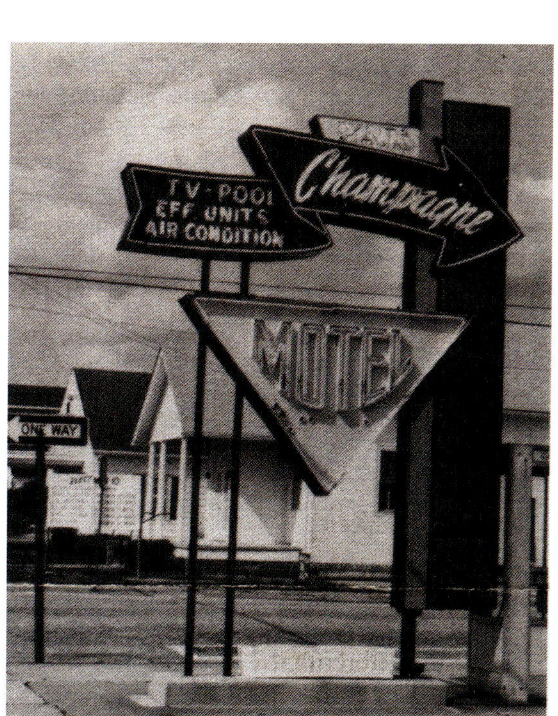

A 1983 view of the sign of the Pink Champagne Motel, before the word "Pink" was enlarged. *Author's collection*

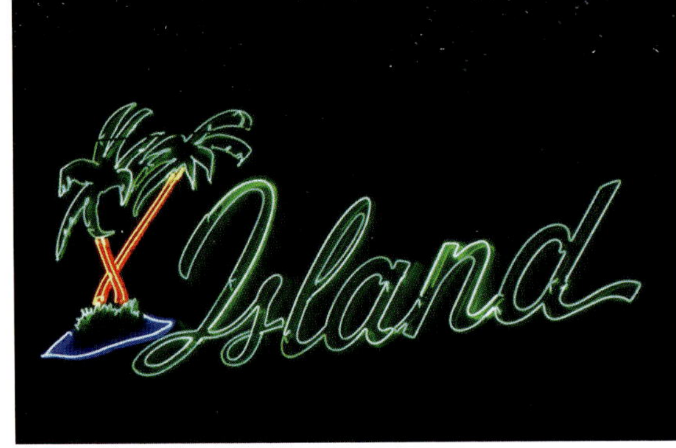

When the Island Motel transitioned to condominium ownership in 2005 or so, its new owners preserved the neon sign, removing only the word "Motel."

in what the Doo Wop Preservation League termed "electric persuasion," saw the word "Pink" enlarged in the 1990s but is otherwise original. Manager Maria Enos has witnessed the motel evolve from a run-of-the-mill beach motel to a more sophisticated destination. "Booking.com and Expedia have changed things," she says. "Now the people we get are more metropolitan—people from New York and Philly looking to get away. It's changed the motel a little bit."

[144] Island Motel (5001 Park Boulevard)
In 1956, plumber Henry Kilmer decided to cash in on the Wildwoods' motel craze and build a tourist court. The one-story Island was expanded in the 1970s with a second story and a large rooftop neon sign. Today, the motel has gone condo but most of the sign remains, albeit at a different location on the motel's roof.

[145] Sea Ray Motel (5006 Ocean Avenue)
In the early 1970s, Alexander Sabetta expanded his summer residence with a second story of motel units. He made his living room into an office, added a neon sign with a stingray-like cloud of flashing neon tentacles, and called it the Sea Ray. The motel survives today, notwithstanding an early eighties fire, and the neon sign shines brightly following a recent restoration.

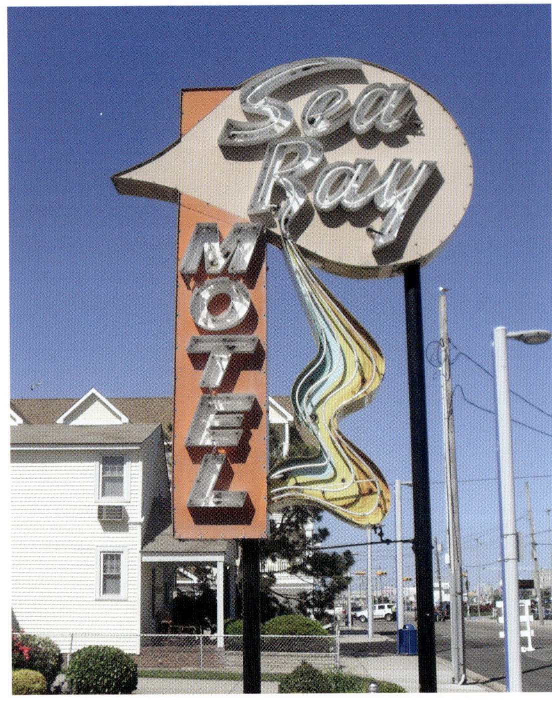

The Sea Ray Motel's neon sign dates to the early 1970s. At night, its multicolored tentacles flash.

[146] Starfire Motel (5100 Ocean Avenue)
Around 1958, the Wade and Russo families built the Starfire Motel on Ocean Avenue, across the street from Wildwood's boardwalk. With its yellow paint scheme, railings punctuated by pillars and keystones, V-shaped window sashes, octagonal pool, and neon sign spelling the word "Motel" in red bubbles, the Starfire was packed with exemplary midcentury modern detail. The motel has since been modified, but its current owners maintain it well.

[147] Lu Fran Motel (5106 Ocean Avenue)
Around 1954, John and Margaret Giacalone had an L-shaped motel built along Ocean Avenue, across the street from the boardwalk. The motel used the same blueprints as the Capri Motel in nearby Cape May, potentially indicating a common builder. In the 1960s, new owners moved the sign to the roof, then added a second, wall-mounted porcelain sign featuring neon lettering and an

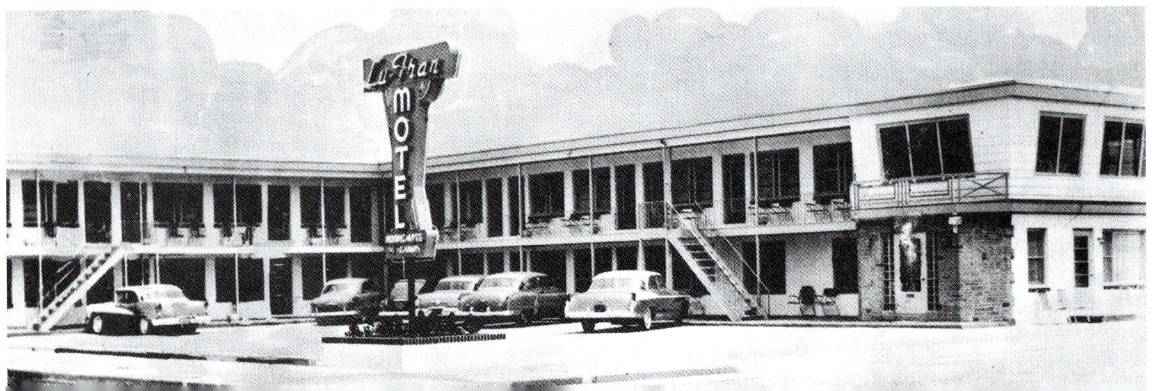

This early 1950s brochure photo of the Lu-Fran Motel shows the motel's first neon sign; a newer one adorns the motel today. *Author's collection*

incandescent-bulb-outlined arrow. The original sign disappeared soon after, but the sixties sign still beckons to travelers (minus its neon tubes).

[148] Blue Jay Motel (5111 Atlantic Avenue)

In 1965, Thomas and Mary Gallagher expanded their small Gallagher Apartments into a fully fledged motel. They added two stories (for a total of three) and a neon blue jay silhouetted against a background of chasing lights and Bauhaus letters. Upon the motel's 2005 demolition, Fred Musso saved part of the neon sign, which now resides in Lancaster, Pennsylvania.

[149] Dolphin Inn (5201 Atlantic Avenue)

Today's Dolphin Inn opened as the Eden Roc Motel. Built by Lou Morey in 1957, the motel took its name from Morris Lapidus's Eden Roc in Miami, a postwar revival of art deco. Wildwood's Eden Roc, first owned by Charles Masciarella, didn't take any obvious architectural features from its Miami namesake. Rather, it was a classic L-shaped Wildwood motel, featuring brick façades, two huge wall-mounted neon and grid-light signs spelling the motel's name in a script (one of which disappeared in the early 1970s), a peanut-shaped pool, a second-floor overhang decorated with a

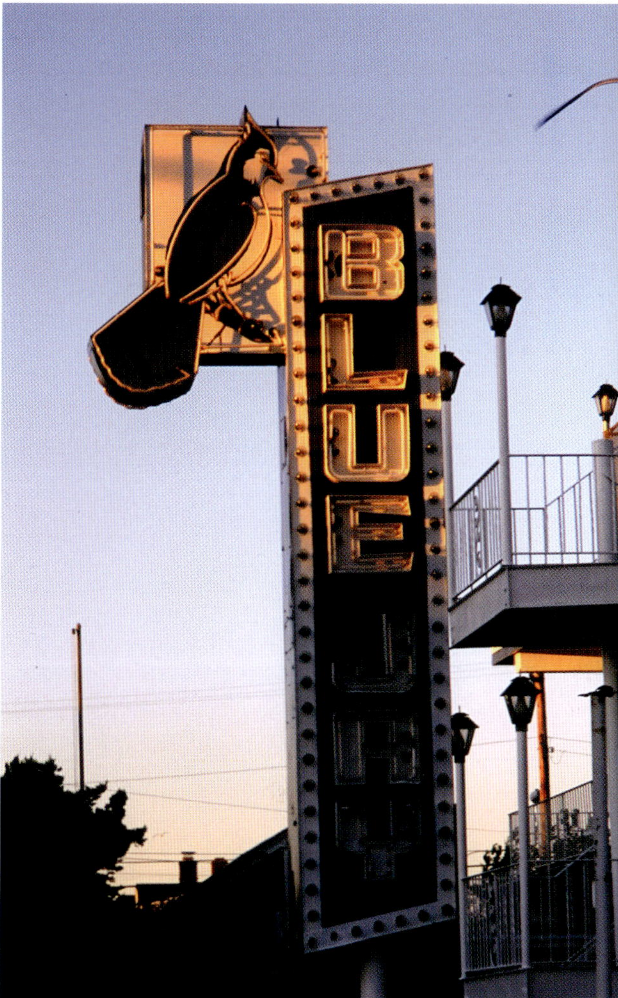

The Blue Jay Motel's neon sign combined neon lettering with flashing incandescent "chasers." *Courtesy of Steve Weir*

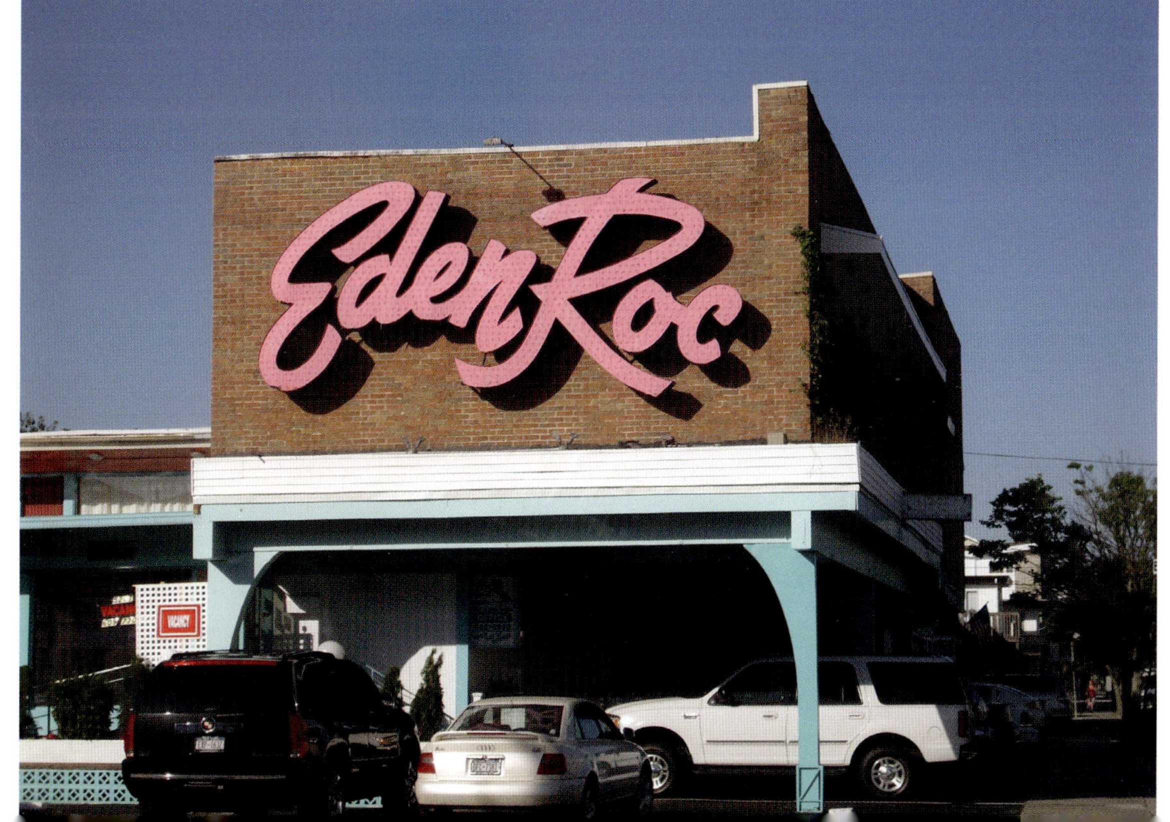

The Eden Roc still had one of its original wall-mounted signs in 2012; the next year it was revived as the Dolphin Inn.

driftwood sculpture, and a coffee shop enclosed in canted glass walls. The Eden Roc radiated exotic modernity, and its early owners played this sophistication up with advertising photos showing women driving by in a red convertible.

By the first few years of the 2000s, the Eden Roc had lost its original luster. As current manager Theresa Robey remembers, "Somebody did a write-up about it, and it became one of the ten worst motels in the United States. Tim Patel, who bought it, walked in here, and there were fleas in the lobby. There were gnats everywhere. The rooms were so run down!"

Patel, who bought the motel in 2012, had his work cut out for him. "I really wanted to keep that Eden Roc name, but I can't," Patel said in a 2012 *Press of Atlantic City* story. Instead, he renamed the motel the Dolphin Inn and commissioned a new ABS neon sign. Thanks to Patel's efforts, the Dolphin Inn remains a vibrant part of the Wildwoods' Doo Wop scene. Aside from necessary improvements to the rooms, Patel has maintained the motel's original features, though as Robey says, he wants to keep his options open: "They want to make it a historic site down here. The only problem is, when you put it in the history books, you can't remodel it anymore. And with the wear and tear on hotel rooms, we really don't want to do that." Still, Patel has spearheaded an exceptional retro renovation, creating a modern Wildwood landmark.

[150] Poolside Motel (248 East Bennett Avenue)
Nicholas Vinci's Poolside Motel evolved from a rooming house in the late 1950s. Vinci added a pair of colorful neon signs to drum up business, and one of these, a pole-mounted sign featuring a ball of flashing incandescent lights, remained until the complex's demolition just after the turn of the twenty-first century.

[151] Sea Kist Motel (5210 Ocean Avenue)
This motel, built by John Smyton in the late 1950s, has seen a series of neon signs over the years. Today the motel is embellished with a variety of plant life and an endearing 1980s neon sign, though an original blue neon "Office" arrow recently disappeared.

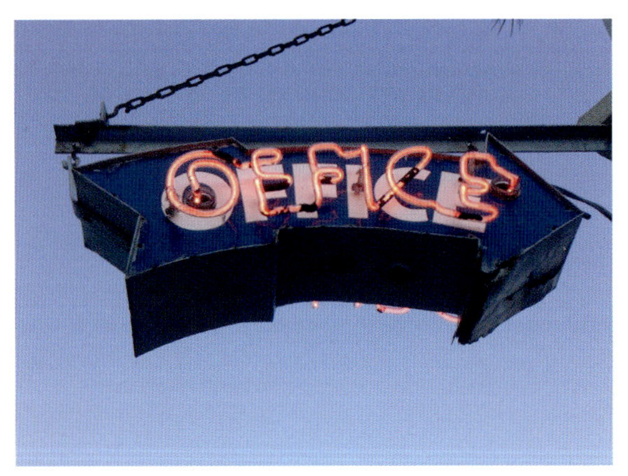

Several motels in the Wildwoods once had neon "office" arrows; this one at the Sea Kist Motel hung on until 2020.

[152] Jay's Motel (5210 Atlantic Avenue)
One of the Wildwoods' first motels (though not the first), Jay's opened in 1952. The Morey Brothers designed Jay's (named after its first owner, Josephine Juvino) like a motel court, with a bungalow situated in the center courtyard of an L-shaped unit of rooms. The motel, the house, and a free-standing neon sign on the street corner all were faced with pink stucco in the Florida tradition. Later owners expanded the motel, added a pool, and added elements to the neon sign (first a yellow arrow, then a metal orb outlined in chasing lights). In 1996, Sal Ferro bought the motel, then in a dilapidated condition, and revitalized it. Eight years later, though, he sold out to developers, who demolished it. Fred Musso salvaged a blue neon "Office" arrow, which now graces a private collection in Portland, Oregon.

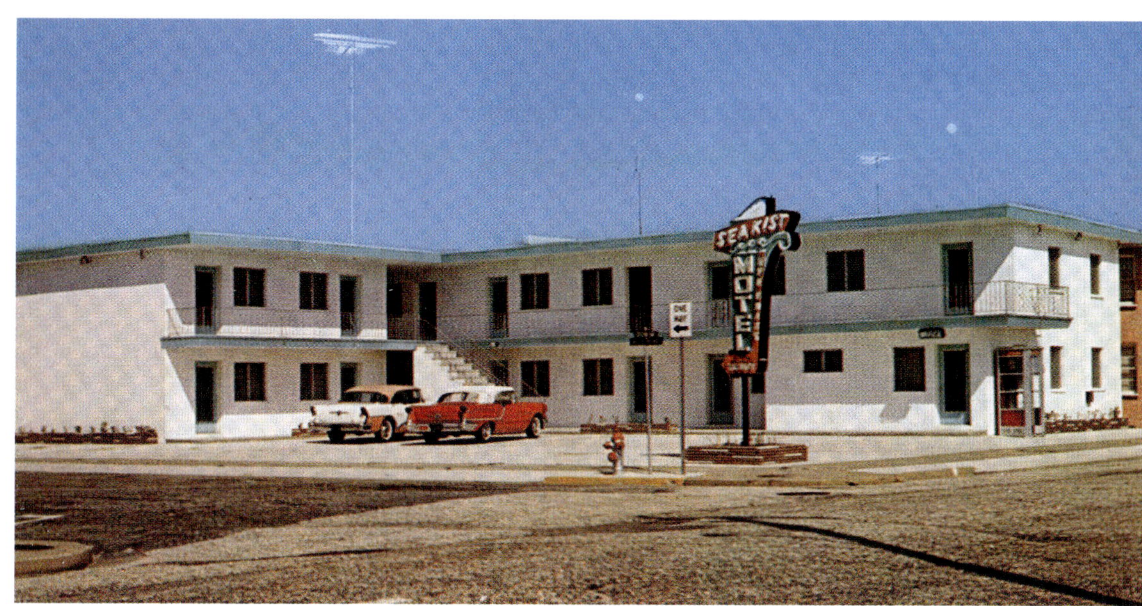

When first built, the Sea Kist Motel had no frills except for a rather extravagant neon sign with animated crashing waves. *Author's collection*

[153] Sea Gull Motel (5305 Atlantic Avenue)
Harry Marin built the Sea Gull Lodge in 1952 and expanded it four years later. This renovation gave the motel several notable modern characteristics, such as a huge pylon adorned with neon signage and a gull-wing office roof. In 1964 Marin sold to William and Betty Nichols, whose family has owned the motel since. "I remember what the color scheme was like when we first bought the motel," says Ginny Nichols, their daughter. "It was called chartreuse, and it was an intense yellow green."

In 1971, the Nichols family expanded the Sea Gull further. "The third story was my dad's idea," Ginny says. "The original office had a gull-wing roof—that was our living quarters for about eight years. It was two rooms—my brother and I had a room with bunk beds, and my parents had a sofa that folded out. What was strange about the original living quarters was that they had heating coils on the floor, so when it was cold, we used to lie on the floor and watch TV."

The renovation added a gull-wing roof atop the entire structure, rather than just the office, and a third story of units. Ginny wants to maintain original elements such as the motel's vintage bath tile. These original fixtures tend to baffle modern travelers, though: "I had someone call me the other day and say, 'I was looking on your website and there was a photo of a toilet that's green. That can't be right!' And I said, 'Oh yeah, we're midcentury modern. That's original!' And she said, 'No, thank you.'"

Also in 1971, the Nichols family bought the neighboring Midway Apartments on Cresse and Ocean Avenues. A new ABS "Sea Gull" neon sign, complete with animated arrows, now hangs on the original Midway Building. "When I was a kid, my parents always said, 'Should we run it for another year?'" Ginny says. "But then we blinked and thirty years went by."

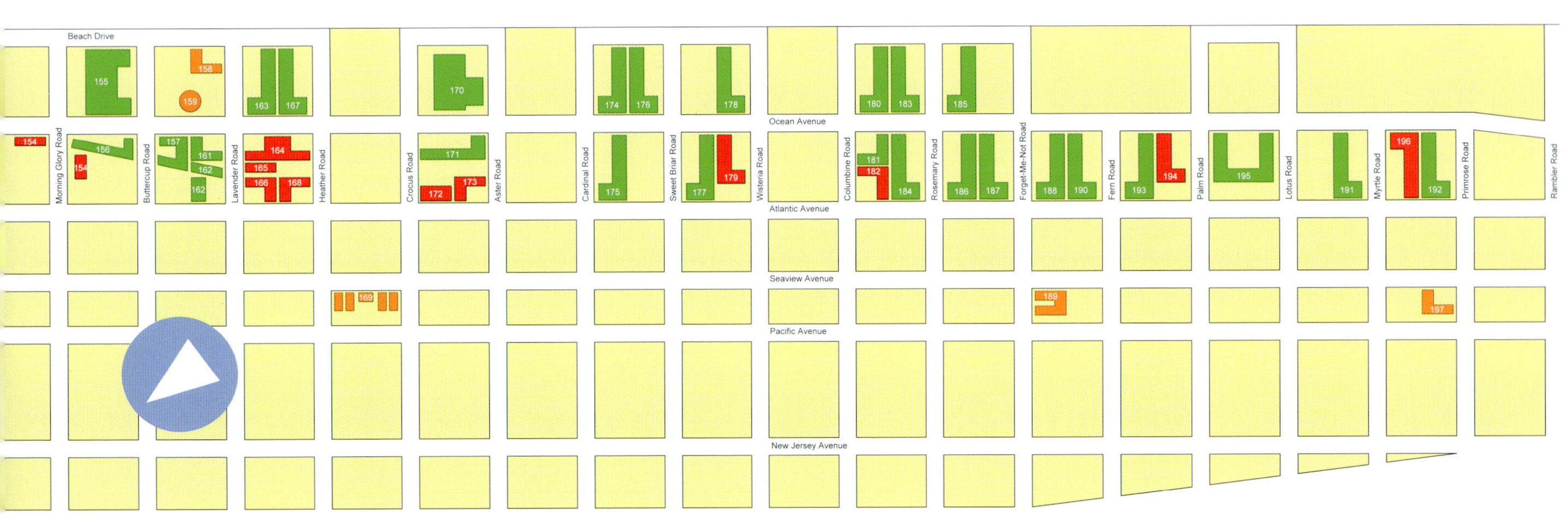

Wildwood Crest

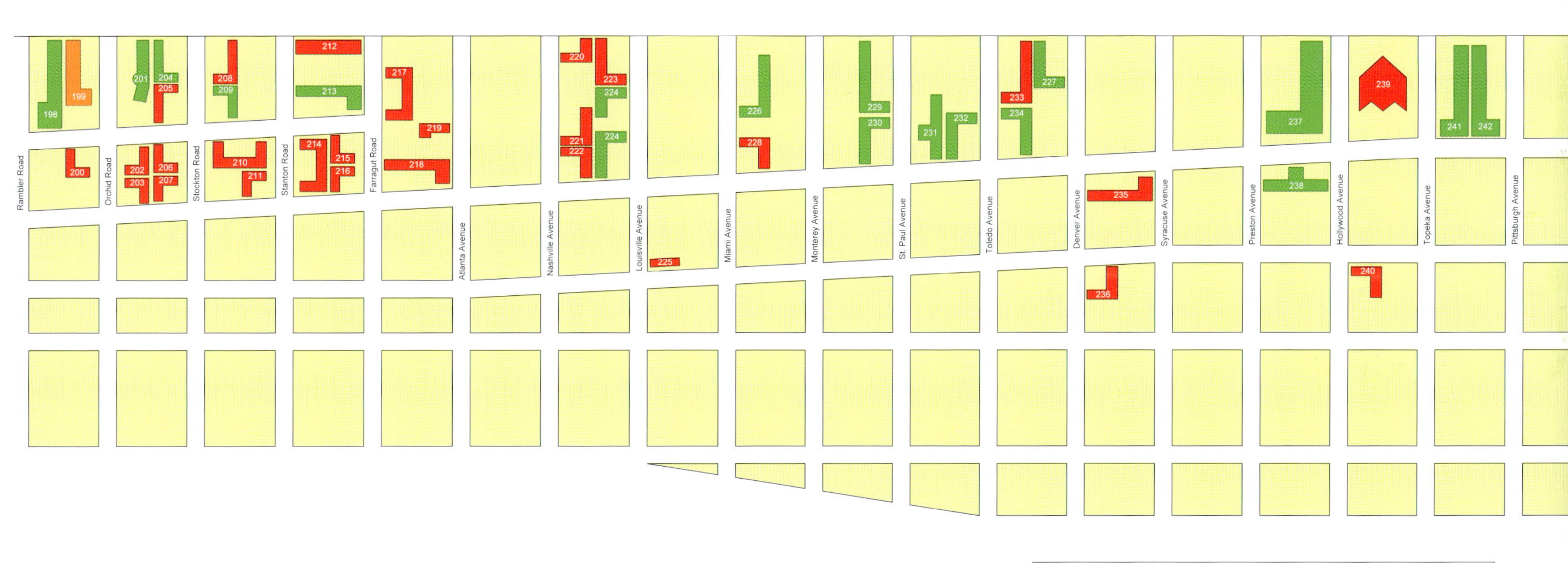

Buildings that have been demolished

Buildings that have been modified

Buildings that are standing and still used for their original purpose

BUILDING KEY (SEE MAP ON PREVIOUS SPREAD)

The southernmost borough on the island is quieter than the city of Wildwood. Unlike North Wildwood, which is today mostly residential, Wildwood Crest still has a thriving motel economy, including many with notable midcentury designs. The Crest, as it is colloquially known, has seen some innovative motels come and go through the decades. Unfortunately, the Crest was hit particularly hard by motel demolitions between 2002 and 2006, and now several once-vibrant motel strips have lost their cohesion.

[154] Siesta Resort (5410 Ocean Avenue)

John and Pearl Batts built the one-story Siesta Motel along Ocean Avenue in 1960 and commissioned a freestanding neon sign with a neon-outlined cactus. Despite several expansions over the years, the motel (and an annex around the corner on Morning Glory Road) succumbed to development in 2005.

[155] Aqua Beach Hotel (5501 Ocean Avenue)

Today's Aqua Beach, a high-rise motel, has elements from two sixties motels. The former Aqua, built by Joseph and Margaret DiAntonio in 1960 and expanded in 1963, forms the northern half (though minus its original stylish, freestanding neon sign and the diamond motif on its blank walls). The All Star, a 1962 construction by the Buckingham Brothers Builders, had a Florida-style carport and rooftop script neon sign and makes up the southern portion of today's Aqua Beach. The 1992 merger, which expanded the two motels and ironed out most midcentury flavor in the process, added a wall-hung neon sign, but that has since been replaced with a plastic one.

[156] Bel Air Motel (5510 Ocean Avenue)

Jean Lucas built the Bel Air, one of the Wildwoods' most recognizable motels, in 1956 on a trapezoidal lot (which, according to current owner Steve Reeser, was once divided by a bulkhead). Because of these site constraints, the motel was shaped like the number 7. The Bel Air had one story, an expansive parking lot, and an extravagant freestanding sign featuring neon lettering and a field of incandescent lights.

In 1967, new owners Edward and Lotte Brown added a pool and second floor to the motel and painted the motel aqua blue. The Browns outfitted the motel with louvered doors, scrapped its original neon sign, and commissioned from ABS a new rooftop sign with a wavy blue banner on a yellow base. "Since they added the second floor and the pool, the exterior has remained the same as it was," says Reeser, who bought the motel in 1996. "We're one of the few motels that still have louvered doors. I think those really add to the look. The louvers still move—when we get a cross-breeze, we open the louvers on the doors and the back windows and it creates a nice breeze."

In 2004, Reeser had KC Sign dismantle the motel's neon sign and bring it to Fred Musso, who built a new version. "It was galvanized sheet metal, and it was all rusted out," Reeser says. "It needed a total rebuild. I went for an exact replica with more plastic on it. This close to the shore, it's more durable than the metal." The original sign survives in a private collection; the new one still surmounts the motel today, lined with rope lights instead of neon tubing.

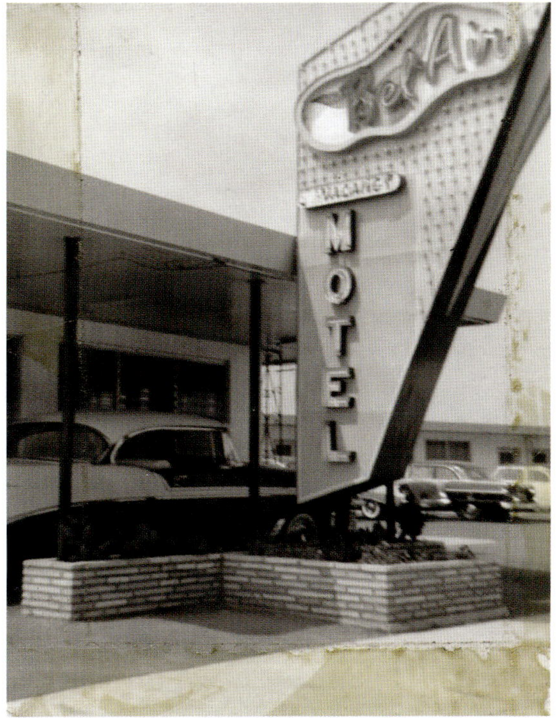

This 1956-vintage neon sign for the Bel Air Motel lasted until the motel was expanded in 1967. *Courtesy of Wildwood Historical Society*

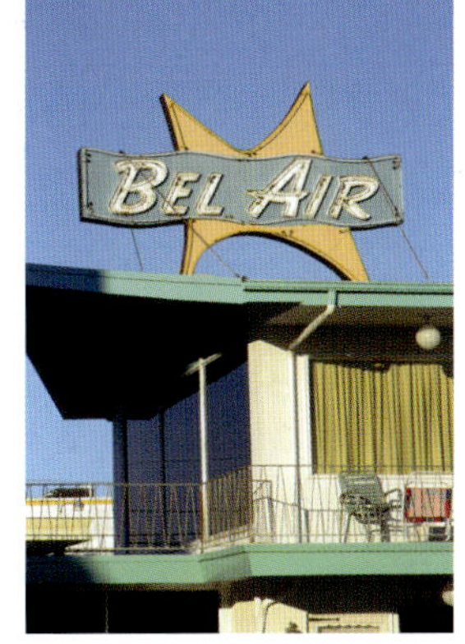

The Bel Air's 1967 neon sign gleams in the morning sunlight in a late 1990s photo. A few years later, this sign was replaced with a similar version manufactured from plastic. *Courtesy of Dorothy Kresz*

Reeser has maintained the motel's original fixtures over the years. "Everything is still original in the bathrooms. They used good materials back then—the tiles are still shiny. The first floor, there's about five different color combinations of tile. The second floor is a tan color, which I guess was more appropriate for the late sixties." He plans to stay put, despite the recent demolition craze. "I don't have any plans to leave. I will eventually, but I'll be here for a while!"

[157] Caribbean Motel (5600 Ocean Avenue)

In the fall of 1957, Dominick and Julia Rossi hired Lou Morey to build a motel at Buttercup and Ocean Avenues. Lou Morey took design inspiration from his trips to Miami. "Lou and Will Morey took their sketch pads when the season ended here," says the motel's current co-owner George Miller. "They would go down to Florida, to Miami, and they would see what was being built on Collins Avenue and Ocean Drive. And they would then come back and build their version. The Caribbean was one of their sketches."

Morey's design for the Caribbean was outlandish, even for the Wildwoods. The L-shaped motel, painted an eye-popping chartreuse, had a second-floor lounge encased in canted glass walls, accessed by a curved ramp, and topped by a sheet metal trellis and an Allied Signs–designed rooftop sign (not pictured in Morey's original drawings, but an integral part of the motel's appeal in retrospect) that spelled out a script "Caribbean" in chasing incandescent lights, and "TV POOL" in neon beneath. "They had to get a special variance from Wildwood Crest to allow that sign," says Miller. "That's such a classic piece of neon."

Astroturf paved the motel's balconies and surrounded a C-shaped pool in the center of the courtyard, and plastic palms decorated the entire property. While the motel was extravagant, budget problems forced Morey to abandon an additional wing of rooms (these were added in 1960). The motel was barely completed in time for summer vacationers to arrive; Morey and the Rossis announced the motel's opening with a public reception on June 6, 1958.

The motel met success, if not (immediately) the acclaim its design merited. The Rossis owned the motel until the 1980s and made few changes to the motel's structure along the way. In 1970, Allied installed a new neon sign that substituted the original chasing lights with turquoise neon installed inside red-painted channel letters. By the late 1990s, though, the Caribbean had deteriorated. In 2004, Carolyn Emigh and her business (and life) partner George Miller decided to branch out from their business in Washington, DC, and rental properties in other shore towns and buy a motel in the Wildwoods. They settled on the Caribbean (which they bought for a hefty price in the middle of the Wildwoods' condo boom) but were alarmed at its condition: "It needed so much work," Emigh exclaims. "It was about twenty years of deferred maintenance. The rooms were really gross." However, they set to work renovating the motel as a twenty-first-century vision of the 1950s. "Our vision was a boutique motel."

Miller and Emigh hired New York City designer Darleen Lev to design new carpets and curtains in a midcentury style. Then, in 2008, shortly after renovating the rooms, they hired Philadelphia neon sign designer Len Davidson to design a new neon sign for the motel's office. In a sign of the times, the new sign mentions the motel's free Wi-Fi.

The Caribbean Motel's current neon sign was installed in 1970 by Allied.

OPPOSITE PAGE: This brochure for the Caribbean Motel was published in 1958, the year the motel opened. Note the scaffolding under the motel's signature circular ramp, which was not yet finished. *Courtesy of Wildwood Historical Society*

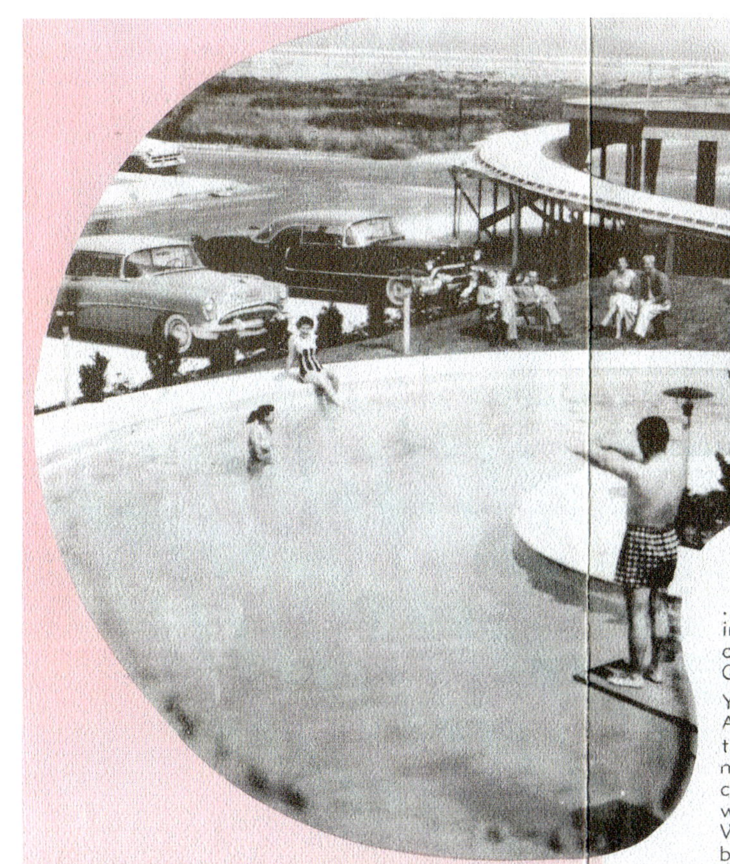
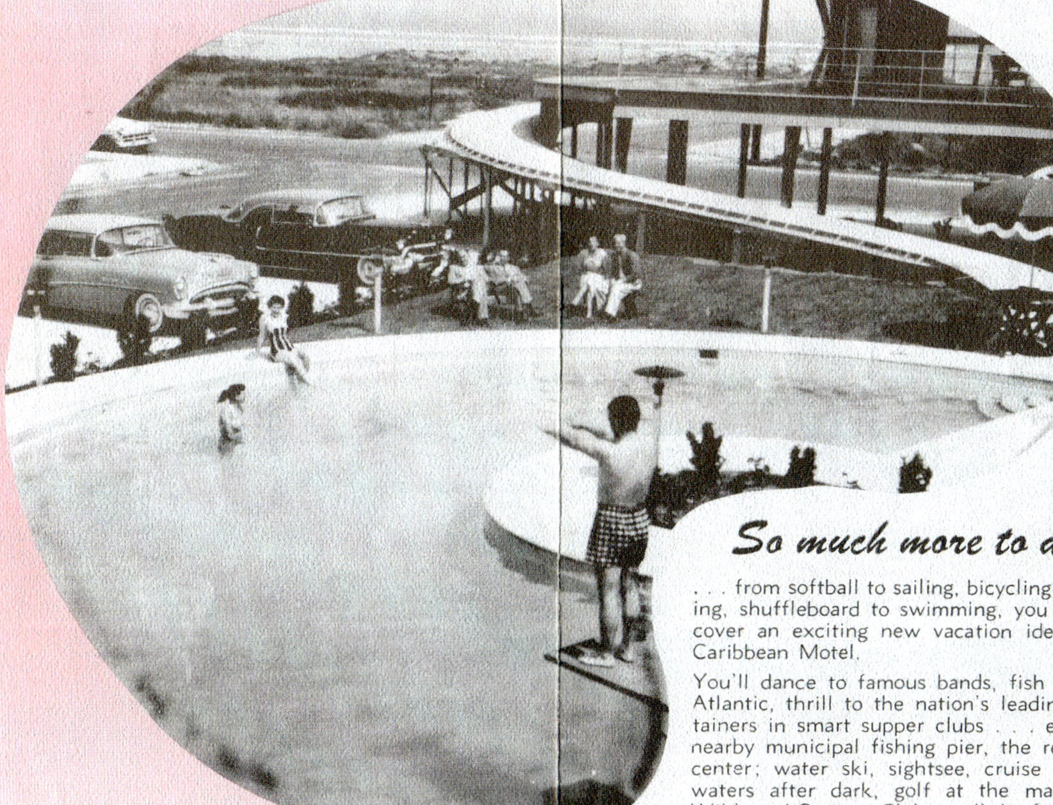

So much more to do!

. . . from softball to sailing, bicycling to bowling, shuffleboard to swimming, you will discover an exciting new vacation idea at the Caribbean Motel.

You'll dance to famous bands, fish the blue Atlantic, thrill to the nation's leading entertainers in smart supper clubs . . . enjoy the nearby municipal fishing pier, the recreation center; water ski, sightsee, cruise romantic waters after dark, golf at the magnificent Wildwood Country Club, stroll the fun packed boardwalk, and just relax in pure luxury at Wildwood's most exciting resort motel.

Ocean Front

From the luxury of your air-conditioned room to the spacious lounge overlooking the Atlantic to the big, beautiful Caribbean pool to the beckoning beachfront there is a complete schedule of resort activities to thrill and please you every moment of your stay.

Phone or write for your reservations, today.

MR. and MRS. DOM. ROSSI
Owners-Managers

OCEAN AVE. AT BUTTERCUP ROAD
WILDWOOD, N. J.

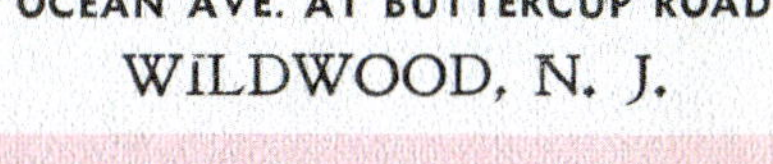
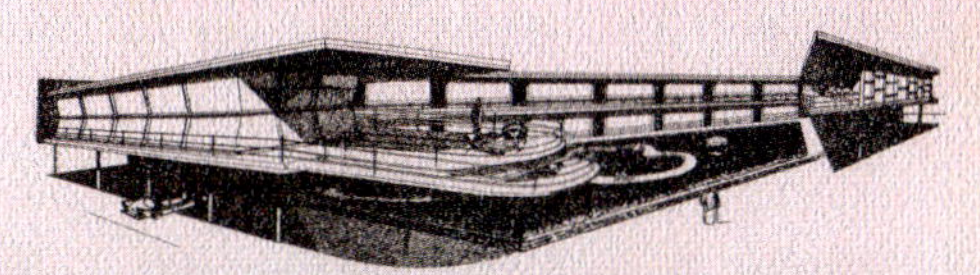

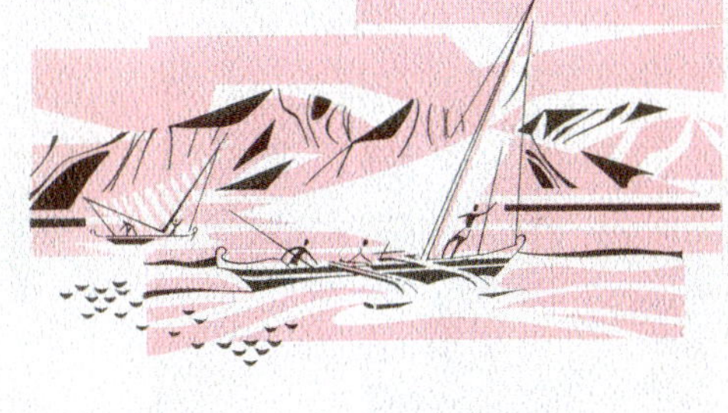

Caribbean motel

OCEAN AVE. AT BUTTERCUP RD.
WILDWOOD, N. J.
Phone 2-8292

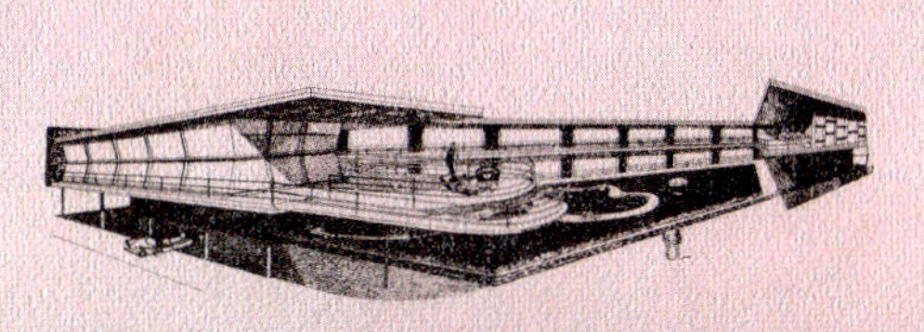

Miller and Emigh tried unsuccessfully to drum up support from their neighbors for a Doo Wop historic district, but they found willing allies in the New Jersey State Historic Preservation Office. Miller remembers, "New Jersey was going to try to keep this from being torn down. And as soon as we told *The Ledger* that our intention was to operate this as a motel into the future, New Jersey got wind of this and put us on the historical register. They then helped us qualify for the secretary of the interior's register."

In 2005, the Caribbean Motel joined the National Register of Historic Places, the second Wildwoods motel (after the Chateau Bleu) to do so. Miller and Emigh also listed the Caribbean in the Historic Hotels of America database, which gives members discounts to listed historic hotels throughout the country. The Caribbean was the first motel on the list, and this listing has helped business. "We usually get customers from referrals, the HHA website," Emigh says. "Some people say, 'We were [in town] last summer, and we were walking by and we saw everybody here seems so happy, having fun!'"

Miller and Emigh have preserved the original look of the Caribbean and plan to keep going. "Between our exterior and room renovations, we're constantly working," Emigh says. "But it's just so pricey." In 2013, they spent $80,000 repairing the motel's HVAC systems. "You can't even see that! If we put $80,000 into the exterior, it would be like the Gardens of Babylon or something."

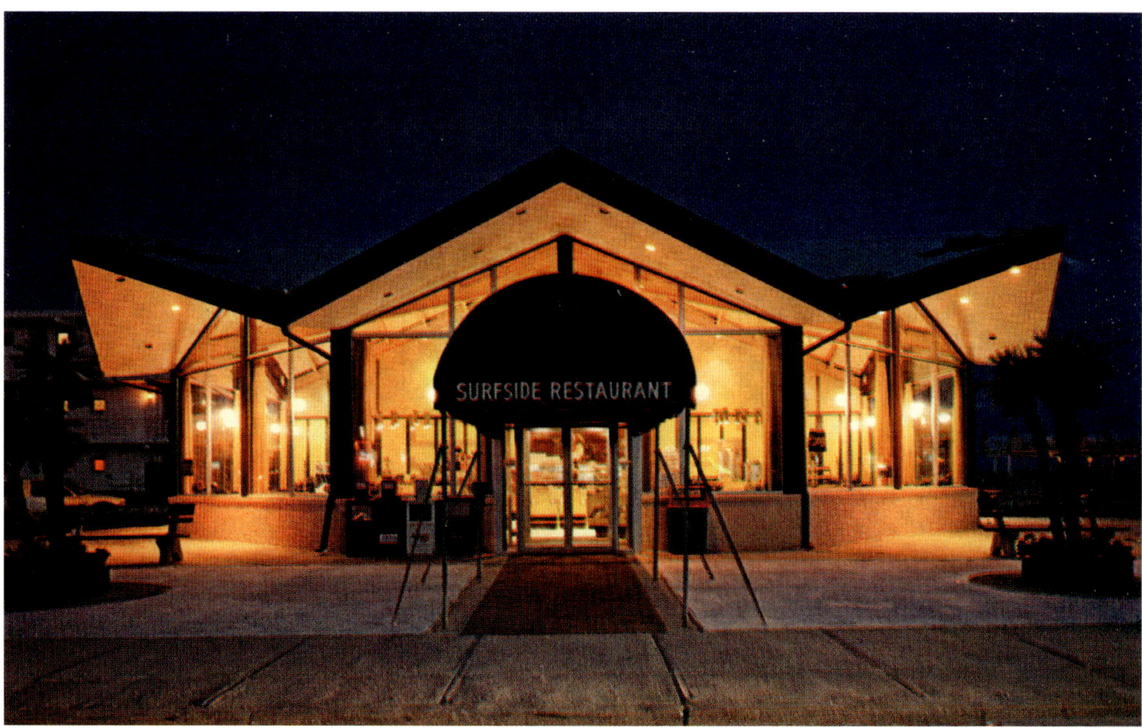

A classic 1991 postcard view of the Surfside, taken by Doug Hunsberger, shows the restaurant's distinctive angular roofline. *Author's collection*

They remain delighted with their slice of fifties escapism. "I'm happy when I can drive by and see 'no' [lit up] above the 'vacancy,'" says Miller. "I'm an innkeeper!"

[158] Flagship Beach Motel (Lavender Road and Beach)

Will Morey built the Flagship Beach in 1962 on an empty beachfront lot. The Flagship Beach had sawtooth balconies that resembled waves ebbing and flowing, which would be widely imitated around the island in the ensuing decade. In 1995, Jim Ranalli, the owner of the Water's Edge Motel next door, merged the two motels, expanding the Flagship Beach and lopping off its zigzag balconies in the process.

[159] Surfside Restaurant (5611 Ocean Avenue)

[159] Doo Wop Experience (4500 Ocean Avenue)

[160] Surfside West Diner (5308 New Jersey Avenue)

Thomas (known to all as Tomi) John and his family arrived in the United States from Macedonia, Greece, on July 4, 1940. His family made a beeline for the Wildwoods, and in the 1950s Tomi entered

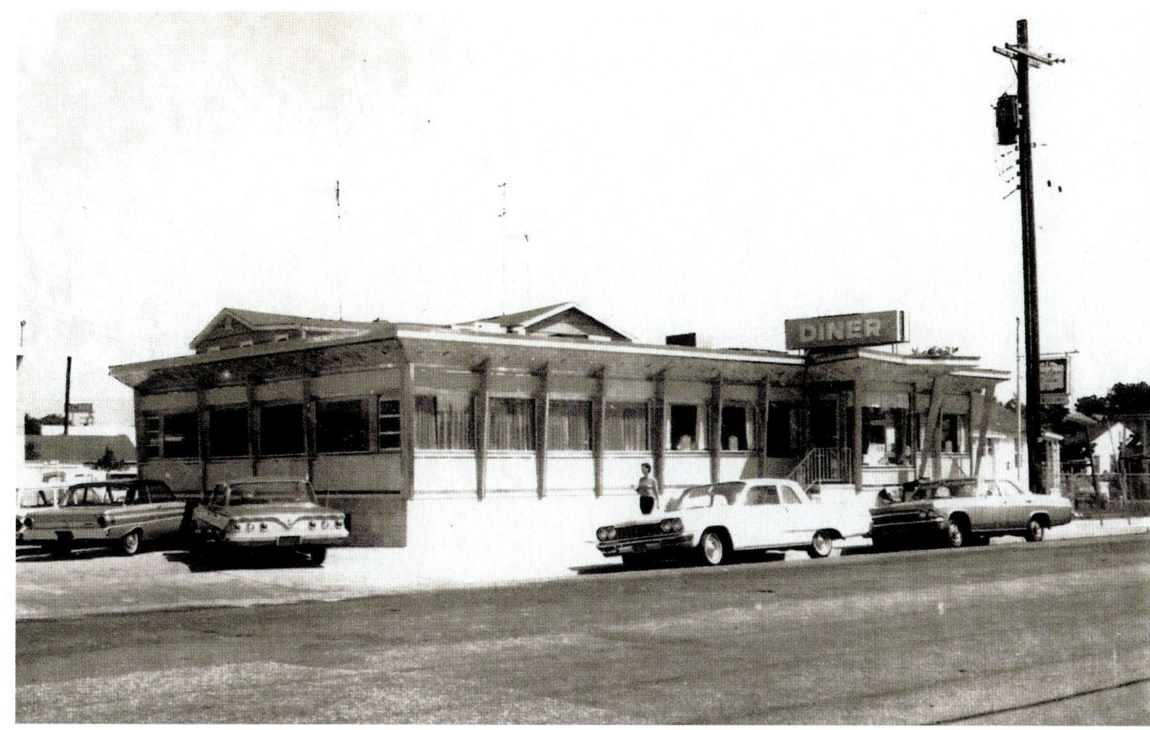

The Crestwood Diner shortly after it opened. Today, Michael John operates this diner as the Surfside West. *Courtesy of Wildwood Historical Society*

the food service business, first by selling pretzels on the boardwalk. Then he opened a restaurant, Tomi John's, which was successful enough to move into a storefront in the flashy Shore Theater late in the decade.

In 1962, John decided to open a location in Wildwood Crest. "He wanted to build a diner there, but my understanding is [that Wildwood Crest] had ordinances against diners," his son, Michael John, remembers. "So he got together with a group of people he knew from Tomi John's, and they built that on that piece of property."

The Surfside Restaurant, John's new venture, opened on July 4, 1963, and created a sensation. Its round, angular roofline had a distinctive profile, and its large plate glass windows and roof-mounted spotlights allowed light to spill out into the neighborhood at night. Inside, exposed beams and an angular ceiling created a unique, cavernous dining space. "At the Surfside, waiting tables was probably the only thing I didn't do," Michael says. "I was a busboy, I washed dishes, I worked the beach grill, and pretty early on I got involved in cooking. The Surfside was open at six, and at that point it had a Beach Grill that was open until five or six for breakfast, lunch, and dinner. And we had ice cream that we did until midnight." With several other restaurants on the island, the John family was busy in the 1960s.

In 1994, Tomi bought out his partners in the Surfside. Seventeen days later, on July 4 (a date that carries a persistent significance in the John family), he suffered a fatal heart attack. His son, Michael, kept running the restaurant, but "then it just got too big, and my heart wasn't in it." In 2002, Michael sold the Surfside to Jim Ranalli, owner of the high-rise Water's Edge Motel next door, who had gobbled up the Flagship Beach Motel in 1995. Ranalli was now eyeing the Surfside's lot and planned to tear it down to build an addition to the Water's Edge.

Jack Morey, one of Doo Wop architecture's chief advocates, argued with Ranalli about the proposed demolition. "I first tried to convince the hotel owner, Jim Ranalli, to turn it into his lobby. I gave him all these suggestions, and he didn't take any of them. So I said, 'Can you do me a favor—can you give the building to us?'" After protracted negotiations, Ranalli allowed Morey and the Doo Wop Preservation League to fundraise the money necessary to dismantle, rather than demolish, the Surfside so that it could later be reassembled for an as-yet-undetermined purpose. The fundraising effort resonated with Wildwoods residents, and, inspired by their donations, the prominent Byrne family contributed a large sum of money. The Surfside, unlike several other buildings on the island of a similar vintage, had been constructed with steel beams, allowing it to be easily disassembled. "It was coming down and it was sort of movable," says Morey. "And it was steel. If it was wood, we wouldn't have been able to do that."

Crews started dismantling the Surfside on October 15, 2002; the quick turnaround meant that some key relics had to be left behind. "It's a shame they didn't save the booths and everything," says Michael John. "We had really neat chandeliers in there. But they only had a few days to go in there and get what they needed."

After kicking around several ideas for how to use the building, the Doo Wop Preservation League finally reassembled it in 2007 in downtown Wildwood's Fox Park, where it serves as a visitors' center, Doo Wop Experience, and band shell. The Surfside's preservation exemplifies the impact that citizens can have on historic architecture, and it is a success story of the Doo Wop Preservation League.

Meanwhile, Michael John, feeling restless after selling his restaurant, had bought the Crestwood Diner on New Jersey Avenue and renamed it the Surfside West. Manufactured by Superior Dining Car Company in 1963, the Crestwood, originally a jet-age relic with flared eaves, had been updated in the 1980s with a mansard roof and wood paneling. "[The Surfside West] is a smaller place to operate, and a lot easier to take care of," says John. "[The original Surfside] was 152 seats, and this is 105." The move allowed him to keep serving longtime customers. "Some of these people have been coming to me for a long time. I'll be here for a while. I'm not going anywhere."

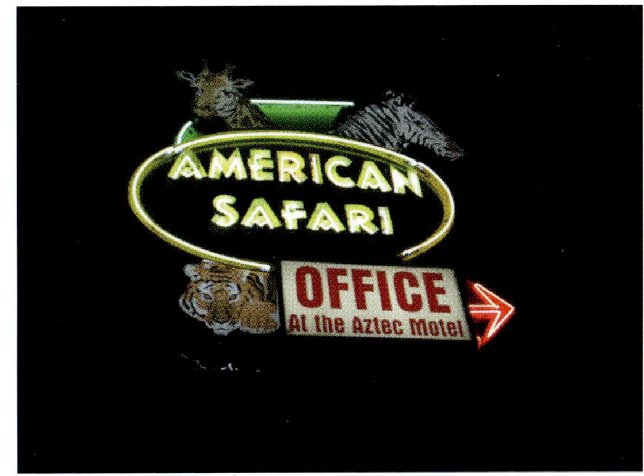

ABS Signs designed this plastic-and-neon sign for the American Safari Motel in 2006.

[161] American Safari Motel (5610 Ocean Avenue)

[162] Aztec Motel (411 East Lavender Road and 5607 Atlantic Avenue)

These two motels began as three: Alf and Grace Davis built the Coral Sands in 1956 on what was then an oceanfront lot, painted it pink, and installed dark-wood railings and a freestanding, candy-striped neon sign. A year later, the Aztec Motel opened next door, with an old western theme and a neon sign with Playbill letters. The Aztec underwent a series of expansions and changes of décor and signage until the 1990s, when its owners bought the Coral Sands and annexed it with the addition of a rooftop neon "Aztec" sign. In 1999, the Aztec received one of the last neon signs built by Allied Signs, though this freestanding sign was replaced with a plastic one in 2017.

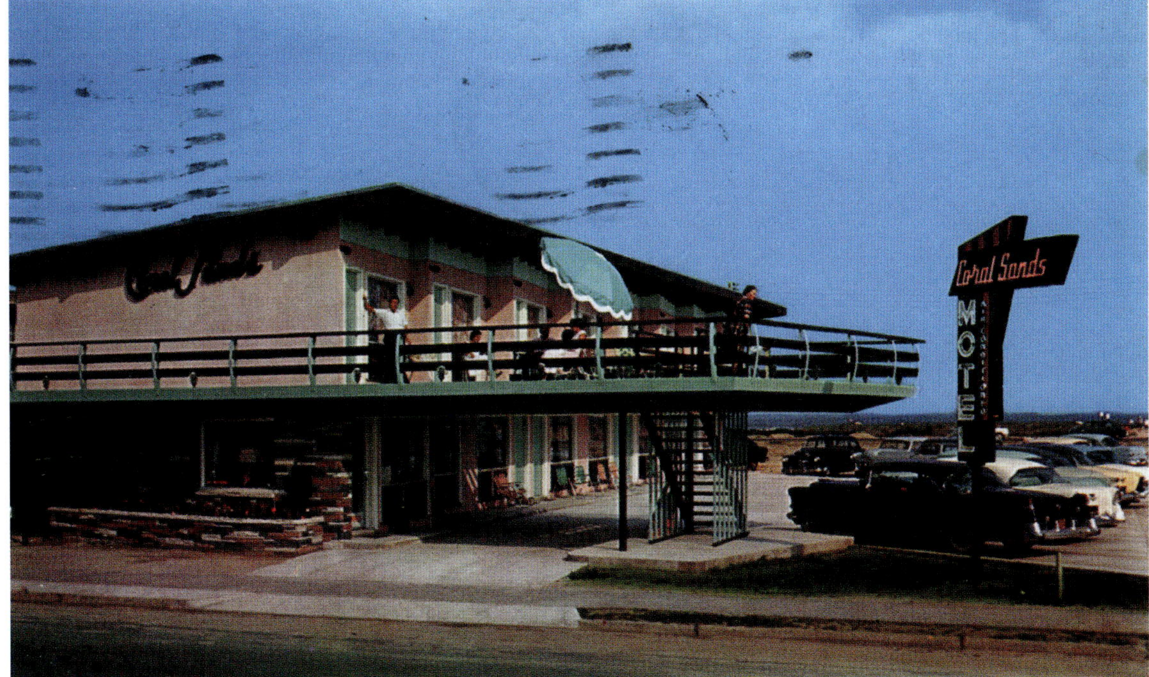

When the Coral Sands Motel opened in 1956, it had an oceanfront location. Today the building is situated two blocks inland and has become part of the Aztec Motel. *Author's collection*

The Aztec Motel has had several signs throughout its history. This plastic one, shown in 1986, lasted until the 1990s. *Courtesy of Ed Steinerts*

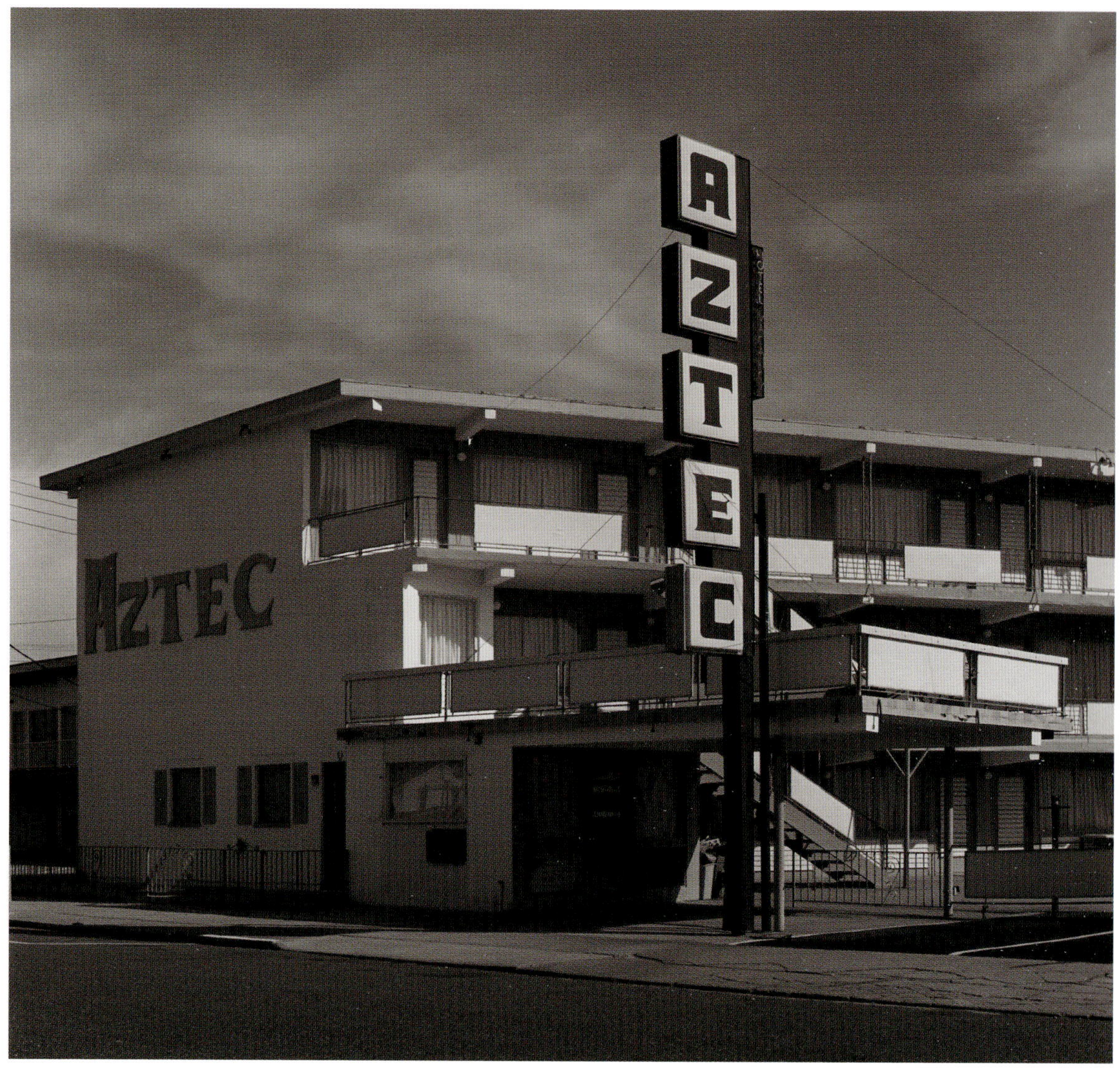

In 1960, meanwhile, William and Dorothy Miller built the two-story, L-shaped Safari Motel and installed a neon sign on the street corner. Today, the American Safari (as it was renamed in the 1990s) remains in place, complete with a distinctive 2006-vintage ABS neon and plastic sign. The American Safari and Aztec Motels (and their neighbor the Gondolier) operate in tandem and proudly wear their midcentury heritage.

[163] Gondolier Oceanfront Motel (5701 Ocean Avenue)

The Guzzone family built the Gondolier Motel in 1965. The jet-age-style motel with curvy railings did not look much like Venice, as its name suggested (a series of Italianate arches on a blank wall that were shown on an architectural rendering did not make the final design), but a rooftop neon sign, which survives today (several expansions later), gives the motel plenty of vintage flavor.

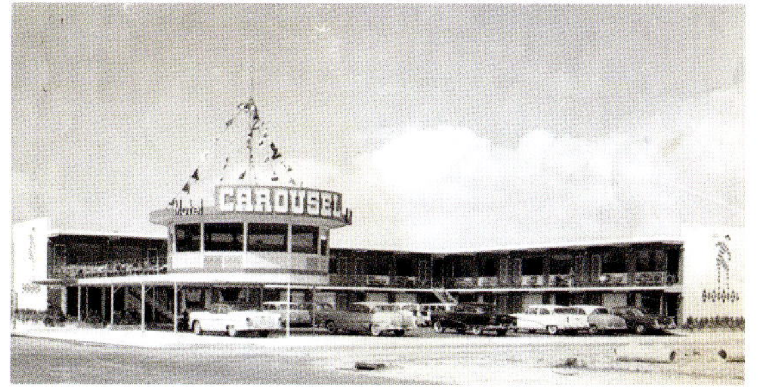

This photo of the Carousel Motel was taken in 1956, the motel's first season. In the coming decade, owners Earl and Ralph Johnson would expand the motel significantly. *Courtesy of Wildwood Historical Society*

[164] Carousel Motel (5700 Ocean Avenue)

[165] Avanti Motel (406 East Lavender Road)

Ralph and Earl Johnson built the vibrant Carousel and the more prosaic Vogue Motel in 1956 on an empty lot in the sand dunes of Wildwood Crest. The Carousel was an L-shaped motel with two stories; in the center of its parking lot was a second-floor circular lounge, perched on piles, encased in glass, and topped with a neon "Motel" sign. Photos from the motel's first season show the parking lot full of cars and the circular lounge bedecked with circus-like flags. The next year, the Johnsons expanded the Carousel with another L-shaped wing, a coffee shop, a pool, and a lounge with a cantilevered roof like that of the Fantasy Motel. In 1965 the Johnsons elicited good press by allowing Sammy Davis Jr. to stay at the Carousel after hotels and motels in downtown Wildwood had rejected him for the color of his skin.

At the end of the 1960s, the Johnsons decided to scrap both lounges and splurge on a new office, located at the base of the motel's T-shaped floor plan, along Ocean Avenue. With brightly colored railings and a striped awning over the office door, the newly expanded motel exuded pop art luxury. In the late 1990s, ABS installed a colorful wall-hung neon sign. After the Carousel was demolished in 2005, this sign briefly sat in the parking lot of the New Carousel (formerly Hialeah) Motel a few blocks south but was never installed. The former Vogue, later renamed the Avanti Motel (and stripped of a sixties-vintage "Vogue" neon sign), was demolished at the same time.

This postcard image shows the Markay Motel shortly after opening. Note the satellite tower, outfitted with neon lettering. *Author's collection*

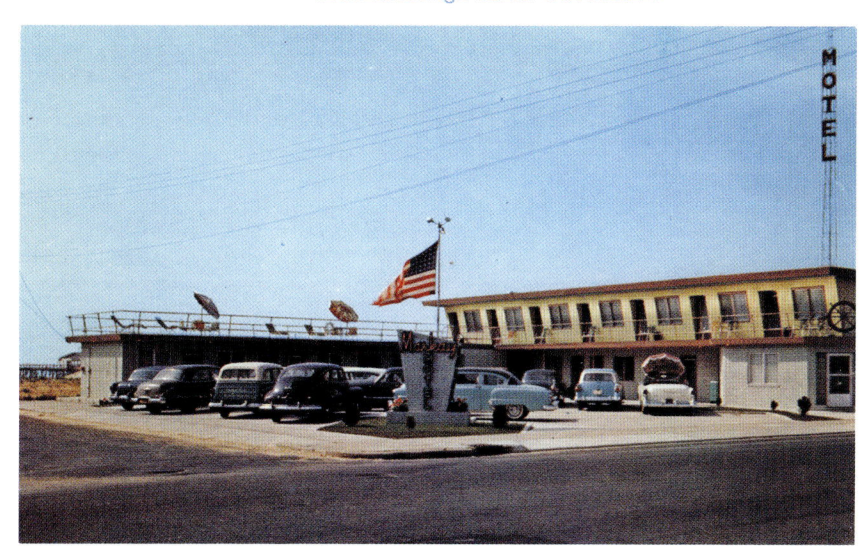

[166] Island Time Motel (5701 Atlantic Avenue)

Ernest and Anna Schoellner hired Lou Morey to build the Markay Motel in 1956, at the same time as the Ebb Tide next door. It began life nearly identical to the Ebb Tide, with a yellow color scheme and leaning walls, but evolved differently from its more famous neighbor over the years. A freestanding neon sign included a life preserver, establishing a nautical theme also visible in ship's-wheel decorations on the motel's railings. Around 1957, new owners added a pool and a new neon sign, and a decade later, a lounge with a peaked roof. The Markay survived in this state until 2001, when a new owner renamed it the Island Time and commissioned a rooftop neon sign from ABS. The Island Time did not last long: developers bought the motel in 2003 and knocked it down.

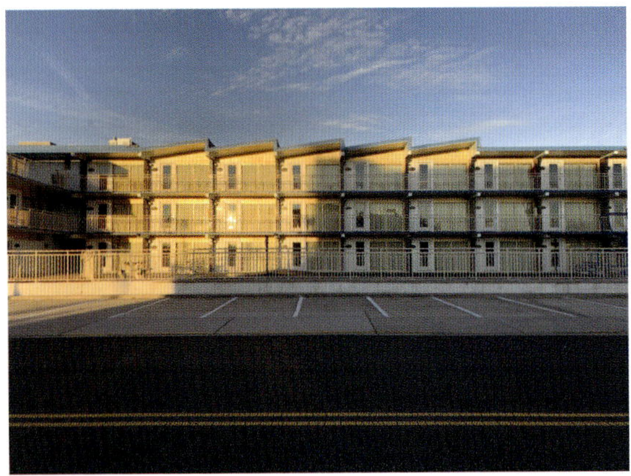

The Attaché Motel still sports its original stepped roofline.

[167] Attaché Oceanfront Resort (5711 Ocean Avenue)

Though its name would seem to court traveling businesspeople, the Attaché's oceanfront location makes it a family-oriented motel. Roman Weiser, who had built the Astronaut Motel three years earlier, built the Attaché for the 1965 season, situating it on what had been an informal beach parking lot. The motel featured modern details such as black brick dividers between the rooms, a rooftop neon sign (featuring the motel's name surrounded by a star-studded amoeba, a logo that inspired the motel's letterhead for its first few years), blue louvered doors, and a terraced roofline, with five asymmetrical steps adding visual interest. Today, it remains in good shape, minus the original neon sign, but with a 1980s-vintage neon-rimmed clock surrounded by art deco accents.

[168] Ebb Tide Motel (5711 Atlantic Avenue)

Al Beers and Harry Stokes hired Lou Morey to build an L-shaped motel a block away from the beach in 1956. Because of budget constrictions, they arranged for construction to happen in stages over the next few years. At first one and a half stories, then two, then three, the motel gradually evolved into a Wildwood Crest landmark.

Painted bright yellow, the Ebb Tide's first-story cinder-block walls sloped inward, and its second- and third-floor wood-framed walls sloped outward, creating a precarious appearance. A curvy freestanding neon sign, installed by Ace in 1957 (and photographed for a postcard before Morey

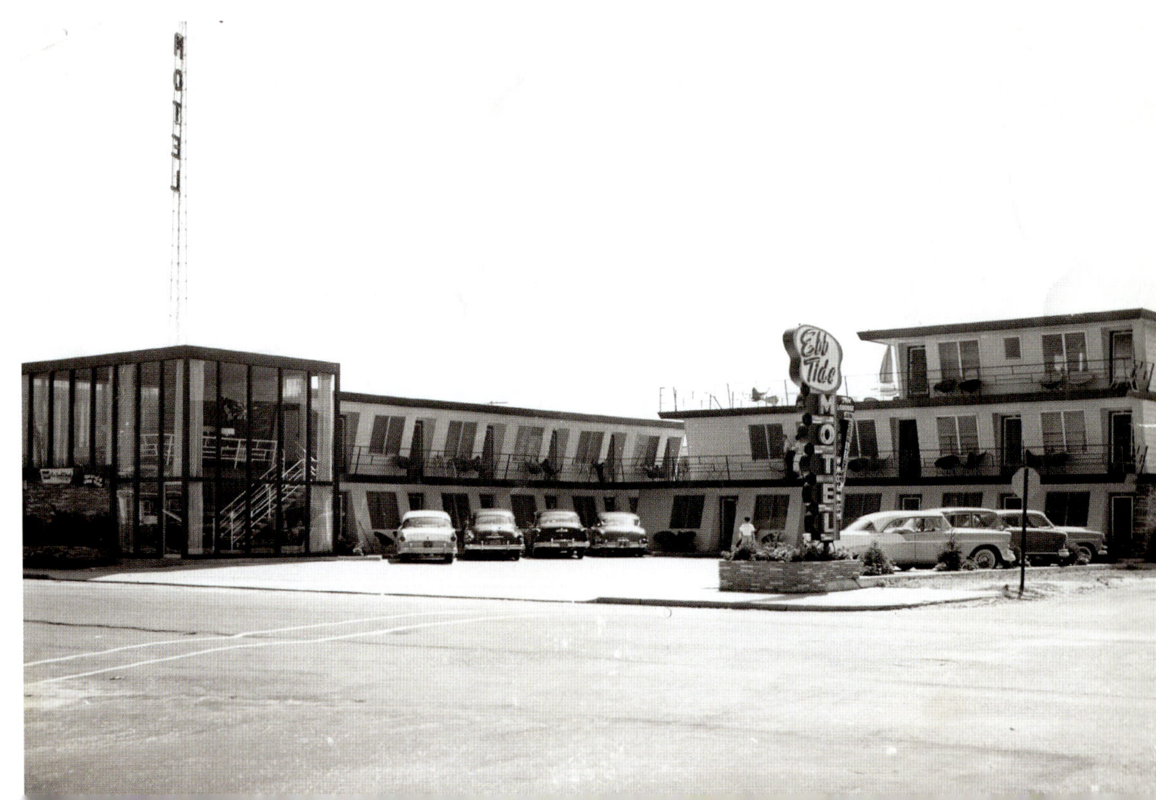

Note the leaning walls, then considered a novelty, and the Ace-built neon sign in this late fifties shot of the Ebb Tide. *Courtesy of Wildwood Historical Society*

had finished landscaping a small garden around it), beckoned to travelers on Atlantic Avenue. A 1958-vintage, glass-enclosed office cubicle gave the motel an additional modern twist, its orthogonal form contrasting with the motel's tilted walls.

While postcards touted "Wildwood's most modern, triple-deck oceanfront motel," the Ebb Tide, which lacked a pool, lagged behind other motels in the neighborhood. The freestanding neon sign, which took up valuable parking lot space, was replaced around 1970 with a new wall-mounted one with a yellow flashing arrow. In December 2003, the motel was torn down to build condominiums, but not before Fred Musso had saved its second-generation sign, which survives in a private collection.

[169] Lantern Lane Cottage Colony (5800 Seaview Avenue)

Constructed around 1945, the Lantern Lane Cottage Colony typified the Wildwoods' postwar motel court architecture, with four lengthy buildings facing each other over grass courtyards. A central office building, facing Seaview Avenue, had unique glass block corners, a stainless-steel porch overhang, and a neon marquee, combining the commercial with highbrow art deco. The complex survives today as condominiums, missing only its neon sign.

[170] Pan American Hotel (400 East Crocus Road)

In 1963 Will Morey bought a beachfront block between Crocus and Heather Roads to use for a new project he was planning. The Pan American, unlike most of the island's motels, did not feature common balconies but, rather, revived the vintage concept of the hotel. A large lobby and on-site restaurant offered classic hotel luxuries, running counter to the Wildwoods' new motel-centric beachfront lodging culture, which saw hotels as regressive. While Morey initially shunned the word "hotel," branding the Pan American as a motor inn for its first couple of decades, he need not have worried; the Pan American was thoroughly midcentury modern.

Morey surrounded the Pan American's exterior balconies with alternating metal railings and cream-colored concrete panels and started the show on the sidewalk with a semicircular carport, topped by a neon sign. Inspired by the escalating space age, Morey installed a rotating plastic sphere on top of the motel's elevator tower, printed with the letters "PA." This sign created such a sensation in the neighborhood that the Wildwood Crest Planning Board banned rotating

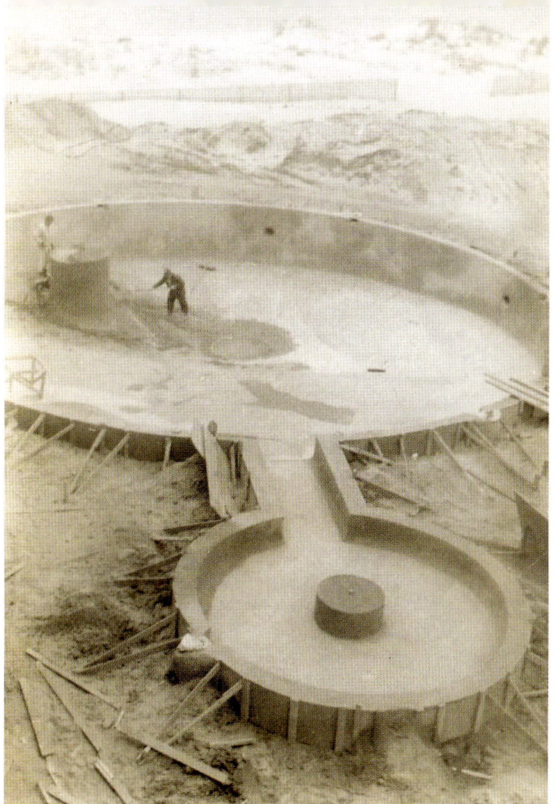

Building the unique circular pools at the Pan American Motor Inn. *Courtesy of Morey Family Archives*

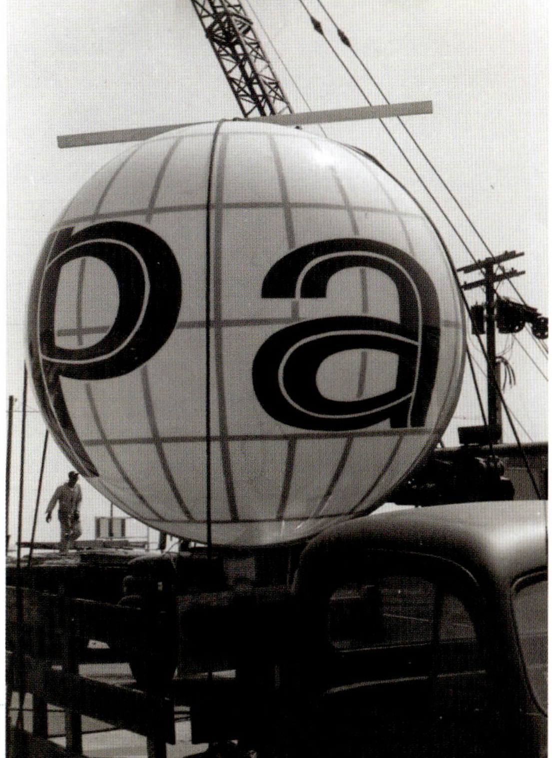

In this 1964 photo, the Pan American Motor Inn's distinctive Sputnik-shaped sign arrives on a flatbed truck. *Courtesy of Morey Family Archives*

A newer replica of the Pan American's sign still sits proudly atop the hotel today.

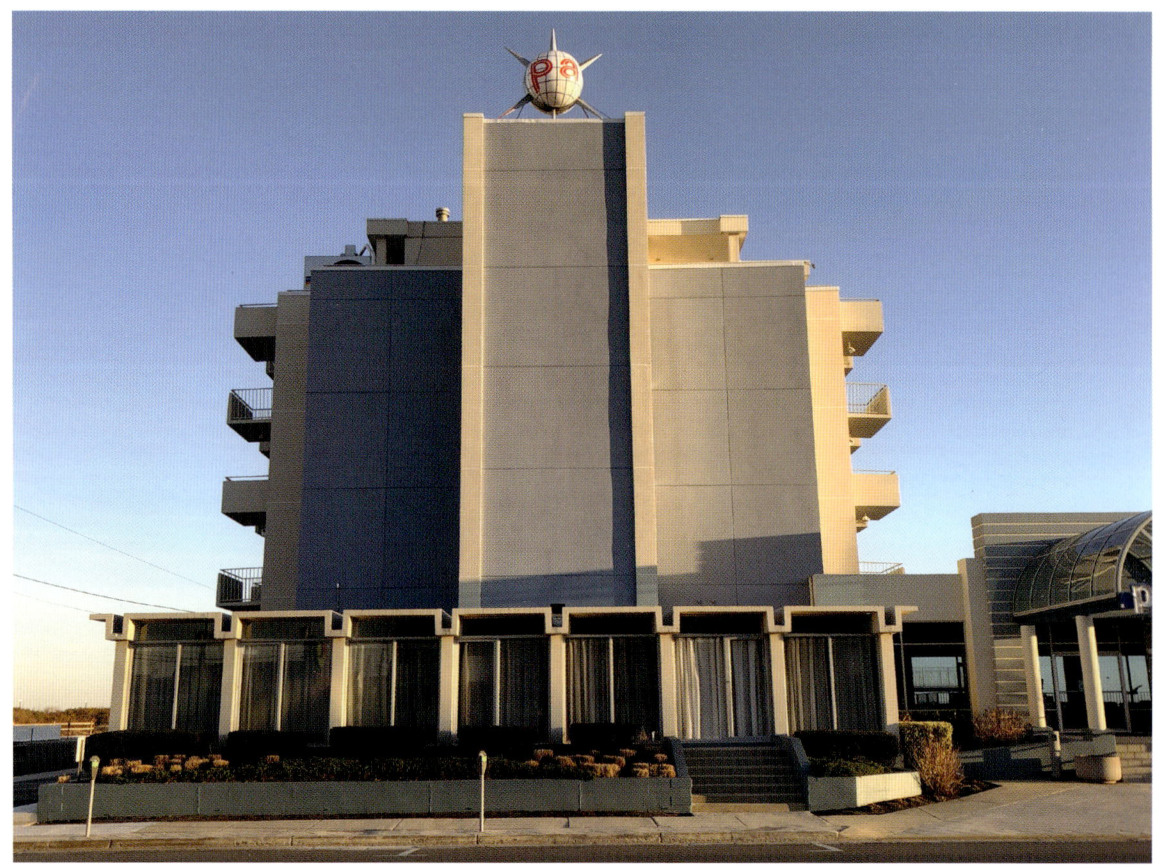

signs two years later. The gambit worked, though: while the Moreys had previously been scrimping and saving, the success of the Pan American allowed Will to take some time off and vacation in Florida. "That was the first building that gave them some financial security," says Will's son Jack. "That one was the one where they sustained their nose above water, even though my mother would throw up every day [in the months before it opened] because she was afraid she couldn't pay the bills. Absolutely true story!"

"This was the first hotel that appeared on the east side of Ocean Avenue," says current manager Jim Kelly, who has worked at the hotel since 1983. "Because of delays at the time, the original hotel opened in 1964 with three stories. The elevator tower was built to sustain a fourth floor. And that floor did happen two years later." Additions in the 1970s and 1980s included a larger restaurant and a penthouse suite. "This hotel was built in 1964, so we're over the fifty-year mark," says Kelly. "But if you look around, it looks like it was built a couple years ago. Once again, we want to keep everything fresh and new."

Kelly thinks the era of Doo Wop enthusiasm has passed, but wants to maintain a modern version of a sixties-vintage experience at the Pan American. Thanks to continued renovations (including a recent overhaul of the hotel's penthouse suite that was featured in *New York Lifestyles* magazine), the Pan American shows its age well. "As long as the Moreys are going to continue running the piers and the hotels, I feel that they'll always keep investing back into this property," Kelly says. "As for me, I'll be here for a few more years!"

[171] Park Lane Resort (5900 Ocean Avenue)

John and Anna Poksay built the Park Lane in 1963 in the then nearly empty beachfront blocks of Wildwood Crest. The three-story motel borrowed the sawtooth balconies Will Morey had used the year before on his Flagship Beach Motel, and a blue freestanding neon sign drew drivers' attention. The Park Lane still stands, and recent owners have taken the motel upscale, adding glass railings, faux brick corners, and a green "PL" logo in place of the original neon sign.

[172] Hudson's Restaurant and Ice Cream Parlor (5901 Atlantic Avenue)

In 1956, Wilbert Schumann hired Will Morey to build a restaurant on the corner of Atlantic and Crocus Avenues, across the street from the Crest Pier. While several motels, restaurants, and

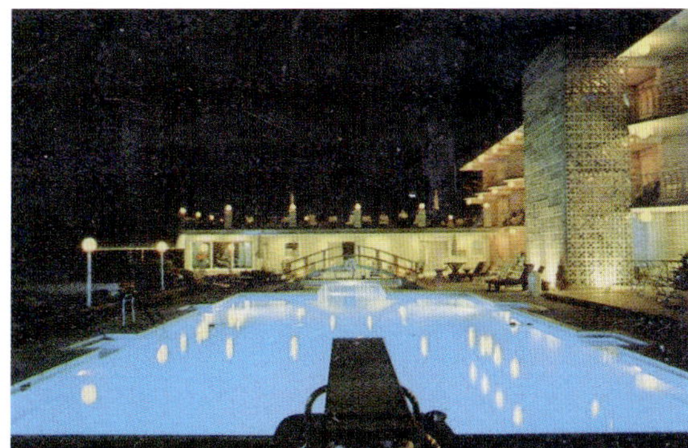

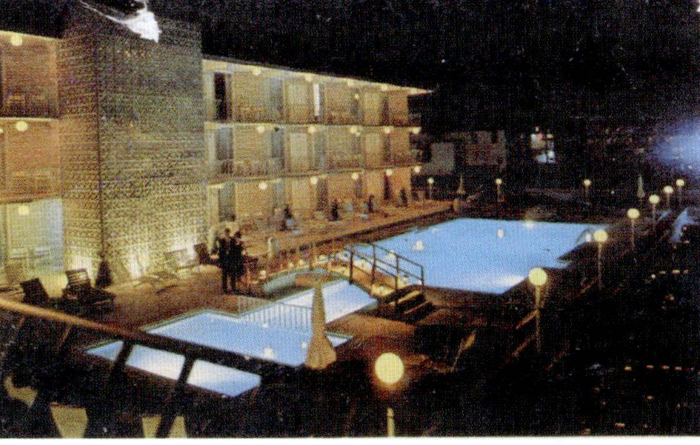

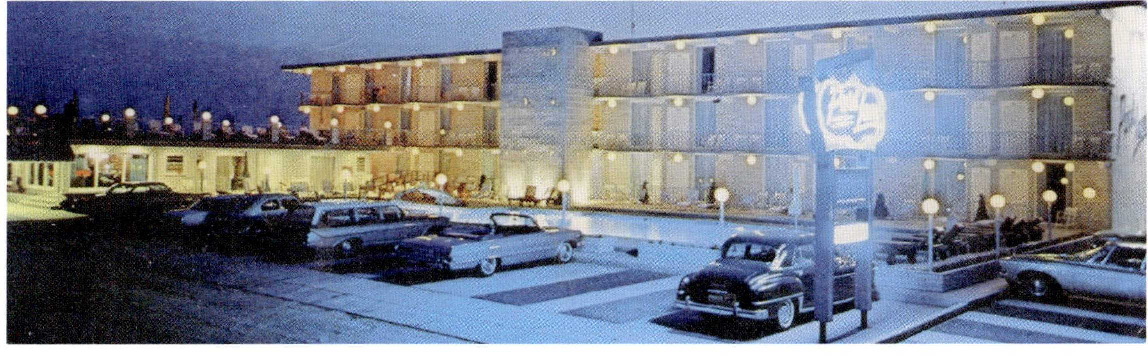

In this memorable 1963 postcard, the Park Lane Motel's neon sign casts a blue glow over cars in the motel's parking lot. *Courtesy of Wildwood Historical Society*

businesses in the Wildwoods borrowed aspects of California coffee shop design, Morey went all out with Schumann's Restaurant. From its flagcrete and driftwood façade and beachfront picture windows to its asymmetrical roof, which came to a point above the front door, Schumann's created a local stir and became a popular breakfast spot. In the 1960s, Schumann briefly renamed the restaurant the All Star in a merger with the nearby All Star Motel, but he returned it to its original name, complete with a new rooftop neon sign, a decade later.

In the late 1990s, new owners renamed the restaurant Hudson's Restaurant and Ice Cream Parlor, and ABS installed a new sign that starred a smiling ice cream cone man. However, in 2003, a few years after the remodel, developers bought the restaurant and tore it down. The ice cream cone man now resides in arcade owner Randy Senna's collection, but the loss of such a distinctive building is priceless.

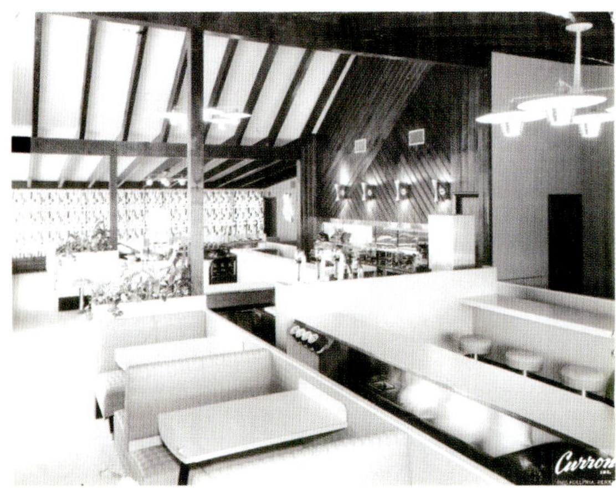

The prowed roof that Will Morey designed for Schumann's Restaurant created a uniquely angular interior dining space. *Courtesy of Wildwood Historical Society*

[173] Satellite Motel (5909 Atlantic Avenue)

Jack Morey recalls that his father, Will, would build a motel closer to the beach every two years. In 1956, Will had built the Fantasy, far from the ocean. Two years later, he bought a lot on the beach block of Astor Avenue (facing away from the ocean). Inspired by the increasingly outlandish designs his brother Lou was building (such as the recent Ebb Tide and the Caribbean, then in progress), Will set a new bar for the Wildwoods' commercial architecture.

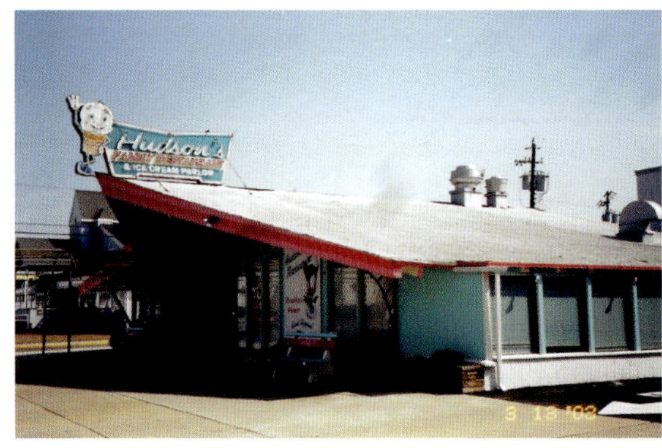

In its later years, Schumann's Restaurant was rebranded as Hudson's and given a cartoonish rooftop neon sign. *Courtesy of Wildwood Historical Society*

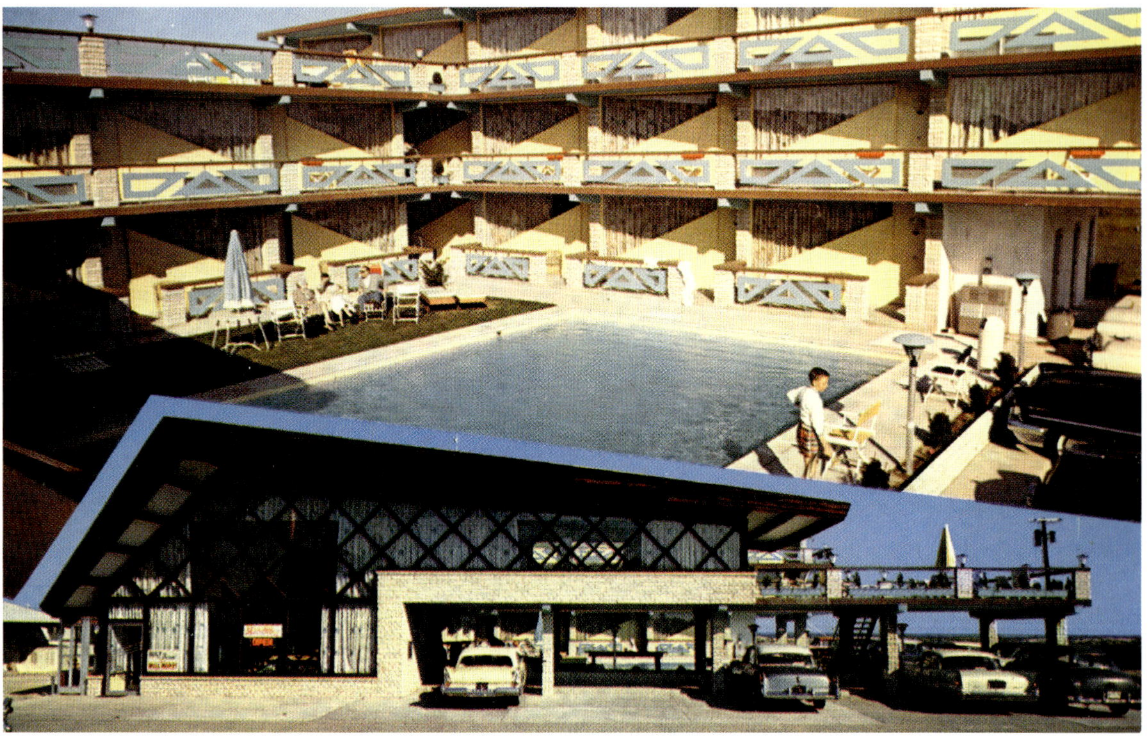

This postcard of the Satellite Motel was produced in 1958, the year the motel opened, and shows how different the motel looked from most other contemporaneous construction on the island. *Courtesy of Martin Melucci*

The Satellite featured a giant asymmetrical gable, which housed an office and a lounge. Atop the gable was a script sign in blue neon. Cutout plywood railings, triangular room windows, and bright-yellow walls contrasting with dark-wood trim contributed to what Thomas Hine, author of the 1986 book *Populuxe*, describes as "a rather elaborate piece of space age folk art." Morey sold the motel in 1964 to Edward Jastremski, who kept the motel in more or less original shape for several years. In the early 1970s, Jastremski replaced the original neon sign, which had begun to malfunction, with a new version with a similar "Satellite" script, surrounded by neon stars, planets, and orbs on a green (then red in the early 1980s, and finally blue) metal background.

The Satellite's original effect was diluted by time: a series of owners in the 1980s and 1990s installed generic railings, encased the motel's original dark-wood gable in clapboard siding, and painted the whole motel off-white. The original asymmetrical lounge and overhang remained a focal point of the Doo Wop preservation movement, though. In 2004, developers bought the motel's lot. Despite a postcard drive and preservation effort, the motel was demolished in October 2004. "The Satellite broke my heart," says Jack Morey. "We couldn't save it. But we saved a piece of art—it's in the Pan American meeting room."

Preservationists saved several elements of the Satellite too. Fred Musso salvaged the motel's mid-seventies neon sign. "I didn't find that sign very interesting but did not want to lose it, given the importance of the motel," Musso says. Unfortunately, the motel's owner was not receptive to the prospect of saving it and charged Musso an exorbitant price. "The American Sign Museum in Cincinnati was asked to purchase it, but it didn't appeal to them either. I did buy it for way more than I paid for any other sign. It was an eleventh-hour save that was an unsettling experience." Fortunately, Musso grabbed the sign in time, and in 2007, ABS installed it in two parts at the Doo Wop Experience museum, where it shares space with a Sputnik-shaped balustrade and an original rug from the motel.

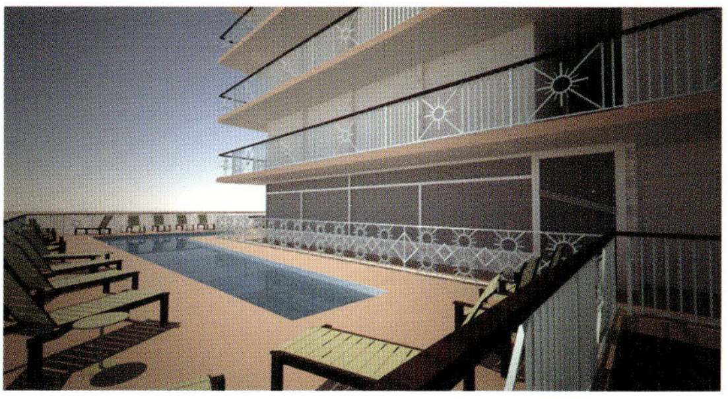

Martin Melucci has designed a "21st-Century Satellite" high-rise motel concept. Even though the Satellite was demolished in 2004, it continues to influence architects and designers. *Courtesy of Martin Melucci*

[174] Crusader Oceanfront Resort and Restaurant (6101 Ocean Avenue)

Local contractor John DeFrancesco built the block-long Crusader, one of the island's few medieval-themed motels, in 1969 for the 1970 season (according to city records, contradicting several sources that put the date at 1968). It featured two Old English neon signs and a mosaic façade depicting a knight and a shield. One of the neon signs still shines brightly today, and the mosaic tiles remain as well, though current manager John Hawes says the tiles have worn out their welcome: "Originally, with all the grout nice and white, it probably looked pretty cool. But now it's just not worth it."

[175] Yankee Clipper Resort Motel (6101 Atlantic Avenue)

Lou Morey built the Yankee Clipper in 1965 on Cardinal Road, placing a neon sign featuring a ship's wheel on its roof. The original louvered room doors are gone, but several rooms feature original wood paneling and a green color scheme that evokes the sixties.

[176] Fleur De Lis Beach Resort (6105 Ocean Avenue)

After building the La Vita Motel a mile south, Frank and Maria Lacivita built this larger motel in 1966. Until a 2010 renovation that added a penthouse suite and dormer windows, the Fleur De Lis sported an original vertical, wall-hung neon sign that advertised its unique French theme.

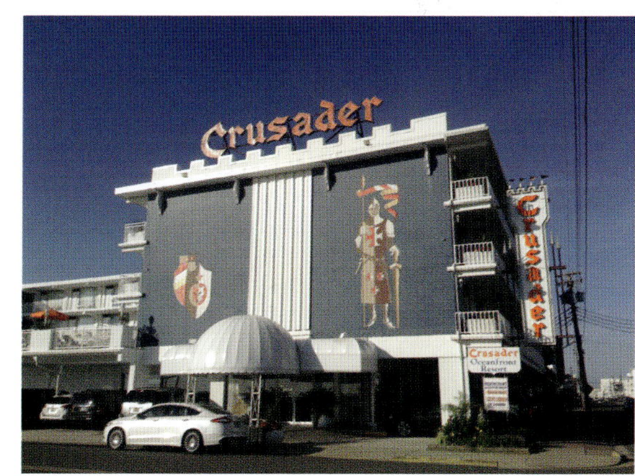

The troublesome mosaic tile façade of the Crusader Motel gleams in the morning sunlight.

[177] Tangiers Motel (6201 Atlantic Avenue)

While Lou Morey was building the Caribbean Motel, he was also busy six blocks south. The first block-long motel in the Wildwoods, the Tangiers perfected a template that would soon proliferate in Wildwood Crest, with a long, rectangular room unit surrounded by street parking and operating in tandem with a separate office unit that emphasized the motel's theme. The Tangiers opened on June 14, 1958, a week after the Caribbean. The lobby building, which also housed the motel's first owners, Henry and Ann Balut, and a small coffee shop, resembled nearby Schumann's Restaurant in its use of California coffee shop tropes such as herringbone wood paneling, a sharply sloping roof, and a rooftop neon sign dotting the "i" in Tangiers with a star. Among the rooms, tan brick furthered this California escapism.

In 1964 the Baluts sold the Tangiers to Pat and Jean DiStasio, who replaced half of the original lobby building with a new tiki-hut-like front office. Office manager Scott Hand says, "This tiki hut was added on because the year this motel opened up, Hunt's up on the boardwalk built Jungleland. Everybody at that time started getting interested in Hawaii." Despite the fact that the motel's namesake city was in Morocco and not in the tropics, the DiStasios also added several plastic palms. In the 1980s, ABS added a second rooftop neon sign, and about ten years later the original sign

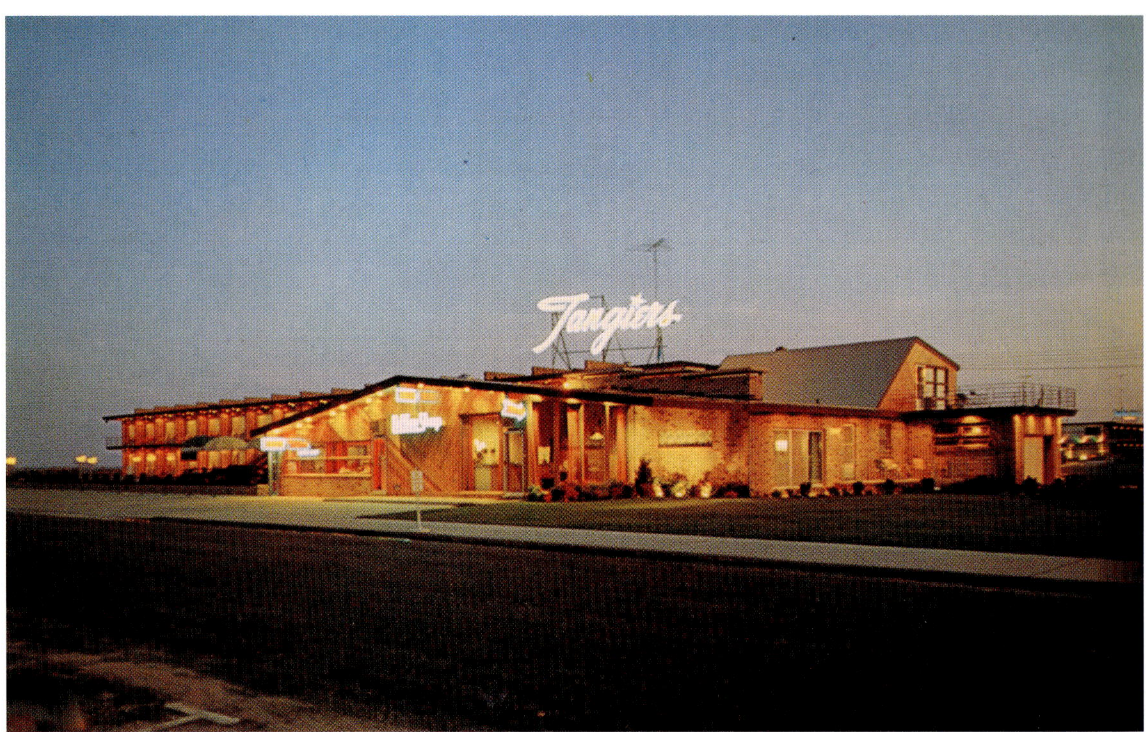

This 1958 postcard photo shows the Tangiers Motel as it looked when built. Less than a decade later, new owners added a new office shaped like a tiki hut. *Author's collection*

disappeared. Despite shifting color schemes over the years, the Tangiers has held on to most of its sixties-vintage structure (though its sign was removed after a 2020 storm). The A-frame profile of the motel's tiki hut office building remains a popular subject for photographers of the Wildwoods' midcentury architecture.

[178] Waikiki Oceanfront Inn (6211 Ocean Avenue)

Lou Morey built the high-rise Waikiki for the 1970 season. Like at his earlier Royal Hawaiian, Morey installed a lava rock façade and four neon signs, one of which (a wall-mounted one along Ocean Avenue) remains today.

[179] New Carousel Motel (6211 Atlantic Avenue)

Built in 1965 by John Juliano, the large-scale Hialeah, named after the beachfront Florida city, featured a gull-wing roof punctuated by flagpoles, and a neon sign that spelled the motel's name in a script typeface, as well as a grand fountain on the Atlantic Avenue end. In the 1970s, the Stratoti family built a large shore house to serve as the motel's owners' quarters, and early eighties owners tempered the motel's original bright color scheme with an odd American Colonial makeover.

In 2005, developers demolished the Carousel Motel on Lavender Road. The Carousel's owner bought the Hialeah Motel nearby, revived the original Warholesque color scheme, and renamed it the New Carousel. The New Carousel was sold and demolished after the 2006 season.

[180] Olympic Island Beach Resort (6401 Ocean Avenue)

Lou Morey built the large Olympic Motor Inn for the 1970 season. On a large, blank façade facing Ocean Avenue, Morey placed an anatomically correct statue of a discus thrower, which drew

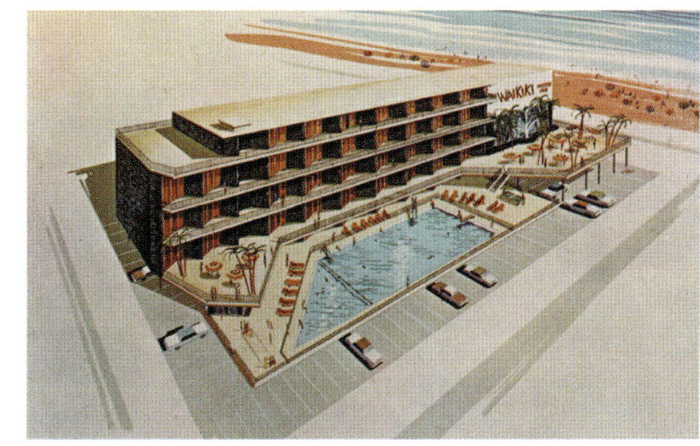

An architectural rendering of the Waikiki Motor Inn that appeared in early 1970s accommodations guides. *Author's collection*

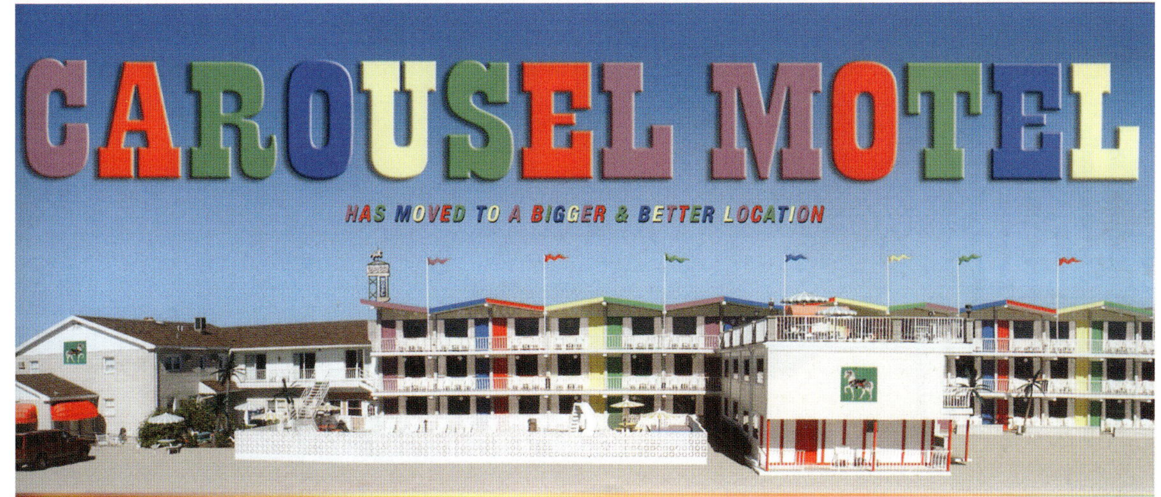

For one year, the Hialeah Motel briefly became the New Carousel Motel. Even though a Carousel Motel neon sign is shown on the roof in this brochure rendering, the sign was never actually installed. *Courtesy of Wildwood Historical Society*

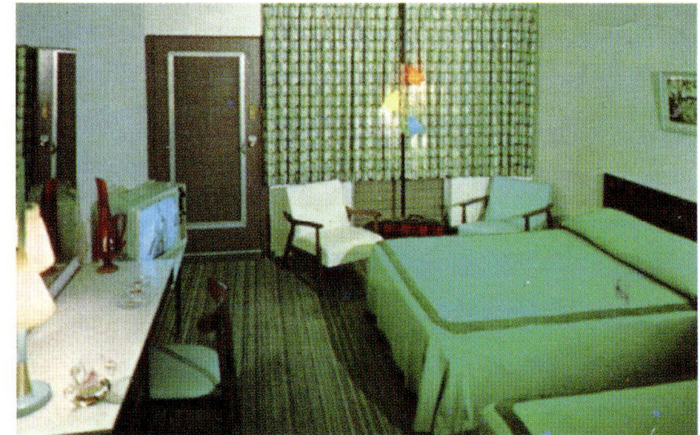

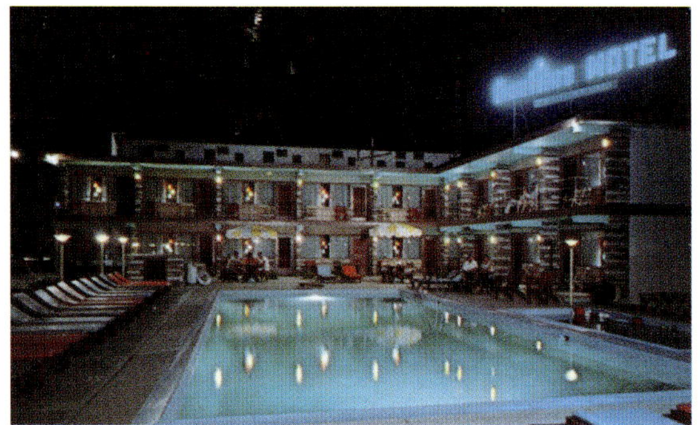

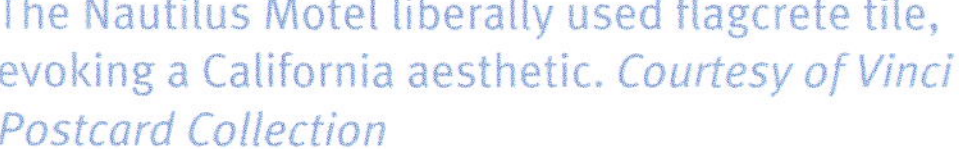

The Nautilus Motel liberally used flagcrete tile, evoking a California aesthetic. *Courtesy of Vinci Postcard Collection*

controversy and which the motel's owners replaced with a façade of classical columns a year or two later, similar to the one shown in original 1970 architectural drawings. In 2000, new owners renamed the motel the Olympic Island Beach Resort and had ABS Signs design a spectacular wall-mounted sign with this name.

[181] Viking Motel (6400 Ocean Avenue)
The Barrish and Grassi families built the Viking Motel for the 1963 season. The motel featured rooms whose windows were angled toward the beach but whose doors were relegated to the side walls, an odd design that forced families staying in different rooms to mingle. Today the Viking Motel survives in mostly original shape (though now overshadowed by taller neighbors), minus its original rooftop sign.

[182] Nautilus Motel (6401 Atlantic Avenue)
When Robert Hart built the Nautilus Motel in 1958, it was situated in a largely empty beachfront neighborhood. It featured a flagcrete façade that was likely inspired by Schumann's Restaurant down the street, and a neon sign with an "i" dotted by a star. After the addition of a full second story in the early 1960s, the Nautilus remained remarkably intact until 2002, when it was demolished.

[183] Bristol Plaza Oceanfront Resort Motel (6407 Ocean Avenue)
The Bristol Plaza opened for the 1970 season (possibly built by Lou Morey, who built the nearly identical Waikiki). The motel was adorned with eye-catching fins and a wall-mounted neon sign, though these have been removed.

[184] Shalimar Resort (6405 Atlantic Avenue)
Elmo Baldassari (who had previously owned the Magnolia and 24th Street Motels) and Edward Schiavi built the three-story Shalimar for the 1964 season. Aiming for a vaguely Egyptian theme, Baldassari and Schiavi added a plastic onion dome on top of the office building, saw-tooth balconies, and plenty of flagcrete. The motel remained mostly unchanged for over thirty years, including its original neon sign.

"We got this motel in 2000, and then we waited a few years before we did the renovations," said Maria Tenaglia in 2017. "We had to find the right architect to take this project on." Maria and her husband, Aldo, eventually hired Richard Stokes, who had designed the critically acclaimed Starlux. "We liked the signs on the boardwalk piers, with the fifties flair. It looked retro and different, but also modern at the same time." Stokes added two more stories to the Shalimar, a task that proved difficult because of the scarcity of the flagcrete that made up the motel's original façade. "We could not find those bricks any longer—we could not find the right grain," said Maria. "The fourth floor is really stucco, but we added a texture to make it look like the bricks." Thanks to this clever trickery, the addition neatly complements the original portion of the motel.

Stokes also designed a five-story addition with a conference room and other business-related amenities. "At other motels, the conventions set up on the sundeck, outside, because there's no other place for them to gather," Maria said. Stokes and the Tenaglias sought out authentic sixties fixtures, including wheel-shaped chandeliers from the Bolero Motel in downtown Wildwood, whose original lobby was demolished in 2003.

With its plastic signs in an angular typeface ("We had to keep it simple but still identify for the time; my daughter designed it"), its row of tall plastic palms in front, and its light-purple stucco, the Shalimar exemplifies a sympathetic expansion of a classic sixties-vintage motel. In 2020, the owners of the Bolero in downtown Wildwood bought the Shalimar.

[185] Ocean Holiday Motor Inn (6501 Ocean Avenue)

Lou Morey may have built the high-rise Ocean Holiday, which opened in 1972. It sported an incandescent wall-hung neon sign depicting a seahorse and, according to vintage postcards, rooms evocatively decorated in orange. In late 2019, Icona Resorts began renovating the motel. As of 2021, its neon sign survives; hopefully it will remain in place for the next chapter of the Ocean Holiday's history.

[186] Compass Family Resort (6501 Atlantic Avenue)

Harry and Jo Templin built the Compass Motel (its original name) in 1965. The motel had a rooftop neon sign and a modern lounge that

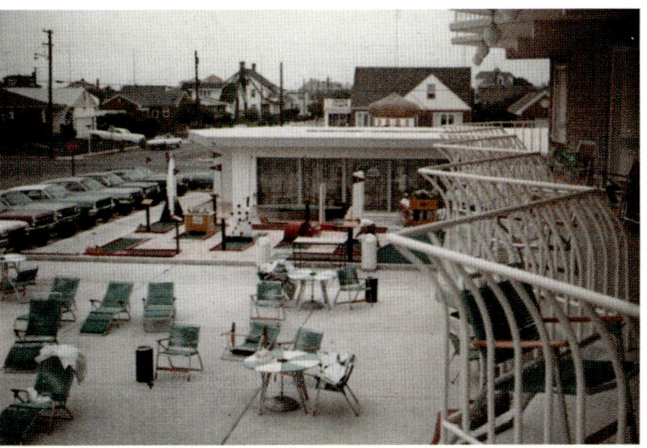

The Shalimar Motel opened in 1964; note the sawtooth balconies and the onion dome that originally sat atop the motel's office. *Courtesy of Fedele Musso*

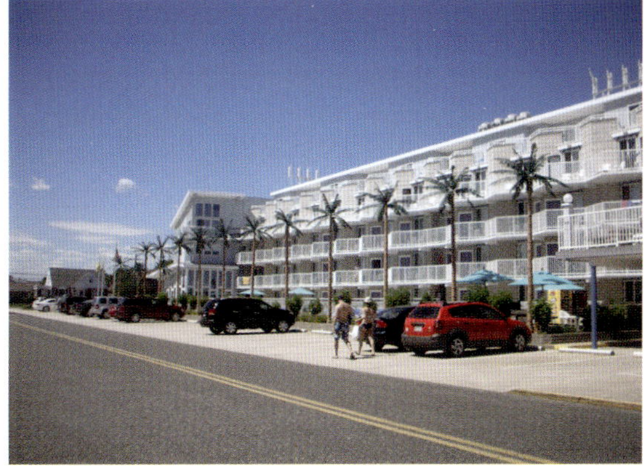

Richard Stokes's expansion of the Shalimar in 2005 added two stories and a new lounge building that offsets the rectangular shape of the original motel.

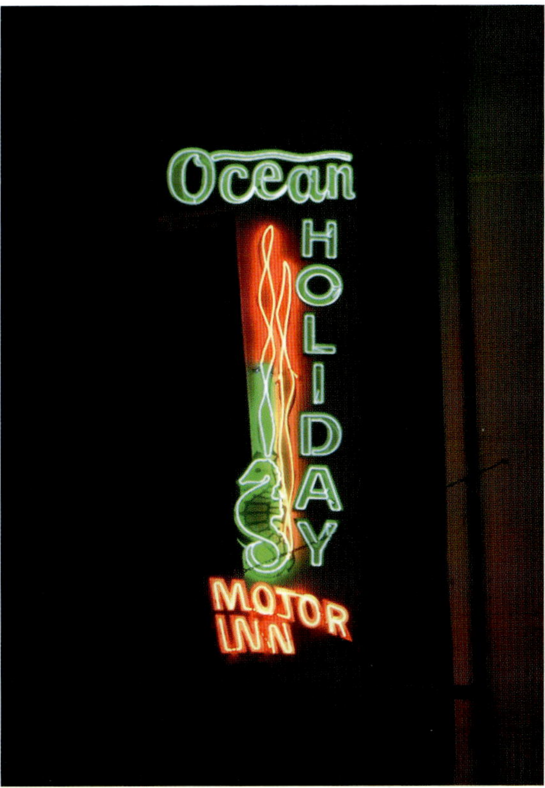

The Ocean Holiday Motor Inn's original neon sign, one of many wall-mounted neon signs on Wildwood Crest's Ocean Avenue strip.

liberally used plate glass windows. Modern renovations have added an American Colonial–style office (though the motel's railings retain their pop-art-like translucent blue panels).

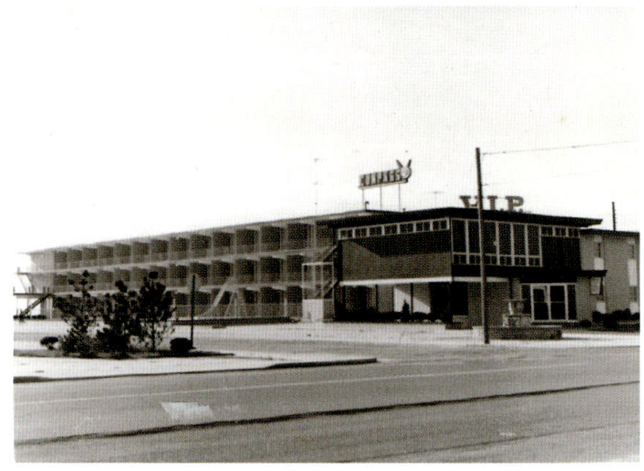

This 1965 view of the Compass Motel shows its original midcentury modern lounge and neon sign. *Courtesy of Wildwood Historical Society*

[187] VIP Family Motel (6505 Atlantic Avenue)

Jim, John, and Katherine Roy and their families built the two-story VIP in 1964 and opened it the next summer. The motel featured a California coffee shop–style office with a pitched roof, flying buttresses, and stained-glass windows; on top, Allied Signs installed a green neon sign with red tubes. The Roy family has maintained the motel's original sixties feel, including preserving its green translucent railing panels and keeping it at two stories. "My father [Jim] always spoke about his plans for a third floor . . . but I don't think it would be financially feasible," says current owner Melissa Roy. The original neon sign still shines, now with green neon tubes. "I would love to keep what's left of the original design," she says.

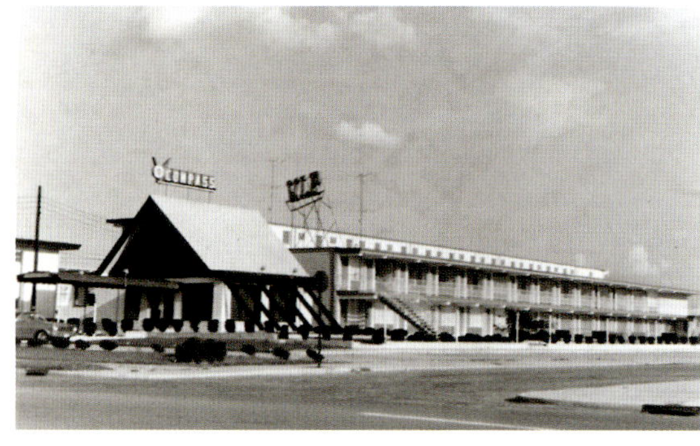

The buttresses supporting the office have disappeared, but the VIP Motel still looks remarkably similar to its appearance in this 1965 photo. *Courtesy of Wildwood Historical Society*

[188] Imperial 500 Motel (6601 Atlantic Avenue)

In 1964, fresh from his recent successes with the Golden Nugget and Le Voyageur Motels, Nazareno Regalbuto built the Imperial 500 Motel. His design was meant to represent luxury, including cut-stone end walls, a lounge building with a gull-wing roof, and individual semicircular balconies that bulged from the motel's façade and sported outward-bowing railings. A red-and-white rooftop neon sign topped the motel.

In 1972, Regalbuto sold the Imperial 500 and built the Newport Beach Motel on Rio Grande Avenue. The same year, Joe and Connie Salerno bought the Imperial 500. Since then, they have maintained its splendor through decades of changing tides in the Wildwoods. "We were fighting

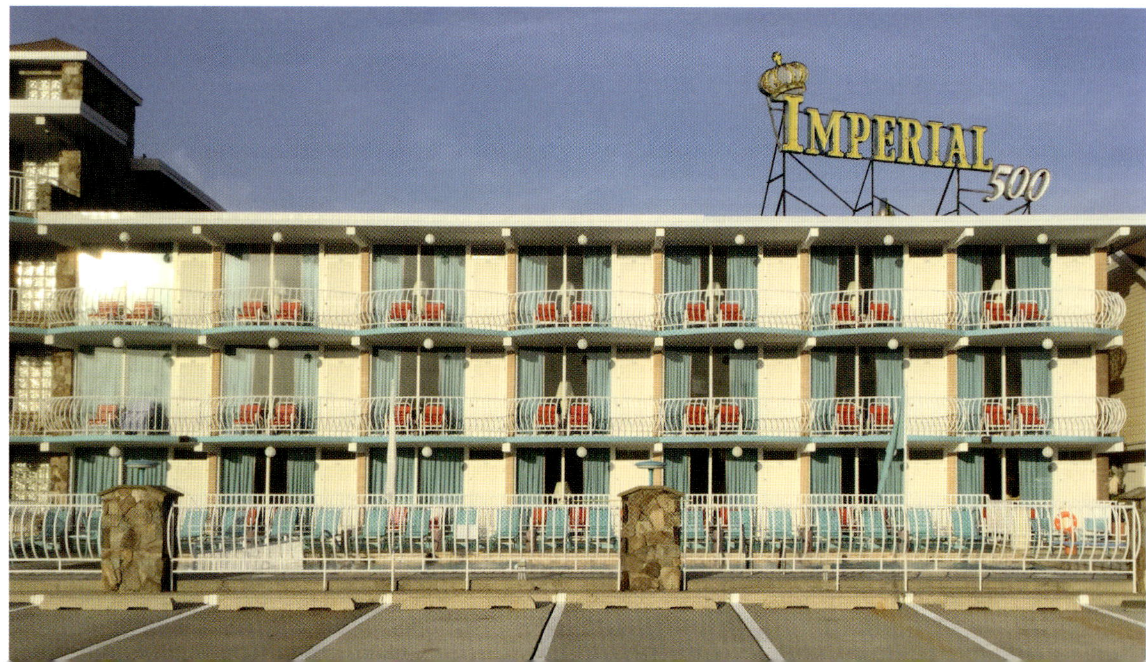

The Imperial 500 still looks much the way it did when it opened in 1964, largely due to a loving renovation by the Johnson and Salerno families in 2000.

the teardowns," says Jim Johnson, the Salernos' son-in-law and co-owner. "We went to the city and tried to slow the process down because we didn't want to see the town torn apart."

In 1999, the families decided to expand, building a partial fourth story (a full fourth story would have required more parking than could fit), an elevator, and expanded living quarters. "We actually took out three rooms because our elevator is internal, instead of building a block wall like other people do," says Johnson. "We didn't want to block the view." The most difficult part of the renovation, much of which Johnson built himself, was forming new replicas of the motel's signature bulging balconies. "The balconies were very difficult. Every one of those balconies has to be formed and poured." They also still maintained the motel's 1964-vintage neon sign. "That needs a lot of maintenance," Johnson says. "I could go to LED and not have to worry about it. But neon is our look, and I wouldn't want to change it. Fred Musso does all my work if I need neon done."

The Imperial 500, like the Shalimar, is a shining example of a sympathetic addition to a vintage motel. Jim Johnson plans to stay for the long haul; his son will inherit the motel soon. "I was offered very big money about ten years ago. I was up here working in the winter, and I told a guy to get off the property. Our customers are like family. We could've been retired right now, but we're still here."

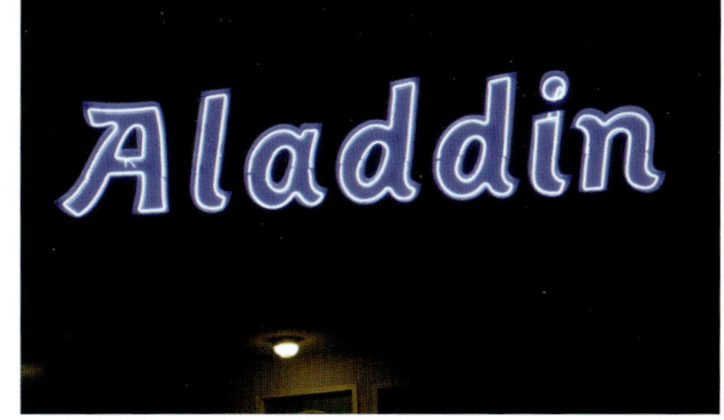

The rooftop neon sign that graced the Aladdin Motel was removed when the motel went condo in 2010. *Courtesy of Jeff Sumberg, www.flickr.com/jeffs4653*

[189] Aladdin Motel (208 East Forget-Me-Not Road)

The Aladdin evolved from the Brentwood Apartments, a 1920s rooming house. Around 1966, its owner built a motel addition, then demolished the original apartments in 1970 to expand the motel. Over the years, the motel featured two rooftop neon signs—first a red one depicting a lantern, then a nineties-vintage blue one in a script font. The motel was converted to condominiums around 2010. Fred Musso salvaged the motel's blue neon sign; an "A" hangs inside the Doo Wop Experience.

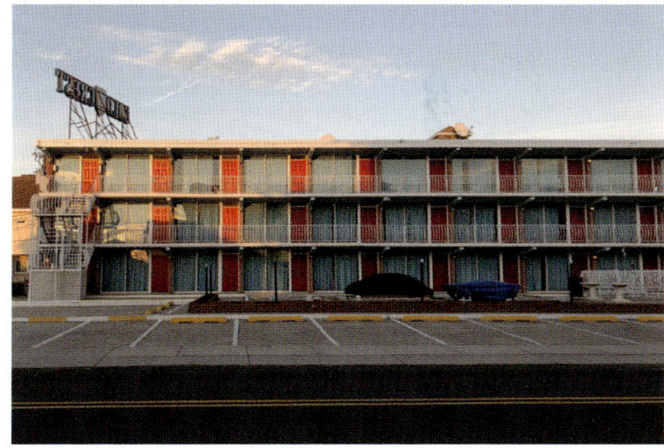
The Gold Crest Motel, shown here, was one of three nearly identical motels built in Wildwood Crest in the early 1970s; all three stand today.

[190] Gold Crest Motel (6611 Atlantic Avenue)

[191] Sand Dune Motel (6905 Atlantic Avenue)

[192] Diamond Crest Motel (7011 Atlantic Avenue)

These three motels share the same blueprints; the Gold Crest and Diamond Crest both opened in 1970, while the Sand Dune opened a year or two later. All three were clad in eye-popping shades of orange and pink when first built; today, only the Gold Crest holds on to a dynamic color scheme of red and blue. All three today feature rooftop neon signs: the Sand Dune's was refurbished by ABS in 2007; eight years later, ABS renovated the Diamond Crest's original sign.

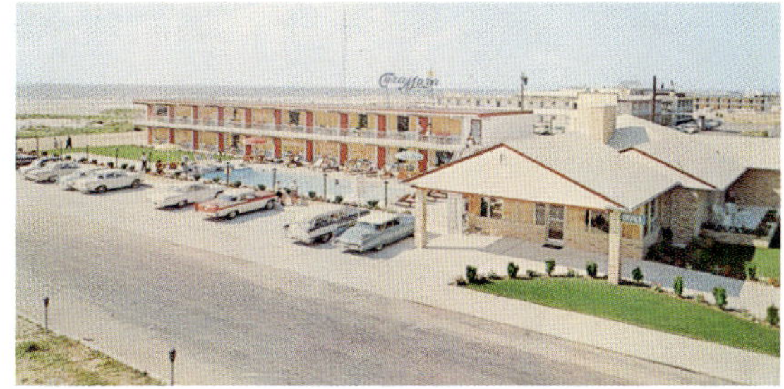
The Cara Mara Motel retains its original midcentury appeal, notwithstanding a series of additions since this 1962 postcard was produced. *Courtesy of Wildwood Historical Society*

[193] Cara Mara Vacation Resort (6701 Atlantic Avenue)

In 1962, Lou Morey built the Cara Mara, one of many projects he took on after the March 1962 nor'easter. The two-story motel had a California cool reminiscent of the nearby Tangiers and a blue rooftop neon sign punctuated by a crisp yellow star. Despite several additions (including a third story) and a switch to condominium ownership in the 2010s, the motel and its 1962 neon sign remain in good shape.

From the east (*shown here*), Lou Morey's Palm Beach Motel resembled a typical L-shaped Wildwoods motel. From its western side, the influence of Will's Pan American Hotel was visible. *Courtesy of Steve F, www.flickr.com/electrospark*

[194] Palm Beach Motel (Palm Road and Atlantic Avenue)
Lou Morey expanded on his brother Will's concept for the Pan American Motor Inn with the Palm Beach, opened in 1966. A theatrical western façade featured private balconies and a dramatic walkway, lined with plastic palms, that led into the motel office. On the motel's eastern side, the same rooms had common balconies, keeping the Palm Beach grounded in the Wildwoods' typical motel aesthetic. Despite its excellent condition, in 2005 developers leveled the Palm Beach and replaced it with condominiums.

[195] Jolly Roger Motel (6805 Atlantic Avenue)
After building the Satellite and Fantasy Motels, Will Morey partnered with Palmer Way Jr., who had served as the mayor of Wildwood Crest and was active in the island's civic life, for his next big motel project. In the winter of 1959–1960, Morey and Way constructed a U-shaped motel facing the beach, borrowing from the California modernism that had proliferated in the Wildwoods over the previous three years by judiciously using plate glass and flagcrete. Morey installed railings in a chevron pattern, and blue curtains and yellow louvered doors added color and movement. He also experimented with a novel floor plan: communal balconies on the outer edges granted vacationers access to their rooms, while internal private balconies faced a pool and courtyard. An asymmetrical

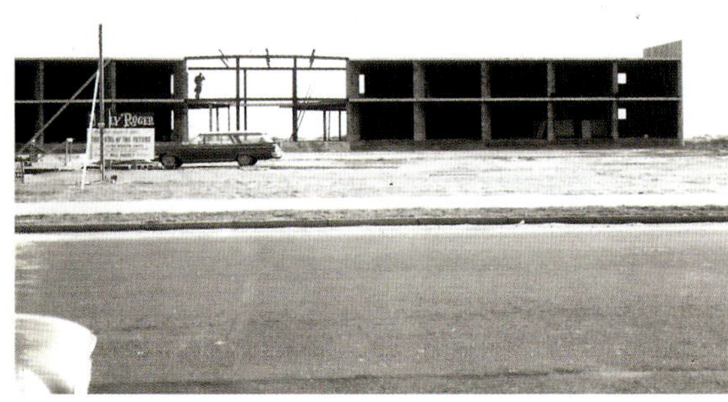

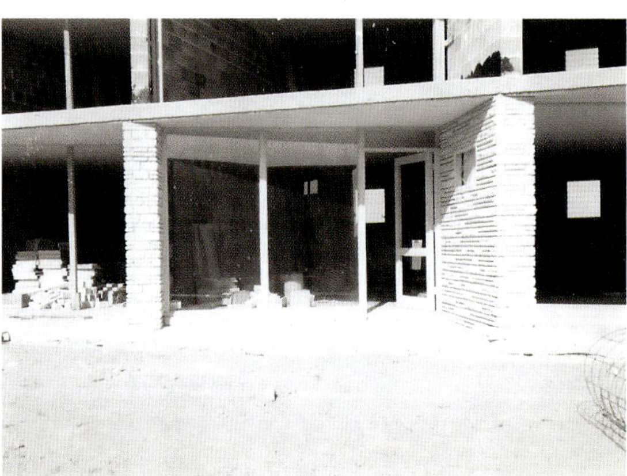

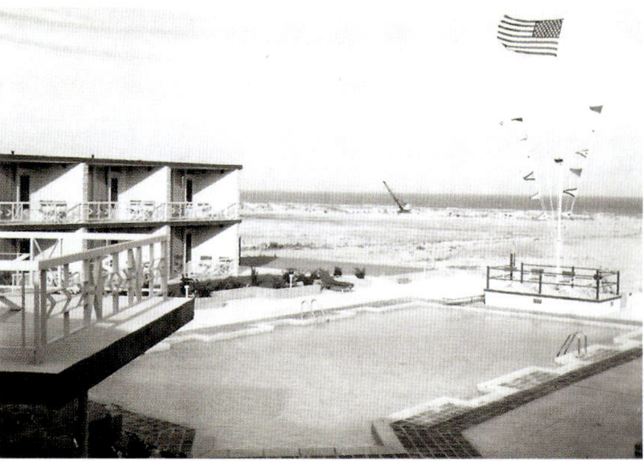

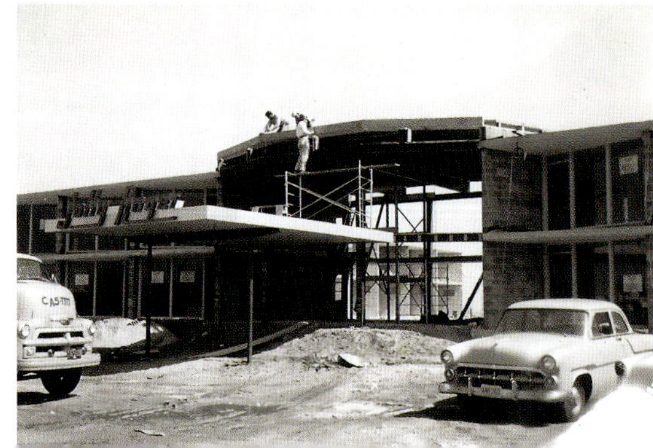

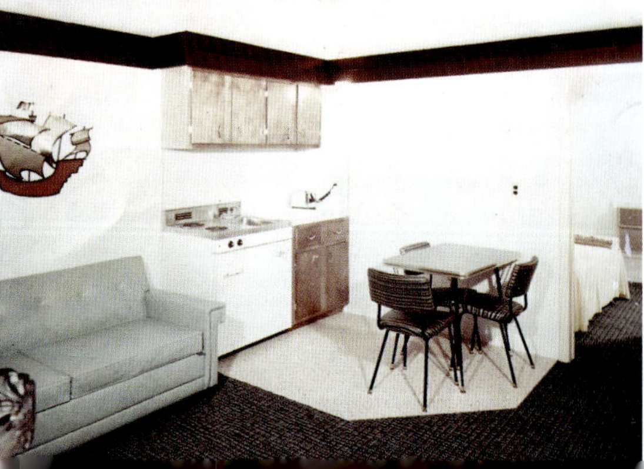

Palmer Way kept a photographic record of the construction of his Jolly Roger Motel. This sequence shows the first cinder-block walls rising, a room taking shape between flagcrete walls, the motel's lobby and neon sign, the nearly complete courtyard (showing the motel's unique chevron railings), and the interior of one of the motel's rooms, showing a muted nautical design. *Courtesy of anonymous collection*

plate glass–faced coffee shop dominated the pool area. Facing the traffic of Atlantic Avenue, a yellow neon sign and a large pirate statue sat atop a carport.

When built, the Jolly Roger had a beachfront location. After the 1962 nor'easter, beach expansion allowed the borough of Wildwood Crest to create an additional oceanfront block that snatched away the Jolly Roger's oceanfront status. Will Morey had designed the motel to be viewed from Atlantic Avenue, but because new traffic approached the motel from the Ocean Avenue side, Morey realized he needed to overhaul the motel's appearance. "When it was built, there was no Ocean Avenue, only Atlantic Avenue," says John Way, son of Palmer Way and a longtime owner of the Jolly Roger. "But after the majority of traffic started coming down Ocean Avenue, you get a different view of the property than what was originally meant to be. It was just very difficult to give it curb appeal coming down Ocean Avenue."

In the late 1960s, Morey and Way expanded the Jolly Roger with a third story. Then, in 1972, they built the Port Royal Hotel across the street from the Jolly Roger, on the new beachfront block the borough had delineated after the 1962 storm. "When they built the Port Royal, they kept in mind the view from the Jolly Roger," John Way says. "Instead of blocking the whole view, the Port Royal sits rectangularly on half of the property. The Port Royal has the patio, but the Jolly Roger gets more light and a bit of a view of the ocean."

For a while, the Way family entertained the idea of engaging noted architects Venturi, Scott Brown, to combine the Port Royal and Jolly Roger into a larger mega-resort. But this expansion never materialized. Recently, the Ways and Moreys sold the Jolly Roger to concentrate their efforts on the Port Royal. The Jolly Roger's new owners have already replaced its original yellow doors with sliding patio doors. Still, with its flagcrete tile, neon signs, and chevron railings, the Jolly Roger remains one of the Wildwoods' outstanding examples of budget modernism.

[196] Nomad Resort Motel (7001 Atlantic Avenue)

Between 1962, when Lou Morey built it, and 2005, when developers tore it down, little changed at the Nomad, including an original grass courtyard surrounding its office. "On the ground level, it still had its original coffee shop," marvels Fred Musso. On top of the Nomad's roof sat a neon sign featuring a white-outlined ship's wheel.

[197] Topaz Motel (7010 Seaview Avenue)

Mike Branca, a former employee of Lou Morey who also built the groundbreaking Casa Bahama, built the Topaz in the early 1960s as one story and later expanded it to two. The motel survives as condominiums, minus the original pink-outlined neon shell that once illuminated the parking lot.

[198] Oceanview Motel (500 East Rambler Road)

Lou Morey's ambitious 1963 Admiral Motel renewed the race with his brother Will to build the most daring motel in the Wildwoods. The Admiral had a groundbreaking 30-foot-tall asymmetrical lobby structure with a gable whose two sides did not meet, creating an illusion of instability. This roof housed a three-story atrium, an office, and a coffee shop. One end of the roof extended to cover

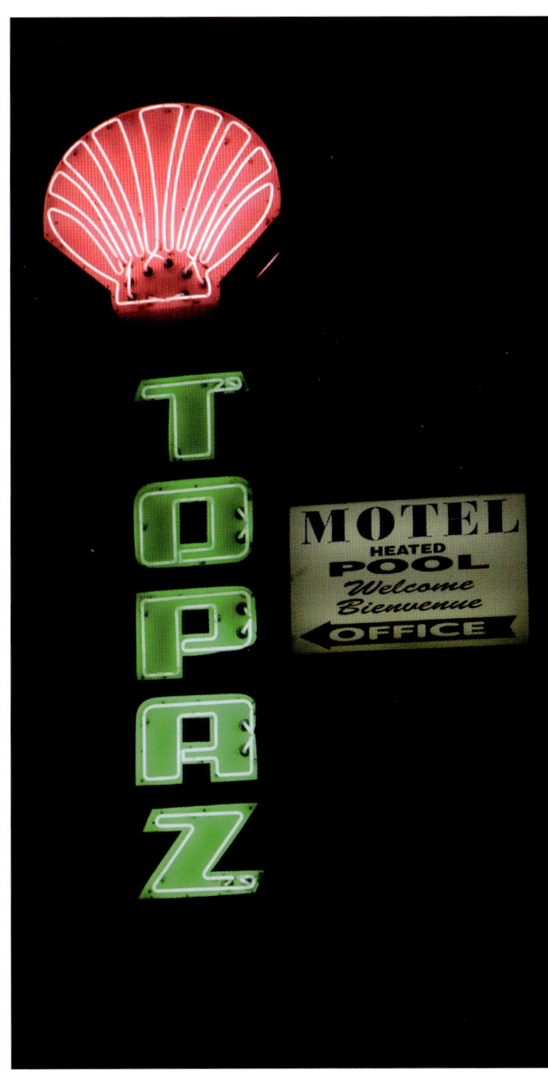

The Topaz Motel building still stands, but this beautiful neon sign was removed around 2015, when the motel was converted to condominium ownership. *Courtesy of Jeff Sumberg, www.flickr.com/jeffs4653*

Lou Morey's design for the Admiral (now Oceanview) Motel's lobby called to mind the sweeping lines of early sixties airport terminals.

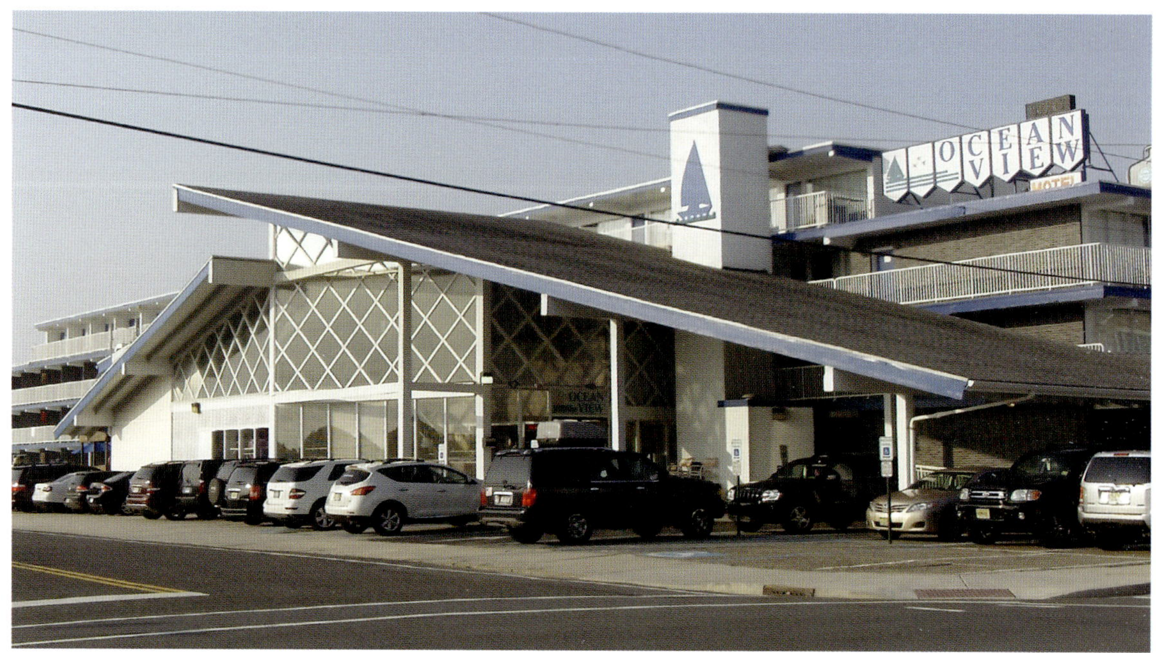

a manicured garden and driveway, and a colorful paint scheme (yellow railings, navy-blue curtains, brown-painted steel beams, and black-painted brick) added exotic appeal. The Admiral's bold shapes and spacious interior are reminiscent of several airport terminals of the early 1960s, notably Eero Saarinen's TWA Terminal in New York City, which shows that Lou Morey's influences had shifted from art deco to neofuturism. While many Wildwoods motels had flashy neon signs, the Admiral's architecture itself was a billboard.

In the late 1960s, the motel's first owners, Eugene and Anne Davolos, commissioned Lou Morey to add a partial fourth floor, and around 1971 they had him build another motel across Ocean Avenue. The Admiral West (the original motel was now renamed the Admiral East) was attractive but had little midcentury flair. The Admiral East and West operated in tandem until about 2000, when they were sold separately; the latter became the Admiral. The original 1963 showplace, meanwhile, was renamed the Oceanview Motel. The Oceanview has survived the condo boom (and weathered rumors on several occasions that it would be demolished) with its remarkable lobby intact.

[199] Singapore Motel (501 East Orchid Road)

Along with the Jade East Motel in North Wildwood, the Singapore was one of the Wildwoods' few examples of what MAC, the organization that had planned the earliest Doo Wop trolley tours in the 1990s, classifies as the "Chinatown Revival" style. The Weil family built the Singapore in 1964 and gave it an "Oriental motif," in the words of a 1967 ad. This motif included an eye-catching lobby building in the shape of a Chinese pagoda, with multiple levels of mansard roofs and a plastic rooftop sign. This pagoda also included room units (which contemporaneous ads described as "honeymoon temples in the sky"). Red horizontal railings, a landscaped garden starring an ivory sculpture of an elephant, and French doors lent the Singapore a unique Eastern flavor. A stucco fence around the pool was emblazoned with (mostly meaningless) Chinese characters.

The Singapore retained most of its remarkable original structure through the first decade of the twenty-first century. Renovations around 2005 removed many of the motel's original midcentury details, such as its garden and distinctive railings (architectural scholar Stephanie Hoagland describes its state in that era as "stylistically confused"). As built, though, the Singapore was a monument to the power of motel builders to transport working-class vacationers to exotic destinations.

In 2020, a developer bought the Singapore and set about renovating the motel for condominium ownership, removing all of the building's original architectural characteristics and leaving only its basic structural elements. This renovation continues during the summer of 2021.

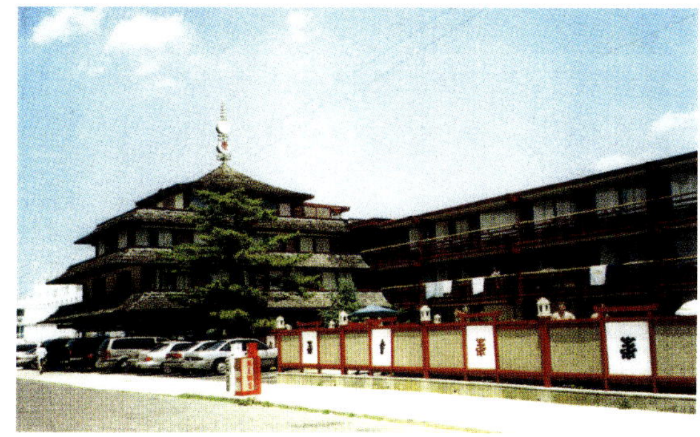

This 1990s photo of the Singapore Motel shows its evocative melding of Asian and American styles. *From Zerbe et al. 2003*

[200] Waterways Motel (7204 Ocean Avenue)

The Schafer family built the Waterways Motel at Orchid and Ocean Avenues in the late 1960s, installing outward-bowing railings that imparted sixties style. Around 2000, its owners turned up its visual volume by replacing an original neon sign with a much-larger one featuring a bubble motif. In 2004, developers tore it down and built condos on its site.

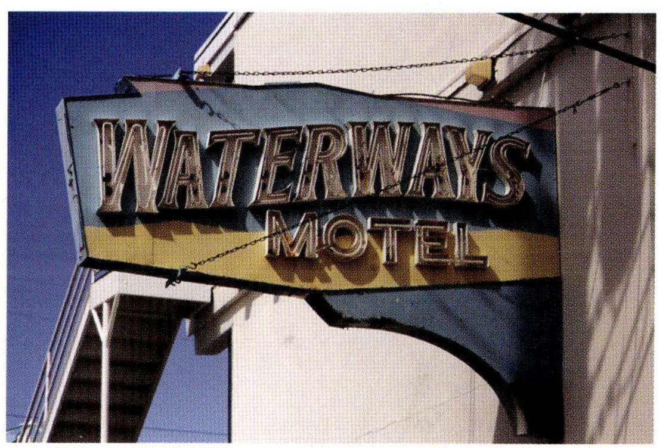

A few years before the Waterways Motel's demolition, its owners replaced this original late-1960s neon sign with a newer one. *Courtesy of Steve Weir*

[201] Royal Hawaiian Resort (500 East Orchid Road)

Lou Morey built the large-scale Royal Hawaiian in 1969 and topped it off with a rooftop neon sign reading "Hawaiian" in wedge-shaped letters and plenty of plastic palms. By 1978, the motel's beachfront location had netted its owners enough to fund an addition, which they again hired Morey to build. The new segment, which featured a prominent lava rock façade and a penthouse suite shaped like a flying saucer, made the motel a high-rise presence in a neighborhood otherwise populated with two- and three-story motels. Despite its incongruous size, its neon sign, relocated to the façade, continues to glow brightly; Allied refitted it with pink neon in the late 1980s. Today, the lava rock façade has been replaced with stucco, but the motel remains in excellent condition.

[202] Kona Kai Motel (7300 Ocean Avenue)

One of the later products of the Wildwoods' tiki mania was the Kona Kai, a 1968 Lou Morey construction commissioned by Manuel and Mary Santos. While the motel's red doors, green neon signage, and plastic palms put it firmly into the realm of midcentury modernism, a lava rock–faced façade underlined the Kona Kai's Polynesian theme in a novel way (Morey would repeat this trick at several other motels in the coming years). In 2006, the Kona Kai succumbed to redevelopment, the last motel on its block to do so. Fred Musso salvaged the motel's neon sign, which had occupied a few different locations on the motel's roof over the years. He sold its letters separately, but, as he says, "they later wound up together again in one ambitious collector's garage!"

This 1976 photo of the Kona Kai Motel shows its liberal use of lava rock. *Author's collection*

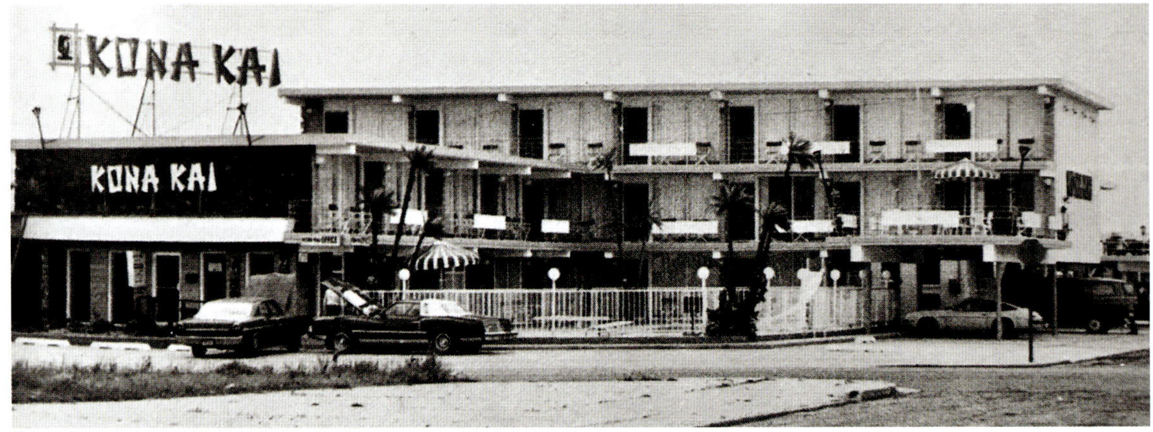

[203] Casa Bahama Motel (401 East Orchid Road)
The Wildwoods' first overtly tiki-themed motel, the Casa Bahama drew on the American enthusiasm for Polynesia and the Pacific islands that flourished in the 1950s. Mike Branca, a former employee of Morey Brothers Builders, left the business in 1959 and set out on his own. The Casa Bahama, his first major project, showed that he had taken Lou Morey's creative lessons to heart: the two-story, L-shaped motel's rooms were situated behind nine ornamental A-frames, which reminded vacationers of the tiki huts that Hollywood associated with Polynesian culture (even though the Bahamas are located in a different area of the world). Other details reinforced this confused, but dynamic, theme: a freestanding neon sign painted in dayglo colors connected this diverse concoction with the Wildwoods' usual modernist aesthetic. Elsewhere, decorative tiki masks and plastic palms magnified the motel's cultural ambiguity. Chester Jastremski, the motel's first owner, kept this glorious stylistic potpourri intact through the 1970s.

Later owners modified the motel little, even keeping it two stories, until developers bought it in 2005 and leveled it, along with the sign (which had appeared, along with the Sea Star and Ebb Tide Motels' signs, in early concept drawings for the Doo Wop Experience's sign garden). The Casa Bahama, which combined a variety of exotic ideals in a uniquely American package, was an unfortunate loss to the Doo Wop preservation movement.

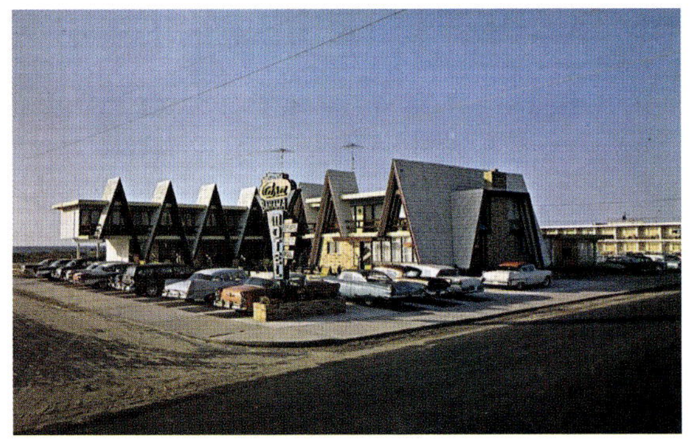

When it opened in 1959, nothing stood between the Casa Bahama Motel and the ocean. *Author's collection*

[204] Astronaut Motel (515 East Stockton Road)
Lou Morey built the beachfront Astronaut Motel in 1962 for Roman Weiser, facing it with an unusual red brick but adding jet-age elements such as a kidney-shaped pool and a rooftop neon sign in an atomic typeface. In 1969, a later owner replaced the motel's rooftop neon sign with a wall-hung yellow sign with vertically stacked white letters and a flashing atom. This sign did not last long: "It got blown down in a storm," remembers current owner Ed Pangburn. "But the original brackets are still out there." ABS removed the letters from this wall-hung sign and mounted them horizontally

on the roof, where they remain today. Pangburn has managed the motel since 1987, three years after a third story was added. He plans to preserve the motel: "I'll be here until the day I die. This is a great job; it's a fantastic lifestyle."

[205] Bonanza Motel (501 East Stockton Road)
Lou Morey built the Bonanza in 1963 while also building the Oceanview a block away. First owner Felix Klayman probably named the motel after the popular western television show, but except for the Playbill lettering in the motel's red rooftop neon sign (later refitted with blue neon to match the sign's paint color), the motel projected jet-age modernism instead, with a circular lobby and translucent blue fiberglass dividers between the rooms. The Bonanza was demolished in 2004 to make way for a high-rise condominium. Before it met the wrecking ball, Fred Musso rescued the motel's rooftop sign; its letters have wound up in collections far and wide.

[206] Hi-Lili Motel (407 East Stockton Road)
Adeline Anginoli built the Hi-Lili Motel for the 1964 season. Named after a relative (not a Dinah Shore song, as is often claimed), it featured a rooftop red neon sign in a whimsical red script, facing

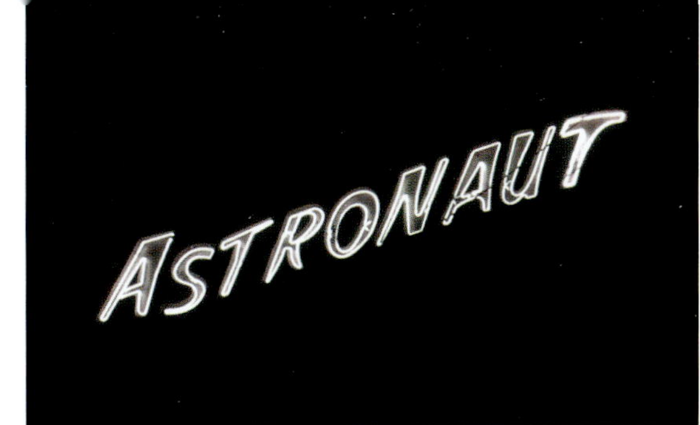

These funky late sixties letters on the Astronaut Motel's neon sign were originally mounted vertically on a sheet metal background, but that sign was damaged in a storm, necessitating this rooftop installation.

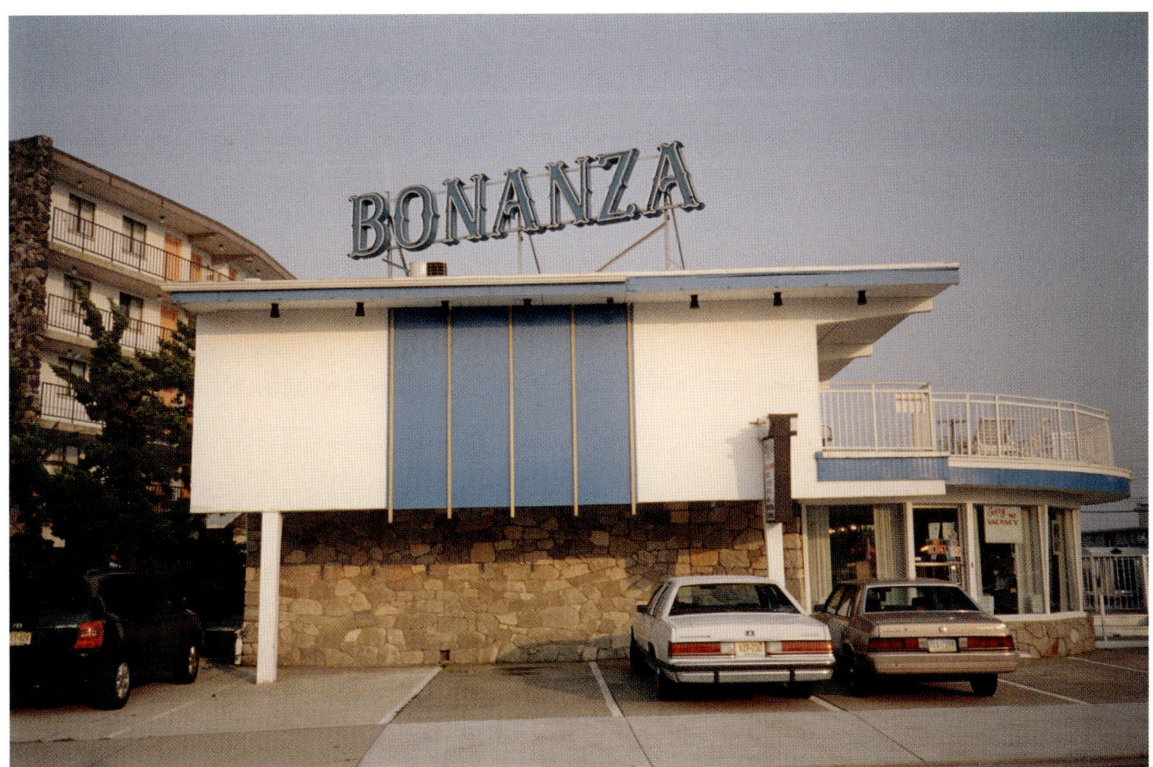

Though the Bonanza's name evoked the Wild West, its architecture was pure jet-age splendor. *Courtesy of Scott Stowell*

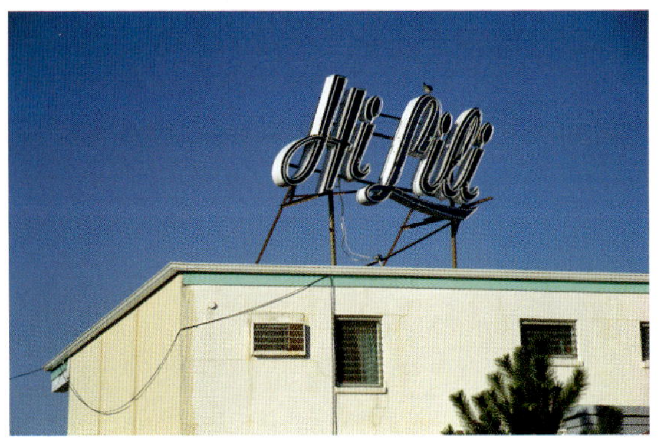

A seagull perches on the Hi-Lili Motel's rooftop sign, positioned to face traffic arriving from the downtown. *Courtesy of Dorothy Kresz*

north (away from the motel's façade) to be readable to vacationers arriving from downtown. When the motel was demolished in 2006, ABS saved the sign, but it has since disappeared from storage.

[207] Dunes Motel (7401 Atlantic Avenue)
The Sergiacomi and Masciarella families opened the one-story DiLido Motel for the 1958 season and expanded it to two stories soon thereafter. The DiLido had an undulating balcony ceiling, jalousie picture windows, and a purple amoeba-shaped neon sign. This sign was modified in the 1990s to reflect a name change to the Dunes Motel (at which time the motel was repainted mostly white). The Dunes was demolished in 2004.

[208] Swan Motel (520 East Stockton Road)
Albert Caffo opened the Swan Motel, one of the Crest's earliest beachfront motels, in 1958. Lou Morey built an L-shaped, Spanish-inspired motel on a spacious lot, and, a few years after the motel

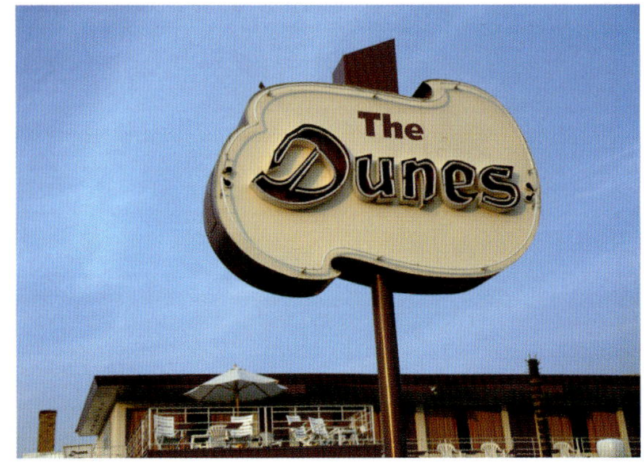

In the 1990s, the DiLido motel was renamed the Dunes, and its neon sign (now minus the stone pillar) was modified to match. *Courtesy of Dorothy Kresz*

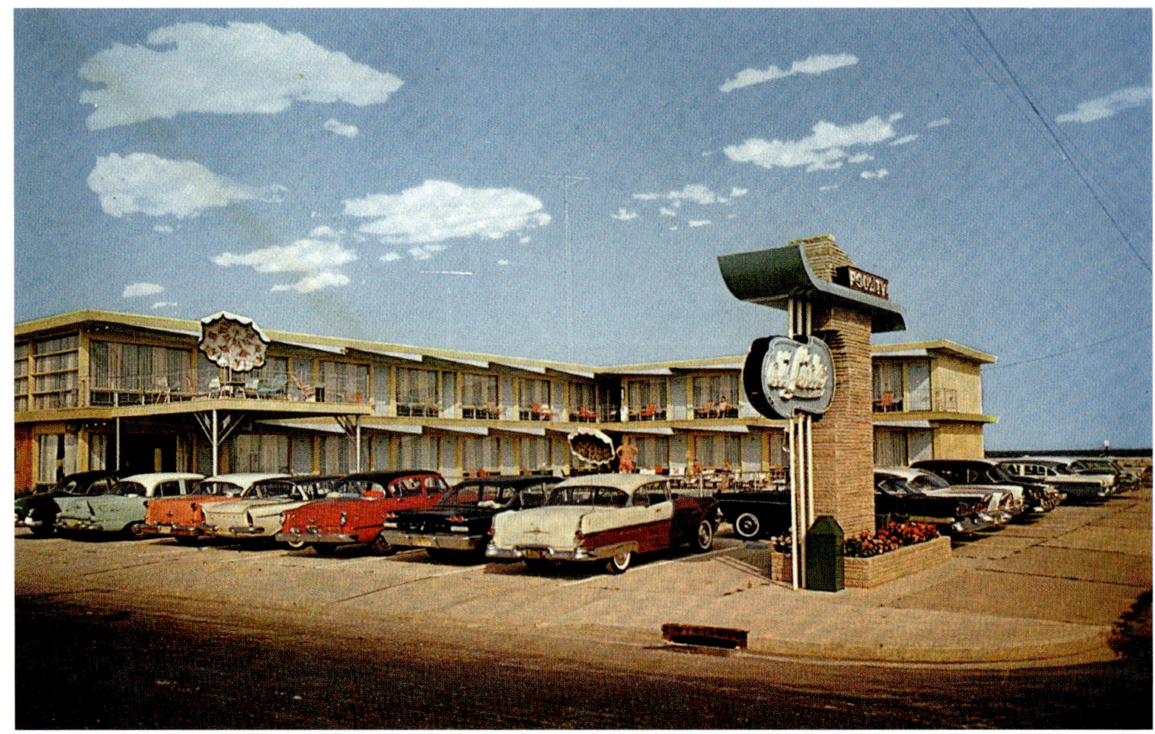

This postcard, printed in 1959 or 1960, shows the DiLido Motel after its second story was added. Note the neon sign, embellished with a stone pillar and a streamlined cornice, both of which were later removed. *Author's collection*

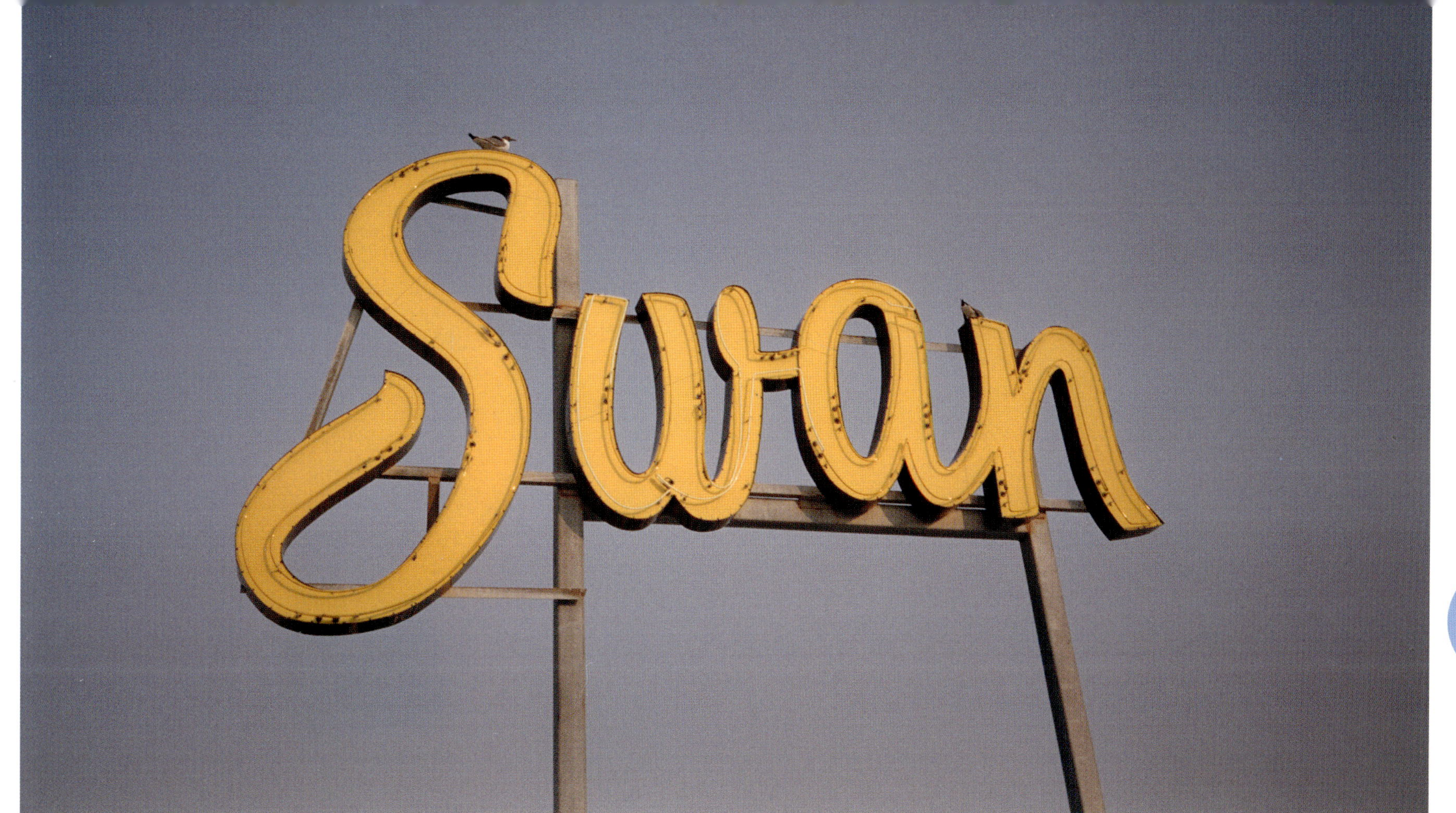

The Swan Motel's iconic sign, shown here a couple of years before the motel's demolition, can today be seen at the Doo Wop Experience. *Courtesy of Scott Stowell*

opened, Allied Signs installed a stunning freestanding sign that spelled the motel's name in huge yellow script letters studded with chasing lights (replacing a neon-outlined swan that had originally sat atop the motel's roof). In the early 1980s, a later owner replaced this sign with a similar version that outlined the letters in yellow neon. The Swan remained in mostly original condition until being demolished in 2005, whereupon ABS saved its neon sign. Two years later, they installed the sign at the Doo Wop Experience in downtown Wildwood, where it commands attention as one of the Wildwoods' greatest neon artworks.

[209] Beach Colony Resort (500 East Stanton Road)
In 1961, Nazareno Regalbuto built the Golden Nugget Motel. He built a typical L-shaped Wildwoods motel but, intriguingly, added a faceted wall on the west-facing façade, painted in alternating colors.

Though today surrounded by condominiums, the Beach Colony Motel and its ca. 1981 plastic sign hint at the onetime glory of Wildwood Crest's motel district. *Courtesy of Tyler Haughey*

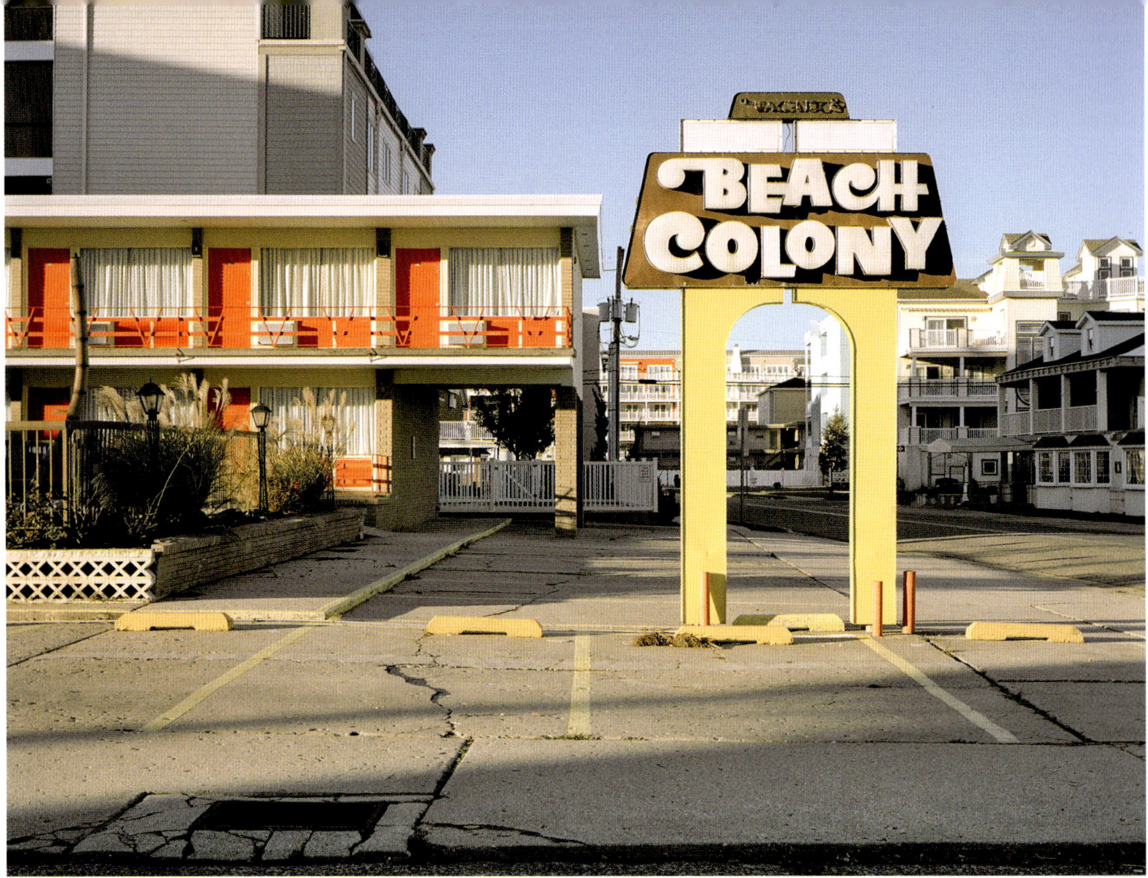

This use of a blank wall to make an artistic statement exemplified the Wildwoods' budget modernism and remains a popular subject for photos.

In 1964, Regalbuto sold, presumably because he was busy farther north building the Imperial 500 Motel. Around 1981, a new owner removed the original neon sign and installed a new freestanding one on which a lopsided disco-era typeface spelled out a new name: Beach Colony. In the 1990s, the Beach Colony opened its doors to pets, which guaranteed it a steady clientele during the condo boom. In 2017, new manager Leslie Zechman gave the motel a new paint scheme of blue and cream, a contrast from the reds, yellows, and oranges it had sported before. Today, the Beach Colony evokes a dynamic combination of sixties and seventies aesthetics.

[210] Sand Castle Motel and Restaurant (402 East Stockton Road)

The Stan-Crest, as the Sand Castle was briefly originally known (named after the Stango family, its first owners), opened for the 1960 season. By the mid-1960s, it had grown to a U shape and gained a rooftop neon sign spelling a new name, "Sand Castle Motel," in boomerang-shaped letters. The word "Motel" later vanished from the sign; the other two words spent several years in decay before

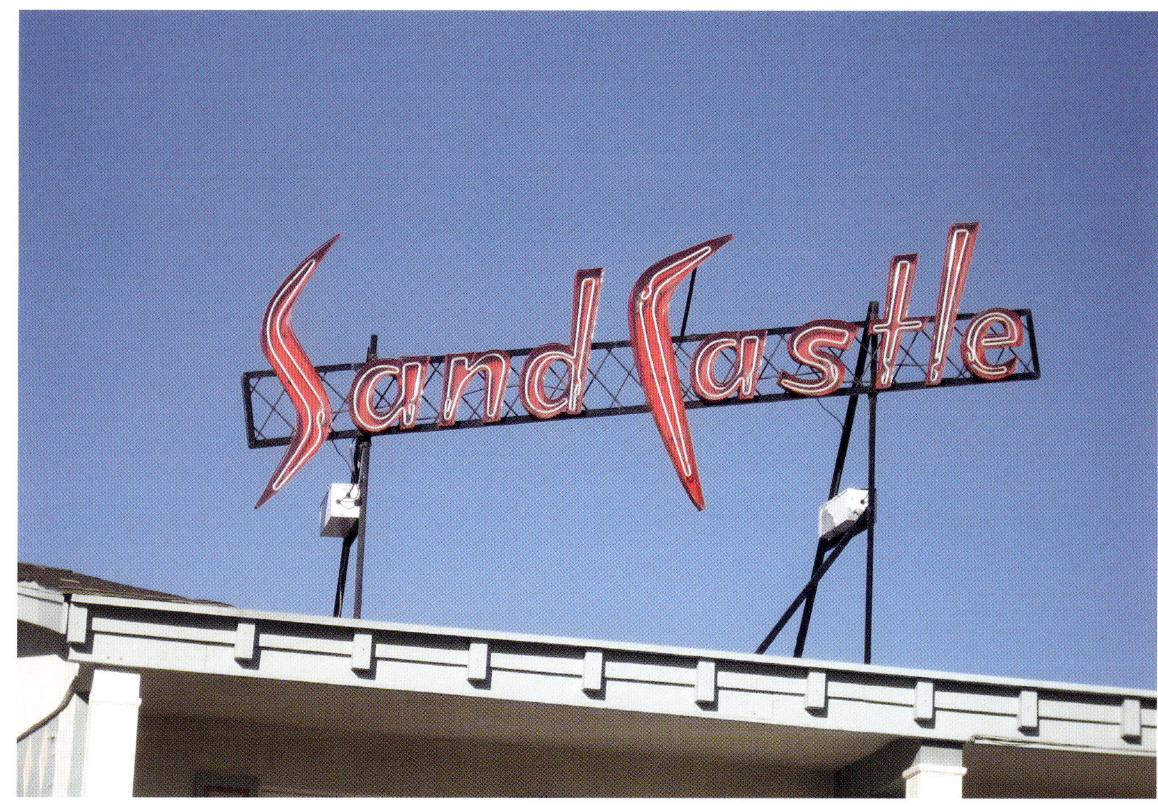

Two-thirds of the Sand Castle Motel's original neon sign sat atop the motel's roof until the motel was demolished in 2015.

a 2007 renovation. In 2015, when developers tore down the Sand Castle, Chuck Schumann salvaged its neon sign, which survives in a private collection.

[211] Tahiti Motel (400 East Stanton Road)
After Mike Branca built the Casa Bahama in 1959, local builders took to heart its muddled but dynamic vision of Polynesia. Robert Gerhardt built the Tahiti in 1963, and it shared the Casa Bahama's vernacular qualities. The L-shaped Tahiti's two end walls each culminated in a large hut-like gable; these were visible from blocks away and likely inspired Lou Morey's 1964 tiki hut office building at the Tangiers Motel, farther north.

In addition to its pair of tiki-like gables, the Tahiti boasted lava rock wall accents (which foreshadowed the more extensive use of lava rock at the nearby Kona Kai), a thatched overhang above the office, and a freestanding neon sign surrounded by a garden landscaped with tiki torches (this being the Wildwoods, several plastic palms kept the motel grounded in its East Coast setting). Like several other motels on the island, the Tahiti's effervescence was diluted by time. Later owners replaced the neon sign with a plastic replica and gave the motel an incongruous multicolored paint

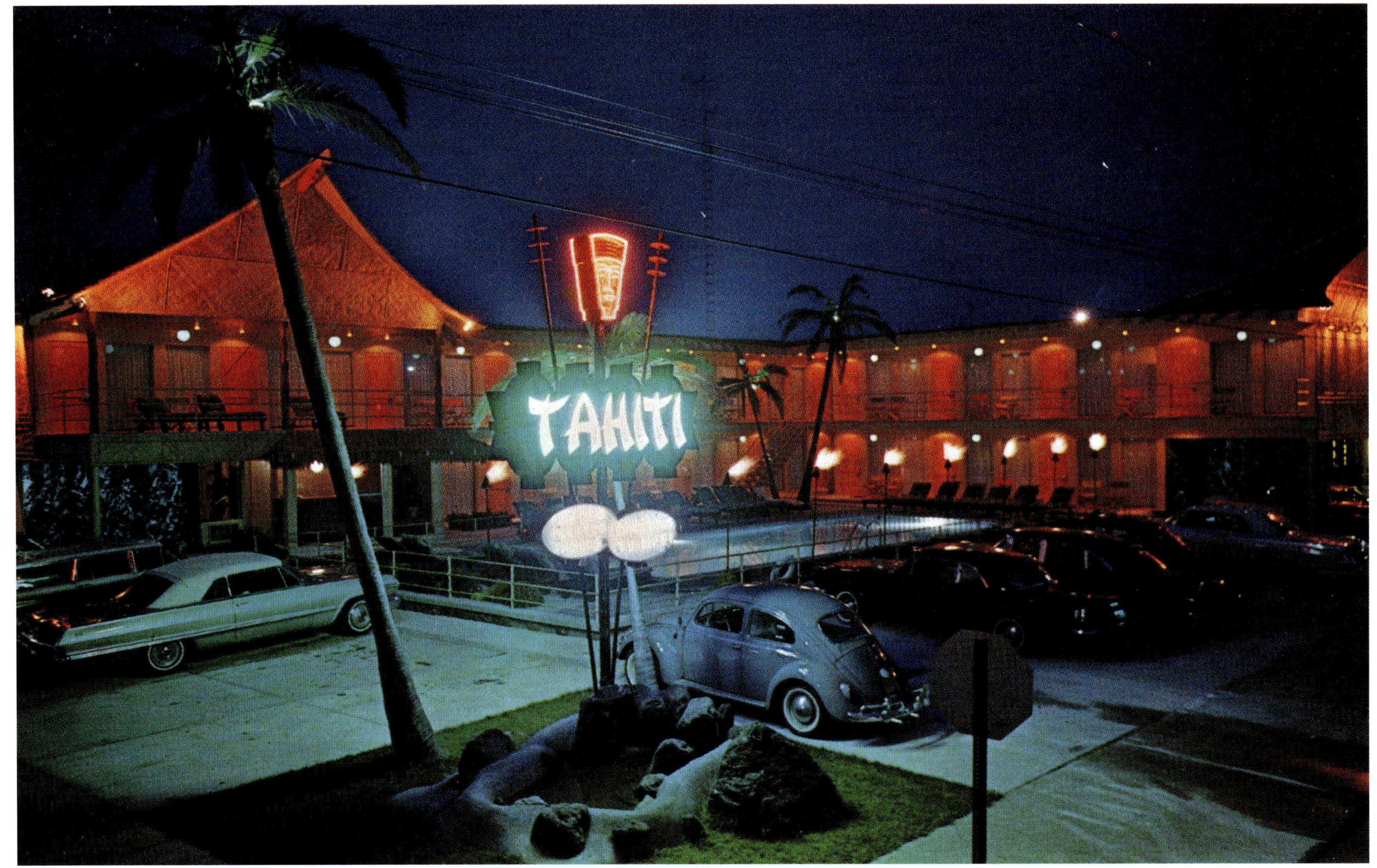

This spectacular early 1960s postcard shot of the Tahiti Motel shows how theatrical many Wildwoods motels were. The neon sign casts a blue glow over a Volkswagen Beetle in the parking lot, and spotlights illuminate the motel's atmospheric lava rock and plastic palms. *Author's collection*

scheme. When the motel fell to the wrecking ball in 2004, the Wildwoods merely lost a toned-down version of a landmark.

[212] Beach Waves Motel (508 East Stanton Road)
The first motel (1956) in Wildwood Crest's soon-to-be motel district, the Beach Waves was a

trendsetter. A few years after it was built, owners Erich and Anita Jung commissioned Ace Signs to embellish a rooftop satellite tower with an animated neon sign featuring crashing waves, which were bright enough to attract complaints from nearby homeowners. Despite amenities such as an on-site restaurant and a lengthwise orientation that made every room oceanfront, the motel was razed in 1972 and replaced with the high-rise Bal Harbour Hotels, which stand today.

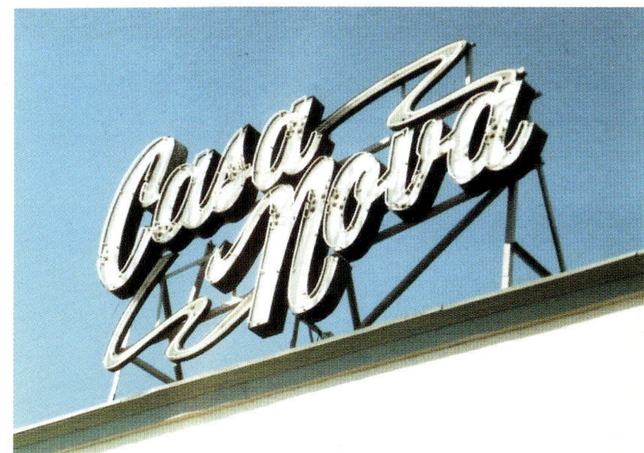

The Casa Nova Motel had the Wildwoods' first indoor pool. *Courtesy of Fedele Musso*

[213] Saratoga Inn (7501 Ocean Avenue)
As an American Colonial building in a neighborhood dominated by modernist motels, the red-brick-clad Saratoga stood out from its surroundings when Will Morey built it in 1960. Since then, aside from the addition of a coffee shop, it has remained remarkably well preserved.

[214] Casa Nova Motel (401 East Stanton Road)
The Del Conte Motel opened in 1963, named after its owners, Louis and Rose Del Conte. The expansive motel had the Wildwoods' first indoor pool (in addition to an outdoor one). After a mid-1960s addition doubled the size of the motel, an early 1970s owner changed its name to Casa Nova and installed a script neon sign with that name, which remained intact until the motel's 2004 demolition.

[215] Hawaii Kai Motel (7504 Ocean Avenue)
This motel, which opened around 1958 with a single story, was initially named the Wishing Well and had a modest neon sign mounted atop an eponymous well in the motel's courtyard. Later expansions (including a name change to Hawaii Kai around 1973) expanded it to three stories and turned up the visual volume with Polynesian decorations. In 2005, the Hawaii Kai was demolished and replaced with a condominium building painted an eye-popping aqua blue.

[216] Three Coins Motel (7511 Atlantic Avenue)
In 1966, Vince Stoker built the Three Coins, an L-shaped motel with gray panels mounted on its

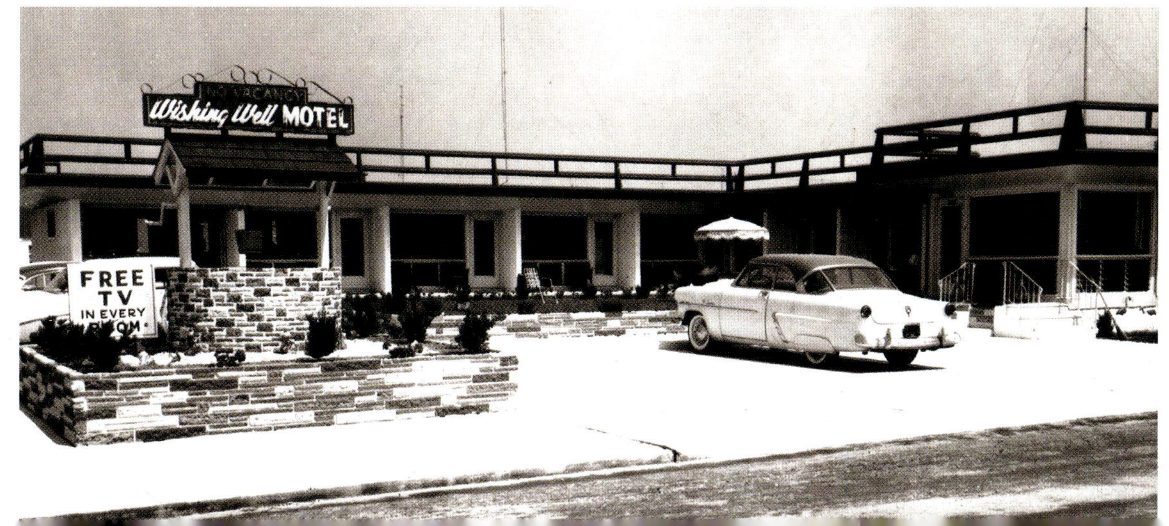

Later expanded and renamed the Hawaii Kai, the Wishing Well Motel, shown here in the late 1950s, was one of the earlier motels in the Wildwood Crest motel district. *Courtesy of Wildwood Historical Society*

end walls (which a nineties owner replaced with brightly colored pastel ones, enhancing its mid-century flavor). A freestanding neon sign lasted only a decade or so before being replaced with a plastic one; the motel itself was demolished in 2004.

[217] Town and Country Motel (420 East Farragut Road)

The Bada Brothers Builders (Bernard and Joseph) built the Town and Country Motel around 1956. Like Will Morey often did, they proceeded to operate the motel they'd built for the next couple decades.

The Town and Country exuded California-style Googie modernism, with patterned railings incorporating translucent orange panels, louvered doors, several neon signs, and a coffee shop enclosed by angular plate glass walls. The Bada brothers kept modifying the Town and Country to keep up with fashion and industry standards, adding a pool, additional stories, and, in the 1980s, a wall-hung neon sign in a Broadway typeface. Although it was one of the more colorful motels in its neighborhood, the Town and Country succumbed to development in 2004. Its lot has remained empty since.

[218] Memory Motel (7601 Atlantic Avenue)

George and Ann Bundschu built the Georgeanna Motel for the 1957 season. According to their daughter, Vicki Bundschu, the motel was the first in Wildwood Crest to have a pool. It also had a red-script

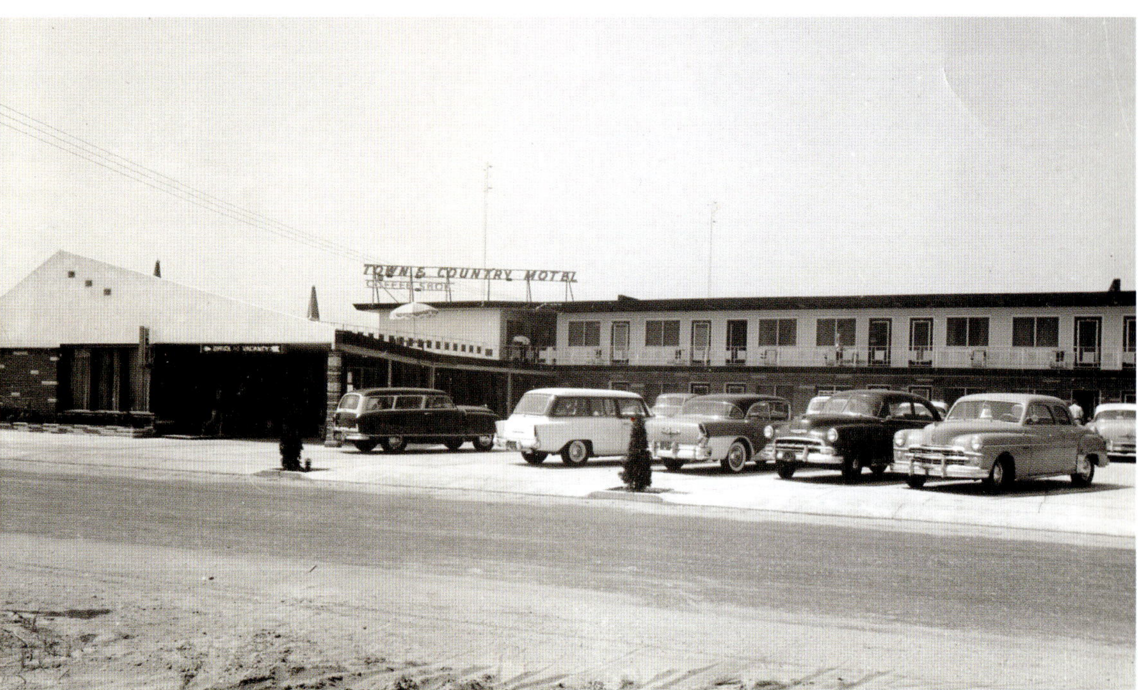

This view of the Town and Country Motel shortly after it opened shows its Googie style and neon signage. *Courtesy of Wildwood Historical Society*

neon sign, zigzag railings, and orange louvered doors. Sixties owners expanded the motel, which remained mostly intact until 1996, when Peter Ferrerio, a local developer, attempted to inject some overt vintage appeal. He renamed it the Memory Motel, after a Rolling Stones song, and outfitted the entire building with a classic rock theme, including a guitar-shaped rooftop neon sign and a pool slide decorated with the Stones' famous tongue logo. This adaptive reuse failed to turn a profit, and in 2001 the Memory Motel was one of the Wildwoods' first motels to be leveled for condominiums.

[219] Catalina Motel (405 East Atlanta Avenue)
The Catalina Motel, which began as a rectangular apartment building set sideways to the street and gained another wing in the 1960s, was well known for its vintage neon sign— the "i" in the motel's name dotted by a star. The motel was razed in 2003 to make way for condos.

[220] Silver Beach Motel (420 East Nashville Avenue)
Nicholas Bianchi built the Silver Beach for the 1957 season. The motel liberally used flagcrete, giving it a California coffee shop cool, but it is best remembered for a rooftop neon sign, installed in the late 1960s. Fred Musso says, "I wish I'd gotten that one. It was four-stroke neon, and some of the tubes were white and others were turquoise. Between the two colors, it really looked silver at night." The motel and sign were unexpectedly torn down in 2004, even though its owners had planned to stay open for another year.

[221] Frontier Motel (404 East Nashville Avenue)
Charles Rice built the western-themed Frontier for the 1966 season. His design included a distinctive lopsided office structure enclosed by plate glass windows, and ABS designed a neon sign that spelled the motel's name in a red Playbill typeface and featured white-outlined bull's horns. The motel remained mostly original until its 2002 demolition, whereupon Fred Musso rescued its sign.

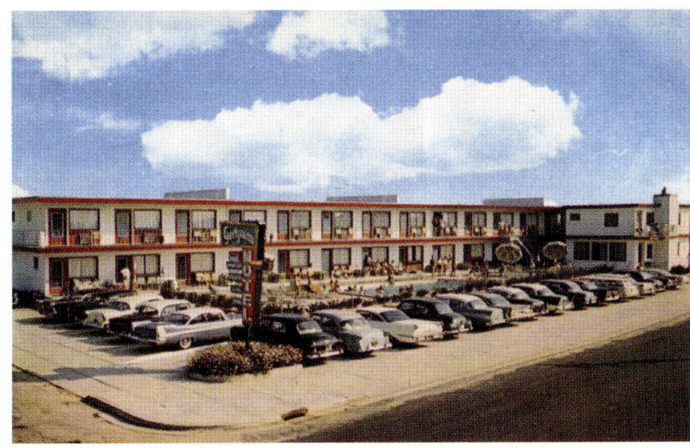

The parking lot is full in this late fifties postcard of the Georgeanna Motel. *Courtesy of Vicki Bundschu*

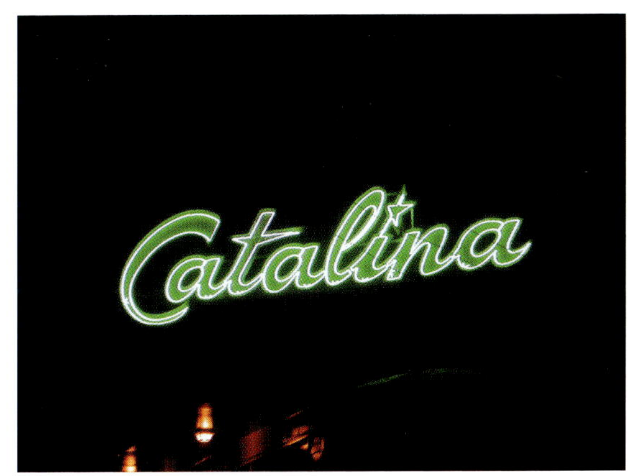

This neon sign elevated the Catalina Motel from a plain midblock apartment building to a midcentury classic. *Courtesy of Jeff Sumberg, www.flickr.com/jeffs4653*

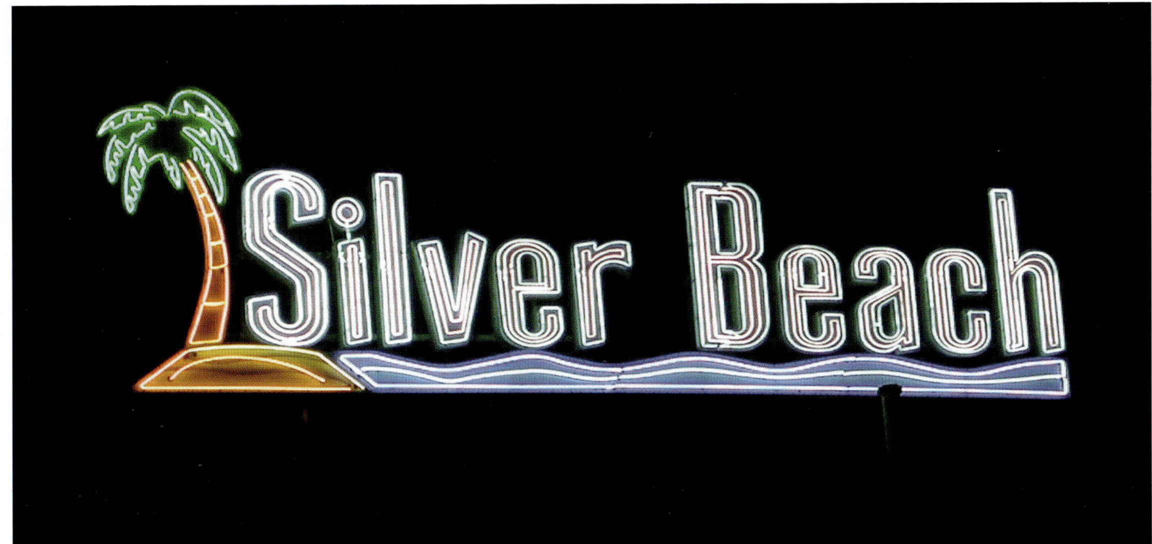

The Silver Beach Motel's late 1960s neon sign combined white and turquoise neon tubes to produce a silver glow at night. *Courtesy of Jeff Sumberg, www.flickr.com/jeffs4653*

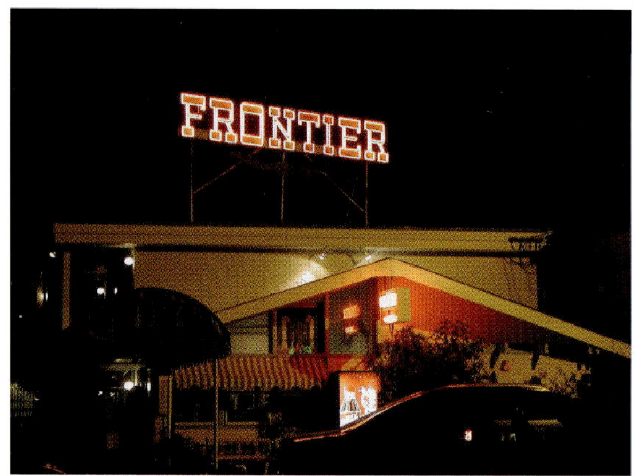

A Playbill typeface gave an American western flavor to the Frontier Motel's neon sign. *Courtesy of Jeff Sumberg, www.flickr.com/jeffs4653*

[222] Tempo Motel (400 East Nashville Avenue)

The early-sixties-vintage Tempo was, oddly, one of the few motels in the very musically inclined Wildwoods to have a musical theme. Originally bar shaped (and expanded to an L in the early 1970s), it had a bulging roofline that was mirrored in individually formed semicircular balconies like those of the Imperial 500 Motel farther north. When built, the motel had a freestanding neon sign that featured a music note. A decade later, its owner replaced that sign with a rooftop one, this time with letters in the shape of music notes.

By the 1980s, the Tempo had gained intricate metal railings adorned with a musical design (a rare example of a motel's midcentury credentials improving with age). The 1990s saw the motel gain a new rooftop sign in a less ornate font, Astroturf-paved balconies, and doors painted in diagonal white and blue triangles. Unfortunately, developers bought and razed this midcentury gem in 2002. The Doo Wop Preservation League tried to save the motel's sign, but Fred Musso recalls that he and other preservationists were told to stay off the property. After several years of negotiation, the Tempo's sign was destroyed.

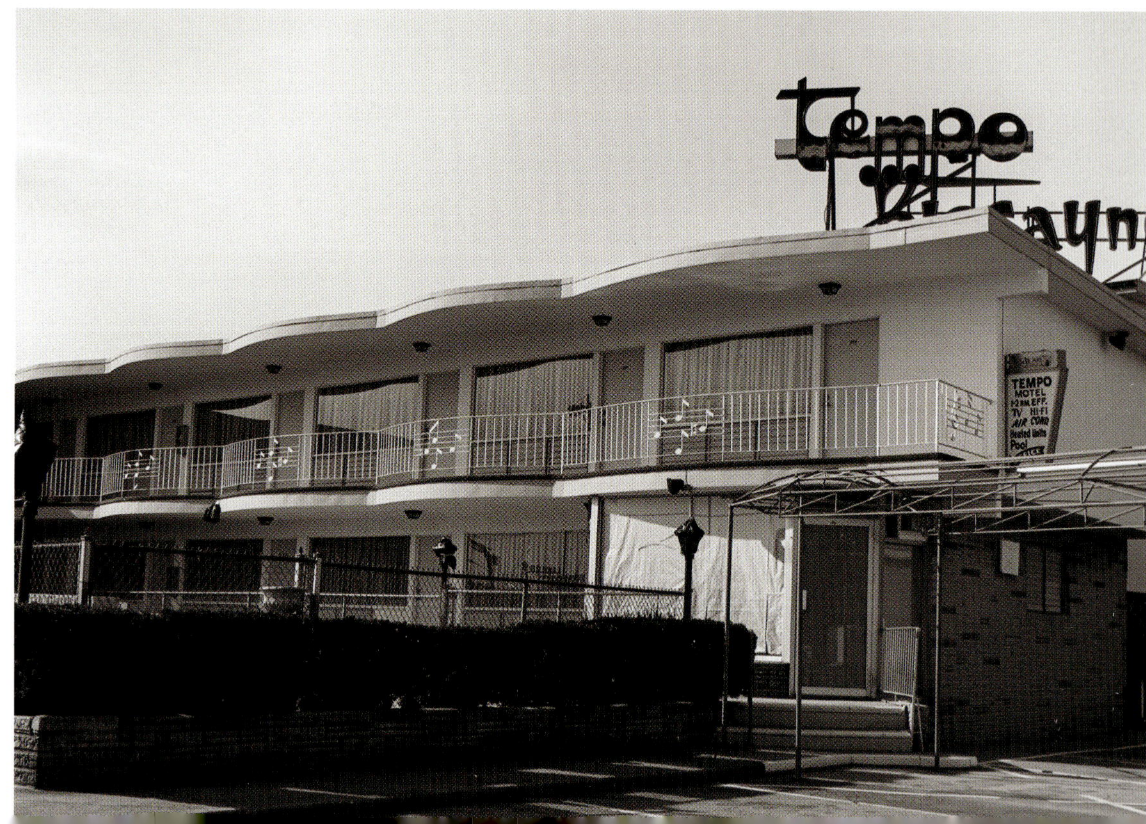

This 1986 photo shows the second of the Tempo Motel's three neon signs. *Courtesy of Ed Steinerts*

[223] Crown Motel (415 East Louisville Avenue)
John Patitucci built the Crown Motel in 1962 during the poststorm avalanche of motel construction on the island. Despite not having any of the dramatic gestures that characterize the island's heavyweight motels, the Crown had several classic midcentury modern elements, such as an amoeba-shaped pool and an exaggerated roof overhang studded with spotlights. Its tan-brick façade harkened back to the California coffee shop aesthetic of the 1950s, while railings fitted with red, yellow, and lavender panels pointed the way toward the late 1960s explosion of color. The motel sported a pair of blue neon signs in an angular Bauhaus typeface (one advertising an on-site coffee shop). Although an early seventies owner replaced the original neon sign with a new one (in green neon, with the letter "C" resplendent underneath a yellow crown), the Crown retained much of its original structure until being demolished in 2005. New construction began on its lot in 2020.

[224] Biscayne Family Resort (7807 Atlantic Avenue)
"My grandfather built this building that we're in right now," says Patrick Davenport. "We own several buildings now, but my grandfather actually built this building himself. It opened for business for the 1968 summer. Anthony Luglio was his name."

The Biscayne features sawtooth balconies like those of the Shalimar a mile north. Unlike the Shalimar, the Biscayne still has its original ship's-prow railings, which come to a point at the corners of the balconies. "Because of deterioration, we cut off and redid the third floor, using the original style of the railings, in 2001 or 2002," says Davenport. "The railings were original, but we had to form each balcony separately." On top of the motel's roof, facing north to attract traffic arriving from downtown, sat an ABS neon sign with the motel's name in blue, the "i" dotted by a yellow star. The neon sign survives today. "That's completely original," Davenport says. "It's been rebuilt and repaired numerous times, but it's original. The sign is an important part."

In 2001, Davenport bought the Bali-Hi motel next door at 425 East Louisville Avenue. Built around 1960 by Victor Quintavalle, it had originally sported a bright-red-and-green paint job, a candy-striped awning, and a neon-outlined palm tree. "We completely redid [the Bali-Hi] for the summer of 2005. We replaced the front doors—they used to have this square pattern on them. One regret that I have—we should have somehow saved that motel's sign." Davenport has kept his two motels in sterling condition. "I think when [the Biscayne] was opened, it was always geared towards families," he says. "It's the same thing now!"

[225] Breezy Corner Motel (7901 Seaview Avenue)
John Moyer opened the Breezy Corner, one of Wildwood Crest's first motels, for the 1953 season. A single-story court with a green rooftop neon sign, the motel was unimposing but provoked an outcry among motel opponents. The Breezy Corner never expanded and was later overshadowed by more-extravagant motels in the Crest. Longtime owner Jessie Clippinger sold out to developers in 2005, and Fred Musso recalled that the sign had deteriorated so much that he could not salvage it.

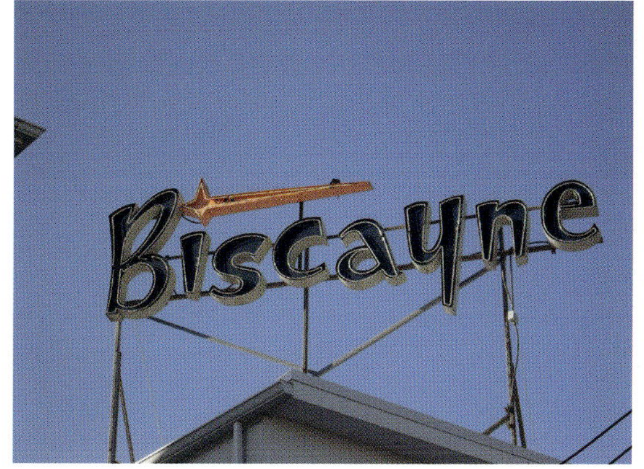

The neon sign of the Biscayne Motel evokes the fun, psychedelic aesthetic of the late 1960s.

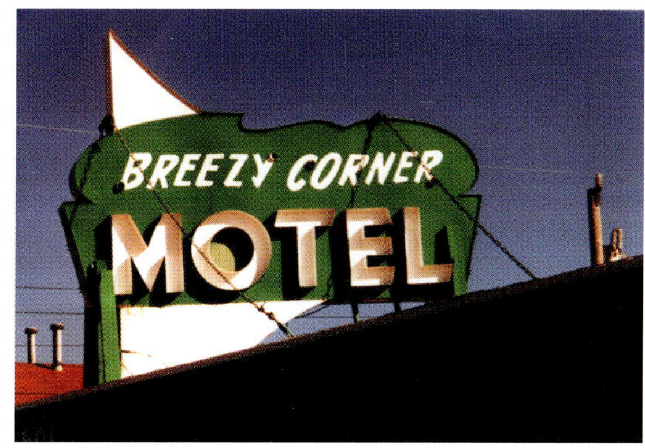

The Breezy Corner Motel's neon sign was one of the older ones on the island when the motel was demolished in 2005. As seen in this photo, its neon tubes have been removed, a cost-saving measure. *Courtesy of Fedele Musso*

[226] Coliseum Ocean Resort (416 East Miami Avenue)

[227] Paradise Oceanfront Resort (405 East Denver Avenue)

Both of these two sixties-vintage Crest motels (the Coliseum was known as the Chalet until the mid-1970s) have been retrofitted with modern resort-style amenities and detailed, ABS-designed rooftop neon signs. Wally Carty, manager of the Coliseum, wonders if the neon signs are worth the hassle: "A lot of the older people like the Doo Wop, and they like to take pictures, but they don't like to stay at places like this," he says.

[228] South Beach Motel (8001 Atlantic Avenue)

In 1958, Nick Pindale and Steve Skvarcek hired Lou Morey, busy elsewhere in the Crest building the Tangiers and Caribbean Motels, to build the El Reno Motel. Morey sprinkled midcentury modern details throughout, including fins on the motel's end walls, doors painted in a chevron pattern, diamond-patterned railings, and a candy-striped neon sign. After decades of modifications (throughout which the original fins survived), the motel was rebranded by nineties owners as the South Beach. In 2005, developers tore down the motel to build condominiums.

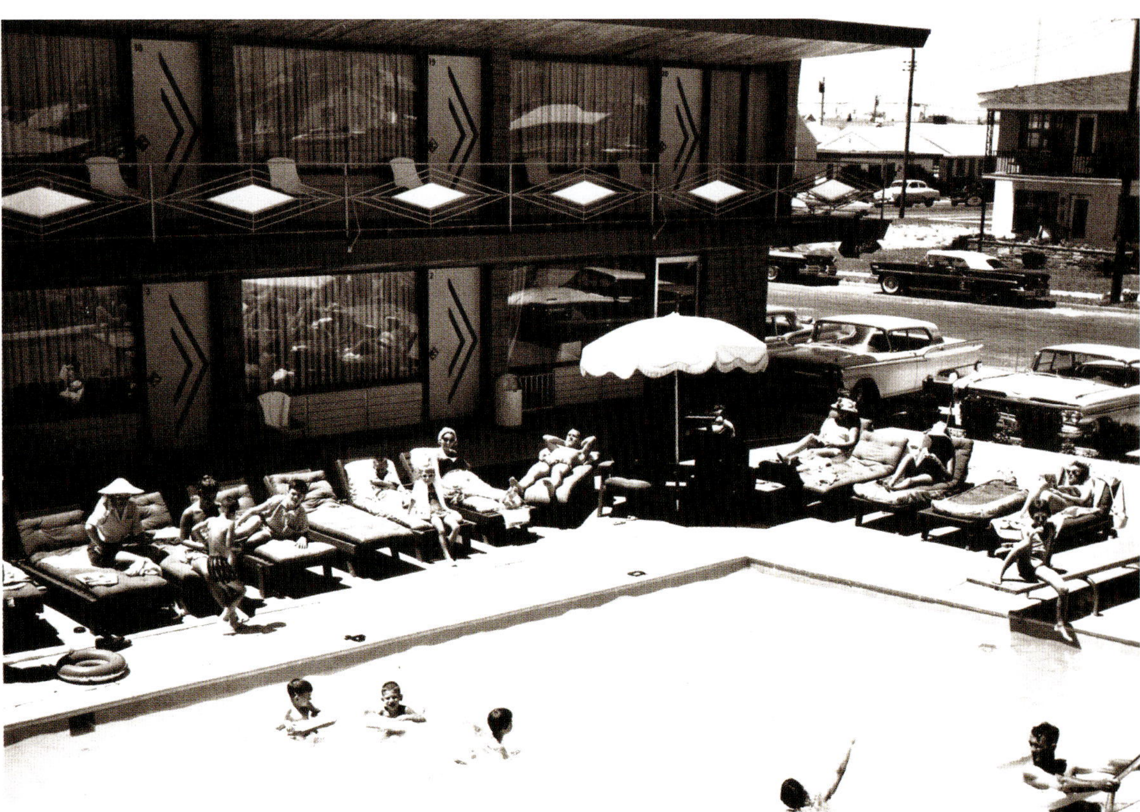

The El Reno Motel did not have any grand architectural gestures, but patterns such as the chevron symbols on its doors and the diamond panels interspersed among its railings imparted midcentury flavor. *Courtesy of Wildwood Historical Society*

[229] Apollo Resort Motel (407 East Saint Paul Avenue)
Today's Apollo is made up of what were originally the St. Paul and Apollo Motels. Ernie and Fay Decina built the Apollo on the beachfront in 1963. Seven years later, another entrepreneur bought the lot next to the Apollo and built the St. Paul Motel, which the Decina family in turn bought in 1971. Both motels had neon signs, though the St. Paul sign disappeared in 2000, when the Decina family merged the two motels under the name Apollo.

Ernie Decina Jr., who owns the motel today with his brother, still remembers the Apollo's rooftop sign fondly. "It was a really nice sign. There were three Grecian columns and spearmen. When it lit, it was really beautiful. The columns were white neon, and I think the letters were blue. It was rusting out—the transformer and stuff were dropping out. It was rotting away. The original one was one of the best neon signs I've ever seen." The Decinas removed the original neon sign around 2007, and in 2013 they had ABS build a new wall-mounted sign in white-and-blue neon, using an angular Mediterranean-style font.

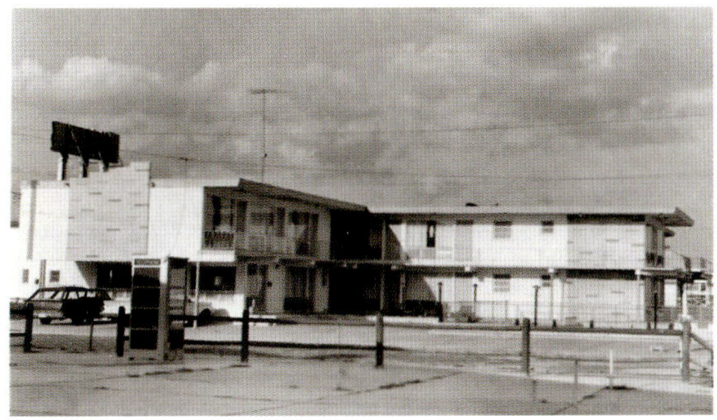

This 1960s photo of the Apollo Motel was taken three decades before the Decina family merged it with its neighbor, the St. Paul. *Courtesy of Wildwood Historical Society*

[230] Pyramid Resort Motel (8105 Atlantic Avenue)
Anthony Cangialosi built the Pyramid Motel for the 1962 season. A vaguely Egyptian theme included an Allied neon sign with Mediterranean lettering and a pyramid in chasing lights. The sign was painted blue, but the neon tubes glowed an effervescent red. Today the motel survives with a partial third story and a later-vintage gable roof. The original sign, one of the island's oldest, still shines.

[231] Carriage Stop Motel (410 East Saint Paul Avenue)
Lou Morey built the Carriage Stop Motel for the 1959 season, when it was one of the Wildwoods' first American Colonial–style motels. The red-brick-faced motel was a novelty for the island (and

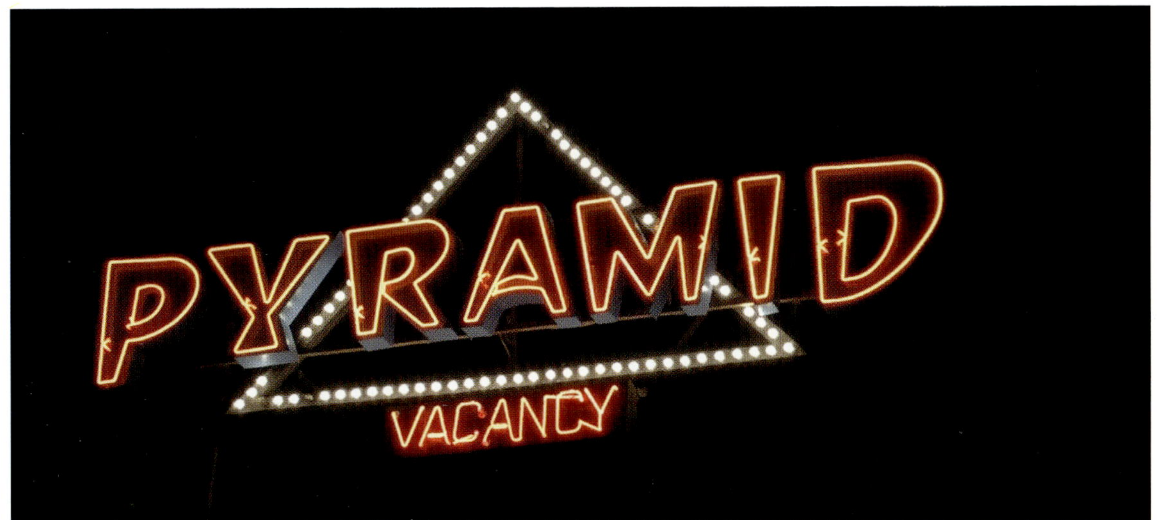

Refitted with new neon tubes and incandescent lights, the Pyramid Motel's original neon sign continues to glow.

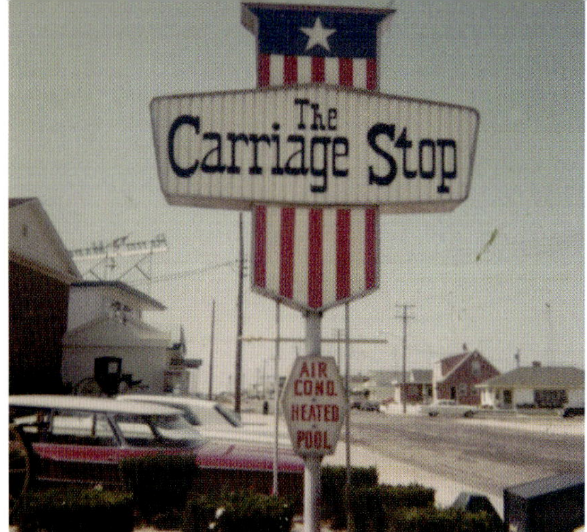

When the Carriage Stop Motel was built in 1959, Ace Signs installed this plastic sign, which was replaced with a rooftop neon one a decade or so later. *Courtesy of ABS Sign Co., Inc.*

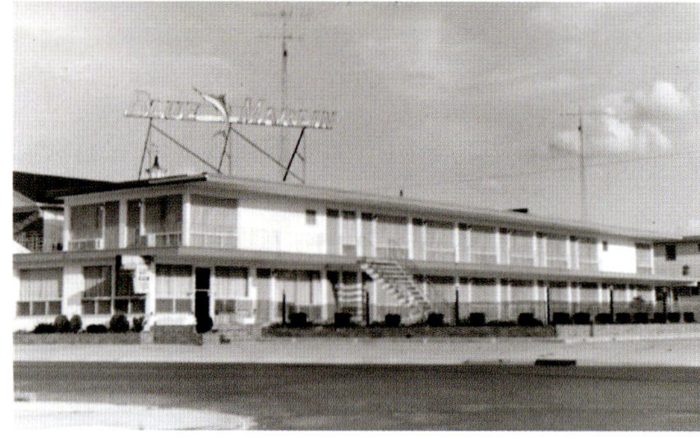

The Blue Marlin Motel has been expanded since this 1965 photo was taken. *Courtesy of Wildwood Historical Society*

probably inspired Lou's brother Will to build the similar Saratoga Inn the following year). Later owners expanded the motel and added a neon sign. In 2005 or so, developers converted the rooms to condominium ownership while leaving intact most of the motel's structure, including its sign (minus its neon tubes).

[232] Blue Marlin Resort (401 East Toledo Avenue)
The Blue Marlin opened in 1963 and might have been built by Michael and Edna Leopitizi, shown as its owners in a city directory from the following year. The Blue Marlin featured arresting geometric railings, blue rooflines, gold curtains, and dark-wood paneling. A well-loved rooftop neon sign featured a white-outlined marlin. Today the motel has been expanded and covered in beige vinyl siding, and the neon sign has been replaced with an LED replica.

[233] Cavalier Resort Motel (410 East Toledo Road)
The Leopoldo family built this large motel in the late sixties, commissioning from ABS a rooftop neon sign spelling out the motel's name in four-stroke neon. Originally two stories, it was expanded in the 1970s with a third story. In the mid-1990s, ABS added a second, wall-hung sign, which Chuck Schumann rescued after the Cavalier was demolished in 2005. ABS installed the wall sign outside the Doo Wop Experience in 2007; Fred Musso installed an "A" from the rooftop sign inside the museum. "Still works perfectly and still as bright as the day it was made fifty years ago," Musso says.

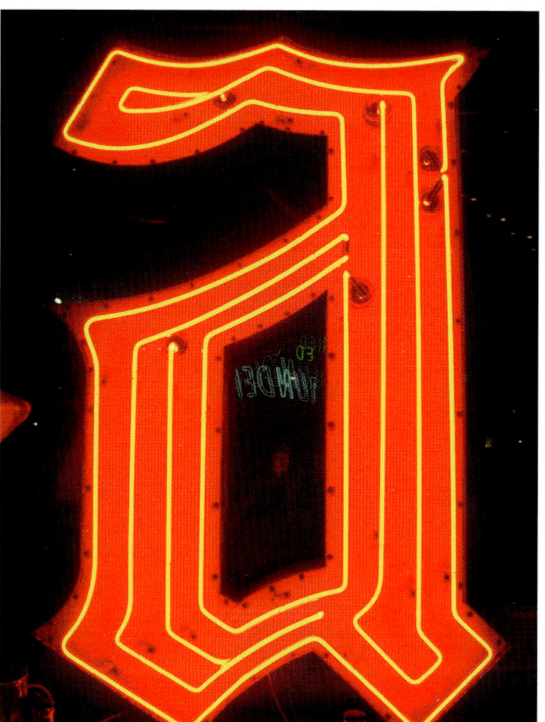

Thanks to sign preservationists' efforts, this "A" from the Cavalier Motel's original rooftop sign is visible inside the Doo Wop Experience in downtown Wildwood.

[234] Ala Kai Motel (8301 Atlantic Avenue)
Kurt and Gertrude Burghold built the Ala Kai for the 1963 season. The two-story, L-shaped motel juxtaposed a yellow roofline, tan brick, and a rooftop neon sign spelling "Ala Kai" in yellow bamboo-like letters surrounding a girl on a surfboard. Aside from the addition of a partial third story and a larger office, the motel has seen little alteration since then. In 2007, ABS renovated the neon sign, which had spent the previous decade deteriorating. Despite the replacement of a small neon "Office" sign with a plastic one in 2020, the Ala Kai remains well preserved.

[235] La Vita Motel (8400 Atlantic Avenue)
The block-long La Vita opened in 1963; first owners Frank and Marie Lacivita named the motel after a variation of their last name. Three years later, after

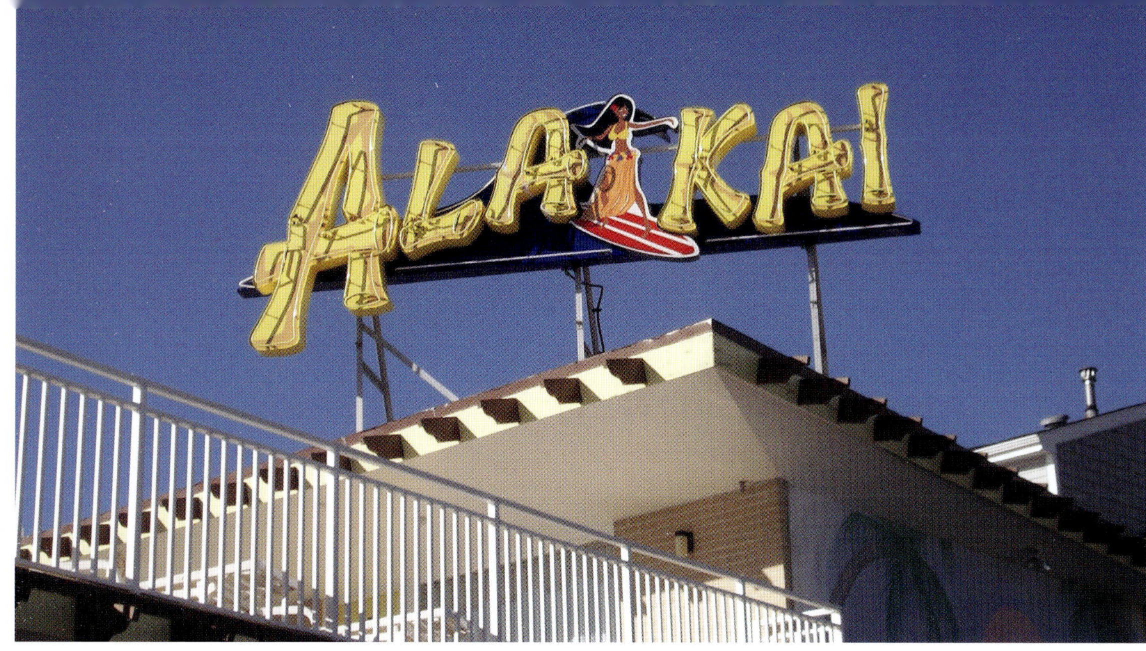

The Ala Kai Motel's bamboo-shaped neon letters help express the motel's Polynesian theme.

the La Vita had lost its oceanfront location to construction across Atlantic Avenue, the Lacivitas sold the motel to Anne and Charles Weyhmiller and built the Fleur De Lis Motel farther north. The Weyhmillers expanded the La Vita's office and added a script rooftop neon sign in place of the original freestanding one and new diamond-patterned railings.

The La Vita survived, remarkably intact, into the twenty-first century. In 2005, developers modified it, removing its decorative railings and covering it in stucco. The motel never reopened, and seven years later the developers tore it down altogether; Fred Musso salvaged its neon sign, whose letters now reside in four states. Musso recalls that the developers threw out furniture and appliances that had never been used.

[236] Monta Cello Motel (8400 Seaview Avenue)

After the Wildwood Crest Planning Board voted to allow motels in their borough, the Monta Cello was one of the first motels to open, around 1954. The single-story American Colonial motel featured a freestanding brick pillar topped with a neon sign. After a half century in existence (during which it gained a two-story addition), the motel met the wrecking ball in 2004. Fred Musso saved part of the motel's neon sign, which now hangs in a pizza shop in Pottstown, Pennsylvania.

[237] Villa Nova Motel (8601 Atlantic Avenue)

Alfred and Jenny Mele, who built the Villa Nova in 1964, designed a spacious, two-story, L-shaped motel and coffee shop complex that occupied an entire beachfront block. On top of the coffee shop was a red neon sign spelling the motel's name in serif letters; in the 1970s or 1980s, ABS replaced this sign with a new sans serif version that still sits atop the motel today.

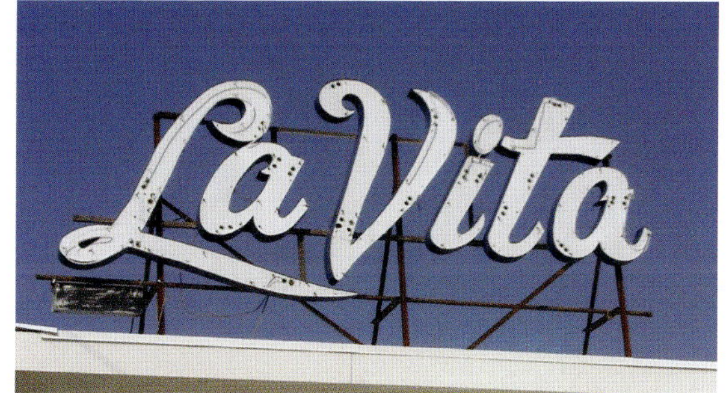

The La Vita Motel's sign in its later years, missing most of its neon tubes.

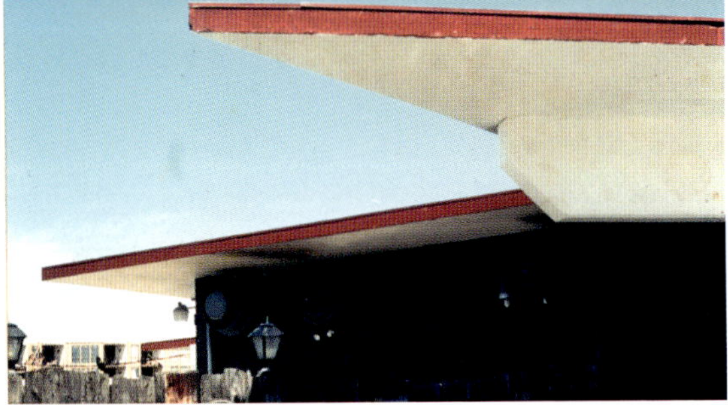

This rear view of the Captain's Table Restaurant shows a detail of its angular roof. *Courtesy of Fedele Musso*

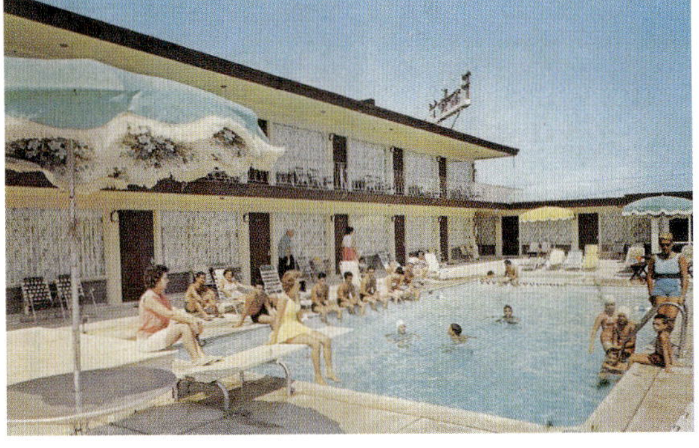

When the Earle Motel opened, it featured unusual black doors and roofline trim. *Courtesy of Wildwood Historical Society*

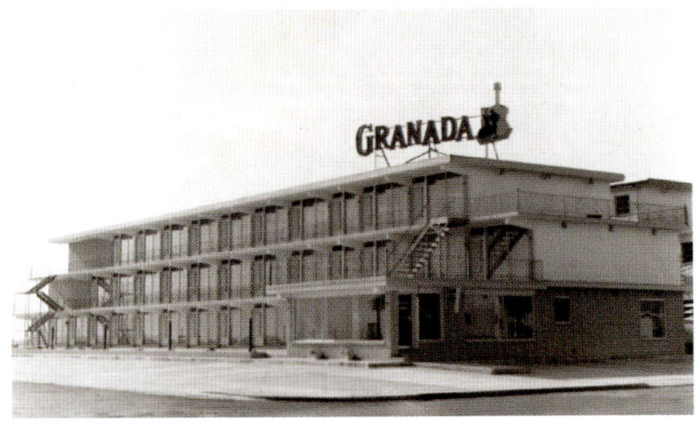

Except for the recent loss of its neon sign, the Granada Motel still looks much the same as it does in this late 1960s view. *Courtesy of Wildwood Historical Society*

[238] Blue Water Motel (8600 Atlantic Avenue)
Austin and Jennie Long built the Blue Water in 1962 or 1963 and installed an appealing blue neon sign whose channel letters survive today, lined with LED rope lights.

[239] Captain's Table Restaurant (8700 Atlantic Avenue)
In 1963, Lou Morey and prominent local builder John DeFrancesco formed a partnership, Captain's Table Enterprises, to build what would become one of Morey's crowning achievements. They built a restaurant with a shield-shaped floor plan and a pitched roof that rose to a peak above the beach, much like the popular 1960s Phillips 66 gas station design. The beach side of the restaurant was lined with picture windows, giving its customers panoramic beach views that were shaded by the restaurant's roof overhang. Morey and DeFrancesco lighted the whole structure with multicolored spotlights at night, and in the restaurant's early years the rooftop was lined with neon to make it visible to passersby overhead. Although the Captain's Table was a modernist monument and local landmark, developers tore it down in 2005 to build houses.

[240] Earle Motel (8700 Seaview Avenue)
Earl Taylor built the Earle Motel, presumably named after himself, for the 1963 season. Southern Wildwood Crest was sparsely populated at the time, and Fred Musso remembers that the Earle's sign, painted green but lined with orange neon tubes, was visible for several blocks. In 2004, developers tore down the motel, but Musso saved its sign. Today its channel letters are scattered around the globe.

[241] Granada Ocean Resort (8801 Atlantic Avenue)

[242] Commander-By-the-Sea Motel (8803 Atlantic Avenue)
These two motels opened for the 1967 season and used mirror images of the same blueprints. Lou Morey is reported to have built the Commander, while John DeFrancesco built the Granada; Morey and DeFrancesco were occasional collaborators, as with the Captain's Table Restaurant, so they may have shared plans. The symmetry vanished in the early 1970s, when the Commander was slightly expanded on the beach side. Both motels had neon signs; the Granada's rooftop sign, complete with a yellow-outlined guitar, was refurbished in the late 2010s but mysteriously vanished in 2020, while the Commander's freestanding sign was removed in the early 1970s.

Bibliography

Books and Pamphlets

Ascough, Rob, and Al Alven. *Images of America: Hunt's Pier*. Charleston, SC: Arcadia, 2011.

Boyer, George. *Wildwood: Middle of the Island*. Wildwood, NJ: Laureate, 1976.

Capitman, Barbara Baer, and Steven Brooke. *Deco Delights: Preserving the Beauty and Joy of Miami Beach Architecture*. New York: E. P. Dutton, 1988.

City of Wildwood. *A Century of Memories*. Wildwood, NJ: One Off Marketing, 2012.

Davidson, Len. *Vintage Neon*. Atglen, PA: Schiffer, 1999.

Dubie, Carol, Donald Jackson, and Susan Shearer. *Wildwood Workbook*. Little Rock, AR: Society for Commercial Archaeology, 1983.

Francis, David W., Diane DeMali Francis, and Robert J. Scully Jr. *Wildwood by the Sea*. Fairview Park, OH: Amusement Park Books, 1998.

Gabriele, Michael. *The History of Diners in New Jersey*. Charleston, SC: History Press, 2013.

Gabriele, Michael. *Stories from New Jersey Diners: Monuments to Community*. Charleston, SC: History Press, 2019.

Genovese, Peter. *Jersey Diners*. New Brunswick, NJ: Rutgers University Press, 1996.

Gutman, Richard J. S. *American Diner Then and Now*. Baltimore: Johns Hopkins University Press, 2000.

Hand, Scott, and Diane Pooler. *Fun Pier: 1957 to Adventure Pier*. Charleston, SC: Arcadia, 2012.

Hastings, Kirk. *Doo Wop Motels*. Mechanicsburg, PA: Stackpole Books, 2007.

Havens, Mark. *Out of Season: The Vanishing Architecture of the Wildwoods*. London: Booth-Clibborn, 2016.

Henry, Taylor. *Wildwoods Houses through Time*. Charleston, SC: Fonthill Media, 2018.

Hine, Thomas. *Populuxe: From Tailfins and TV Dinners to Barbie Dolls and Fallout Shelters*. New York: MJF Books, 1986.

Hirsch, Anita. *Wildwood By-the-Sea: Nostalgia and Recipes*. Wildwood, NJ: Holly Beach, 2009.

Hirsch, Michael Lorin, Richard Stokes, and Anthony Bracali. *How to Doo Wop: Wildwoods-by-the-Sea Handbook of Design Guidelines*. Wildwood, NJ: Doo Wop Preservation League, 2004.

Hirschorn, Paul, and Steven Izenour. *White Towers*. Cambridge, MA: MIT Press, 2007.

Margolies, John, and Emily Gwathmey. *Ticket to Paradise: American Movie Theaters and How We Had Fun*. Boston: Little, Brown, 1991.

Martino, Vincent. *Postcard History Series: The Wildwoods, 1920–1970*. Charleston, SC: Arcadia, 2007.

Miller, Ben. *The First Resort: Fun, Sun, Fire and War in Cape May, America's Original Seaside Town*. Cape May, NJ: Exit Zero, 2009.

Remington, Vernick & Walberg Engineers. *Design Guidelines for the Wildwoods Boardwalk*. Cape May, NJ: Granigan Design, n.d.

Smith, Ian, and Dean Davis. *Wildwood Moments: New Jersey's Most Beloved Boardwalk*. Atglen, PA: Schiffer, 2008.

Stern, Rudi. *Let There Be Neon*. New York: Harry N. Abrams, 1979.

Van Meter, Jonathan, and Dorothy Kresz. *Neon-Lit Kidney-Shaped Low-Rent Flat-Roofed Doo-Wop Commercial Architecture*. New York: Pentagram Papers, 2001.

Venturi, Robert, Denise Scott Brown, and Steven Izenour. *Learning from Las Vegas*. Cambridge, MA: MIT Press, 1977.

Wildwood Crest Centennial Celebration. *The First Hundred Years . . . 1910 to 2010: The People and the Places . . . A Pictorial History of Wildwood Crest*. Cape May, NJ: Exit Zero, 2010.

Williams, Robert O., and Melinda M. Williams. *Wildwood's Neon Nights and Motel Memories*. Atglen, PA: Schiffer, 2010.

Wright, Jack, ed. *Fab-O-Rama: The Story of Morey's Piers, Planet Earth's Greatest Seaside Amusement Park*. Cape May, NJ: Exit Zero, 2009.

Articles and Essays

André, Sara. "Neon and Angles: Motels of the Wildwoods." *Historic Preservation Bulletin*, Summer 2006.

Bollinger, Daniel. "Those Wildwood Days Still Shine Bright." *New York Lifestyles*, June 2017.

Genovese, Peter. "Diehards Design a Doo Wop Do-Over." *Star-Ledger*, July 10, 2004.

Gilfillian, Trudi. "A Doo Wop Kind of Place." *Press of Atlantic City*, October 6, 2003.

Gilfillian, Trudi. "Another One Bites the Dust." *Press of Atlantic City*, May 12, 2005.

Gilfillian, Trudi. "New Owners Review Doo Wop Motels in Wildwoods." *Press of Atlantic City*, December 13, 2012.

Gilfillian, Trudi. "State Gives Wildwood Crest Motel Historic Designation." *Press of Atlantic City*, July 2, 2005.

Gilfillian, Trudi. "Wildwood Boardwalk Motel Rebuilds after Fire." *Press of Atlantic City*, April 14, 2012.

Gilfillian, Trudi. "Wildwood Crest's Old Motels More Did-Wop Than Doo-Wop." *Press of Atlantic City*, May 30, 2005.

Goldstein, Steve, and Jacqueline Urgo. "Tacky Motels? No, Treasures." *Philadelphia Inquirer*, May 11, 2006.

Hine, Thomas. "Detecting Treasures from an Era Barely Past." *Philadelphia Inquirer*, August 7, 1984.

Hirsch, Michael. "The 2012 SCA Conference: Wildwood Daze!" *Society for Commercial Archaeology Road Notes*, Spring 2012.

Izenour, Steve. "What Is Popular Culture?" *Learning from the Wildwoods*, 1998.

Lev, Darlene. "Wildwood: The Last Mid-century Modern Resort." *Modernism*, Winter 2005–2006.

Mallon, Thomas. "A Shore Fling." *Preservation*, July/August 2003.

Milgrom, Melissa. “Learning from Steve Izenour.” *Metropolis*, January 2002.

Musso, Fred. “Readers Reply.” *Society for Commercial Archaeology News Journal*, Spring 2000.

Nark, Jason, and Michelle Gloria. “Our Neon Neighbor.” *Cape May Magazine*, July 2016.

“Opinions Mixed on Building Motels in Wildwood Crest.” *Wildwood Leader*, August 27, 1953.

Rosenello, Regina. “Crest Motels Come Tumbling Down.” *Wildwood Leader*, July 24, 2004.

Sachs, Andrea. “Ocean Air and ’50s Flair, Together in Harmony.” *Washington Post*, September 28, 2014.

“Stalking the Wild CA in Wildwood, NJ.” *Society for Commercial Archaeology News Journal*, July 1983.

Stewart, Doug. “Doo Wop by the Sea.” *Smithsonian Magazine*, June 2003.

Thomas, George. “Wildwood at Heart.” *Penn Gazette*, September/October 1998.

Thomas, George. “The Wildwoods by the Sea: Learning from ‘Other Directed’ Style,” *Learning from the Wildwoods*, 1998.

Urgo, Jacqueline. “Historic Sites: Shore Motel, Burlco Store.” *Philadelphia Inquirer*, October 6, 2003.

Websites

Cherkasky, Bill. “Memories of Wildwood, New Jersey: Motels.” Dark in the Park. www.darkinthepark.com/Wildwood/wildwood3.htm.

Doo Wop Preservation League. “Doo Wop Preservation League.” www.doowopusa.org.

Grassi, Ralph. “Funchase.” www.funchase.com/Funchase.htm.

Hastings, Kirk. “The Doo Wop Architecture of Wildwood Crest.” Wildwood Crest Historical Society. https://cresthistory.org.

Hoagland, Stephanie. “The Rise, Fall and Resurrection of Wildwood’s Doo Wop Motels.” Garden State Legacy. http://gardenstatelegacy.com/files/The_Rise_Fall_Resurrection_of_Wildwoods_DooWop_Motels_Hoagland_GSL20.pdf.

Melucci, Martin. "The 21st Century Satellite." Website inactive.

New Jersey Turnpike Authority. "Garden State Parkway: A Historic Journey." New Jersey Turnpike Authority. www.njta.com/gsphistory/index.html.

Other

Accommodations Directory. Wildwood, NJ: Greater Wildwood Hotel and Motel Association, 1952, 1954, 1956, 1960, 1961, 1966, 1967, 1970, 1972, 1973, 1974, 1979, 1980, 1981, 1982, and 1984 editions.

Granigan, Beth, Richard Stokes, and George Thomas. "The Guide to Wildwood's Doo Wop Architecture." Wildwood, NJ: Doo Wop Preservation League, 2008.

Hoagland, Stephanie. "Stymied by Success: Preservation Stagnation on the Jersey Shore." Talk given April 10, 2018. Transcript: www.ncptt.nps.gov/ blog stymied-by-success-preservation-stagnation-on-the-jersey-shore-2.

Musso, Fred. "List of Wildwoods Neon Signs." Compiled 2019.

Polk's Wildwood City Directory. Detroit, MI: R. L. Polk, 1946, 1949, 1955–56, 1957–58, 1960, 1964, and 1967 editions.

Rosenberg, Kim, and Josh Silber. "Wildwood: The Kimpendium." Compiled 2015.

Zerbe, Nancy L., Stephanie M. Hoagland, and Kevin D. Murphy. "National Register of Historic Places Multiple Property Documentation Form: Motels of the Wildwoods." Washington, DC: US Department of the Interior, National Park Service, 2003.

Interviews with Al Alven, Sue Bianchi, Al Brannen, Vicki Bundschu, Wally Carty, Gordon Clark, Kathy Crane, Shirley Cruz, Patrick Davenport, Len Davidson, Ernie Decina, Gail DeFeo, Jim DeFeo, Carolyn Emigh, Rick Geers, Scott Hand, John Hawes, Randy Hentges, Michael Hirsch, Michael John, Jim Johnson, Jim Kelly, Agnes Knoll, Jane Lawrence, Steve Lawrence, Dan MacElrevey, George Miller, Jack Morey, Fred Musso, Virginia Nichols, Ed Pangburn, Steve Reeser, Theresa Robey, Melissa Roy, Paul Russo, Chuck Schumann, Richard Stokes, Maria Tenaglia, Bob Van Eman, John Way, and Leslie Zechman.

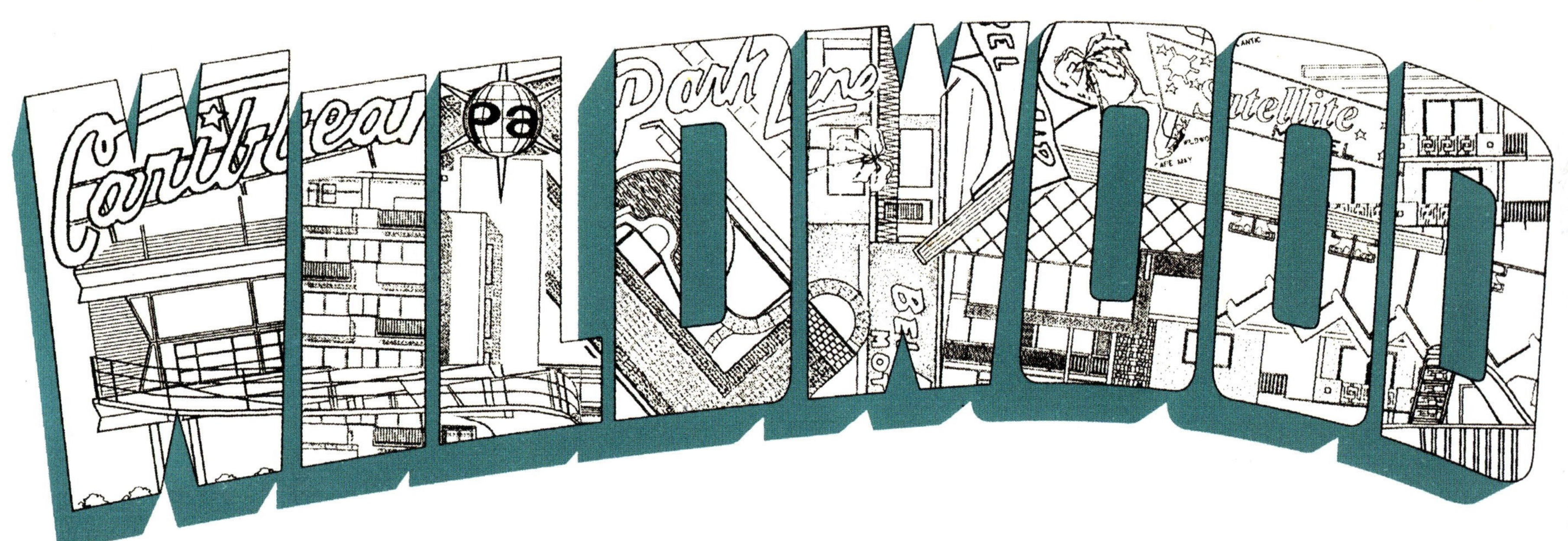
WILDWOOD
Park Lane
Satellite

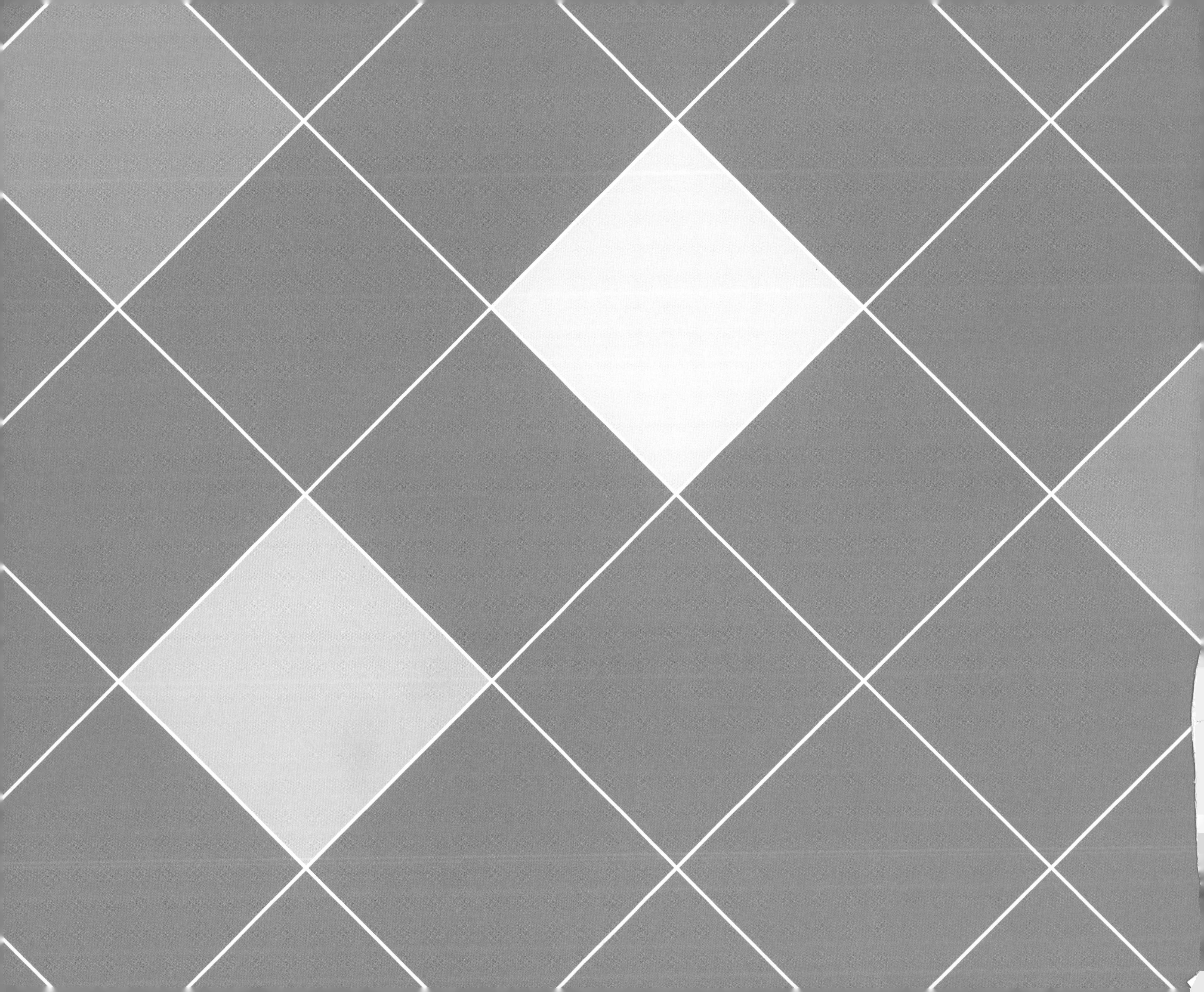